T0295647

The Frontiers of Corporate Food in Egypt

MIDDLE EAST POLITICAL ECONOMY SERIES

The Middle East Political Economy Series seeks to profile research monographs that will advance the theory, practice, and teaching of the political economy of the Middle East and North Africa for a new generation of scholars, students, and practitioners. Critical scholarship is especially encouraged within the spirit of political economy as an interdisciplinary and applied field, dealing centrally with national and global processes of inequality, structural transformation, economic reform, and political change.

Series Editors
Don Babai and John Sfakianakis

The Frontiers of Corporate Food in Egypt

Marion W. Dixon

OXFORD
UNIVERSITY PRESS

Great Clarendon Street, Oxford, OX2 6DP,
United Kingdom

Oxford University Press is a department of the University of Oxford.
It furthers the University's objective of excellence in research, scholarship,
and education by publishing worldwide. Oxford is a registered trade mark of
Oxford University Press in the UK and in certain other countries

Published in the United States of America by Oxford University Press
198 Madison Avenue, New York, NY 10016, United States of America

British Library Cataloguing in Publication Data

Data available

Library of Congress Control Number: 2023935898

ISBN 978–0–19–284298–5

DOI: 10.1093/oso/9780192842985.001.0001

Printed and bound by
CPI Group (UK) Ltd, Croydon, CR0 4YY

Links to third party websites are provided by Oxford in good faith and
for information only. Oxford disclaims any responsibility for the materials
contained in any third party website referenced in this work.

To all who have sacrificed for a more just world before,
at, and after the January 25, 2011 uprising

Contents

List of Figures and Tables

Figures

Tables

Acknowledgments

When I first arrived in Egypt, on January 2008, at the height of the world food price hike, the political environment was contentious, to say the least. Yet, people were willing to meet with me and collaborate with me over the years—agreeing to sit down with me, interview with me, introduce me to someone else, make data available to me, invite me to a village or to an event, advise me. I can't adequately express my gratitude to each and every one of them. If they are in Egypt, I do not want them to be inadvertently associated with this research, and I choose to keep most of them anonymous.

I firstly acknowledge Bashir, who was a father in a home away from home. Mark helped me with Egyptian Arabic—even how to read it—working with me week after week. I met Joel Beinin during my preliminary visit to Cairo, and he gave me resolve to keep going. Ray Bush, whom I also first met in Cairo, encouraged and supported me and this project from the very beginning. During the first years of this research, he invited me to present my research and to submit my reflections from the 2011 popular uprising as I was experiencing it. That reflection, "An Arab Spring," remains one of the most read articles in the *Review of African Political Economy*. That publication and this project would not have been possible without Ray. Before I began writing this book in 2020, two Egyptian icons had died, and I will honor them here: Nawal El Saadawi and Shahinda Maqlad are two women I admire, and both have inspired, in their own ways, this book.

I also thank the research, public, and other institutions in Egypt that accommodated my research inquiries: Arab and African Research Centre, Desert Development Centre at American University in Cairo, Egyptian Centre for Economic Research, General Authority for Investment, Land Centre for Human Rights, National Nutrition Institute, Social Research Centre at the American University in Cairo, and World Food Programme.

My research in Egypt was made possible by funding from the Mario Einaudi Centre for International Studies, the Polson Institute for Global Development, the Institute for Social Sciences, and the Richard Bradfield Research Award. All funding was graduate support from Cornell University. At Cornell University, I also thank Phil McMichael, who was more than willing to hear me out when I decided to expand this research to corporate agriculture and food, even though nothing had been written about it at the time. Fouad Makki has always provided assuring guidance, and both Phil and Fouad will see how I strayed from and have come back to world systems analysis in this book. They both made that journey possible. Vilma Santiago-Irizarry provided anthropological insights, and Timothy Mitchell, as an external member, encouraged me to turn this project into a book manuscript. I am grateful to them for their guidance and encouragement. Johannes Plambeck, who at the time was working at the Maps and Geospatial Information Department at Olin and Uris Libraries, worked with me to produce many of the figures in this book. Nimat Barazangi mentored me from the beginning on participatory action research. The dissertation may have taken much longer to finish if it hadn't been for Elyshia Aseltine's wise advice in 2011. Special thanks also go to Kathleen Arthur, Djahane Banoo, Muawia Barazangi, Upik Djahlins, Emme Edwards, Nicole Fisk, Lori Freer, Ilene Gaffin, and Rich Entlich, Muthoni Kamau, Holly and Michael Kazarinoff, Dela Kusi-Appouh, Karuna Morarji, Sudeshna Mitra, Vinay Pagay, Sara Rzayeva, Mindi Schneider, Alicia Swords, Marygold Walsh-Dilley, and Rob Young.

My friends, colleagues, and students in the School of International Service at American University helped me take this project well beyond the dissertation. My involvement with colleagues in the Ethnographies of Empire Research Cluster and the International Development Program's Friday Forums was especially helpful in developing the ideas presented in this book. I enjoyed and benefited greatly from the many conversations about all things agriculture and food that I shared with Adam Diamond and Garrett Graddy-Lovelace. I thank Claire Metelits as well as the Center for Teaching, Research and Learning (CTRL) for providing the initial resources to turn this project into a manuscript.

I appreciated the invitation to present my research at the workshop on "Spatialities of Food—the Urban Case of Cairo" that Jörg Gertel organized at the Collaborative Research Centre at the University of Leipzig. I was also grateful for the invitation to present my research at the workshop on "The production of knowledge for research: understanding rural well-being in the Arab world" that Martha Mundy organized at the American University of Beirut for Thimar, the research collective on agriculture, the environment, and labor in the Arab world. I also appreciated the invitation to submit articles for consideration in special issues: I thank Timothy Mitchell and Anupama Rao, editors of the special issue on the Politics of Food in the *Comparative Studies of South Asia, Africa, and the Middle East*. I thank Toby L. Moorsom, Sheila Rao, Heidi Gengenbach, and Chris Huggins, the editors of the special issue on Food Security and the Contested Visions of Agrarian Change in Africa in the *Canadian Journal of Development Studies*. I thank Hilde Bjørkhaug, André Magnan, and Geoffrey Lawrence, the editors of the Routledge volume on *The Financialization of Agri-Food Systems: Contested Transformation*.

My involvement in the Political Economy of the World System section of the American Sociological Association in more recent years has been especially helpful for me developing the world systems perspective in this book. A special thanks to Amy Quark and Bill Winders, in particular, for their camaraderie and support. The same goes for the World-Ecology Research Network, led by Jason W. Moore and Diana Gildea. This book would not be what it is without Jason's continual mentorship. Also, I want to acknowledge the broadly defined research community of Middle East and North Africa (MENA) studies, including especially Habib Ayeb, Sylvia Bergh, Koen Boegart, Omar Jabary Salamanca, Angela Joya, Karen Rignall, Reem Saad, and Sami Zemni. From Rural Sociology, I thank Pablo Lapagna for his help with the book-writing process. I am grateful to my editor, Adam Swallow, and project editor, Vicki Sunter, at Oxford University Press, as well as two anonymous reviewers, for providing the opportunity to turn the culmination of years of research into a publishable book.

I could not have asked for better colleagues at Point Park University, where I have been while writing this book, and at our local unit, the Pittsburgh Post-Gazette. My colleagues have reinforced for me that collective struggles matter in the face of formidable social structures. Our collective struggles animate this text.

Sadly, I lost friends, colleagues, and family members along this long journey, and during the last year of writing, I lost my father, Sandy Dixon. I carried his memory while writing. I owe much to my family, near and far. Anouar and Elias, who share every day with me, were incredibly patient and generous as I wrote this book. Anouar's contributions cannot be easily summarized.

Portions of Chapter 3 have appeared in Dixon, 2020, "Agrarian Question Revisited: Smallholders and Corporate Food in Egypt," *Canadian Journal of Development Studies,* 41(2): 279–295. Portions of Chapter 7 have appeared in Dixon, 2018, "Riding on Waves of Crises: Finance, Food, and Political Tumult in Egypt," in *The Financialization of Agri-Food Systems: Contested Transformation,* edited by H. Bjørkhaug, A. Magnan, and G. Lawrence, pp. 135–155, New York: Routledge; and Marion Dixon, "The Land Grab, Finance Capital, and Food Regime Restructuring: The Case of Egypt," *Review of African Political Economy,* copyright@ROAPE Publications, Ltd, reprinted by permission of Taylor & Francis Ltd, www://www.tandfonline.com on behalf of ROAPE publications Ltd. Portions of Chapter 8 have appeared in Dixon, 2015, "Biosecurity and the Multiplication of Crises in the Egyptian Agri-food Industry," *Geoforum.* 61: 90–100; and Marion Dixon, "Plastics and Agriculture in the Desert Frontier," in *Comparative Studies of South Asia, Africa, and the Middle East,* vol. 37, no. 1, pp. 86–102. Copyright, 2017, Duke University Press. All rights reserved. Republished by permission of the publisher. www.dukepress.edu. All reprints have been heavily revised for this book.

List of Abbreviations

CAIRNS	Group of 19 Agricultural Exporting Countries
CEA	Controlled Environment Agriculture
EARIS	Egyptian American Rural Improvement Service
EGP	Egyptian Pound
ERSAP	Economic Reform and Structural Adjustment Programme
FAO	Food and Agriculture Organization of the United Nations
H5NI (HPAI)	Avian flu (Highly Pathogenic Avian Influenza)
HEIA	Horticultural Export Improvement Association
IFC	International Finance Corporation
IMF	International Monetary Fund
LCHR	Land Centre for Human Rights
LDP	Low-Density Polyethylene
MALR	Ministry of Agriculture and Land Reclamation
MNC	Multinational Corporation
MRS	Mubarak Resettlement Scheme
NAC	New Agricultural Country
NCD	Non-Communicable Diseases
NDP	National Democratic Party
OECD	Organization for Economic Cooperation and Development
TNC	Transnational Corporation
USAID	United States Agency for International Development
WFP	World Food Programme
WHO	World Health Organization
WNRD	West Noubariya Rural Development Project
WTO	World Trade Organization

Reader's Note

Where there is an English word commonly rendered for the Arabic, I use the English translation to appeal to the non-specialist reader. It will be useful to keep the following two terms in mind, in particular: A *feddan* is a unit of land equal to 1.038 acres; in all cases, except in quotations and in proper names, I use acre to refer to *feddan*. *Fellahin*, commonly translated as cultivators of the soil, are referred to as peasants (in the past) and as smallholders (in the present).

Where conveying the original Arabic seemed important, I have provided transliteration in parentheses or endnotes. For both Egyptian Arabic and, in fewer cases, Modern Standard Arabic, I use a simplified version of the *International Journal of Middle East Studies* transliteration system, removing all long vowels and using diacritical marks only for the letters ʻayn and hamza. All translations of Arabic conversations are my own.

1
Introduction

Frontier Making and the Ecology of Commercial Agriculture in Egypt

August 8, 2010. I had returned to a government office in Cairo for the second part of an interview. The Egyptian government official who was meeting me was in the middle of negotiations with the Russians over wheat imports. Wheat and other food prices had begun to rise again after falling from a historic high in the beginning of 2008. There had been a drought in Russia that year, and Russian wheat prices were rising dramatically. The price increase was set to elevate Egypt's wheat import bill by 20%, the official told me. That day the interview lasted three and a half hours, while we drank tea copiously, and I had a sneaky suspicion that the official wanted to stay in the interview room to get out of the negotiations.

It was hot in the room. Perhaps because it was August in Cairo. Perhaps because the political environment in Cairo and the rest of the country was bubbling. Tension was in the air. There had been spats of sectarian violence and growing political dissent and organizing, especially throughout 2006 and 2007 among workers in the Mahalla textile factory, who were waging strikes and other actions for higher wages in the face of climbing domestic prices beginning in 2005–06 (De Smet 2016: 184). Between 2005 and March 2008, inflation reached 15.8% (Beinin 2008). When prices pinnacled, in the first months of 2008, subsidized bread shortages led to long bread lines (Beinin 2008; *IRIN,* April 10, 2008). As people in the lines clamored for bread, clashes led to injuries and even death. The army was brought in to stop the deadly clashes and began to take charge in distributing bread (Abul-Magd 2017: 146–147). A mobilization among different political groups called for a general strike on April 6, 2008, which was called off as activists were arrested. In Mahalla, though, the striking workers and thousands of other townspeople went to the streets, demanding the government lower the price of bread. Clashes with the police ensued and ended in the arrest of hundreds and the death of one boy (Joya 2008; De Smet 2016: 183–185). The Egyptian government also responded to growing popular discontent with a host of policy measures to try to absorb the impact of world price volatility and domestic inflation. The government increased the expenditure on consumer food subsidies, not just because of the growing import bill, but to cover the vast majority who spend a sizable percentage of their income on food and who became more food insecure as a result of the price hike (Harrigan 2014). The People's Assembly (Parliament) also

The Frontiers of Corporate Food in Egypt. Marion W. Dixon, Oxford University Press.
© Marion W. Dixon (2023). DOI: 10.1093/oso/9780192842985.003.0001

passed an increase in public sector wages, and because Egypt was a net rice exporter, the Parliament placed a temporary ban on rice exports (USDA 2009).

For some the growing popular tension in Egypt from the 2007–08 world price hike marked a critical moment in the bourgeoning revolt that culminated in the 2011 uprising (Joya 2011; Bogaert 2013). The official whom I was interviewing in 2010 understood at some level that a critical threshold was about to be reached: The government conducted an undisclosed study, which concluded that 83% of the time people in Egypt will revolt if the price of a few key food stuffs (wheat, sugar, rice, tea) goes above a certain percentage of their income. As prices rose that year, the official calculated that there could be an explosion in protest. Sure enough, by the first months of 2011, world food prices reached the highest level since recording began in 1990 (FAO 2012) and food inflation in Egypt reached over 20% (Harrigan 2014: 107). This time the price hike coincided precisely with a mass popular uprising that began in Tunisia and then Egypt and the rest of the region—what became known as the Arab Spring. This book addresses the question of why food prices have been volatile and what the relationship is between food prices and the popular legitimacy of ruling governments by looking at the development and growth of a corporate agri-food system in Egypt.

Of the vast literature that has been published during the past decade to explain the popular uprisings in the region, there has been a debate recently about the so-called Arab Inequality puzzle (Achcar 2021; Hlasny and Verme 2021). The Arab Inequality puzzle is the puzzle that income inequality in the region was low or moderate during the decade or more before the 2011 uprisings, suggesting that income inequality does not explain the uprisings. What the literature on the puzzle fails to consider is that income inequalities around the world are high historically: In 2021, the top 10% of income earners in Egypt captured 50% of the total national income.[1] This top 10/bottom 50 income ratio, which can also be understood as the bottom 50% of income earners earning 16–19 times less than the top 10%, is about average—comparable to the United States and much of Southeast Asia (Chancel et al. 2022: 32). This level of income inequality can only be deemed low in a relative sense, relative to other countries at a time of historically high inequality within countries.

The Arab Inequality thesis fails to take into account the great march toward economic equality during the twentieth century and the reversal at the turn of the twenty-first century to levels comparable to the nineteenth century. To get a sense of this historical change in Egypt, consider that income inequality had been lowered significantly from the 1950s onward with the bottom 50% of income earners having a larger share of total income than the top 1%. This ratio switched dramatically after 2000. From an intergenerational perspective, this change is significant: one generation holds more income than the top 1%, the next less income.

But to capture the extent of the change in opportunities intergenerationally, the attention should be on wealth inequality, which has been even higher. As the World Inequality Database has been at pains to highlight, the bottom 50% of wealth holders hold close to no wealth at all in all regions (Chancel et al. 2022: 37).[2] In Egypt, between 1995 and 2021, the capture of the top 1% of total wealth nationally stayed above 30% on average. As I show in this book, this statistic and others like it do not even reflect the extent of capital concentration given that the numbers are individual rather than family based.

The Arab Inequality thesis further fails to consider the spread of protest activity from the region during the past decade. The past decade of global protest has, in fact, been comparable to previous world-revolutionary moments (Karataşash 2019)—and at a time in which warnings abound of the return to the rule of inherited wealth. While writing this book, from 2020 to 2022, the COVID-19 (SARS-2) pandemic raged. According to the WHO dashboard, more than six million people (and counting) have died. It is still too early to know all of the impacts from the pandemic, but it is likely that even in countries like Egypt that have seen relatively low loss of life from COVID-19, the pandemic has exacerbated economic inequality due to the loss of income during lockdowns and sickness, the collapse of certain economic sectors like tourism, and the like (Chancel et al. 2022: 15). The concentration of capital globally has meant that the share of wealth globally of billionaires rose from 1% to 3% of total wealth since 1995 (Chancel et al. 2022: 15). And the first year of the pandemic, 2020, "marked the steepest increase in global billionaires' share of wealth on record" (Chancel et al. 2022: 15).

This concentration of wealth is partially an outcome of debtor–creditor relationships, of wealth being transferred from debtors to creditors. Sovereign debt, corporate debt, and personal debt have risen exponentially since the 1980s, and banking, in turn, has concentrated into what Jerome Roos (2019) calls a creditor's cartel. The five biggest banks got bigger: "the share of the world's five biggest banks in the total assets of the top-1,000 banks roughly doubled between 1998 and 2009" (Roos 2019: 63). Within nation-states, the average percentage of creditor-assets controlled by the five largest banks for each country rose from 37.9% in 1980 to 57.1% in 1999 (Roos 2019: 63). International credit markets have not only concentrated among a handful of banks "too big to fail," but these creditors' interests have become structurally interlocked (Roos 2019: 69).

In Egypt, sovereign debt rose sharply in the 1980s: Debt servicing costs nearly doubled, increasing from 24% of exports in 1980–81 to 46% in 1989–90. In 1986, the government's outstanding installment and interest payments on its loans had reached $9 billion (Soliman 2011: 102–103). The government went into default on its foreign debt, and by the early 1990s, received restructuring of that debt for its stance on the U.S. Gulf War and on conditions that the government implement structural adjustments (Soliman 2011; Abul-Magd 2017). That respite from foreign debt did not last long as imports rose faster than exports. Despite having paid a total of $24.6 billion in debt repayments between 2000 and 2009, the government fell back into the debt trap: the level of debt increased by around 15% during the same time period (Mossallem 2017). By 2010, the country's public debt, which remained largely domestic, had risen to 73.7% of GDP (Adly 2020). With the 2011 uprising that forced President Mubarak to step down and those closely associated with the president to be arrested, a Popular Campaign to drop the debt quickly formed, calling for an audit for the onerous debt accumulated under the decades of the Mubarak administration (Mossallem 2017).

Several presidential campaigns, the Union of Independent Syndicates, and the Socialist Coalition Party, among others, adopted this campaign, which was articulating how the balance of power between states and creditors had decidedly shifted toward the latter.

The creditors' ability to exercise financial discipline over indebted states has been aided by the more interventionist tendencies of creditor states, central banks, and international financial institutions like the IMF (Roos 2019: 68). This shift in the power balance has also meant that the balance of power within the borrowing countries has tipped in favor of financial firms and wealthy elites (Roos 2019: 68). These social groups have the most to gain from states continuing payment of debt interest, even though states will never be able to pay off the debt. This structural power of private creditors was apparent when the Ministry of Finance (2009: 8) announced in 2009 that the government "is committed to carrying ahead its reform progress set in motion since 2004," despite the fact that the food price shock of 2007–08 had driven large segments of the population into food insecurity. It was these so-called reforms—namely, financial liberalization—that had contributed to the vulnerability of lower-income population groups to world food prices in the first place.

The country's corporate agri-food system, and the corporate food regime, or global food economy, of which it is an integral part, grew through the structural power of private creditors. The corporate agri-food system is both an outcome and cause of concentrations of credit—and capital more generally. The creditors' market discipline structured the Mubarak administration's decisions, which enabled the development and growth of this system. The financial firms, large family business groups, transnational corporations (TNCs), and multinational corporations (MNCs) concentrated their wealth within the country, in part, through investments in agriculture and food.[3]

The corporate agri-food system has not only contributed to the greater vulnerability of population groups to world food prices, but this system has been at the center of two public health crises. The first involves the shift in national diets toward foods/drinks high in unhealthy fats, sugars, and sodium. These dietary changes have contributed to the exponential growth in overweight/obesity and related chronic diseases. The second public health crisis is the spread of infectious diseases—namely, zoonotic diseases like the Avian flu. Infectious zoonotic diseases, like COVID-19, can skip from animals to humans and cause illness and death. Increases in chronic diseases have, in turn, exacerbated the spread of and risk from infectious diseases. The commercialization and industrialization of agriculture has further led to a host of environmental costs, which further exacerbate these public health problems. These so-called costs include, for example, the contamination of soil and waterways from agrochemicals. The spread of infectious diseases and the degradation of local ecosystems are also threats to production and were factors in pushing agribusiness into new lands. I refer in shorthand to those who invest in agriculture and food as agribusiness.

The book's thesis is that the development and growth of a corporate agri-food system depended on the horizontal and to a lesser extent vertical expansion of reclaimed lands from agricultural areas in the Delta and Nile Valley. This dependence on new lands, or frontiers, can be explained not only by how commercial agriculture and its industrialization degrades so-called local environments, but by the ecology of commercial agriculture and its industrialization. By ecology, I refer specifically to processes of genetic homogenization and production intensification—both of which necessarily lead to vulnerabilities, which have multiplied and become bigger threats like infectious zoonotic disease. These threats coupled with other forces that have degraded agricultural land in the Delta and Nile Valley, such as real estate development and soil salination from the sea level rising with global warming, have pushed agribusiness to reclaim land. Also, political struggles and conflicts over agricultural land in the Delta and Nile Valley incentivized investors to invest in land reclamation. This contestation arose, in part, due to increases in land prices in the 1990s, which also pulled agribusiness to reclaimed land, which was cheaper to buy and/or reclaim. These risks to capital have moved agribusiness from the Delta and Nile Valley to the frontiers of reclaimed land.

Land reclamation has long been criticized as unsustainable. Government agricultural revenue, irrigation water, and laborers are all being drawn from agricultural areas in the Delta and Nile Valley to reclaimed lands. In addition, land reclamation has led to the draining of inland lakes, the degradation of coastal ecosystems, and the depletion of the underground aquifer. Land reclamation has not only degraded local ecosystems, but as I show in this book, this degradation has then led to new lands to be reclaimed. Historically and presently, the frontier continually expands. The ecology of commercial agriculture and its industrialization—from the loss of genetic diversity between and within plant and animal species to the degradation of top soil to the depletion of irrigation water sources—compels this continual movement to virgin soil, farther from existing farms and residential areas. The continual expansion of reclaimed land has shaped the extent of, and limits to, capital accumulation in agriculture in the longue durée and in the development of a corporate agri-food system more recently.

Corporate Agri-food System in Egypt

Corporate agriculture and food is a system that began to be built in the 1970s and rapidly developed by the 1990s. As a system, it depends on both domestic production and imports. Its most basic components include food processing and an animal protein complex largely for the Egyptian market, and so-called fresh fruits and vegetables (and ornamentals) for export. This system has two interconnected sides: the formal agri-food industry and the informal sector of agricultural producers and vendors. As such, there have been many actors involved in the system—and predominantly among them are large Egyptian family business groups, Egyptian and foreign financial firms, MNCs, and TNCs. The system's development and growth has depended on the (re-)entrance of MNCs and TNCs but also on the (re-)emergence of two types of capitalist enterprise within Egypt—family business groups and finance. Most of these corporate actors are invested in many economic sectors and have consolidated their market shares through integration into agriculture and food.

The dual character of this system—the formal/informal—also means that its development has depended on farmers of all sizes, including smallholders (with five acres or less). The relationship of the corporate agri-food system to smallholders is a complicated one. Smallholders participate in this system as producers of crops, wage laborers, and vendors. Members of smallholder households, even children, may work as daily wage laborers in agroexport farms, as I discuss in Chapter 6. Small-scale vendors may sell adult broiler birds (to be slaughtered) in open-air markets that the poultry industry bred, as I discuss in Chapter 8. Smallholders may grow crops for food processors or the agroexport market, informally or formally, as I discuss in Chapter 3. Smallholders, who maintained their status as the majority of agriculturalists in the country in 2009–10, have been supplying crops for agribusiness, and at the same time, have been a main source of staples (especially wheat), which is for subsistence, local markets, and the bread subsidy program.[4] Paradoxically, then, smallholder production has enabled the growth of this system and helped meet the subsistence needs of the rural poor.

The development and growth of the corporate agri-food system also depended on an expanding frontier of reclaimed lands—lands made suitable for cultivation and/or settlement. Corporate food often comes from processing facilities that are concentrated in industrial zones in the satellite cities in reclaimed lands. It is then transported via the highways, ports, and airports of the frontier to the consumer markets of Cairo and other sizable markets like Alexandria and tourist resorts as well as the hypermarkets and supermarkets of the Middle East and Europe.

The system's dependence on the frontier has meant that spatially this system has been drawing irrigation water, laborers, state agriculture revenue, and even crops from the Nile Valley and Delta to reclaimed lands. Upstream, agribusiness farms and facilities are concentrated in reclaimed lands, although they can be found in the Nile Valley and Delta as well. Labor on agribusiness farms (horticulture farms and processing facilities, especially) is gendered: there is a permanent workforce of male managers, supervisors, professionals (agronomists, engineers, etc.) and a daily and seasonal, lower-wage female workforce. Agricultural inputs include both imported corporate and government high-yielding seed varieties, vaccinations and other pharmacological interventions, plastic agri-technologies (including drip irrigation), agrochemicals, and the like. The use of genetically modified (GM) seeds has been heavily contested: The Egyptian government had banned GM imports in 1997, and then approved and discontinued the testing of GM crops between 2008 and 2012.[5] It should be noted that most agribusiness, at least during the time of this research, between 2008 and 2012, was not vertically integrated with their own farms. Rather, agribusiness relies heavily on contracting with commercial farms and on informal arrangements with smallholders, both of whom are on reclaimed lands and in the Nile Valley and Delta. The heavy reliance on contract farming is a reason for the dual character of the system.

Downstream, a main component of this system is food processing, which is largely for the Egyptian market but is also exported. Most investments in the agri-food industry were in food processing, which grew from 12.6% to 71.1% of the country's total manufactured value added between 1992 and 2002 alone (IMC 2005). Food processing is designated for a fairly wide spectrum of corporate consumer food markets—both food retail (e.g., supermarkets and hypermarkets) and food service (e.g., fast food franchises). Hypermarkets as a percentage of total grocery sales were projected to rise from 13% in 2003 to 26% in 2011 (USDA 2010a). Supermarket sales have been even larger: Supermarket sales reached an estimated total of $1.6 billion with 550 supermarkets in 2008 (USDA 2010a). And supermarkets cross the social class spectrum—with discount markets and the lower-middle-end of the market (e.g., Ragab Sons) to the high-end of the market (e.g., Metro). Likewise, the food franchise market rose from seven chains in 1993 to 45 in 2010, and valued at more than $300 million in 2010 (GAFI 2010). In terms of agricultural exports, they rose threefold from $278 million to $863 million between 2004 and 2006 alone, and then during the food price hike, increased nearly 130%, from $863 million to $1.983 billion, between 2006 and 2010 (EDF 2011).

In conclusion, the corporate agri-food system is one significant, and largely overlooked way, in which Egyptian society and economy have become increasingly integrated into the expanded world economy of the neoliberal period. Theoretically, this system's integration has taken the form of becoming a constitutive part, or a node, of the corporate food regime.

Corporate Food Regime

Food regime analysis brings a structural and historical perspective "to the understanding of agriculture and food's role in capital accumulation across time and space" (McMichael 2009: 140). The latest and present-day corporate food regime emerged in the 1970s and 1980s when the restructuring of capitalist relations and the hegemonic state system led to agriculture and food changes worldwide (McMichael 2013). The corporate food regime has deepened the process of agribusiness creating transnational supply chains; new regions have been incorporated into animal protein and food processing chains and a so-called supermarket revolution has swept the globe. Enabling these developments has been the dramatic growth of the size of the financial sector relative to the rest of the world economy. Specifically, financial firms "massively expanded their involvement in the food commodities trade" (Bjørkhaug et al. 2018: 2–3). Plus, agribusinesses have developed their own financial firms.

Corporations of all types and financial firms have consolidated what is grown, how it is grown, and for whom it is grown. They have been able to do so in part through formal and informal arrangements with smallholders (Watts 2009; Ouma 2015; Bisoka and Ansoms 2020; Gengenbach 2020). In Yıldız Atasoy's (2017: 4) words, small-scale producers are "a dynamic element in the deepening commodification of agriculture."

The process of agricultural commercialization and industrialization has further deepened the steady homogenization of the biological material in agriculture—from seeds to soil to animals. Both crop species diversity and genetic diversity within species have dwindled (Weis 2007, 2013). This genetic homogenization has led to vulnerabilities of industrial agriculture and is associated with multiplying and intensifying threats from pests and pathogens, including zoonotic diseases like the Avian flu (Davis 2005; Weis 2007, 2013; Wallace 2009).

Further characterizing the corporate food regime is both a widening dietary gap between the rich and the poor and a convergence of diets across class toward foods and drinks high in unhealthy fats, sugars, and sodium (Weis 2007; Otero 2018; Swinburn et al. 2019). These dietary changes are associated with the rise of overweight/obesity and a host of related chronic diseases, such as heart disease and diabetes 2 Prentice 2006; Monteiro et al. 2013; Otero 2018; Swinburn et al. 2019). As the Lancet Commission warned in their 2019 report on the Global Syndemic of Obesity, Undernutrition, and Climate Change, the "concentrated power of the large food corporations is the most powerful source of policy inertia for actions that create healthier food environments" (Swinburn et al. 2019: 803).

Social movements that emerged to challenge the growing role of corporations in agriculture and food are also constitutive of the corporate food regime. As the regime emerged so did social movements like La Via Campesina, an umbrella organization made up of many local, regional, and national groups seeking to halt or reverse these processes (Holt Gimenez and Shattuck 2011; McMichael 2013). Because world food prices have become increasingly volatile as the corporate food regime has grown (Winders 2011; Winders et al. 2016), its growth is also associated with rising popular unrest in many countries, as will be explored further in Chapter 2.

The corporate food regime emerged out of growing competition in global agri-food trade. New countries in the global North and global South—particularly the CAIRNS group of second rank agroexporters—began to compete with the trans-Atlantic powers in an expanding global agri-food trade (Friedmann 1993). The inclusion of agriculture in the World Trade Organization (WTO) (1995)—and the bilateral and multilateral trade agreements that followed—enabled the growth of agroexport markets, industrial animal agriculture, and corporate food markets in member countries. Food regime analysis came up with the concept of New Agricultural Countries (NACs) to capture these new agroexporting countries that have also developed corporate food markets nationally.

New Agricultural Countries

I theorize Egypt as a New Agricultural Country (NAC). The concept captures the multi-layered, multi-faceted character of corporate dominance: Grain and food/drink TNCs in the global North have consolidated their global commodity chains (Fold and Pritchard 2005; Burch and Lawrence 2007), while national corporations and family business groups along with other investors, public corporations, and the military in the NACs have consolidated national agri-food industries and even began to spread regionally.

The concept also captures how the development of corporate food markets and agroexport markets has been uneven. There is a core of NACs that tend to be competitive in high-value agriculture as well as animal feed grains and processed foods (e.g., Brazilian soy, citrus, and poultry), and an "underbelly" that has, for example, like much of sub-Saharan Africa, returned to exporting colonial crops (Watts and Goodman 1997). In between, there is a range of less significant agroexporting countries like Egypt and Kenya that have developed their own corporate agri-food systems.

A set of industry standards and protocols institutionalized within the WTO governs global agri-food trade, and, in effect, reinforces this hierarchy within the NACs (Busch and Bain 2004; McMichael 2013). Corporate food retailers and their third-party certifiers (e.g., Codex standards, Good Agricultural Practices (GAP)) designed these rules that regulate production and trade—what is referred to as private governance or quality governance. Many of these standards and protocols fall under the umbrella of biosecurity: technologies, governance mechanisms, institutions, and discourses that seek to manage and explain the knowns and unknowns (e.g., invasive species, zoonotic diseases, etc.) that are impacting and potentially threaten economy and society. As I show in Chapter 8, biosecurity determines the conditions of participation of countries and local suppliers in global agri-food trade, thereby, contributing to the consolidation of corporate agri-food systems. Only the most capitalized investors can afford to adopt these practices and technologies (Ponte 2009; Ouma 2010). At the same time, the institutionalization of biosecurity does not mean uniformity of implementation; "place-specific diversity happens together with the expansion and deepening of globalized standards and normative practices of commodification" (Atasoy 2017: 246).

As an NAC, Egypt has acted as a regional hub: MNCs, TNCs, and financial firms entered the country and competed and cooperated with Egyptian family business groups and financial firms to process and distribute food for largely the supermarket and hypermarket shelves in Egypt as well as the Middle East and Europe. Gulf investors have become one of the largest sources of investment in the Egyptian agri-food industry (Henderson 2019). However, much of the influence of the Gulf Cooperation Council (GCC) countries as a regional hegemon (Hanieh 2013) appears to have become more significant after the 2011 uprising. If looking at Egypt's main trading partners between 2000 and 2019, there is a notable shift from the West to the GCC, China, and Russia. In 2000, all of Egypt's main trading partners were Western. By 2008, India and China were added to the list of top trading partners, and in 2019, three GCC countries joined three Western countries plus Turkey, China, and Russia.[6] Plus, from the perspective of the corporate agri-food system's development, investments have not simply moved unilaterally from the GCC to Egypt. Investment historically is far more complicated. Some of the largest corporate actors in this account began with an Egyptian and spread regionally with co-investors (for example, EFG-Hermes). Egyptian financial firms that have spread regionally have co-investors including Gulf investors as well as multilateral funders. Large family business groups and multinationals regionally, if not throughout the global South, have grown in part through subsidiary relationships with transnationals.

A more important theoretical point about the country's corporate agri-food system as an integral part of the corporate food regime is that the system's integration is one of uneven and combined dependency. As Gerardo Otero (2018: 165) emphasizes, the core countries have increased their imports of fruits and vegetables as well as wine and other alcoholic beverages. These two groups are luxury rather than basic foods, and they make up a small percentage of total food intake. Conversely, the NACs have become dependent on the importation of basic foods. Although exports of fruits and vegetables (and ornamentals) to the North increased considerably, these exports have not caught up in value to basic food imports. This imbalance matters—but not for the reasons that many commentators claimed at the time of the price hikes in 2007–08. International development agencies and multilateral organizations were claiming that food import dependency in Southern countries, which was attributed to government-subsidized bread and other foods, was a main culprit behind trade imbalances. As I show in Chapter 2, this claim is false: Most food imports in Egypt were for corporate food processing and animal feed—not for the consumer food subsidy program. Also, food imports represented a small share of the total value of imports in Egypt at the time of the crisis. On average, around 50% of imported wheat at the time of the price shock was designated for the bread subsidy program—the rest was for the private bakeries, bread distributors, food processors, and the like. And on average, imported wheat was 3.9% of the total value of imports in the inter-crisis period (between 2007–08 and 2010). Contrary to what is often assumed, the Mubarak administration had achieved a level of economic diversification as reflected in the country's imports and exports at the time. The other major food imports—corn, dairy, fish, horticulture, meat, and oilseeds—are all heavily, if not exclusively, for corporate food service and retail.[7] Many of these imported foods can also be considered basic foods, in Otero's (2018) terms, because corporate food markets skew toward global consumers but also cut across class to a certain extent and intersect with informal food markets.

Why does import dependency on basic foods matter, then? A loss of self-sufficiency increases a country's vulnerability to price fluctuations (Otero 2018: 158). Food prices have grown volatile as the corporate food regime has developed, and price fluctuations disproportionately affect the lower-income groups in any country. These groups tend to spend larger shares of their household budgets on food. Further, price fluctuations are intricately tied to political instability as food prices impact the popular legitimacy of ruling governments. In Egypt, the corporate agri-food system has greatly expanded corporate food markets by lowering the costs of processed foods/drinks, yet, the system has not succeeded in lowering the cost of food as a percentage of income on average: This percentage was around 38% in 2011 (Harrigan 2014: 110).

Since the 2007–2009 food and financial crises, there has been growing attention to the social similarities between the beginnings of the twenty-first century and the beginnings of the twentieth century. During both periods of globalization, there was the aforementioned food insecurity among the masses and heightened economic inequality (as well as global pandemics). These and other similarities are often understood as colonial legacies, and what I suggest in this book is that these social patterns are rather characteristic of so-called globalization, born out of processes of uneven and combined development.

Uneven and Combined Development

In the most basic sense, uneven and combined development refers to the co-existence and interactive development of all societies throughout history (Rosenberg 2005 cited in Allinson 2016: 27). This interaction is between societies of different social structures, and their interaction shapes unevenly the patterns of social relations within each society (Allinson 2016: 13; see also Anievas and Nişancıoğlu 2015: 48). The resultant social formations, in turn, combine into and shape the international or world order, from which they came. In the capitalist world system, societies have interacted the most during the periods of global expansion of capitalist social relations: the two periods of so-called globalization, in the long nineteenth century (c. 1780–1914) and in the neoliberal period (c. 1980–2012). For the purposes in this book, this expansion was under the first colonial-era food regime and the third corporate food regime.

I argue that in Egypt there were three combined social formations that have enabled the heightened integration of Egyptian society and economy into the two food regimes: two types of capitalist enterprises—family business groups and finance—and commodity frontiers of reclaimed lands. I do not claim that these are the only social formations that enabled participation in the world system. Rather, these three social formations are the most relevant to the genealogy of the corporate agri-food system that I offer. Family business groups, finance, and commodity frontiers of reclaimed lands emerged in the long nineteenth century; transformed in the post-independence period (roughly the 1950s through the 1970s); and re-emerged by the 1980s. They are not colonial legacies in the sense of representing a continuity with the colonial past. Rather, they are the resulting social formations under the impact of the global expansion of capitalist social relations (see Allinson 2016 13). In Fouad Makki's (2015: 478) terms, how one region interacts with the world-system is

> as much a historical as a structural relationship, and rather than being unilaterally determined by the structural imperatives of the wider system, emerges out of the historically variable relationality between them.

The uneven and combined development that I am referring to is specific to these regimes that expand capitalist social relations across and within borders and heighten the interaction of societies.

Family Business Groups

Contrary to the widely held belief that corporations are public companies managed by outside professionals, corporations are both public and private, and many are family owned and/or family controlled, as scholars in the 1970s were pointing out (Burch 1972; Zeitlin 1974; Barnes and Hershon 1976). Approximately 60% of private companies with revenues of $1 billion or more were owned by families and founders in 2010 (Björnberg, Elstrodt, and Pandi 2014). A 2014 McKinsey report on Southern, so-called emerging markets found that the trend toward family-based big companies was increasing worldwide: In the Middle East, an estimated 60–70% of large companies were family owned (Björnberg, Elstrodt, and Pandi 2014).[8]

In William K. Carroll's (2010: 133) terms, corporations have produced and reproduced great fortunes. As I was finishing this book, Morgan Stanley, the global investment bank, announced that its family offices, which had opened in 2021, had grown to $5.5 trillion in assets (Son 2022). Often these fortunes are understood and measured as individual, but they are rather largely family-based—and in anthropological terms, based in patriarchal kinship social units. It would be difficult to analyze the oligopolistic character of today's world economy without considering the breadth and depth of inherited wealth (see Piketty 2014 on inherited wealth worldwide).[9]

In Chapter 7, I explain how family business groups, in cooperation and competition with TNCs and MNCs and financial firms, have concentrated their holdings across the sectors of the formal economy—including agriculture and food. Following Robert Vitalis (1995: 22), I define a family business group as, firstly, a diversity of holdings across different economic sectors. Secondly, rather than a separation of ownership from management, the ownership-management structure often involves several individuals or families, though a single individual is typically designated as the group leader. Thirdly, the core leadership is bound by personal, family, ethnic, or other communal ties.

Large Egyptian family business groups (e.g., Mansour group, PICO group) helped build the country's corporate agri-food system by diversifying into and within agriculture and food largely following the privatization and liberalization policies under the 1991 structural adjustments and, then, Egypt's membership in the WTO in 1995 and the many bi-lateral and multi-lateral trade agreements that followed. As they consolidated the formal economy, family business groups got larger and began to look and act more like corporations: with some level of separation of ownership from management, the establishment of a Board of Directors, legally binding regulatory and accounting procedures, a legal framework for mergers and acquisitions, and on and on.

Finance

The growth of the corporate agri-food system was possible through two phases of financialization. As I show in Chapters 2 and 7, family business groups grew in part by setting up their own investment arms starting in the 1990s—a process of non-sectoral financialization. Second, during the global economic boom of 2003–2007, and following the passage of the 2003 banking law in Egypt, existing financial firms grew and new kinds of financial firms proliferated. Private equity funds alone rose from $533 million in 2004 to $6.4 billion in 2008 (Ismail 2009: 16, 61). This process of sectoral financialization further led to rapid concentration in agriculture and food.

I argue that finance not only played a role in the country's corporate agri-food system through processes of non-sectoral and sectoral financialization, but that finance re-emerged as a social class. In Egypt, as a social class with some political and economic power, bankers and other finance capitalists became a target of popular discontent because of a widely perceived association of this class with Gamal Mubarak, the son of the former President Hosni Mubarak. More importantly to understanding the broader connection between the growth of the corporate food regime and eroding popular legitimacy of ruling governments is that both family business groups and finance represent two very direct ways to transfer wealth and privilege to individuals and within families. They are among the least meritocratic ways of ordering the social classes.

Frontiers

Reclamation is the process of repurposing, transforming for a new purpose. Land reclamation is inseparable from human settlement historically: land is transformed for a new use or uses. As I show in Chapter 4, with capitalist development, beginning roughly in the twelfth to thirteenth centuries in western parts of Europe, land reclamation became a type of commodity frontier as well: a place for the production and/or extraction of commodities to get a return on investment. Land reclamation is costly, requiring often the remaking of local ecosystems, which is why states have relied on private persons or entities to bare part of the cost in reclaiming the land. With capitalist development, investors, firms, and elites have dominated reclaimed lands.

As I show in Chapter 4, this type of frontier differs from other types—say, resource frontiers of the neoliberal period (Tsing 2005; Cons and Eilenberg 2019), or commodity frontiers in historical capitalism that require the right type of politics and not much more than an axe and hoe to make the land profitable (Moore 2015). This type of commodity frontier requires considerable investment, and with the development of the capitalist world-system, ever newer types of land became subject to reclamation—from coastal lands to riverine and deltas to swamps and marshlands to steppes and (most recently) to drylands.

Since the world price hike of 2007–08 and the near Northern financial crash, there has been renewed attention to reclaiming drylands—and arid lands, in particular. Drylands is a broad designation that includes desert (hyper-arid), semi-desert (arid), grassland (semi-arid), and rangelands (dry-subhumid).[10] The focus in Chapters 6 and 8 is on arid lands. Hyper-arid and arid lands typically receive less than 200 mm average annual rainfall, and combined make up about 20% of land around the world

(Davis 2016: 12). And both are characterized not only by scarce rainfall but the high variability of rainfall (Davis 2016: 15). As I show in Chapter 8, so-called greening the desert narratives and programs re-surfaced as a sustainable answer to the problem of food insecurity. Technical feats such as solar-powered irrigation systems with desalinated water and hydroponic methods that grow crops without soil were presented as saviors in the face of ignited fears from limits to production as a result of desertification, depleted fresh water sources, soil salination, and other threats from environmental degradation and global warming.

I argue that land reclamation as a commodity frontier, and commodity frontiers in general, should be included in food regime analysis. As the corporate food regime developed and grew, many highly capitalized production zones in arid regions were developed to produce cash crops for corporate food service and retail at home and abroad—from western Peru to the São Francisco River Valley in northeast Brazil to the Sous Valley in southern Morocco. The expanding frontier into arid lands has been important to the growth of the corporate food regime because of the ecology of commercial agriculture and its industrialization. The loss of genetic diversity between and within plant and animal species, the loss of top soil, the absorption into soil, and the run-off into waterways of agrochemicals, the depletion of underground fresh water sources—generally, the degradation of the ecological conditions of production over time—leads to the volatility of industrial agriculture. Volatility means threats to production, especially from pests and pathogens. Threats, in turn, lead to greater controls over the production environment. These controls include movement to lands with virgin soils (lands that have not been cultivated recently or cultivated intensively) and to lands farther from existing farms and residential areas.

Land reclamation in Egypt has been rather narrowly analyzed, and throughout this book, in Chapters 4, 5, 6, and 8, I attempt to broaden the perspective. The focus has largely been on state reclamation post-1952 independence—and especially on large reclamation projects like Toshka in the southwest of the country that began in the 1990s (Mitchell 2002; Sims 2018). I offer a much longer view of land reclamation by identifying three waves of frontiers in modern Egypt: The first modern frontier was in the long nineteenth century, during the first colonial-era food regime. This frontier was a commodity frontier. The second frontier was from roughly the 1940s through the 1970s and was a state frontier. The third frontier developed under the corporate food regime beginning in the 1980s and represents a second commodity frontier. Land reclamation as a commodity frontier is referred to as a frontier of capital, and both frontiers of capital enabled expanded commodity production, thereby, deepening Egypt's integration into the respective food regimes.

What distinguishes the second frontier of capital that has been integral to the development of a corporate agri-food system is that land reclamation involved both agribusiness production and state reclamation for the redistribution of small land plots to various marginalized social groups. A focus in this book is on the relationship between the frontier of capital and state (and informal) reclamation. Also, unlike the colonial-era frontier, today's frontier of capital is for the production of cash crops for both the national market and for export.

When discussing frontiers, how much land has been reclaimed? From the state frontier onward, the numbers provide only estimates, or a sense of the order of magnitude of the frontiers. According to the General Authority for Reconstruction Projects and Agricultural Development (GARPAD), the main government agency in charge of land reclamation since the 1970s, from 1950 to 1997, a total of 2.6 million acres were reclaimed with an average of 71,000 acres per year, with a peak period (1987 to 1991) when there was a high of 170,000 acres annually (Sims 2018: 105). Only a portion of these reclaimed lands would have been devoted to the production and processing of agricultural crops.

Reclaimed lands from the 1952 Free Officers coup onwards are often referred to as "the desert." However, most of these lands have not been hyper-arid and are technically not the desert. As an agribusiness manager corrected me during a farm visit, the soil is silted, rather than sandy as in the desert, and has good water absorption capacity.[11] Despite this misrecognition, I keep to the convention and refer to the second frontier of capital, in shorthand, as the desert frontier. I do so to allay any confusion because of the pervasive designation of these areas as the desert. It should be kept in mind, though, that these areas are good for particular types of industrial agriculture because they are arid (rather than hyper-arid).

While much attention has been on the state's mega project, Toshka, a ten-year project to reclaim 540,000 acres in a remote area 150 kilometers west of lake Nasser, little has actually come of this project since it was announced in 1997 (Sims 2018). In contrast, what has received little attention is the rapid development of agribusiness farms and facilities, to the extent that agribusiness is vertically integrated, with concentrations along the two main highways from Cairo that surround the Delta— the Alexandria-desert road to the west and the Ismailia-desert road to the east (Figure 1.1). Agribusiness also exists in other reclaimed lands, for example, along the northern strip of the Delta, into the southern Sinai, and southward to the west of the Nile Valley. Also, there has been comparatively little attention on the industrial zones of the new satellite cities that the state built in the 1980s and 1990s as part of the desert development program. These cities are concentrated in greater Cairo and along the two main highways (e.g., 10th of Ramadan, 6th of October, Sadat City, and Borg El Arab).[12] Food processing is concentrated in these industrial zones, which are near to agribusiness farms and main transportation routes.

The three primary nodes of the corporate agri-food system predominate in the desert frontier: In terms of animal protein, aquaculture farms dominate cultivation north of the Damanhur—Kafr al Sheikh—Mansoura strip of the Delta, while poultry (and to a lesser extent, beef and dairy) are found throughout the reclaimed lands. Industrial poultry is the farthest from residential areas, and at the time of research, led the way to the south, especially around Minya in Middle Egypt. Between 1992 and 2002, aquaculture production (in reclaimed and traditional lands) increased 800% and contributed 47% of total fish production in 2002 (DAI 2002: 109, 111). By 2008, the FAO (2010: 21) had named Egypt one of the top 15 aquaculture producers in the world. The focus in this book is on poultry: In just two decades, from the early 1980s to the turn of the twenty-first century, the country transformed from a net importer

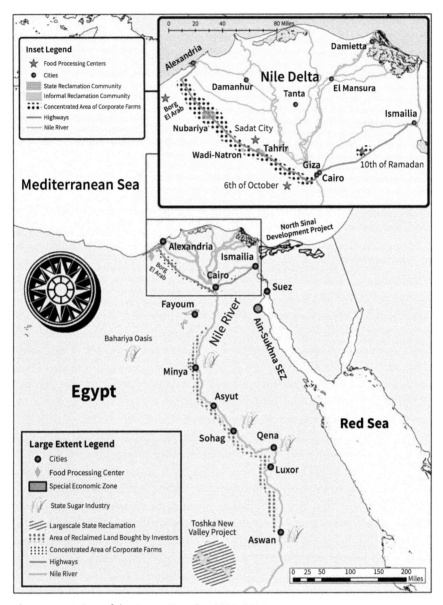

Figure 1.1 Points of the Desert Frontier, 2008–2011.
Source: Johannes Plambeck.

of poultry into a self-sufficient producer with a full-scale corporate poultry industry. Much of the animal protein complex is designated for the Egyptian market.

Horticulture (fruits, vegetables, and ornamentals) is found throughout the desert frontier. However, there was rapid development of industrial horticulture in the southwest of the Cairo-Alexandria desert road, in Wadi Natrun—what Sims (2018: 93) calls the "hottest land reclamation area in Egypt." This area is about 300,000 acres, and has experienced rapid population growth, an increase from 25,000 in 1996 to 71,000 in 2006 (Sims 2018: 93). To the extent that reclaimed lands are devoted to cultivation, much of this cultivation is devoted to fruits and vegetables: According to 2011–12 Ministry of Agriculture and Land Reclamation (MALR) data, of the 2.78 million acres under cultivation in the desert frontier, 1.18 million or 42% were under permanent crops (crops from trees/shrubs)—mainly orchards (olive trees, date palm trees, grape vines, etc.) (Sims 2018: 111). While the animal protein complex is largely for the Egyptian market, most "fresh" fruits and vegetables are destined for export.

Food processing, a cornerstone of corporate food markets, is largely in the new cities. From packaged to frozen to canned/preserved, food processing made up most of the total output of domestic manufacturing activity by the turn of the twenty-first century. As I show in Chapter 3, animal protein and food processing are closely intertwined, with dairy being a key ingredient of food processing. Processed food is both for export and the Egyptian market, which covers a wide class spectrum.

I argue in Chapter 8 that one of the unique characteristics of the desert frontier (from the previous frontiers) is the extent to which agribusiness farms and facilities, whether they are animal agriculture or horticulture, for the domestic market or export, are organized around biosecurity rules and protocols. These controlled environment agri-technologies and structures shape the organization of production, and they function as a type of gatekeeper in the field of agribusiness as only the most capitalized investors are able to invest in biosecurity.

Also, unique to the desert frontier is the role of the military. The military has had various uses for reclaimed areas—from revenue-generating activities like toll roads and commercial farms to national security measures like detention and training facilities. And its role in land reclamation appears to have grown over time. By 2002, under the Ministry of Defense's decree no. 146, so-called desert land (reclaimed or not) falls under two categories: areas of strategic importance and open areas where public and private projects could be erected (Abul-Magd 2017: 138). As Zeinab Abul-Magd (2017: 141–144) highlights, the military has had a role to play in agribusiness—and in agribusiness in reclaimed lands, in particular. For example, the military developed commercial farms and processing facilities for export both in Noubariya in the northwest Delta and in East Uwanayat in the southwestern part of the country (with Gulf investors).

Because the desert frontier includes both private reclamation (agribusiness and others) and state reclamation (part of the broader desert development programming), many actors have been involved in frontier development and expansion: the military, private investors, international development agencies, state agencies, various classes of marginalized settlers and laborers. Nonetheless, agribusinesses have rapidly concentrated their share of cultivated reclaimed lands. Agribusiness of various sizes could easily be argued to dominate reclaimed lands devoted to cultivation (as opposed to real estate, industry, infrastructure (e.g., roads), mining, or other purposes).[13]

Frontiers broadly defined hold a special place in nation making and building in modern states. In Hegel's (1967) terms, a frontier is a way to resolve the tension inherent in modern societies: the tension from the gap between the haves and the have nots (cited in Harvey 2001: 286). As I show in Chapter 6, frontier making in Egypt since the 1940s has been a distinct way to deal with the resulting social problems from this polarization—i.e., landlessness, unemployment and underemployment, lack of affordable housing, and on and on. The new towns around Cairo have come to embody, in Sims's (2018: 284) terms, the nation's "desert dreams," becoming

> vessels for everything modern Egypt desires, including mega shopping malls, golf courses, foreign language schools, private (and expensive) hospitals, shiny corporate headquarters, fast-food outlets, private universities […]

Is land reclamation especially important in Egypt compared to other nation-states, as Sims (2018) claims? Perhaps. In the region, a significant percentage of the land mass was historically not cultivated intensively or at all as it was dominated by nomadism. The extent of nomadism in arid and hyper-arid areas certainly favored state-led land reclamation. Also, in Egypt, the lands that have not been cultivated intensively or cultivated recently are relatively easy to access, being to the west and east of the Delta and Nile Valley, and largely on flat land. This ease of access compares, to say, the Sous Valley in Morocco, an arid area that has been subject to reclamation and that is separated from the areas to the north by a mountain range.

Research Methods

This study is based on mixed-method research that I conducted in Egypt during the 2008–2012 period. By chance, I first arrived in Egypt to conduct preliminary research in January 2008, which was the height of the food price hike of 2007–08. In January 2008, food prices in Egypt had reached a historic high. I had arrived to study the political struggles over agricultural land, which had intensified in the country since the land liberalization policies in the 1990s. Before that spring, there had been a flurry of activity among what Ray Bush (2011) calls "fluid networks of resistance to rural dispossession"—networks of smallholders, civil servants, Left activists, and legal and human rights organizations mobilizing against the dispossession of the rural poor from their livelihoods.

This first phase of my research was downward within agriculture and food in Egypt—among those with the least power and control over change. My research methods included participant observation within these fluid networks of resistance to rural dispossession. I was invited to press releases, conferences, and actions in Cairo and the Delta in 2008, 2009, and parts of 2010, whereby the multiple grievances of the rural poor were expressed. They were grieving private and state violence and coercion to push them off their land. They were grieving mounting debt to pay for inputs that used to be affordable. By invitation, I visited villages in the Delta and the Nile

Valley (Middle Egypt). I proposed a collaborative research project with a local NGO, whereby smallholders would design and carry out an inquiry, asking questions relevant to their communities, and the research findings would then lead to an action plan to address community needs (Kindon et al. 2007).

At the same time, going between sites—Cairo, the Delta, and the Nile Valley during the 2007–08 food crisis and its aftermath—I began to question the framing of debates around the country's food insecurity. Among the networks, the crisis was one of local elites and agents of the state threatening smallholder and other rural folks' livelihoods, and within policy making and international development circles, the crisis was one of government policy failure. In these debates, the food landscape in the country was painted very narrowly—of peasant foods, on the one hand, and subsidized food, on the other hand. But I saw corporate food everywhere—from packaged snacks to soft drinks to fast food outlets to supermarkets and hypermarkets. Yet, my research among these networks confirmed that the rural poor were not largely suffering losses to agribusiness development, but rather, pushing them from their land were real estate developers, the military, and others taking advantage of rising land values.

To address the question of how corporate food grew if not through the dispossession of the rural poor, I began the second phase of research upward with the elites who have the most power and control over agriculture and food—that is, large capitalist enterprises (large family business groups, financial firms, and trans/multinational corporations), policy-making elites, and international development professionals. Much of this second phase was conducted in 2009 and 2010. I conducted participant observation in a family business in the commercial district of Cairo to investigate the networks of elites and their connections to international institutions of higher education, finance, and so on (Ong 1999; Collier and Ong 2005). I conducted semi-structured interviews with consultants, journalists, researchers, government officials, and development professionals with direct involvement in, or knowledge about, the agri-food industry. I collected additional data on industry growth, corporate holdings and profits, agribusiness investment and agri-food trade from published and unpublished documents of industry, government and multilateral institutions as well as news reports. Interviews were secured through snowball sampling.

Through the second phase of research, I learned the enabling and limiting factors in the development and growth of a corporate agri-food system—or what I began to think of as a system—including especially the role of land reclamation. I was able to sketch the corporate food markets, thereby, expanding greatly the view of the food landscape in the country. Also, I discovered that kinship-based elite networks at the time of my research in Egypt were similar to those in the colonial and quasi-independence periods. I then began to connect empirically capitalist enterprise and class formation in the neoliberal period with that in the long nineteenth century.

The third phase of research in 2011—the frontier phase—connected the downward and upward streams of agri-food system change and the present with the past. My methods included semi-structured interviews in Cairo with the executives and managers of ten of the largest agribusinesses in Egypt; tours of agroexport farms in the desert frontier to the west and east of the Delta; and attendance at a food safety conference and an agriculture and food exhibition in Cairo. The farm tours and interviews with agribusiness executives and managers, in particular, heralded a marked shift in how I understand processes of corporatization and financialization. Threats to production—from the Avian flu, the tomato leaf minor (a pest), the wind, the sun, and so on—were omnipresent on farms and in investment and production decisions. These interactions and observations made me take seriously the unwanted and unanticipated in processes of planned change.

The research design of this three-phased project is broadly based on global ethnography (Burawoy 2000), which explores connections between sites and delves into external actors in and across time. Although there is a considerable amount of research on the development of agroexport markets in the global South (e.g., Freidberg 2004; Gibbon and Ponte 2005; Ouma 2015), there are few other examples of book-length studies offering the type of methodology that I attempt in this book. Methodologically, the growing role of corporations in agriculture and food in the country creates a system that operates nationally and is intricately connected to the corporate food regime. The few other examples that offer a similar methodology, and have been useful to me, are Sekine and Bonanno (2016) and Atasoy (2017), who both attempt to show how national agriculture and food changes, in Japan and Turkey, respectively, are tied to global forces and structures. This book shows the development and growth of a corporate agri-food system—and does not describe the current reality. In Karen Rignall's (2021: 204) terms, my account represents a genealogy of the present.

Plan of the Book

This book begins with the moment of crisis of the corporate food regime: world food prices rise to a historic high by early-2008, fall sharply, and then rise again in late-2010. I show how food price shocks and price fluctuations, more generally, including in 2008 and 2011, are characteristic of the corporate food regime. In the most basic way, industrial agriculture's heavy reliance on oil-based energy has coupled agriculture prices with oil prices, and as oil prices rose during the first decade of the twenty-first century, agricultural commodity prices rose. The vulnerability of population groups in Egypt to world prices—i.e., the extent to which world prices impact domestic prices—is the result of the growth of the country's corporate agri-food system and the concomitant decline of what Farshad Araghi (2016) calls the agrarian welfare state of the post-WWII period. Yet, mainstream explanations of food insecurity in Egypt and other indebted countries in 2008 elided corporate food altogether and instead pointed to the failure of government policy. The claim was that governments wrongly focused on subsidizing food, a policy which was supposedly leading to greater demand of wheat imports, thus, exacerbating trade imbalances. What I show in Chapter 2 is that consumer food subsidies in Egypt remained a miniscule contributor to the country's import bill and were the most significant social safety net to alleviate hunger and malnutrition.

In Chapter 3, I describe the dual character of the corporate agri-food system: the formal agri-food industry, on the one side, and the informal sector of independent producers, street vendors, and open-air markets, on the other side. I show that the system's dual character helps explain how national dietary changes—toward foods/drinks high in unhealthy fats, sugars, and sodium—mirror changes in what the majority of agriculturalists have been growing, especially that which is made from/for animals (e.g., clover as animal feed for dairy cows). While the corporate agri-food system relies on agricultural imports, many of the inputs come from agriculturalists in the country—and of all sizes. I focus on smallholders, who have been facing various pressures, including outright dispossession from their land, and through informal arrangements, have turned to the production of crops for food processors as a livelihood strategy. Smallholders, in turn, have become a source of key corporate foods (e.g., raw milk, potatoes).

Throughout this book, I stress that popular struggles matter to the extent and the limits of this system. The intense struggles over agricultural land and rural livelihoods, which I introduce in Chapter 3, inform the movement of investors from existing agricultural lands to new, reclaimed lands. In other words, popular struggles are one of a number of risks that push and pull agribusiness to the frontier of reclaimed lands. I devote Chapters 4, 5, 6, and 8 to developing a world-ecological theory of this type of commodity frontier. Why are frontiers of reclaimed lands central to capital accumulation in agriculture and food?

Chapter 4 addresses this question by looking at the longue durée of land reclamation—of land reclamation undergoing slow (and uneven) transformations over long periods of time. I focus on the transformation of land reclamation as a commodity frontier in parts of western Europe in the late medieval period, and I contrast state land reclamation in the Islamic empires and then the Ottoman state with land reclamation as a commodity frontier in the proto-capitalist states of western Europe and territories through the early modern period. This historical comparison illuminates two interconnected pillars of this type of frontier that distinguish it from state land reclamation and from other commodity frontiers: The first pillar long proceeded the capitalist mode of production and concerns the state incentivizing individual men or private entities to reclaim the land, thereby, gaining revenue, offsetting costs, building (potential) political allegiances, and so on. The second pillar is unique to historical capitalism and involves the grantee transforming the land so that it is suitable for the extraction or production and sale of commodities that returns more money than was put in.

In Chapter 5, I show how land reclamation as a commodity frontier developed in the Ottoman state in Egypt, beginning in the early-1800s. Land reclamation, especially of the Delta, was possible because of the introduction and development of finance. The resulting sovereign debt furthered frontier making, which became important to the expansion of commodity production for export both under the Ottoman state and the British colonial state. I argue that land reclamation during this global expansion of capitalist relations became a distinct social formation—a distinct way that Egyptian society and economy became more deeply integrated into the world system, and the first food regime, in particular.

Chapter 6 continues the typology of frontier making by showing how the frontier of the colonial era gave way to a new type of frontier post-independence. I call this frontier the state frontier, and I show how state land reclamation informed and was informed by the agrarian reforms in the Nile Valley and Delta. By the end of the Gamal Abdel Nasser administration, land reclamation as a commodity frontier slowly returned. The administrations of Anwar Sadat and Hosni Mubarak in the 1970s and 1980s, respectively, sold state reclaimed lands and farms to investors. A new type of frontier emerged—the desert frontier—that combines the redistributive (and select other) aspects of the state frontier with the drive for private wealth accumulation of the long nineteenth century. I explore, in particular, the historical relationship between agribusiness farms and facilities and settler/reclamation communities.

Land reclamation as a commodity frontier was a particular social formation of the first food regime as were two types of capitalist enterprise—finance and large family business groups. In Chapter 7, I focus on the emergence of finance and family business groups in the long nineteenth century as they were both types of enterprises and social classes (or factions within the capitalist class). Their dominance faded considerably in the aftermath of the 1952 coup. But they returned—and indisputably as two dominant capitalist enterprises by the turn of the twenty-first century. They are the main private actors, along with MNCs and TNCs that entered the country, behind the development and growth of the corporate agri-food system. I also address how these actors negotiate the Western standards and protocols of the new world economy.

In Chapter 8, I delve into the so-called international standards and protocols of global agri-food trade in particular. The umbrella term for these standards and protocols (and accompanying technologies) is biosecurity. I detail how biosecurity measures have come to increasingly shape on-farm organization and production in the desert frontier. I offer the case studies of industrial horticulture and industrial poultry to illustrate these processes of standardization. In doing so, I contest the premise of biosecurity: that there is a direct positive relationship between ever greater controls over production zones and protection of these zones.

Chapter 9 concludes with reflections on the methodology that this book offers for studying and analyzing agri-food change: What does the relationship between frontiers and corporate food reveal about the way the capital accumulates in agriculture and food and even how capital forms initially and develops in land? Some key developments related to Egypt's corporate agri-food system since the period covered in this book are also highlighted.

An epilogue addresses the 2021-2022 food price shock that unfolded while writing and finishing this book. World food prices were rising sharply in 2021, during the COVID-19 pandemic, and then when Russia invaded Ukraine in the beginning of 2022, world food prices reached a new historic high—yet again. My analysis explores what is unique about this ongoing food price shock and what many commentators are calling a polycrisis—of hunger, geopolitics, finance, and more.

The appendix explains some of the challenges that I faced and opportunities that opened for me while conducting research in Egypt during the 2008–2012 period.

Notes

1. Economic inequality numbers in Egypt are taken either from the 2022 World Inequality Report (Chancel et al. 2022) or from the online World Inequality Database. If I don't cite the report, the numbers are from the database.
2. Net household wealth is equal to the sum of financial assets owned by individuals, net of their debts (Chancel et al. 2022: 38).
3. In this book, I use both the terms TNC and MNC to distinguish corporations based on the breadth of their market reach. TNCs are corporations that are truly global and largely Western historically, and MNCs are regional.
4. According to the 2009–10 Egyptian Agricultural Census, farmers with less than five acres made up 51.1% of all agricultural producers (Ayeb and Bush 2019: 143).
5. For more on the complicated history of GM crops in Egypt and across the GM debate, see Sawahel 2008; Sarant 2013; Gakpo 2019; Turnbull, Lillemo, and Hvoslef-Eide 2021.
6. This trade data was compiled from the Observatory of Economic Complexity (OEC).
7. These 2007 food import numbers were compiled from resourcetrade.earth. The top non-cereal food imports nearly equaled in value cereals.
8. This regional average ranks fourth out of six regions in terms of the percentage of big companies that are owned by families. The Middle East was tied with Eastern Europe, and had a lower percentage than Southeast Asia, Latin America, and India.
9. For an introduction to the connection between corporations and family fortunes, take the Forbes billionaire lists: Of the 22 billionaires on the 2021 Forbes Arab Billionaires list, six are Egyptian, and of those six, five are from two families—two family business groups, in particular. Two are from the Sawiris family (Orascom), and three from the Mansour family (Mansour).
10. This classification is a United Nations classification, from the UN Decade for Deserts and the Fight Against Desertification (2010–2020).
11. Farm visit, 10/18/11, Noubariya.
12. According to Sims (2018: 287), by 2005, there were a total of 41 industrial zones, and 2,304 industrial projects licensed, but only 983 of these projects were operating.
13. Reliable numbers on what is happening on reclaimed lands, and who is doing what, have been notoriously difficult to find. Sims (2018: 11) ventures that more than 75% of all reclaimed lands during the last 20 years have been captured by "private investors and corporate modes of farming." This estimate is reasonable, but is only an estimate.

2
Food Crises and Revolt

The stage was set for the demise of food subsidies in Egypt in the period between the 2007–08 price shock and the 2011 popular uprising. In the midst of the price shock and in the aftermath, multilateral organizations, think tanks, corporate media, scholars as well as Egyptian government agencies began to blame food insecurity on consumer food subsidies. The Egyptian government, and governments around the world, had increased food subsidies in response to inflation (FAO 2014). The mainstream claim was that food subsidies were placing an inordinate demand on wheat imports, thereby exacerbating the import bill. The Hosni Mubarak administration immediately announced that it was looking into completely revamping food subsidies, whose universal character had already been chipped away at. Nonetheless, food subsidies had remained accessible to most at that time.

This mainstream, neoliberal policy consensus paved the way for the structural weakening of food subsidies in 2014 under the new military government of Abdel Fattah El-Sisi. The Sisi administration replaced food (non-bread) subsidies with a registered card system (called Tamween) as well as cash transfers (for targeted population groups like the elderly and disabled) (Abdalla and Al-Shawarby 2017; *Mada Masr*, April 19, 2018). Those who apply and register receive a so-called smart card: a determined value is added every month to the card (50 EGP in 2015), and recipients can only use the card at designated Tamween shops for food and non-food items (Breisinger et al. 2021). The bread subsidy was greatly restricted to a rationing system—a limit of five bread loaves per recipient per day. These austerity measures paved the way for the 2016 IMF loan of $12 billion (IISD 2014; IMF 2016).

In this chapter, I show that blaming the country's food insecurity on food subsidies was (and is) wrong. The significant increase in the cost of subsidies at the time of the first price shock reflects the fact that food subsidies were at a 30-year low in 2007 (as a percentage of total government expenditure) (Gertel 2015). As I demonstrate in this chapter, food subsidies had a relatively miniscule budget and contributed a small percentage to the country's import bill. In fact, most imported grains (wheat and corn) were (and are) for animal feed and for food processing—that is, industrial uses—and not for feeding people directly.

Rather than being an outcome of government food subsidies, food insecurity was more directly an outcome of Egypt's integration into a volatile world market. This integration led to vulnerabilities to food price fluctuations on the world market, and these vulnerabilities indelibly linked to political instability as the popular legitimacy of the government eroded. The lens offered on this integration—and on the 2007–08

The Frontiers of Corporate Food in Egypt. Marion W. Dixon, Oxford University Press.
© Marion W. Dixon (2023). DOI: 10.1093/oso/9780192842985.003.0002

and 2011 food price shocks—in this chapter is the country's corporate agri-food system as a unit of the corporate food regime.

The Twin Crises of 2007–2008 and 2011

World prices rose beginning in 2004 and pinnacled the first months of 2008. From 2004–05 to the spring 2008, world wheat prices alone rose by more than 200%—from an average of $127 per ton to $397 per ton—and rice prices rose by more than 250% to $962 per ton in 2008 (Winders 2011: 83). Then, prices collapsed: By mid-2008, domestic prices for wheat and corn (but not for rice) had nearly returned to January 2007 levels (FAO 2011a: 22). However, by the second half of 2010, world prices for wheat and corn doubled (FAO 2011a: 22). That summer extreme weather had destroyed corn crops in the United States and wheat crops in Russia, among other crop failures in cereal-producing regions of Australia, Pakistan, and West Africa (World Bank 2012: 2). In response, the Russian government imposed an export ban, just days before my interview in Cairo that I introduce in Chapter 1, and Russia was the largest supplier of wheat to Egypt (Kramer 2010; World Bank 2012).[1]

Smaller, import-dependent countries were impacted the most (FAO 2011a: 8) as world prices tend to have a stronger impact on domestic prices.[2] As prices rose, according to a 2008 FAO estimate, at least 40 million more people around the world began living in hunger (cited in De Schutter 2010: 2).[3] Some form of popular protest erupted in an estimated 30–48 countries throughout the world—in Europe, Africa, South America, the Caribbean (Patel and McMichael 2009: 9; Barrett 2013: 4).

The food price volatility of 2007–08 was the result of increasing financialization of international commodity markets, all of which experienced price hikes. During the first decade of the twenty-first century, trading on commodity futures markets rose exponentially: The volume of index fund trading increased by 1,900% between 2003 and March 2008 (De Schutter 2010: 3), and agricultural commodities typically account for about 30% of the commodities in these funds (Clapp 2009: 1187–1188). From 2005 to March 2008 alone, the value of commodity futures contracts doubled, estimating $400 billion, an increase of $70 billion in the first three months of 2008 (Clapp 2009: 1187). There is a feedback effect between futures trading and prices: futures trading contributes to an increase in price, and a higher price leads to more trading. Crude oil prices fueled this bubble as other commodity prices follow the price of crude oil: Trading in crude oil futures began to increase steadily in 2002 and then quite dramatically in 2005–06 (Dunn and Holloway 2012). Crude oil prices began to rise rapidly in step, between 2002 and 2003, peaking between 2011 and 2012 (OECD n.d.). The trans-Atlantic housing market followed suit and then crashed in 2007–08, precipitating a near financial crash in the United States.

The coupling of crude oil prices and agricultural prices is characteristic of the corporate food regime. Industrial agriculture is heavily reliant on oil as a source of energy—for the production of farming inputs (e.g., chemical fertilizer), the tilling of soil and the harvesting of crops (via mechanization), refrigeration, transportation, and so on. This coupling further tightened as crude oil prices rose from 2002 onward. Public energy security fears rose as oil prices kept rising, fueling the growth of the biofuels economy. For example, by 2007, the U.S. Congress passed the Energy Independence and Security Act, mandating the increase of agro-fuels production from 4.7 billion gallons in 2007 to at least 36 billion gallons in 2022 (Winders 2011: 85). As Phil McMichael (2009: 283–284) argued, this economy is more accurately called an agrofuels project as food for human consumption (corn, sugar, and palm oil) is converted to fuel: corn for ethanol and sugar and palm oil for biodiesel.

The historic high of world food prices in 2007–08 was a conjuncture—of various forces and events coming together at a precise moment—namely, the growth in commodity futures markets and the consequential growth in agrofuels, combined with weather shocks (FAO 2011a; Winders 2011). The food crisis also had structural causes, a process of de-regulating agriculture over decades as the international agreements and national policies that had helped stabilize agricultural prices and production in the post-WWII period were eroded or eliminated (Winders 2011: 84). One such national policy that was designed specifically as a buffer against the world market was grain reserves or stocks. Between the 1990s and the 2010s, most countries stopped using strategic grain reserves to ensure domestic food security (Fraser et al. 2015: 446). For example, most governments of sub-Saharan Africa had been regulating the grain market from independence until the late 1980s (Lynton-Evans 1997). Through a combination of low producer prices and heavy subsidies, low consumer prices were maintained. There were pricing systems and marketing boards (or parastatal companies), which had monopoly rights for the marketing of designated cereals and were normally responsible for the grain reserves. By the end of the 1980s, under conditions of debt management, subsidies were greatly reduced or eliminated; parastatal companies lost their monopoly positions; price controls were relaxed or eliminated (Lynton-Evans 1997).

Private companies came to replace the publicly held grain reserves. Public grain reserves had served at the very least as an emergency source of grains at times of low harvests or high world prices (Davis 2001). In contrast, the private system of grain distribution is highly concentrated in the hands of a few conglomerates like Archer Daniels Midland (ADM), Cargill, and Bunge. These transnational corporations not only hold grain reserves (the size of which is unknown), but they are the largest actors in the commodity futures markets and are able to manipulate prices on a world scale (Fraser et al. 2015: 451).

The very coupling of oil prices and agricultural prices reflects a process of industrialization of agriculture around the world. This process has been uneven and does not just explain the growing reliance of farming systems on oil as an energy source. The industrialization of agriculture also involves the de-coupling of grain for direct consumption as grains have increasingly been directed for indirect consumption (as animal feed, ingredients in food processing, and so on). This decoupling characterizes what Tony Weis (2007) referred to as an industrial grain-livestock complex, which was built long before the corporate food regime. The building of this complex, and the concomitant decoupling of grain as a food grain, has involved a process of homogenization of what is grown. The diversity of crop species and the genetic diversity within species in agricultural systems around the world have been greatly reduced with plant breeding and genetic engineering throughout the twentieth century (Weis 2007). Ten crops (rice, wheat, corn, soybeans, sorghum, millet, potatoes, sweet potatoes, sugar cane/beet and bananas) dominate agricultural systems globally, and the Big Three cereals alone (rice, wheat and corn) account for 85% of the total volume of world grains produced (Weis 2007: 16). Rice and wheat are food grains "that serve as the dietary foundation for most societies and feed most of the world's population" (Winders 2017: 9). By contrast, corn and soybeans (the fourth largest crop) are used principally as animal feed, the ingredients in processed foods, and biofuels (Weis 2007; Winders 2017: 9–10). Notably, this great homogenization of crops grown accelerated on a world scale from the 1990s: Corn, rice, and wheat (as a percentage of world grain production) increased from 81% to 90% from 1990 to 2015 (Winders 2017: 3–4). Corn production grew the most, doubling from 1990 to 2015, while the production of other grains (barley, oats, rye, millet) declined (Winders 2017: 3–4). Significantly, plant and animal diseases have been multiplying, and the virility of the diseases increasing, with the steady erosion of diversity of crop species and of genetic diversity within species (Davis 2005; Enticott 2008; Weis 2010; Moore 2015).

Not only have the types of grains declined but also the regions producing and exporting these grains are limited. Although the institution of the World Trade Organization in 1995 was intended to increase competition in global agri-food trade, as will be discussed in Chapter 7, the global agri-food trade has become rather concentrated. As of 2021, five countries could be considered "breadbasket" regions, accounting for at least 72% of the production of wheat, corn, rice, and soy (Clapp 2022: 6). That concentration means that countries that are dependent on grain imports, like Egypt, are then dependent on a small number of countries. This grain is largely traded to be turned into animal feed and for food processing—often over long distances ("food miles") and destined for supermarkets and hypermarkets. The industrial-livestock complex of the twentieth century essentially became extended in the corporate food regime of the twenty-first century.

In the corporate food regime, food retail corporations have gained tremendous market power, with supermarkets capturing the largest market. By the turn of the twenty-first century, supermarkets had a 55% share of national food retail in South Africa, similar to the share in Argentina, Chile, the Philippines, and Mexico (Weatherspoon and Reardon 2003: 333). Further, the global trend is toward concentration with the top 10 food retailers controlling 24% of the global food market (ETC Group 2005 cited in Clapp and Fuchs 2009: 5). This growth, in turn, coincided with an increase in processed foods traded: Processed food grew from 40% of global agricultural trade in 1985 to 75% in 2002 (IMC 2005). Processed foods have increasingly been foods with animal protein—dairy, meat, fish, animal-based oils/fats. There has been not only an increase in animal protein consumption around the world with the growth of the corporate food regime, but also an industrialization of animal agriculture: Factory farming, or the mass production of animal protein (meat/poultry/dairy) in confined feedlots, has been growing rapidly in many parts of the global South, especially in Asia and Latin America (Weis 2007, 2013). In fact, rising meat consumption by a class of 1 billion new consumers in middle-income countries—those shoppers at the super/hyper markets and customers at corporate food service (e.g., fast food chains)—is cited as a structural cause to the historic high of food prices in 2007–08 (McMichael 2009: 282; Winders 2011: 85–86).

In the simplest terms, there are two consumer markets of the corporate food regime: Wealthy consumers have access to a diverse, healthy diet and poor consumers to more refined, durable foods. At the same time, as Weis (2007: 15) emphasizes, all classes increasingly consume foods and drinks high in unhealthy fats, sugars, and sodium. As I show in Chapter 3, this worldwide shift toward the class-based neoliberal diet (Otero 2018) is recognized as a leading contributor to the rising prevalence of chronic diseases worldwide (Haslam and James 2005; WHO 2005; FAO 2006a; Prentice 2006).[4]

Not only has the growth of the corporate food regime led to dietary changes but the prices of key agricultural commodities (corn, soybeans, wheat, cocoa, coffee) have grown increasingly volatile. Prices declined during the first phase of the corporate food regime; however, as Bill Winders et al. (2016: 80) show, from 1971 to 1995, the average annual change in prices was about double the earlier period. Due to growing competition, price volatility became even more marked after the 1990s. For example, the world market share in corn of the top five exporters fell from 97% in 2000 to 80% in 2009, as the average change in annual corn prices rose to almost 20% (from an annual average of 14% during the 1971–1995 period) (Winders et al. 2016: 80, 86). The steady decline in grain reserves, as discussed above, also corresponded directly with this price volatility: According to Brian Wright and Carlo Cafiero (2011: S68), the wheat price hike in the 1970s, 1995–96, and 2007–08 occurred when world stock-to-use ratios were low.

Theoretically, in McMichael's (2009: 285) terms, there have so far been two phases of the corporate food regime: the first phase (1980s–1990s) "deployed a low world price of traded agricultural commodities against small producers across the world, providing relatively cheap food to match declining wages in the North." The second phase (2000s) has reversed this trend of world prices—prices moving against wage-food consumers around the world (McMichael 2009: 285). The reinforcing combination of rising world prices, increasing price volatility, weakening buffers to price volatility (via grain reserves), and growing inequality of dietary changes has contributed to the declining popular legitimacy of governments around the world.

What declining legitimacy meant for the neoliberal consensus was not clear in the 2007/08–2011 period. Ian Bruff (2014), Janet Roitman (2014), Ian Bruff and Cemal B. Tansel (2018), among others, have correctly argued that the 2007–2009 crises led to a deepening of neoliberal policies and logics, although this outcome was certainly not determined before 2011. In the 2007/08–2011 inflationary period, corporate profits grew[5] and exports intensified.[6] Neoliberal restructuring continued to be pushed in the name of reform in the midst of the crisis: For example, in 2008 and 2010, the World Bank named Egypt as one of the top 10 reformers in its Ease of Doing Business Index (EDBI) (Woertz et al. 2014: 27).[7] At the same time, there was a considerable move away from the neoliberal consensus. Perhaps most significant to the eventual ability of ruling elites to capitalize on their gains in the pre-2007-08 period was what has been dubbed the bailout of Northern banks (Roitman 2014). Also, wealthier states began to circumvent WTO rules when their sovereign wealth funds and investors began to lease large swaths of land and forests and mines in Southern countries largely in Africa and Asia. This land grabbing is what McMichael (2013) has dubbed a type of security mercantilism by which certain states are attempting to guarantee access to food and biofuels by sponsoring land deals offshore in response to heightened food and energy security fears.

States attempted to shield their populations from the vagaries of the market by circumventing the WTO architecture in other ways. One immediate measure that many agroexporting states took was imposing grain export bans or restrictions. These bans/restrictions then further exacerbated the world price hikes (FAO 2011a: 11). When a handful of the largest wheat exporting countries (Kazakhstan, Russia, Ukraine, and Argentina) imposed export bans or restrictions in 2008, a third of the global wheat market was cut off, and bans/restrictions among the largest rice-exporting countries (Egypt included) left only a few export suppliers (McMichael 2009: 287). When prices rose again roughly at the beginning of 2010, and drought struck Russia, returning to the scenario presented in the introduction to Chapter 1, the Russian government again imposed a grain export ban by mid-August. This ban negated any existing contracts that exporters had with clients abroad (Welton 2011: 13). Given that Egypt was Russia's largest wheat importer, the Egyptian government was buckling down in negotiations with Russian sellers—but at prices higher than those in the previous contracts (Welton 2011: 13).

What changed beginning in 2011 was what Immanuel Wallerstein (2011b) called the world revolution—popular protest against ruling elites that spread outward from the Middle East and North Africa. In 2011 alone, protests in the region spread to Israel, Botswana, England, Spain, Greece, the U.S., among other countries, quickly becoming a global protest (Werbner et al. 2014). This global protest continued to spread throughout the 2010s, making the past decade comparable to previous world-revolutionary moments (Karataşash 2019).[8]

Corporate Food and Vulnerabilities to the World Market in Egypt

Egypt's growing participation in the corporate food regime not only meant export intensification, which Western creditors and development agencies alike praised. Economic growth via participation in global agri-food trade also translated into the growth of food processing and of corporate consumer markets (namely, food service and food retail), and the increasing market share of a handful of corporations (national, multinational, and transnational) and financial firms in this agri-food industry. This growth was not expansive but certainly rapid, beginning in the 1990s during the structural adjustments that Economic Reform and Structural Adjustment Programme (ERSAP) of 1991 ushered in. In 1995, annual real investment in the food industry was at roughly EGP 400 million and by 2008 rose to about EGP 1.9 billion—the greatest annual real investment in Egypt for 2008 (Abdel-Latif and Schmitz 2011). The country's trade deficit had declined before the crisis. Between 1995 and 2007, the difference in the value of exports to imports fell from 62% to 38%; however, after 2007–08, this difference rose from 38% to roughly 46% by 2010.[9] Put differently, from 2006 to 2010, Egypt's exports increased on average by 17.7% each year while imports increased on average by 26.7% each year, resulting in a trade deficit of $26.7 billion.[10]

What imported commodities was the country dependent on in 2008 when prices pinnacled? All five of the top imports are the cornerstone of the formal economy including infrastructure: petroleum, iron and steel, grains (wheat and corn), electrical/telecom, and motor vehicles (Figure 2.1). Petroleum imports are the largest import by category; 1.3 times the next import category, iron and steel. In addition, petroleum is intricately connected to the other imports. The country is dependent on imports and yet is an oil-producing country. When crude oil prices rose steadily during the first decade of the twenty-first century, the value of crude oil exports from Egypt rose accordingly: The oil export value was at approximately $2.2 billion in 1995, and began to increase exponentially in 2003, reaching $7.4 billion in 2007. And exports of crude oil decreased while exports of higher-grade oil rose during this period. Yet, the value of finished oil imports rose more quickly than that of exports: Oil imports to exports rose from 39% in 1995 to 55% in 2007.[11] Because the state is cut off from the monopoly market upstream of refined oil,[12] end-user oil had been subsidized—a policy that has long been the ire of multilateral creditors, including the IMF. Fuel subsidies have been consistently three to four times more costly than food subsidies during the 2007–08 and 2012–13 period (Rohac 2013: 4) and are much more regressive. Yet, the cost of fuel imports in 2008 was only a little more than 10% of the total import bill due to the economic diversification that the Mubarak administration achieved.

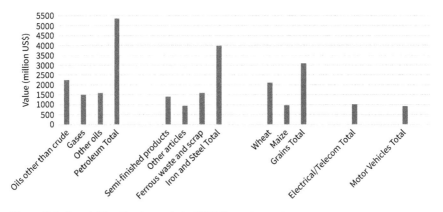

Figure 2.1   Egypt: Top five imports in 2008 (by category).

Source: UN Comtrade 2006–2010.

The corporate agri-food system as an integrated part of the formal economy relies heavily on imported oil for mechanical inputs in the fields (e.g., pumps, tractors), the manufacture of fertilizers and pesticides, refrigeration, transportation, and on and on. In terms of the system's demand on imported wheat, data from the 2010–2013 period shows that more than 50% on average was for the private domestic market (McGill et al. 2015: 3)—bread distributors, bakeries, corporate processors, and so on. The second major imported grain, corn,[13] is for corporate food: food processing and animal feed for industrial poultry in particular (USDA 2009).[14] There are two types of corn: imported yellow corn and domestic white corn. Both yellow and white corn are largely for animal feed: Between 2008–09 and 2013–14, on average 68.2% of corn was estimated to have been for feed, compared to 14.5% of wheat (McGill et al. 2015: 5). While yellow corn is for the corporate sector, white corn is largely for on-farm animal feed (USDA 2009). In fact, much of the on-farm use of corn and wheat for feed is for dairy cows (see Chapter 3). Given that both corn and wheat are used as animal feed—and the value of imported yellow corn was more than half the value of imported wheat in the 2007–2011 period—trends in imported and domestic grains reflect the dietary shift toward animal protein, concomitant with trends within the corporate food regime. Also, most of the other major food imports were essential ingredients of the neoliberal diet—including edible oil, sugar, red meat, and powdered milk (FAO STAT n.d.). More precise measurements of the weight of the corporate agri-food system on the import bill are difficult to capture given the integrated nature of the formal economy. However, the system has impacted the import bill more significantly than the consumer food subsidy program, as will be expounded on in the following section.

Confronted with a growing trade imbalance in the midst of 2007–08, some neoliberal policies were deepened like export intensification. The agroexport market of non-traditional, high-value foods and ornamentals—a cornerstone of the corporate agri-food system—was supposed to counteract the declining terms of trade. Plus, rising world prices of course offered an opportunity for handsome rewards for agroexporters. In interviews in Cairo in 2010 and 2011, development practitioners and government consultants and officials repeatedly expressed pride in the rapid growth of agricultural exports. In one interview, a development manager of a multilateral organization boasted that horticulture exports increased six-fold during the 2000s.[15] There was also a way in which agroexport growth was equated with Egypt's food security. For example, when asked to assess the state of the country's food security, a development consultant replied that food security would grow if exports continued to grow.[16] This expressed confidence in exports mirrored the understanding of food security that had dominated the development discourse since the 1980s—of food security defined as access to food on the world market (McMichael 2017). As exports grew so would dollars, which could then be used to buy food in the world market. Yet, while agricultural export revenues may have grown, import costs grew even more during the inflationary period between 2007–08 and 2011.

Public grain reserves had also dwindled under structural adjustments. Given that public grain reserves are a buffer against world market prices and an emergency in domestic grain production, the Egyptian government issued a three-year mandate to increase wheat production that increased yields in 2010–11 and 2011–12 (FAO 2012) and began to build new silos in 2010 to store more volumes of domestic wheat (Ghoneim 2012: 19). Yet, in the wake of the 2011 uprising, the estimated grain reserves were between 4–6 months (Ghoneim 2012: 6; USDA 2012), but three months of the estimated total supply were virtual (in contracts). When Egypt's main trading partner in wheat nulled all contracts in August 2010, the virtual grain reserves became meaningless.

The dual process of corporate food growth and social protection declines kept food prices high for many Egyptians, thus, making them vulnerable to the volatile world market. After 2007–08, the government attempted to shield vulnerable population groups—via increases in grain reserves, public sector wages, and consumer food subsidies, among other measures—but these measures had minimal impacts given that food as a percentage of total income in the country remained high. In 2011, the percentage of income spent on food on average was hovering at 38%—a percentage that is on par with the regional average of 35–55% of income (Harrigan 2014: 110). This regional trend is consistent with the second phase of the corporate food regime, in which world food prices rose against consumers broadly (McMichael 2009). In Egypt, the crisis was expressed in the increased rates of both food insecurity and poverty beginning in 2007–08. An estimate is that over half a million people fell below the poverty line as a result of the crisis—an increase of around 4.5% (Harrigan 2014: 97). Households spending a higher percentage of their income on food than the average found that they could not afford basic necessities (staple foods, transportation, etc.) when prices rose sharply in 2007–08, and those spending a lower percentage than average found that they were suddenly food insecure, having to make trade-offs between paying for food and paying other rising living expenses like housing and health care. As a result of the sizable percentage of income spent on food, when food prices rise, income can fall—say, when the healthcare costs of an ill member of a household cannot be met and that member can no longer work, or when a member's income rests on the affordability of a commodity, like oil for taxi drivers.

Claiming the Crises: Malthusia Raises Its Head

The mainstream consensus on the food security problem emerged quickly in the midst of 2007–08. The mainstream consensus framed the problem in terms of food import dependency and grain deficits, pointing out that the Middle East and North Africa (MENA) region in particular had the largest food deficit of any region, importing "about half of its overall staple crop consumption requirements" (Ianchovinchina et al. 2014: 1302; see also Lybbert and Morgan 2013: 357). Repeatedly, Egypt, where 'aish means both life and bread, exemplifies this regional problem: As one *Washington Post* article proclaimed, "Egypt's slide from breadbasket of the eastern Mediterranean to net grain importer is elemental to an economic crisis that threatens to convulse the nation" (Glain 2012a).

Further, the consensus was that this slide from breadbasket to net grain importer can be blamed on the imbalance between supply and demand. In terms of demand, population growth (and in part demographic change toward a younger population) and income growth have led to higher demand (Ianchovinchina et al. 2014; McGill et al. 2015; USDA 2015; World Bank n.d.). This higher demand has, in turn, outstripped food supply. More recently, climate change has been added to explanations of the supply problem; as Ianchovinchina et al. (2014: 1302) conclude, import dependency in the region "is because of high population growth and climate change, which can raise the frequency of draughts and water scarcity."

Despite some qualifications, Malthusia, the pervasive ideology that blames crisis in the non-Western world on population pressures (Davis 2001), seems hard pressed to go away when explaining crises in the MENA region (Mitchell 2002).[17] Explanations of food import dependency in the region being rooted in the problem of production not being able to keep up with demand reflect a reality—but a partial reality. It is true that regionally there has been a demographic shift toward a younger population. As is often quoted, more than 30% of the population in the region is between 15 and 29 years (UNDP 2011; OECD n.d.). It is true that per capita income figures have risen regionally despite youth unemployment since the 1990s (World Bank n.d.). But the supply–demand formulas obfuscate questions of what is being produced and imported, by whom, and for whom. Moreover, these explanations do so to justify the policy prescription that resurfaced in the wake of 2007–08 to reduce and replace food and other subsidies. This "claim to crisis" (Roitman 2014) was that demand was outstripping supply not so much because of a younger population and rising incomes but because of food subsidies.

Subsidies as a broad category consist of both direct and indirect subsidies, for consumers and producers. The two main direct consumer subsidies are for fuel/energy and food. Much of the moral outcry was directed toward the food subsidy system, which since the early 1990s covered *baladi* bread and non-bread food (*baladi* flour, cooking oil, and sugar, especially). *Baladi* bread, or bread "of the country," has historically been made of a mix of grains. While it is not whole wheat grain, *baladi* bread can be considered more nutritious than both semi-subsidized bread and refined white wheat bread sold in private bakeries.[18] The bread subsidy program had stood on its own in that it was universal and had accounted for "a major part of the Government of Egypt's safety net program, both in terms of costs and coverage" (WFP 2008: 3). Yet, this program, and food subsidies more generally, had long been the target of neoliberals. By the 2007/08–2011 period, non-bread subsidies had already been slashed and a market-segmented bread subsidy program had developed with both fully subsidized *baladi* bread and semi-subsidized bread. Both types of bread were sold at the Army's numerous bakeries and depots, both for the army and for civilians (Abul-Magd 2017: 146–147). While I was living in Cairo, at any one of the designated fully subsidized bread depots, anyone (Egyptian or foreign) could buy bread; one bag was 20 loaves (*rareef*) for 2 EGP. Semi-subsidized bread was sold for a higher price anywhere, including at private bakeries and other retail outlets.

In the midst of the price hike of 2007–08, questions about the Egyptian govern-ment's ability to maintain its food subsidy system re-surfaced as the country's food import bill grew. The IMF (2008: 5) announced that the subsidies are under "renewed scrutiny" because of the recent sharp increases in food and fuel prices. The fiscal bur-den of subsidies was repeatedly framed as unsustainable given not only the growing food import bill but because the program is inefficient and breeding corruption. The claim was that people were profiting off the system (*IRIN*, April 10, 2008) and those who need the subsidies were not getting them (Slackman 2008). In 2008, the Mubarak government initiated a pilot program introducing a so-called smart card with embed-ded chips with data on the household head's monthly quota of non-bread subsidized goods (Ghoneim 2012: 18). Then, in 2009, the government announced its intention to re-evaluate the entire food subsidy program (El-Fiqi 2014).

After 2011, the mainstream consensus among international creditors, the right-wing think tank the Cato Institute, and the FAO sought to counter the tide toward growing subsidies in most countries around the world.[19] The policy prescription was not to reform subsidies but to replace "indiscriminate food and energy subsidies with targeted aid for the poor" (Woertz et al. 2014: 11), including cash transfers. Again, the significant cost of subsidies was raised (World Bank 2012: 7). The cost is usually represented in one of two ways: as a percentage of total budgetary expenditure and as a percentage of GDP. For example, reports claimed that subsidies made up 31% of total budgetary expenditure in Egypt in 2008 (Woertz et al. 2014: 11), and more than 13% of GDP in 2013 (Rohac 2013: 2). Moreover, the import bill from subsidies was apparently depleting the country's foreign reserves (Rohac 2013: 2), making it diffi-cult for the government to purchase imports of wheat, thereby, placing the country's food security at risk (McGill et al. 2015: xi).

As the consensus against subsidies was reached, subsidies were no longer painted as merely inefficient, failing to reach the neediest and in need of targeting. Rather, subsidies were said to actually benefit the better-off groups, even the wealthy (Rohac 2013: 12–13; FAO 2014: 2). Further, it was argued that the bread subsidy in par-ticular was indirectly encouraging domestic wheat production—another misguided policy. The bread subsidy program relies in part on a producer subsidy, a procure-ment price for domestic wheat, which is then bought by the government for the program. The domestic production of wheat was supposedly wrong-footed given that the country "faces severe resource limitations" (Rohac 2013: 16) and farmers are then disincentivized from producing for value-added and/or exports (McGill et al. 2015: xiv). According to the consensus, domestic production of wheat and the bread subsidy have also been adversely impacting domestic diets: an energy-rich but nutritionally poor carbohydrate-based diet that is supposedly contributing to obe-sity and malnutrition (Ramadan 2015: 2; see also McGill et al. 2015; Alebshehy et al. 2016).

Pinpointing government subsidies as a main policy hurdle in the way of improving food security in Egypt and throughout the indebted, food import dependent world is faulty on a number of grounds. As world food prices soared and the government expanded food subsidies to cover the newly food insecure, the cost of the subsidies undoubtedly went up. According to Ministry of Finance figures, presented in the Cato Institute report, food subsidies nearly doubled from $2.4 billion in 2007–2008 to a high of $4.7 billion in 2010–2011 (Rohac 2013: 4). What does this increase mean, say, in terms of the cost as a percentage of GDP? According to a FAO estimate, the cost of the bread subsidy program in 2010/11 was 0.8% of Egypt's GDP (McGill et al. 2015: xi). This cost (as a percentage of GDP) is much lower than the estimated cost of subsidies stated above (more than 13% of GDP in 2013). In fact, the cost of food subsidies is often obscured in these reports by the cost of food and fuel (and other) subsidies being lumped together. Not only are the two estimates of different years (2010/11 and 2013), the difference here is that one estimate (0.8% of GDP) is an esti-mate of the bread subsidy program alone and the other estimate (13% of GDP) is presumably of all subsidies (fuel, producer food, consumer food). Adding the costs of various subsidies without clarifying which expenditure is for which subsidy could explain at least some of the discrepancy between the perceived and the real costs of food subsidies. Further, it is spurious to claim the significance of cost increases without a point of reference for the increase: Food subsidies had dropped from 14% of government expenditure in 1980/1981 to 4% of government expenditure by 2007 (Ahmed et al. 2001; Youssef 2008; Gertel 2015), following the substantial reduction in (non-bread) food subsidies in 1991 and 1992 as part of ERSAP (Ibrahim and Lofgren 1996: 173).

The second, related claim that food subsidies were leading to foreign exchange difficulties, by increasing the demand for imported wheat, is also spurious. Wheat imports as a percentage of total imports is small: In the intercrisis period (2008 through 2010), wheat was never more than 4.11% of the value of total imports, and on average wheat was 3.9% of the total value (Figure 2.2). Of the five main cate-gories of imported commodities at this time, wheat as a grain does not stand alone: the other main grain import, corn, was 52.5% of the average value of wheat imports for the same time period. Yet, little to nothing is mentioned in policy circles or the

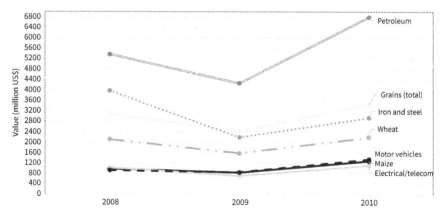

Figure 2.2 Egypt: Top five imports, 2008–2010 (by category).

Source: UN Comtrade 2006–2010.

news media about imported corn. Furthermore, wheat imports that are designated for the bread program are less than 50%: In 2011–2013, an estimated 43% of imported wheat was government purchases (McGill et al. 2015: 3). By multiplying the average wheat import value for 2011–2013 and then dividing that number by the average total import value for the same period, I arrive at the burden of bread subsidies on the import bill for the 2011–12 period: *on average 1.54% of the total import bill can be directly attributed to the bread subsidy program.*[20]

The growing subsidies are a substantial cost to whom, then? Raising alarm about the cost as a percentage of public expenditures—say, that "the government spends more on subsidies, including gasoline, than it spends on health and education" (Slackman 2008)—obscures the fact that the rising cost was being born to secure a most basic need for the growing number of people who were facing food insecurity as commodity prices soared. Even the long-established subsidy reform agenda had acknowledged that the "food subsidy system is widely credited with guaranteeing the availability of affordable staples to the population and helping to reduce infant mortality and malnutrition" (Ahmed et al. 2001: 1). Again, the program ensures the basic food nutrients at low prices, especially for poor households (Ramadan 2015). In fact, Galal (2002) showed that when food (non-bread) subsidies were severely eroded in the early-1990s, caloric intake dropped by 20%. As the World Food Programme (2008: 3), the nearly stand-alone international organization that defended subsidies in the wake of 2007–08, explained:[21]

> [The food subsidy system] provides vital commodities at cheaper prices when compared to regular market prices, and it frees a portion of the household budget to be spent on other important non-food items, such as education and health care.

Food subsidies have been such an important component of the social safety net because it actually reaches many—not all—of those who are in need of food assistance. Despite some leakage, the bread subsidy program had remained progressive; the "poor get more benefits not because of effective targeting mechanisms, but rather, because the social assistance is of such low value that the better-off do not bother to apply to receive it" (WFP 2008: 3). The Cato Institute report lumps together the fuel and food subsidies in a misleading way to claim that subsidies are targeted toward the better-off. At the same time, the report acknowledges that, in theory, food subsidies can be self-targeted in the sense that poorer households will choose to purchase larger quantities of the subsidized food than wealthier households (Rohac 2013: 8). Furthermore, Woertz et al. (2014: 9–10) highlight that food subsidies in the region were effective in absorbing some of the world food price shock, at least temporarily.[22]

By criticizing the direct and indirect role of food subsidies in promoting domestic wheat production, the mainstream's own argument—of subsidies being the main culprit behind demand outstripping supply—is undermined. Not only had the program reduced its reliance on imported wheat over time, the program positively impacted rural household food security. The government offered a price for domestic wheat above the world price for wheat adjusted for the cost of delivery to Egypt ("import parity price") (McGill et al. 2015). Between 2010 and 2013, domestic wheat was on average 42% of the volume of wheat for the program (McGill et al. 2015: 3). For the 2011–2013 period, the government bought 37% of domestic wheat (McGill et al. 2015: 3). The reliance of the program on imported wheat fell from an estimated 77.4% in 1997–98 (Ahmed et al. 2001: xxxi, 145). Plus, the rest of the wheat that is produced is designated for local mills and household consumption at the village level (McGill et al. 2015: 35). The production of wheat (and other staples) for household consumption and for sale in local markets is an important source of income and a main source of calories for rural folk (Kruseman and Vullings 2007: 51, 55). Given that more than half of the bread subsidy is made up of domestic wheat and the government purchases more than 35% of domestic wheat, the program can also be considered an indirect subsidy for smallholder households that are producing wheat. Because of the government procurement price, these households are able to afford to devote more of their fields for on-farm, direct consumption.

The claim that food subsidies undermine nutrition also falsely assumes that wheat demand is for direct human consumption alone. In fact, proponents of cutting the program have long argued that it promotes profligate bread consumption or at least feeds "a hefty appetite for wheat" (Lybbert and Morgan 2013: 357–358)—a supposed cause of health problems (Ahmed et al. 2001; McGill et al. 2015). These assumptions belie the fact that wheat is not only designated for the subsidy program and for on-farm/household consumption, but also has increasingly been used as animal feed. McGill et al. (2015: 26) themselves estimate that between 2005 and 2011 wheat consumed as feed increased by 159%. Over all, what this claim fails to account for is the shift in consumption toward animal protein (Mitchell 2002) and processed food more generally, a point that I elaborate on in Chapter 3. When national dietary surveys depict low meat consumption, as has been noted more recently in McGill et al. (2015), what is missed is the larger category of animal protein—not just animal meat (largely chicken) but also fish, eggs, dairy (butter, milk), ghee, and so on. Claims that the bread subsidy program has led to poor nutrition in the country ignores not only this dietary shift toward animal protein, but an overlapping shift toward the neoliberal diet high in unhealthy fats, sugars, and sodium (Otero 2018).

Although at the time of writing policy makers have not yet accomplished replacing all food subsidies with cash transfers, they have made changes to make that radical departure more likely. If they get their way, it is just a matter of time before policy makers make bread subsidies conditional too. Why replace food subsidies with cash transfers?

Cash transfers came to the center stage of the social policy agenda in middle-to-low-income countries following the 2007–2009 crises. Andrew M. Fischer (2020) argues that cash transfers have come to be part of the mainstream or centrist focus on social protections. Fischer (2020) suggests that the centrists have supported such social policies as part of a type of strategic blindness, seeking marginal gains while failing to consider how they can and are being used by the political Right. The account here of the embrace of cash transfers after 2011, however, does not support this interpretation. As the FAO (2014) document on food and agricultural policy trends since 2007 reported, the vast majority of governments around the world were moving away from liberalization and toward greater direct and indirect subsidies and other supports in the public interest. It is at this precise moment in which governments are seeking greater protection from the vagaries of the world market that the FAO (2014: 63) purports that food and fuel subsidies have emerged as a "major area of policy debate." Where the FAO (2014: 63) stands in this debate that it appears to have taken a role in manufacturing is clear:

> Although attempts to phase out subsidy regimes have often proved challenging, there is growing recognition that universal price subsidies represent a burden on public finances, benefit the rich more than the poor and distort the market.

The FAO (2014: 63) claims that cash-based transfers "have emerged as a preferred policy instrument against poverty" in Latin America, Africa, and Asia. The mainstream rejection of reform after 2011 rather seeks to reverse the trend *toward* social protection that government after government preferred.

Undergirding this policy agenda of replacing food subsidies with cash transfers was an expressed moral outrage at not only government incompetence and corruption but the corrupting influence of social policy on consumer citizens. In the aftermath of 2007–2009, mainstream narratives focused on solutions involving "increased ethical responsibility by individuals" (Amable 2011 cited in Bruff 2014: 21). Bruff (2014) points out that this moralizing involved both individual citizens and the state. There is, in fact, a long genealogy within economics and finance of associating inflation with a breakdown of moral and social order; as a symptom of moral degeneracy (Cooper 2017). Following Melinda Cooper's (2017) analysis of the inflation of the 1970s, consumer subsidies can be understood as re-emerging in the midst of 2007–2009 as both a symptom and cause of the crisis of inflation.[23] Calls to personal responsibility are operative in the recurring claims that bread subsidies are the cause of overweight and obesity in Egypt. These claims appear to have informed the 2014 policy change that replaced the universal bread subsidy with a type of dietary regime—involving quotas of bread loaves per individual.

Revolting Food

First days of the popular uprising
                    —Author's journal (edited), February 1, 2011

On Friday, January 28th, protestors call for a million plus demonstration. And it is massive. The police respond with force and after the nightfall some protestors even died in Tahrir Square. There are clashes between protestors and the police throughout the day and night. In our neighborhood, major clashes break out between protestors and the police in front of the Dar El Salaam police station, down the street from our building. Protestors attack the police station, using what seems like petrol bombs to set the building on fire and smashing the windows of the station. Protestors charge the station with sticks, glass, stones—and then retreat when police respond. It sounds as if the police are responding with tear gas and rubber bullets.

At some point in the night, the police are disbanded and the army comes in to take their place. At around 3 in the morning, President Mubarak gives a public, televised speech stating that he will create a new government. He fires his Cabinet, including the Prime Minister, and tries to distance himself from the police, stating that he and his army will protect the people.

The next day, Saturday, the 29th, in the morning, we go down to the streets to see the destruction. There is debris all over, some evidence of blood spilt, some vandalism (an ATM machine, for instance), and four or five tanks standing in front of the battered police station.

Reports throughout the country are that people are embracing the military— giving flowers to soldiers, kissing soldiers. Demonstrators begin to chant that the people and the military are hand-in-hand.

Mubarak signs in a vice president, Omar Suleiman, head of intelligence and key negotiator with Israel, and then appoints a new prime minister, Ahmed Shafiq, former Air Chief. Both are military men. On Saturday, reports also surface that eighteen prominent businessmen fled Egypt on private jets.

Fears of looting gangs begin to surface. A Ministry of Defense spokesperson addresses the public in a televised address, telling them to stay inside and observe the second day of curfew. He assures the public that the military will protect the people from looters, but he urges young people to be vigilant in protecting their families and neighborhoods throughout the night. And that is exactly what neighbors did that night: They set up popular committees to 'secure the peace'—setting up road blocks with anything they could find, taking shifts throughout the night to keep watch over the streets, and securing themselves with sticks.

Protests continue not just in Cairo but throughout Egypt—in Port Said, Suez, Alexandria, among other smaller cities. The main demand of the protests on Sunday continued to be "Mubarak out!" (Arhal Mubarak), mimicking the protestors in Tunisia.

The curfew is extended by one hour, starting at 3pm not 4pm.

Mubarak's first directive to the new Prime Minister Shafiq is to cut inflation and keep consumer subsidies.

Gunshots are heard throughout the night, into the early morning. In our area, the shots likely came from the nearby, local prison. Rumors are that prisoners are escaping after being stuck inside with no food for three days. People were helping the prisoners by feeding and clothing them.

The U.S. media as well as Egyptian state television are circulating rumors of non-Egyptians being behind the vandalism and looting.

On Monday, fears of food shortages generate intense momentum. News reports of food shortages spark fears and fears spark long bread lines, shortages of tomatoes—yet, prices appear to be relatively stable.

Many commentators agree that food prices triggered the popular uprising throughout the region in 2011 (Lagi et al. 2011; World Bank 2012; Barrett 2013; Harrigan 2014).[24] Protestors in Tunisia were famously holding up baguettes in the streets and a common protest slogan in Egypt was "bread, freedom, social justice" (*'aish, huriyya, adala igtimaiyya*). As my first-hand account of the January 25 uprising above indicates, during the initial uprising, the authorities were also clearly concerned about keeping food affordable and allaying fears about food accessibility. However, it was not the poor and hungry who were leading the protests. In fact, diverse, cross-class, largely urban social groups revolted, often assuming different roles in the protests that led to the ouster of President Mubarak and the activism that followed ("We are All Khaled Said"; Bush and Ayeb 2012; Abdelrahman 2014).[25] So, if hunger, or the inability to access food as prices rise, did not lead to revolt, how were food prices a trigger to the 2011 uprising in Egypt and the rest of the region? Put differently: What explains the high probability (83%) that Egyptians will revolt as prices of a few key staples rise above a certain percentage of income, as the undisclosed government study (from Chapter 1) revealed?

Mass popular backlash against rising food costs—dubbed food riots—is an expression of what E. P. Thompson (1971) called the moral economy of food markets. This moral economy involves popular ideologies of how food markets should work (Hossain and Kalita 2014). Food rioting can be understood as an expression of a "sudden and severe entitlement gap, a gap between what people believe to be their entitlement and what they can in fact achieve" (Patel and McMichael 2009: 25). During the January 25 uprising and the Arab Spring more generally, the entitlement gap was blamed on the long-standing heads of state and their so-called cronies. Naomi Hossain and Devangana Kalita (2014) also found in their comparative research on popular responses to the 2011 price hikes in parts of Africa and South and Southeast Asia that this entitlement gap was often understood as a failure or indictment of government responsibilities and, to a certain extent, economic elites whose interest public officials were understood to be acting to protect.

Neoliberal subsidy reformers, in fact, understood the indelible link between public entitlements and the popular legitimacy of governments. As both the 1996 World Bank report on structural adjustments in Egypt and the 2001 IFPRI report on the country's bread subsidy program acknowledged, food subsidies were "perceived to be important in promoting political stability in Egypt" (Ahmed et al. 2001: 2). Recent history had proven that: The "massive food riots of 1977" (Ibrahim and Lofgren 1996: 159) erupted when the Sadat government, under pressure from the IMF, slashed food subsidies in 1976–77, leading to a 50% increase in the price of bread (Sadowski 1991). The government responded by dispatching the army and reinstating the subsidies (Dethier and Funk 1987; Sadowski 1991). Again, a point is that the popular resistance to subsidy cuts in Egypt demonstrates that "a sudden and severe entitlement gap" is not a gap in absolute terms (from low to high prices) but in relative terms (as a percentage change, to higher prices). Wheat prices had been falling in real terms throughout the 1970s (Dethier and Funk 1987: 25). The government instituted food subsidies as a national program in response not to high prices but to volatility, that is, the government's reduced ability to control domestic prices first during the fuel-food crisis of 1972 and then under austerity in 1977 (Sadowski 1991). And Egypt was not alone: During the first sweep of structural adjustments in the indebted South, between 1976 and 1982, there were at least 146 protests against cuts to consumer subsidies and the like (Patel and McMichael 2009: 9).

As the neoliberals pointed out, the resulting political instability made the Mubarak government cautious in de-funding consumer subsidies (Ibrahim and Lofgren 1996: 159; Ahmed et al. 2001: 2). It was argued that the Mubarak government had been more successful than the Sadat government in implementing the neoliberal policy, by avoiding the backlash, through "reform by stealth"—by maintaining subsidies but the subsidized items themselves gradually disappear and are replaced by slightly modi-fied and costlier items (Waterbury 1989 cited in Ibrahim and Lofgren 1996: 169). At the same time, neoliberals acknowledged that the second wave of structural adjust-ments in the early 1990s under Mubarak had been met with popular unrest; during the first years of ERSAP, they acknowledged that "Egypt witnessed an unprece-dented wave of politically motivated violence, mainly Islamic activists and the state" (Ibrahim and Logren 1996: 159). While being assured at the time that the "survival of the regime itself is not at stake" because of ERSAP (Ibrahim and Logren 1996: 159), the 1996 World Bank report again returned to the problem of legitimacy and concluded that because of this political instability "most of the remaining subsidies (primarily on bread and cooking oil) will be retained" (Ibrahim and Logren 1996: 178). The neoliberals remained on the side of so-called reform—not dismantling but eroding funding for subsidies in the name of targeting.

This stance on reform changed beginning in 2008. The emerging consensus was not just for reform but ultimately for replacing subsidies. Reforming subsidies was no longer a problem primarily because of political legitimacy but because of so-called vested interests (IMF 2008: 6; Rohac 2013: 3). This policy position change becomes clear after the 2011 uprising and the concomitant spread of protest around the word. It is in the context of volatile world prices and popular protest that subsidy regimes grew all over the world—and it is this trend toward growing public entitlements that must be stopped, as the 2014 FAO report spells out. This moment is precisely when the remaining entitlement becomes no longer tenable:

> when price controls or large-scale subsidies have to be scaled back when the state finds it can no longer afford them, the sudden withdrawal of what has become an entitlement can cause unrest akin to that of a market price spike.
>
> (Barrett 2013: 26)

In Barrett's (2013: 14) terms, it was the region with the most generous subsidies that experienced widespread regime change and political upheaval. According to this logic, because so-called food frustrations helped fuel the 2011 uprising in Egypt, the food subsidies must end (Lybbert and Morgan 2013: 368–369). The hope appears to be to do away with the idea that markets should be susceptible to public demands.

By replacing universal social programs with cash transfers, the channel that universal social programs provide—through which citizens make demands on the state, develop solidarities across coalitions, put pressure on public officials, and so on—becomes segmented (Adesina 2020). As Jimi O. Adesina (2020) and Andrew M. Fischer (2020) note, the mainstream position on cash transfers is entirely consistent with the resurgent Right's effort to shield ruling elites from democratic forces. In Egypt, it was only after the military takeover in July 2013, after all, that the "history of failed reforms" (Rohac 2013: 9) had a chance to come to an end. The "ultimate solution" was to end the gradual reforms; "private markets would likely prove popular and create constituencies that would find it in their best interests to defend the new status quo" (Rohac 2013: 14). At the same time, the Cato Institute report contradicts itself as it cannot help but acknowledge that eliminating universal consumer subsidies "will have to be accompanied by a strengthening of the existing safety net or by an increase in compensatory payments to vulnerable groups" (Rohac 2013: 14).

Conclusions

The "claim to crisis" (Roitman 2014: 12) in the post-2007–08 period is operative: Multilateral lenders, international institutions, and ruling parties in indebted countries alike claimed a crisis to justify certain policy prescriptions to address food insecurity. Subsidies (food, fuel, and other) have long been the target of neoliberals, and in the inflationary moment of 2007–2009, the moral outcry over subsidies received renewed attention. In Egypt, the mainstream claim that "out of control" subsidies were causing food insecurity and political instability could only make sense by painting a narrow food landscape in the country: of government subsidies, on the one hand, and peasant foods, on the other, conveniently eliding corporate food altogether. This false landscape is not the product of mere ignorance or deception. Rather, this claim reflects the contradictions of neoliberal development theories: of successes attributed to countries' integration into the international system and failures attributed largely to endogenous factors (Payne and Phillips 2010: 92). Within this theoretical framework, failures—like long bread lines, popular clashes with police, and balance of payments difficulties—"lie purely from endogenous factors, associated in the main with 'incorrect' government policies and institutional deficiencies" (Payne and Phillips 2010: 92). Making sense of non-sensical arguments—how effective can cash transfers be in meeting needs when prices are high and volatile?—is only really possible within this theoretical contradiction.

But more, it is in claiming crisis (Roitman 2014) that their concern becomes clearer. By repeatedly harping on food subsidies, which contributed minimally to government expenditure and even less to the import bill, the neoliberals demonstrate that the call to fiscal responsibility is a justification for their policies, not a concern in and of itself. The particular political solution offered is one involving the disciplining of a cash-strapped, indebted government and the poor and working classes who rely on social assistance. However, a class analysis of the neoliberal consensus as disciplinary measures on the poor and working classes is not sufficient given that food subsidies in Egypt as elsewhere were universal. After 2007–08, an estimated nearly half of the Egyptian population became reliant on subsidies (Lybbert and Morgan 2013: 368–369).

The shift post-2007–08 from a reform only agenda to an agenda to replace food subsidies with cash transfers hints at a qualitative turn in neoliberalism, as others have noted about the post-2007–08 historical moment (Bruff 2014; Bruff and Tansel 2018). By 2011, in the throes of world revolution (Wallerstein 2011b), any remaining entitlement—especially one as significant as consumer food subsidies—becomes untenable, whereas before it was assumed to be necessary. This shift marks the end of the consensus to maintain popular legitimacy through stealth by reform (Waterbury 1989). In Ian Bruff's (2014) terms, institutions are moving away from seeking consent for the hegemonic project (of doing away with popular ideologies concerning the public interest). The term reform, in fact, signals a nod to consent. Abandonment of that project forecasted the rise of global authoritarianism, understood not just as the state exercise of brute force but also in terms of "the reconfiguring of state and institutional power in an attempt to insulate certain policies and institutional practices from social and political dissent" (Bruff 2014: 115). When the Sisi government began in 2014, harsh repressive measures to quell dissent ensued while the universal bread subsidy ended, inflation soared, and the corporate agri-food system remained in place.

Notes

1. From the beginning of 2008–09 through the end of February 2009, Russian exports accounted for 54% of Egyptian wheat imports (USDA 2009).
2. In one study of the direct causal relationship between world food prices and domestic food prices in the Middle East and North Africa region after the 2011 food crisis, this relationship was the strongest in Egypt, Djibouti, and the UAE, in which world prices contributed approximately 40% to food inflation (Ianchovinchina et al. 2014: 1316).
3. In terms of total numbers of the hungry, another FAO estimate calculated that by 2009 more than one billion people were undernourished—an increase from fewer than 800 million hungry people 15 years earlier (Winders 2011: 83).
4. Chronic diseases include, namely, obesity, cardiovascular disease, chronic respiratory diseases, and diabetes. Chronic diseases also have multiplier effects on poor health outcomes. For example, overweight and obesity have been shown to increase the risk for cardiovascular disease, type 2 diabetes, stroke, some cancers, and a host of other illnesses (Haslam and James 2005; Kim and Popkin 2006).
5. For example, in 2007 alone, profits of the top three grain traders (Cargill, ADM, Bunge) rose 103%, while those of the top three global seed/pesticide companies (Monsanto, Syngenta, and Dupont) rose 91% (McMichael 2009: 290).
6. In Egypt, the exponential increase in agricultural exports began in 2006 when the price spike began, and increased by nearly 130% between 2006 and 2010, from $863 to $1,983 million (EDF 2011).

7. See also Hanieh (2013) on neoliberal reforms through 2010 throughout the Middle East.
8. In 2017, the Carnegie Endowment for International Peace began to track this global protest. See the Global Protest Tracker.
9. Total import and export values for both periods (1995–2007 and 2007–2011) were calculated from the Observatory of Economic Complexity (OEC).
10. The second export and import values were calculated from the UN Comtrade 2006–2010.
11. Oil export and import values were taken from EconStats.
12. For a summary of the Seven Sisters—of how the seven energy conglomerates came to market and political power—see Prashad (2007: 176–190).
13. In terms of total cereal consumption (both human and animal), in 2011, wheat constituted half of total consumption followed by corn at around 38% (McGill et al. 2015: 25).
14. This assertion is further supported by the author's interviews with agribusiness representatives, 8/16/2011 and 9/20/2011, Cairo.
15. Interview, 8/9/2011, Cairo.
16. Interview, 6/3/2010, Cairo.
17. To Harrigan's (2014) credit, in her demand–supply equation of regional food insecurity, she qualifies the demand side: With demographic and income changes, there have been changes in consumption (toward meat and dairy) that require more energy (and inputs).
18. My assertion about the level of nutrition in flour is based on the extraction rate of the wheat in the milling process. For example, according to 2012 figures, more than 80% of subsidized bread was made with wheat flour with an 82% extraction rate, a rate lower than the 100% whole wheat extraction rate but higher than the common straight-grade extraction rate (72%) (USDA 2012).
19. On this post-2007–08 worldwide trend, see FAO (2014).
20. This calculation of the bread subsidy burden is based on estimates from the 2014 FAO report.
21. It should be noted that the World Food Programme was awarded the Nobel Peace Prize in 2020 when world hunger was rising during the first year of the COVID-19 pandemic, ongoing conflict in Yemen, sanctions against Iran, and on and on. In the words of the Nobel Committee, the WFP was awarded the Prize "for its efforts to combat hunger, for its contribution to bettering conditions for peace in conflict-affected areas and for acting as a driving force in efforts to prevent the use of hunger as a weapon of war and conflict."
22. Globally, food price increases had a pass-through effect regionally of around 0.3% for every 1% price increase (Ianchovinchina et al. (2014) cited in Woertz et al. (2014: 9–10)).
23. I rely heavily on Cooper's (2017) brilliant analysis of the targeting of the U.S. Aid to Families with Dependent Children (AFDC) to explain the convergence of neoliberalism and new social conservativism in the inflationary moment of the 1970s. Like consumer food subsidies, AFDC had a miniscule budget and became the ire of neoliberals in the United States. For Cooper AFDC came to represent the moral malaise of inflation in gendered and racialized ways.
24. Many thanks to Ray Bush for coming up with the telling phrase "Revolting Food," which forms the heading to this section.
25. "We are all Khalid Said" was a Facebook page.

3

The Dual Character of the Corporate Agri-food System

Corporate food may appear to be separate from the ubiquitous food stalls and street vendors and open-air markets in Egypt. Yet, the formal, integrated industry—of supermarkets and hypermarkets, agroexports, packaged foods and drinks, and so on—is intricately connected to this rather more visible informal agriculture and food sector of small-scale vendors and producers. As national diets have changed toward foods high in unhealthy fats, sugars, and sodium, so has what the majority of agriculturalists grow. Upstream, the corporate agri-food system rests both on the concentration of agribusiness on reclaimed lands and on farmers, including small-holders (*fellahin*), in the Nile Valley and Delta who have become a source of key corporate foods (e.g., potatoes, raw milk) as well as laborers.[1]

When I began research in Egypt in 2008, I was researching the dispossession of smallholders from land. I attended conferences, press releases, and other actions among smallholders, Left activists, bureaucrats, and others who were challenging legal and extra-legal measures pushing and pulling tenant farmers and agrarian reform beneficiaries (smallholders with land titles) from their land and livelihoods.[2] Similar processes of land dispossession were happening around the world as newly created markets in land led to a wave of evictions and violence beginning in the 1990s (Edelman 2003; Borras et al. 2007).[3] Yet, smallholders have not gone away. In fact, around the world more and more people are engaged in small-scale com-modity production (van der Ploeg 2009). In Egypt, while landlessness has risen from a combination of dispossession, de-activation of agricultural land and fragmentation (division of land for the next generations), the number of smallholders rose by 60%, from about 2.3 million in 1990 to 3.7 million in 2010 (Ayeb and Bush 2019: 144–145). As I explore in Chapter 6, government policies to redistribute plots of reclaimed land to the landless help partly explain this paradox. In this chapter, the focus is rather on smallholders who have been able to hold on to land and to farming and have gained at least part of their income from supplying corporate food chains.

The growth of a corporate agri-food system has contributed to social differenti-ation or social class polarization in farming. Agribusiness has relied on imported ingredients and their own farms (including testing sites/fields) and processing facil-ities largely on reclaimed land. Agribusiness has also relied heavily on contract farming, and most contracts are issued to capitalized farms. Thus, contract farming has led to a growing role of investors in agriculture—from entrepreneurs to fam-ily business groups to MNCs/TNCs to financial firms. At the same time, agribusiness

The Frontiers of Corporate Food in Egypt. Marion W. Dixon, Oxford University Press.
© Marion W. Dixon (2023). DOI: 10.1093/oso/9780192842985.003.0003

relies on smallholders—but often on a non-contractual basis. Smallholder integration into corporate food chains has meant borrowing money to pay for seeds and other inputs, and has involved so-called pro-poor development, that is, projects seeking to establish contracts between smallholders and corporate food chains. Their incorporation into these chains is consistent with value-chain agriculture around the world, which is constituted through formal and informal arrangements with smallholders (Watts 2009; Ouma 2015; Bisoka and Ansoms 2020; Gengenbach 2020).

Smallholders have become key growers of crop ingredients in corporate food that is broadly constitutive of national dietary changes since the 1990s—toward animal fats and proteins and processed, industrial foods and drinks. These national dietary changes are completely left out in much of the literature on overweight and obesity in Egypt. This literature tends to paint a picture (stuck in time, perhaps) of food subsidies governing consumption habits in the country. But as I show in Chapter 2, food subsidies were significantly cut in the early-1990s under ERSAP, so while food (non-bread) subsidies were declining, foods high in unhealthy fats, sugars, and sodium were increasing. Much of the research on the tremendous growth of overweight and obesity and non-communicable diseases (NCDs) throughout the global South, in fact, points to the spread of the so-called Western diet and lifestyle (Weis 2007, 2013; Otero 2018; Swinburn et al. 2019).

In these ways, public health and rural livelihoods have become interwoven, reflecting the dual character of the corporate agri-food system. There are many ways to view this relationship. One reasonable view is that smallholders are becoming indebted to grow crops for these food chains because they have few other livelihood choices. This view is one of smallholders persisting through their often informal integration. I argue that persistence is not a sufficient lens, though. The contestations over land should not be overlooked. Even though agribusiness is not behind much of the violent dispossession (and threats of dispossession) that smallholders have faced, contesting claims over land and other livelihood sources have informed the strategies that agribusiness employs. Intense struggles, as with rising land prices and proliferating pathogens, are threats to capital. Contract farming is a prominent way to offset these risks. Furthermore, the corporate agri-food system was able to grow because the agrarian reform institutions and, more broadly, what Farshad Araghi (2016) calls the agrarian welfare state, of the post-colonial, post-WWII period were undermined. Smallholders, in turn, lost power on the national stage. But they—and the larger politicized category of the rural poor—remain a political class, however diversified they may be as households. The rural poor have become relevant not just to corporations but to national dietary changes, to national debates on food security, and to more.

Global and National Dietary Changes

The general shift in Egypt toward a diet higher in animal fats and proteins as well as processed, industrial foods reflects dietary changes occurring worldwide with the growth of the corporate food regime. Wealthy consumers have access to a diverse, healthy diet—what Gerardo Otero (2018) calls luxury foods—fruits and vegetables and specialty food and drink (e.g., wine). Poor consumers have access to more refined, durable foods (Weis 2007). At the same time, there is a space of dietary convergence across social class—a space of processed foods and drinks. The "nature, extent and purposes of food processing has been revolutionized" (Monteiro et al. 2013: 21), and two revolutionary changes in food processing will be highlighted to explain these new consumption habits across social class. So-called staple foods that are mixed with other ingredients, including sugars, oils, and flours, have become more nutritionally deficient (Otero 2018: 172). Also, there has been the growth of what Carlos A. Monteiro and his colleagues call ultra-processed foods and drinks—typically energy-dense; carbohydrate-rich; low in fibre, micronutrients, and essential plant-based chemical compounds; and "high in unhealthy types of dietary fat, free sugars, and sodium" (2013: 22).

Ultra-processed foods are foods that are entirely or mostly made not from food but from industrial ingredients and additives. Frozen food, fast food, packaged snacks and candy, and carbonated drinks are common examples. Transnational corporations brand and own ultra-processed products, which are hyper-palatable, packaged in technically sophisticated and attractive ways, marketed heavily to children and adolescents, and highly profitable (Monteiro et al. 2016: 33).

In terms of global trends of ultra-processed products, between 1998 and 2012, sales have plateaued in high-income countries while sales continued upward in middle-income and even low-income countries (Monteiro et al. 2013: 23–24 cited in Otero 2018: 9).[4] So while the consumption of ultra-processed foods and drinks is much higher in high-income countries, accounting for well-over 50% of dietary energy as opposed to 25% in upper-middle-income countries such as Brazil, this gap is closing (Otero 2018: 9). In fact, the increase in sales has been greatest in lower-middle-income countries, Egypt included (Monteiro et al. 2013: 23–24). In a sample of lower-middle-income countries, between 1998 and 2012, sales of frozen products increased 7.67%, snacks 5.45%, and carbonated drinks 9.9% (Monteiro et al. 2013: 24). It should be noted that these percentages of relative annual growth do not include all types of ultra-processed products; therefore, they are lower than actual trends (Monteiro et al. 2013: 25).

Over all, trends in ultra-processed products are difficult to measure given the nature of the products and the fact that most trade data as well as nutrition surveys do not adequately capture these products if at all. The designation of ultra-processed products is based on Monteiro and his colleague's NOVA classification of food processing. The NOVA classification was designed to better understand the nature and extent of dietary changes around the world—including not only group 4 (ultra-processed) foods/drinks but also group 3 processing that involves adding oil, sugar, salt, or the like to flour or other minimally processed ingredients. This group 3 may contain additives and preservatives and makes up common types of processing at street stalls and vendors as well as in households. Vegetable oil consumption, in particular, has risen exponentially around the world as measured as a percentage of total food supply (Otero 2018: 175). For Otero (2018: 174), the growing consumption of vegetable oil means "increased access to cheap fats and sugars" and traditionally low-fat diets being transformed as a result. Also, refined flours have steadily replaced whole grain flours, not just in ultra-processing but in group 3 processing.

Animal protein (meat, fish, dairy, ghee, etc.) is one of the main processed foods of the corporate food regime. Weis (2013) calls the growth of global meat production— and its industrialization—the meatification of diets around the world. The term meatification could be misleading as it is not only meat that has grown in significance to diets but animal products more generally. Nonetheless, the significance of meat to dietary changes should be highlighted here: As the 2019 Lancet Commission report on the Global Syndemic highlights, global meat production increased 4–5 times from 75 million tonnes annually in 1961 to 318 million tonnes in 2014, and is projected to increase further to 455 million tonnes in 2050 (Swinburn et al. 2019: 806).[5] Poultry meat production, in particular, has increased 844% from 1961 to 2014 (Otero 2018: 10). The "world's most common bird" (Patel and Moore 2017: 3) is explored further in Chapter 8.[6]

The National Nutrition Institute's cross-sectional surveys of 1981 and 1998 capture the order of magnitude of dietary changes in Egypt.[7] During the nearly two-decade period, the surveys show a sharp increase in animal protein consumption, a doubling of meals eaten away from home, and growing inequality in caloric intake (NNI 2000; see also Galal 2002). In the 1998 NNI survey, more than 22% of respondents reported in their diet reports consuming excess fat (defined as more than 30% of total energy intake). Almost half (48.2%) of respondents reported consuming excess animal fat (defined as more than 10% of total energy intake). Group 3 processing at home was nearly universal: More than 90% of the survey respondents used vegetable oil in cooking daily, more than 97% used ghee daily, and less than 33% used hydrogenated oil (with trans fats) daily.

The NNI data is useful because it offers a longitudinal look at national consumption habits. However, like other nutrition surveys, the NNI surveys do not capture well the qualitative shifts in diets. While the high level of (vegetable and animal-based) oil consumption in the home is captured in the surveys, the change in the quality of the flour consumed is not as clear. The army's and private bakeries have spread and appear ubiquitous in urban governorates. These bakeries sell semi-subsidized bread and non-subsidized bread and cakes and the like, which have been replacing subsidized (*baladi*) bread and are made with industrial-grade wheat flour and are less nutritious.

The shift toward ultra-processed foods and drinks is also not clear in the surveys. As I will explain further below, it is reasonable to assume that young people are especially attracted to these new consumption habits. In their 2011 report on young people in Egypt, based on the 2006 census of all governorates, the Population Council accessed the extent to which young people were consuming carbonated drinks and fast food. Nearly a decade after the last NNI survey, the Population Council found that 42% of young people in the highest wealth quintile (WQ) consumed carbonated drinks and fast food more than three times a week, compared to 14% of those in the lowest WQ (24 cited in Alebshehy et al. 2016: 665). At the same time, more than half (53%) of those surveyed in the lowest WQ reported consuming carbonated drinks and fast food once a week (Population Council 2011: 24). Consumption of carbonated drinks went up in urban areas: more than half (55.5%) of respondents in urban governorates reported consuming carbonated drinks 1–3 times a week compared to less than half (46.4%) of those in rural governorates (Population Council 2011: 24). The rural–urban difference became starker with the frequency of consumption: More than double the respondents in the urban governorates reported drinking carbonated drinks more than three times a week. In terms of animal protein, animal protein was consumed across social class, although most animal protein that was consumed among respondents in the lowest WQ was eggs. Only 5.5% of respondents in the lowest WQ reported consuming meat more than three times a week (Population Council 2011: 24–25). Based on the 2006 census, young people's consumption of ultra-processed foods and meat was higher among the wealthiest in urban areas but even the poorest were consuming ultra-processed foods/drinks and eggs weekly. But what about the majority of young people who are between the lowest WQ and the highest WQ? What about the adult population across social class?

The food industry data (of investment, sales, etc.) also offers updated data on the order of magnitude of national dietary changes. The annual real investment in the food industry grew fivefold between 1995 and 2008 (Abdel-Latif and Schmitz 2011). Between 1992 and 2002, food processing alone grew from 12.6% to 71.1% of Egypt's total manufacture value added (IMC 2005). Corporate food retail (supermarkets and hypermarkets) and food service (franchises, snack food kiosks, etc.) grew rapidly: Hypermarkets as a percentage of total grocery sales were projected to rise from 13% in 2003 to 26% in 2011 (USDA 2010a). In 2008, hypermarket sale reached $200 million with 10 hypermarket outlets (e.g., Carrefour, Spinneys), and supermarket sales reached an estimated total of $1.6 billion with 550 supermarkets (USDA 2010a). Egyptian family business groups own many of the largest supermarket chains, which range from the high-end of the urban consumer market (e.g., Metro) to the lower-middle end of the market (e.g., Ragab Sons). The Mansour business group owns Metro, the largest supermarket chain at the time, which had 60 stores in 2011 (Business Monitor 2011) and had sales ($110 million) exceeding those of Carrefour ($54 million) in 2007 (GAFI 2010). Likewise, the food franchise market rose from seven chains in 1993 to 45 in 2010, and valued at more than $300 million in 2010 (GAFI 2010). The growth of corporate food service and retail is important to the qualitative shifts in diets as much of what is sold in these markets is industrial products including ultra-processed foods and drinks.

The growth of corporate food service and retail is also important to understanding the space of dietary convergence across social class as the consumer market for corporate food lies along a fairly wide spectrum from low-end (e.g., street kiosks) to the middle (e.g., discount supermarkets) to the high-end (e.g., European hypermarkets). During research in Egypt, between 2008 and 2012, industrial foods and drinks appeared to be ubiquitous in greater Cairo and the urbanized Delta. I routinely ate street food and snacks, cheap and not so cheap, as did my friends and associates and those I witnessed on the streets of Cairo. Working-class people, students, and others who routinely use public and informal transportation (the metro, buses, mini-vans) would grab fast food, snacks and/or drinks at the street kiosks and food vendors located at transportation hubs throughout greater Cairo (Figure 3.1). The upper-middle class and professionals, who had cars and who may employ drivers to drive them around the city, routinely stopped their cars at the many street kiosks on main roads to grab chips, Coca-Cola and other junk foods and carbonated drinks on their way to work or the sports club or wherever they were heading.[8]

Ultra-processed foods and drinks did seem to be most popular among young people. Early on, I was perhaps most struck by the consumption of these products in homes. This trend appeared to be across social class to a certain extent—and mostly among or for the youth. At a friend's cousin's birthday party in her home in a popular neighborhood of Cairo, a store-bought, American-style birthday cake with food coloring and the works was served with carbonated drinks. At a middle-class colleague's home, I was invited for lunch with her kids, and we ate store-bought chips with a home-made meal of macaroni. Also, it was not uncommon for young people from popular neighborhoods hanging out with friends at McDonalds ("MacDo") in the formal neighborhoods of the city. McDonalds and other franchises were among the few gender-free, smoke-free, air-conditioned hang outs. Although consumption of fast food and carbonated drinks was higher among young people in urban governorates, according to the 2011 Population Council report, both are still consumed in rural governorates. When I visited villages in the Delta on a number of occasions, I saw snack/candy wrappers littering the canals. Given the food industry figures and

Figure 3.1 Snack food/drink kiosk, Cairo.

the nature of the corporate food consumer market, consumption of processed, industrial foods—and ultra-processed foods and drinks, in particular—cannot be reduced to the urban youth, although this group, at least those with higher income, appears to be embracing these consumption habits more than others.

Chronic Health Problems

The change in diets toward unhealthy fats, sugars, and sodium has long been recognized as a leading contributor to the rising prevalence of chronic diseases worldwide (FAO 2006a; Prentice 2006). Obesity, in particular, has risen sharply worldwide over the past four to five decades and "is now one of the largest contributors to poor health in most countries" (Swinburn et al. 2019: 794).[9] Furthermore, the sharp increase in the prevalence of chronic diseases in many parts of the global South has created a so-called double burden of disease, as large segments of the population face both chronic diseases and infectious diseases and underweight/hunger (Prentice 2006). In terms of a double burden of malnutrition, fetal and infant undernutrition are risk factors for obesity later in life (Swinburn et al. 2019: 792–793). The 2018 Nutrition Report concluded that 83 out of 141 countries (59%) had double burdens of malnutrition: a high prevalence of two of three nutrition conditions—childhood stunting, anemia in women, and overweight in women (Swinburn et al. 2019: 799).

The convergence of chronic disease prevalence among the wealthy and poor alike reflects in part the space of dietary convergence across social class. Excess meat consumption and ultra-processed food and drink consumption are both key driving forces in what the 2019 Lancet Commission report calls the global obesity pandemic (Swinburn et al. 2019: 806). Red meat consumption (particularly processed meat) is associated with increased risk of NCDs, including type two diabetes, cardiovascular disease, and (some) cancers (Swinburn et al. 2019: 806). Dietary changes as well as the continued prevalence of undernutrition increase the risk for obesity, and obesity, in turn, increases the risk for chronic diseases.

According to 2008 WHO health statistics, Egypt had the fifth highest percentage of obese women over the age of 15 in the world. An estimated 75% of Egyptian women over the age of 30 were overweight or obese (Alebshehy et al. 2016: 662). Obesity prevalence is more than double among women as compared to men (Alebshehy et al. 2016: 662). In the 1998 NNI survey, 41.9% of surveyed mothers were obese and 31.3% were overweight, while 25.9% of pre-school children were stunted. The percentage of stunted and underweight children has dropped and the percentage of overweight children has risen (FAO 2006a; Manyanga et al. 2014).

According to Petra Nahmias (2010)'s doctoral research, there was a significant increase in obesity rates among women between 1992 and 2005. During this period, the prevalence of obesity between social classes has evened out and has shifted from urban to rural governorates. Changes in obesity among the richest were insignificant while obesity rates among the poorest nearly trebled from 8% in 1992 to 23% in 2005 (Nahmias 2010: 76). Further, the urban–rural difference shrunk: In 1992, the group with the highest predicted probability of obesity was the richest in urban Lower Egypt, but between 1992 and 2005, there were only small increases in obesity in urban governorates, and obesity rates more than doubled in rural governorates. The 2014 study of Mona Mowafi and colleagues, based on the 2007 Cairo Urban Inequity study, confirms Nahmias's finding that the prevalence of obesity cuts across social class. Mowafi et al. (2014) found no significant association between most measures of socioeconomic status (SES) and overweight/obesity in the Cairo areas studied.

Although there are limitations using the body mass index (BMI) to measure overweight and obesity, these BMI figures are still useful in showing patterned changes given the drastic difference in weight over decades—and not just in Egypt but in many middle-income and low-income countries around the world. Moreover, I am not arguing that dietary shifts alone have led to the rise in overweight/obesity and chronic diseases. There are a number of other risk factors identified, including fetal and infant undernutrition and lack of physical activity. An estimated 42% of Egyptian women aged 25–64 years have low physical activity (WHO 2016 cited in Alebshehy et al. 2016: 266). Also, I have highlighted ultra-processed foods and drinks as they are understudied risk factors and they do not squarely fit in the energy balance model (the balance struck between energy in and energy expended), which is limited in explaining weight gain (Guthman 2011: ch. 5). Moreover, the corporate food regime has grown and intertwined with other large-scale societal changes, such as urbanization. In Egypt, the rapid growth of large villages and small towns in particular—what Bayat and Denis (2000) called rural urbanization—is important to understanding the double burden of disease. Not only does rural urbanization denote a move away from agricultural work (which involves physical activity) and a move toward industrial foods, exposure to various other endocrine-disrupting pollutants has also risen—and such chemicals are linked to weight gain (Guthman 2011: ch. 5). These so-called obesogens include food additives, plastics, and the like in ultra-processed foods/drinks as well as other synthetic organic and inorganic chemicals (in the form of pesticides, cosmetics, medicines, and the like) (Guthman 2011: 99–108).[10]

A Corporate Coup?

The Egyptian diet is often invoked in reports and news articles and among friends and colleagues: an energy-dense diet of *ful*, *tameeya*, and *baladi* bread.[11] But there is a contradiction that invocations of the Egyptian diet obscure: Egyptians appear to be clinging to familiar foods, but at the same time, as I have illustrated in this chapter, they are readily replacing some of these old foods with others. Why is it that both statements can be claimed to be true?[12]

In many ways, these dietary changes have been gradual, rather than sudden, and in degree rather than kind. Industrial, processed foods and carbonated drinks (even Coca-Cola) have been part of the food landscape since before the 1952 independence. Poultry birds have long been bred in the country. Vegetable oil has been part of the food subsidy program for decades. In these ways, the changes refer to the spread and growing prevalence of processed foods and animal protein and fat. But what about the qualitative shifts in diet?

Power is often exercised in changing a society's food consumption habits (Mintz 1996: 17). Food corporations spend considerable money in packaging and advertising to reach new consumers. In terms of the proliferation of ultra-processed foods and drinks around the world, there is a type of virtuous cycle between food science technical advances and market consolidation. Food science advances have enabled "the invention of a vast range of palatable products made from cheap ingredients and additives" (Monteiro et al. 2013: 22). Transnational food and drink corporations have derived higher profits from these products and have, in turn, exponentially grown their market reach (Monteiro et al. 2013: 22). The ten top-selling food processors amounted to 28% of the total volume of sales worldwide in 2009 (Otero 2018: 17). Market concentrations are much higher in some countries.[13]

In Egypt, the entrance of the big food/drink TNCs has had the effect of quickly concentrating corporate food service and food retail as well as food processing and the agroexport market. Most of the largest food processors have been the largest agroexporters. By 2004, the agroexport market was already heavily concentrated in the hands of national, multinational, and transnational corporations, including Faragella and Juhayna (two of the largest food processors), Farm Frites (a regional MNC that partnered with Americana, an MNC and one of the largest agribusinesses in Egypt), and Cadbury and Nestlé (two of the world's largest food TNCs) (EDF 2011). In 2005, ten corporations were dominating the production of frozen vegetables and seven were dominating the processing and packing of dairy products (IMC 2005). A handful of Egyptian family business groups, MNCs, and TNCs dominate food processing as they do other parts of the agri-food industry.

When food science advances dropped the price of ultra-processed foods and drinks, the market widened considerably. Low prices are a necessary but not a sufficient condition for market growth. In the street kiosks in Cairo during the 2008–2012 period, the vast majority of products on sale were between 1 and 5 EGP, prices that many Cairenes, even young people, could afford. Through market concentration, food corporations are also able to mass market their brands and create brand recognition and loyalty. In middle-income countries, at least, food corporations have also been found to use marketing to scare customers away from live markets and small-scale food vendors. In their 2012 report, the watchdog group GRAIN found that food TNCs and governments were behind such organized campaigns (GRAIN 2012). In Egypt, there was an organized campaign, a public–private partnership between the Ministry of Health and the dairy industry, to purportedly raise awareness of the dangers of non-packaged milk sold by small-scale vendors (EFG Hermes 2010). Campaign proponents cited a similar marketing campaign in Turkey led by Tetra-Pak, the packaging TNC, in partnership with the Turkish Ministry of Health and dairy industry. The claim was that this campaign raised packaged milk consumption from 32% in 2002 to 60% in 2009 (EFG Hermes 2010: 58).

Can these changes in consumption habits in many societies around the world be explained by the use of corporate power alone—to reduce prices, advertise aggressively, and make these products palatable and even addictive? In Amita Baviskar's (2018) study of the phenomenal fast-rising popularity of Maggi (a Nestlé ultra-processed food) in India, she found that clearly the price and marketing were important. Once the Maggi packets fell to five rupees, with the development of cheap metallized polymer films and other packaging materials, the market for Maggi widened considerably—across social class and caste. The mass marketing was also successful in advertising Maggi devoid of foreignness. However, for Baviskar (2018), corporate power is not a sufficient explanation for this food habit change. After all, Maggi like other industrial foods are products with cultural meanings; "industrial foods are distinctive in that they appear neutral, floating above older classificatory schemes, tethered only to modernity" (Baviskar 2018: 5). Now working-class people can in a modest way enjoy some of the same pleasures as the social classes above them (Baviskar 2018: 5). And young people are particularly attracted to Maggi. Baviskar (2018: 9) explains this popularity in terms of the product's ability to "create and affirm" a youth identity that subverts in some ways the older male patriarchs in the household and in other social institutions. The economic, social, and political conditions made this change easier by changing the daily life conditions including the symbolic significance of certain foods. This is what Mintz (1996: 20) referred to as the outside meaning of the new consumption habit creating inside meaning. In an age of extreme economic inequality, processed foods become popular by enabling consumption across social hierarchies, offering what Baviskar (2018) refers to aptly as consumer citizenship.

Both corporate power and the cultural meanings of food help explain why it can be claimed that Egyptians are clinging to familiar foods and, yet, replacing some of them with new foods. This apparent contradiction is also the result of concomitant changes in agriculture and who is growing what. Just as food consumption habits have changed so has agricultural production. Just as public health conditions have changed so have farmer livelihoods. These changes in agriculture in many ways circle back to a handful of Egyptian family business groups, MNCs, TNCs, and financial firms exercising market power by integrating farmers of all sizes into their chains. Corporations both integrate and exclude the majority of agriculturalists—smallholders. This particular characteristic of these chains illustrates what I call the two sides of the country's corporate agri-food system: the formal, integrated and the informal, independent. Agribusiness would only have been able to rapidly consolidate the formal agri-food industry by relying on smallholders.

Corporate Food Commodity Chains: Integration of Smallholders

During research in Egypt from 2008 to 2012, development organizations I encountered were promoting contract farming as a pro-poor development strategy. Their frequent claims that smallholders were missing out on the economic growth of the agroexport market (IFAD n.d.; IMC 2005) ignored the fact that smallholders were already integrated into corporate food chains under various terms and conditions, but largely non-contractual ones. Smallholders are, indeed, excluded from some chains due to the traceability requirements of the retailers.

Moreover, the contract specifications of corporate retail tend to exclude producers who are less capitalized and not able to meet the specifications of what is grown, how the crop is grown or how much is grown within a given timeframe. However, as food processing for the domestic market has grown exponentially, smallholders have become key producers of crops for corporate processors. The examples offered here demonstrate the dairy industry's dependence on smallholders for raw milk and the potato processors' informal arrangements with various types of farmers, including smallholders. In these two cases, the fact that smallholders are two or more steps removed from the corporate processor obscures the moderate to heavy reliance of both chains on smallholders.

The Dairy Industry: Formalized Integration of Smallholders

To get a sense of how significant the dairy industry is to food processing, consider that two of Egypt's largest food processors at the time of research, Juhayna and Faragello, were among the largest corporations in dairy. Four corporations monopolized the packaged milk market: Juhayna and Faragello, Beyti (one of the largest dairy companies) and Enjoy (which had been switching private equity hands) (EFG Hermes 2010). Seven corporations dominated packaged cheese and three corporations (Juhayna, Danone, and Nestlé) had nearly half of the spoonable yogurt market (EFG Hermes 2010). Most of the dairy products—from packaged milk to yogurt to butter and cheese—were designated for the domestic market. As an agriculture official at a Western government agency in Cairo claimed in a 2011 interview, "There has been a huge demand for milk and milk products, and the big producers can't keep up." The lack of supply was apparently a reason for a couple of the processors to start their own dairy farms. However, at least in the mid-2000s, most dairy processors did not have their own farms; only six farms owned more than 1,000 cows (IMC 2005).[14]

Corporate dairy relies to some extent on imported inputs: 2014 trade data indicates that the country's top food ingredient import, valued at $802 million, was processed dairy products such as powdered milk, butter, whey, and cheese (USDA 2015). More importantly, though, corporate dairy relies heavily on domestic producers of raw milk. Ninety percent of dairy cows and 72% of total milk production were coming from small-scale farms (farms with 10 cows or less), while 7% of dairy cows and 21% of total production were from commercial farms, and 3% of dairy cows and 7% of total production from large-scale, corporate farms (IMC 2005). During the 2008–2012 period, the dairy commodity chain looked like the following: Milk producers sell to medium-sized processors (such as the Egyptian Milk Producers Association), who then process the milk (in a basic form) and sell it to corporate dairy, who processes it further (Figure 3.2).

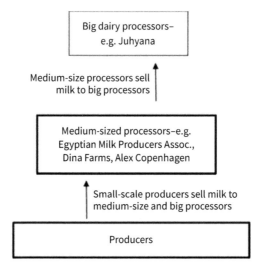

Figure 3.2 Raw milk processing.

The position of smallholders is at the bottom of the milk processing chain. Yet, a more complicated perspective on their position within the milk processing chain is offered if looking at tariff policy. After Egypt joined the WTO in 1995, the state maintained high tariffs (at 40%) on imported milk until 2005 (FAO n.d.), even though corporate dairy would have liked the lowest possible price for raw milk. The state erected barriers to imported milk that protected small-scale dairy farms and middlemen from international competition.

At the same time, corporate dairy continued to grow. A 2008 Presidential Decree (no. 103) reduced the customs tariff for milk substitutes as well as butter, dairy spread, cheese, and other corporate food ingredients like soybean oil (USDA 2009). These reductions helped many corporate processors by lowering the price of key ingredients, while subjecting some (select) end-user products to increased competition. Corporate dairy was also able to cartelize milk processing, thereby, lowering raw milk prices. In 2010, the Egyptian Farmers Association filed a complaint to the Egyptian Competition Authority (ECA) against the three biggest corporations in packaged milk (Juhayna, Beyti, Enjoy) for fixing raw milk purchase prices (OECD 2015). Then, in the revolutionary moment of 2011, just a few months after the January 25 uprising, the ECA publicly warned the three corporations that they would be penalized for violating competition laws (*Reuters*, March 14, 2011). In its 2015 oligopoly report, the OECD announced that one of the top three corporations signed a protocol to observe the government's milk to feed ratio in determining the raw milk purchase price, in effect breaking the cartel.

The monopoly case reveals that the dairy industry was born out of, and is subject to change through, political struggles, which involved a type of formalized integration of smallholders in the milk processing chain. The state, via the intermittent tariff regime and agrarian welfare (and related) institutions—in this case, the Milk

Producers Association, the Farmers Association, and the Competition Authority—helped protect raw milk producers. Yes, small-scale producers are in an exploitable role as they do not exert control over raw milk prices, and presumably their share of the total domestic dairy market has gone down as the corporate processors' share has gone up. At the same time, the growth of corporate dairy depended on small-scale raw milk producers. The shift in small-scale farming toward dairy production, in fact, matched the dietary shift nationally—toward not only (more) dairy but processed dairy. The domestic milk supply per capita rose by nearly 70% in three decades (1970–2000), and clover (*berseem*), the main fodder for animals, has become one of most significant crops cultivated among smallholders (FAO n.d.). This trend may have begun before the 1960s (Issawi 1963). To conclude, in so far as small-scale farming moved toward animal agriculture as the corporate agri-food system grew, smallholders became "the domestic milk supply" through which corporate dairy grew and the concomitant changes in diet were made possible.

Potato Processing: Non-Contractual Integration of Smallholders

Potatoes are another central crop for food processing—for the production of French fries, potato chips, and other potato-based snack foods. Like dairy, potato processing had already undergone consolidation before the research period began: One TNC (TNC1), which had bought a domestic food company in 2001, reported to consume an estimated 60% of all the processing potatoes in the country. Smallholders in the Delta were already growing potatoes and were increasingly devoting production to processing potatoes through informal arrangements with traders and TNC1 agents (for seeds and other specified inputs).[15]

TNC1's commodity chain looked like the following: TNC—agent—trader—farmer. TNC1's seeds were imported from Europe and tested at their in-house farm on reclaimed land. The trader was responsible for delivering the seeds to the farmer in the Delta and the potatoes to the agent, who delivered them to the TNC factory for processing. TNC1 imported palm oil from Malaysia for end user processing (for example, potato chips), and their potato products were for the domestic market. At the time of the interview, 10,000–12,000 farms of various sizes were planting their seeds. As a development agent explained in an interview, in their agency's attempt to take out the middlemen, they found that smallholders, including those with less than one acre, continued to work with traders on an informal basis. The agent asked the smallholders why they did this when they knew that the traders were paying less than the market price at the farm gate. The smallholders explained it was because the traders provided the certified seeds and took care of most of the other costs before the harvest as well as packing and transport. Because smallholders do not have the cash up front, they preferred these informal arrangements with traders.

Cash poverty is also a reason for their exclusion from other corporate food commodity chains like the tomato processing chain. Tomato is like potato in that smallholders were already growing a lot of the crop for the domestic market, and as the corporate agri-food system grew, an increasing percentage of total tomato production was being devoted to processing tomatoes. Like the potato processing chain, tomato processing appeared to be highly concentrated. One TNC interviewed (TNC2) claimed to have 25% of the tomato paste market and 80% of the ketchup market, which was largely for export. Processing tomatoes were more likely than potatoes to be designated for export. TNC2 developed a regional hub based in Dubai, and Egypt was one site of this hub, producing and exporting tomato end products (ketchup, tomato paste). TNC2 only contracted formally, on a yearly basis, with farms of at least 10 acres and with nurseries to plant the certified seeds and grow the seedlings. The corporation's comprehensive contract specifications—from the area of land to be devoted to seedlings to the range and quantities of organic and chemical inputs per land area to the color and condition of tomatoes when they are harvested—made it impossible for smallholders to participate. Furthermore, according to the terms of the contract, farmers paid for the certified seeds as well as a 25% deposit of the value of the tomatoes to be delivered (that would be returned once the specified volume of tomatoes was delivered). The price that farmers would receive for the tomatoes and for the delivery (to the TNC2 factory) were specified in the contract. A USAID-funded initiative found out, when attempting to arrange TNC2 contracts with smallholders, that TNC2 was unwilling to change the contract conditions and provide the money up front, before the tomatoes were delivered for processing. Ultimately, this initiative did not work with TNC2 but instead connected smallholders with domestic processors, for which the traceability requirements were less stringent.[16]

In conclusion, this comparison of a potato processing TNC (1) and a tomato processing TNC (2) demonstrates that the agroexport market was more likely than domestic food processing to exclude smallholders. TNC2's market of tomato paste and ketchup was largely for export to the Middle East, and TNC2 issued contracts with larger-scale, capitalized farms given the traceability requirements of its chain. However, the agroexport market in its entirety did not exclude smallholders. During my research of agroexport farms, I found that smallholders in nearby reclaimed areas regularly supplied to these farms on demand, as will be explored further in Chapter 8. Smallholders as producers were, in fact, integrated in varying ways in corporate food chains: from a non-contractual basis to a routine basis to an on-demand basis. The so-called pro-poor initiatives, wedded as they are to the market calculus, obscure two things in their attempt to (further) integrate smallholders into the market. Market integration problematically results in more debt. Also, these initiatives overlook how smallholder production has been reconstituted through biological homogenization—of animal protein, certified seeds, and so on. This loss of biodiversity in farming, and accompanying vulnerabilities, reflect the politicization of agricultural land, that is, the question of who gets to farm and what they get to farm.

Politicization of the Land

Al-fellah baymut (The farmer is dying)
        —A Delta farmer announces to the author, notes from visit to Delta village, spring 2008

At the Egyptian People's Assembly yesterday, on November 22, President Mubarak gave a speech at the inaugural parliamentary session, and in that speech was confronted by a standing farmer, who said to him, "Mr. President, farmers are suffering." The President tells him to wait, drink some water and the farmer will get what he is asking for. In that speech, the President offers platitudes to the effect that after all he and all Egyptians are farmers.

                                                    Author's notes, November 23, 2009

I began research in Egypt in 2008 among what Bush (2011) calls "fluid networks of resistance to rural dispossession"—resistance that ranged from individualistic and spontaneous to collective and more organized. Groups of smallholders, Left activists, lawyers, civil servants, and others expressed the grievances of smallholders, agricultural workers, fishfolk, among other marginalized rural groups, and they made claims vis-à-vis institutions of political modernity such as Parliament, the courts, the media, and trade unions. These intense struggles over the land had begun in the counter agrarian reforms of the 1990s. The 1991 Economic Reform and Structural Adjustment Program (ERSAP) heralded a new tenancy law (no. 96), which lifted land prices and revoked tenant farmers' usufruct rights in perpetuity and replaced usufruct rights in perpetuity with revocable rents (Bush 2007). This law and accompanying extra-legal measures pushed and pulled tenants and small-scale landowners from their land. Yet, land appropriation was generally not for agricultural purposes.[17] The military, quasi-/state agents, local elites, and heirs of feudal landlords appropriated newly valuable agricultural land for public infrastructure projects (for example, a highway, a subway line in greater Cairo) and for private wealth accumulation (for example, private sports clubs or tourist resorts).

    In response, urban networks linked to and supported this resistance, and included leftist, legal aid, and human rights groups and organizations, such as the Land Centre for Human Rights (LCHR) and the Peasant Solidarity Committee (PSC) (Bush 2011, 393, 402–403). These networks claimed to represent the rural poor, a term which was often used interchangeably with smallholders (*fellahin*) but is much broader, encompassing family farm landholders, tenant farmers, widowers, the landless, and fisherfolk. As the PSC articulated in one of many publications, solidarity means political struggle with the rural poor, who face eviction, imprisonment, sabotage, and other forms of oppression (Sakr 2010). Land dispossession has, indeed, been the most dramatic and urgent issue facing smallholders. According to the LCHR, which had been documenting the abuses perpetuated against the rural poor and providing legal aid for those prosecuted and abused, nearly a million tenant farmers were evicted within the first years of implementation of the new tenancy law (LCHR 2000).

Tenant farmers found that they could not pay the rents after state controls were lifted and rents increased multifold (Bush 2007, 2011). During participant observation among these networks in Cairo, the Delta, and Middle Egypt, I found that not only were tenant farmers being displaced from land but so too were landowners through extralegal measures—including manipulation through the presentation of false documents, intimidation, and humiliation through confiscating papers and sabotaging cultivated fields, and arrest, detention, and torture. State and quasi-state agents (for example, thugs (*baltagiyya*)) often worked on behalf of landlords, feudal heirs, local businessmen, the military, and other state agents to appropriate their newly valuable land.

For those who had maintained access to land, the advocacy networks voiced the full gamut of grievances from a liberalized and privatized agriculture and food sector, in particular, from the dismantling of the cooperative system to the rising costs of farming inputs (like chemical fertilizer), curtailed access to agricultural credit and the volatility of the agricultural market (see also Ashmawi n.d. cited in Saad 2004). Repeatedly expressed within these networks was a double-faced grievance that is directly related to the growth of the corporate agri-food system. On the one hand, there were calls for access to public sources of credit (to purchase seeds, fertilizers, and so on). As was expressed at a seminar hosted by LCHR in Cairo in 2009, "What are the borrowing options for the poor? The government has no money!" On the other hand, the networks were regularly seeking protections for the rural poor over mounting debt to various private lenders. Systemic debt was acknowledged. Smallholders were borrowing in the face of volatile markets, not knowing how much they would get for any given crop. For example, the international NGO CARE in Egypt had arranged a contract with a group of smallholders to produce green beans for European supermarkets. The participating smallholders borrowed to pay for the seeds and other required inputs. Then, the agroexporters backed out of the arrangement after the Egyptian government apparently raised shipping costs to Europe. Consequently, the indebted farmers had no market for their crop and organized with LCHR to file a complaint against CARE to cover the debt (LCHR 2006).

The politics of the rural poor in these fluid networks of resistance concerns what Partha Chatterjee (2004) called political society—not civil society—groups calling for national recognition as having legitimate claims over certain rights and resources.[18] Political society exists in relation to the legal-political forms of the modern state (Parliament, the courts, the police, and so on) and involves appeals to ties of moral solidarity across social groups nationally (Chatterjee 2004: 24). The combination of legal and extra-legal measures in rural dispossession is important for understanding the work of political society. Not only had smallholders lost legal rights, but the national political consensus over which groups have legitimate claims to certain rights and resources had changed. A window opened for newly powerful actors to legitimately assert claims over smallholders' land. Yet, smallholders remained a political class, however weakened they had become. Their engagement with the People's Assembly (Parliament) is a case in point. Since the agrarian welfare state of Gamal

Abdel Nasser, a parliamentary quota reserved half of the seats in the People's Assembly for workers and farmers (Charbel 2016). Although the law specifies what a farmer means—a person whose sole work and main source of living is cultivation, who resides in the countryside with his family and who has no more than 10 *feddan* [acres] (Government of Egypt 1972)—large landlords were able to consolidate their position in Parliament and push forward policies favorable to them in the neoliberal period (Bush 2009: 55). Yet, the farmer's stance before President Mubarak during the 2009 inaugural parliamentary session, as shown above, is not anathematic but rather is a glimpse onto this terrain of struggle.

On April 30, 2010, I attended the Day of Peasant Struggles (the "Commemoration of the Martyrdom of Salah Hussein" (*Ahtfaleya zakara sheed alfalaheen almanadl Sallah Hussein*)) in the village Kamshish in the Delta (Figure 3.3). Landlords had been behind the assassination of Hussain, who was investigating continued social inequalities in Kamshish at the time of the agrarian reforms of the 1960s. Hussain's martyrdom has since symbolized the political struggles of the rural poor, and this day of commemoration is celebrated yearly.[19] One of the speakers at the podium in 2010 was Hamdin Sabbahy, then a member of Parliament, who announced that smallholders in the northern Delta had created an independent union. This announcement signaled the proliferation of independent smallholder unions that appeared in the revolutionary moment following the January 25 uprising. In that moment, Sabbahy himself ran for President on a Left political platform.

Sabbahy and others in Parliament, within this broader network, were mobilizing for recognition of the rural poor as a group with rights, and this mobilization was rooted in claims of a moral and political order (Saad 1999). As Reem Saad (1999) eloquently articulated, smallholders understood the systematic undermining of the agrarian reform institutions as a disruption to the moral and political order that those institutions helped build and as a signal to a return to feudalism. During my participant observation with this network, the power struggle was often referred to as a struggle with the feudal successors, the feudal system. The new tenancy law was repeatedly referred to as illegal and the regime (*al-nizam*) and various government organs implementing it as criminal. Conversely, those within the networks appealed to the rights of permanent tenancy bestowed under agrarian reforms as inalienable rights, and hailed Gamal Abdel Nasser as a hero for ending the feudal order, a type of slavery. Nasser's portrait was commonly displayed on walls and at rallies. Painting the laws as illegal and the government as criminal suggests, in Chatterjee's (2004: 57) terms, that the networks were investing the rural poor with a collective identity with a moral content. They used the broad and blurry designation of the rural poor, and smallholders were often wearing the traditional dress (*gallabiyah*) signifying that they are tillers of the soil, to demonstrate shared interests and to make collective claims despite their differences.

In these intense struggles over the land and rural livelihoods, smallholder households who were able to hold on to land employed a number of livelihood strategies— from sending members to do off-farm, wage work to saving and sharing seeds to borrowing money to pay for the seeds and other inputs of corporate food processors.

Figure 3.3 The 44th Commemoration of the Martyrdom of Salah Hussein.

Source: *The Farmer: Special Issue.*

As Michael J. Watts (2009: 277) argued, "the subsumption of peasants directly into the firm as growers represents a distinctive, although not necessarily totally original, way in which peasants may persist." More than a persistence lens, though, Watts continued to ask what he called Antonio Gramsci's Southern question: What might new forms of global accumulation and imperialism mean for the politics of the rural poor? Here the lens on the politics of the rural poor has focused on Chatterjee's (2004) concept of political society, which takes this "politics of the governed" to the national stage and asks how and why the struggle of class forces plays out and certain social groups gain and lose recognition to make legitimate claims over rights and resources within the body politic.

Conclusions

The politicization of agricultural land has been one force behind the reliance of the corporate agri-food system on smallholders. Dependence on smallholders is important for a number of reasons. Contrary to the assumption of international development actors that smallholders were excluded from the agricultural growth model and limited by so-called static agriculture, smallholder production has been reconstituted during the neoliberal period. Smallholders have been farming under changed conditions and have been changing what they grow—toward more animal protein (for processing), in particular, clover as feed for dairy cows and dairy cows for raw milk. These changes represent processes of biological simplification. These changes also involve debt accumulation as smallholders have been borrowing on a non-contractual basis in an increasingly volatile market, as has been illustrated with the example of an NGO-driven pro-poor supply chain connecting smallholders directly with corporate consumer markets. At the same time, the reconstitution of smallholder production has been part-and-parcel of national dietary shifts—toward foods high in unhealthy fats, sugars, and sodium across social class—and the concomitant chronic health problems.

By addressing the relationship between smallholders and capital accumulation in agriculture and food, this chapter is concerned theoretically with the agrarian question of the twenty-first century. The subsumed position of smallholders in corporate food certainly helps explain rural poverty (Boltvinik 2016). However, my analysis takes the theoretical relationship beyond attributing the persistence of the rural poor to their functional role in capital accumulation to politics on the national stage. The networks of resistance to rural dispossession (Bush 2011)—made up of coalitions of the rural poor (broadly defined to also include the landless and fisherfolk), Left activists, Parliamentarians, bureaucrats, and others—have been engaging directly with agrarian reform (and related) institutions, as I demonstrate with the case of the dairy industry and the response of the Competition Authority (and other state and quasi-state actors) to the industry's exploitation of small-scale raw milk producers. These groups are part of Chatterjee's (2004) political society, making claims vis-à-vis the legal-political order of the state, and in this case, responding to the distribution of power in society as a whole. During the neoliberal period, the rural poor have become a political class because they lost out while corporations and investors have benefited. Yet, agrarian reform and related institutions of political modernity, however weakened, remain relevant to rural livelihoods and to capital accumulation in agriculture and food.

The intense struggles over the land—over who gets to farm and what and how they get to farm—also help explain another strategy of corporations to grow their market share of agriculture and food: land reclamation, or the frontier. Agribusiness has relied on new or reclaimed lands—lands that have been transformed to become suitable for cultivation and/or settlement. Just as they have been offsetting risks onto contract and other independent growers, agribusinesses have been minimizing risks by moving testing fields, farms, processing facilities, and other fixed capital to the frontier.

Notes

1. Smallholders is a term used interchangeably with peasants, small-scale farmers, and, in Arabic, *fellahin*, which roughly translates into "cultivators of the soil." A smallholder is someone who cultivates land for household/own consumption, often in combination with small-scale commodity production. A smallholder today will likely also work for a wage or have household members who are engaged in off-farm income generation.
2. The term Left activists refers to activists on the political Left, embracing a range of political platforms from communism to socialism to Nasserism, and holding a range of positions, often volunteer.
3. In many ways this wave of land dispossession was eclipsed in the scholarship by a larger wave that followed the 2007–2009 food-financial-energy crises, as will be discussed in more detail in Chapter 7.
4. The Monteiro et al. (2013) data is of relative annual growth in retail sales by country from the Euromonitor passport global market information database.
5. In their 2019 report, the Lancet Commission introduces their concept of the Global Syndemic, a synergy of three epidemics—obesity, undernutrition, and climate change.
6. The bird is not just any poultry bird but a particular species of poultry that was bred intensively and spread globally throughout the twentieth century: *Gallus gallus domesticus* (Patel and Moore 2017: 3).
7. I thank Dr. Sahar Zaghloul from the National Nutrition Institute in Cairo for pointing out this data and making it available to me.
8. The 2019 Lancet Commission report on the Global Syndemic suggests that the rapid growth of supermarkets in low-income and middle-income countries could exacerbate the problem of access to nutritious foods as supermarkets compete with small retailers and "encourage consumption of inexpensive processed foods" (Swinburn et al. 2019: 812). Here I extend the warning from supermarkets to the full spectrum of the consumer market of corporate food to understand these threats.
9. Obesity is generally measured by the body mass index (BMI) of 30 or greater, and overweight by the BMI range of 25.0–29.9. Guthman (2011) notes that part of this reported increase in obesity around the world can be attributed to the change in the measurement of obesity. Suddenly with the change many people who were not considered overweight or obese became so.
10. Another significant consumption change that should be explored more is pharmaceuticals (over the counter and prescription), some of which are shown to contribute to weight gain. Big Pharma has grown in tandem with the corporate food regime, and in

Egypt, consumption of medicines appears to have grown exponentially (see, for example, Moneim 2020 on the level of capital concentration in the industry).

11. *Ful* is a fava bean dish, *tameeya* is falafel (also made with fava beans), and *baladi* bread, as explained in Chapter 2, was fully subsidized wheat grain bread.

12. Sydney Mintz (1996: 24) raised this contradiction and question.

13. For instance, by 2000, Nestlé had a market share of 61% for many packaged foods in Latin America, while Unilever held similarly dominant shares in other markets (Otero 2018: 17).

14. The data on the dairy commodity chains is largely from interviews with two agriculture program officers at a Western government development agency in Cairo on August 14 and September 15, 2011. The interview data is further corroborated by data from the Egyptian Competition Authority and Industrial Modernisation Centre.

15. The data on TNC1 is based on interviews with TNC representatives in Cairo on September 13 and 21, 2011 and on corporate brochures, contracts with growers and other internally circulated documents.

16. The data on TNC2 is based on an interview with a TNC representative in Cairo on September 20, 2011. This sub-section also draws on data from interviews with international development agency representatives on pro-poor commodity chains in Cairo on January 18 and September 26, 2011.

17. There are a few examples of agribusiness taking part in this land grabbing; see, for example, Glain (2012b).

18. I thank Timothy Mitchell for drawing my attention to Chatterjee's work.

19. See Mitchell (1998) for a description of the Hussein assassination and its aftermath.

4
Land Reclamation in the Longue Durée

If an observer in the early twenty-first century was to look upon any of the world's great cities—say, Jakarta or Mexico City or San Francisco—and then map the city onto the landscape that existed before its transformation, the observer would get a sense of what land reclamation can entail. Islets may have been turned into seaside downtowns with towering skyscrapers. Swamps may have been made into international ports. In any such landscape, water was harnessed and redirected, land was leveled, and settlement and the development of infrastructure made possible—and often over centuries.

In the most general sense, land reclamation is inseparable from human settlement. To reclaim land is to transform the land for use in a novel way or novel ways. In the longue durée, land reclamation has been for four general uses: cultivation, extraction, pasturage, and settlement. When and where settlement became civilizations, with fixed-field grain agriculture, states would be involved in land reclamation to exercise territorial control and for territorial expansion. Ferdinand Braudel (1972) argued that land reclamation made civilization possible on the plains of the Mediterranean, and this claim was not hyperbole. The plains of the Mediterranean are susceptible to flooding, marshes, and the like; therefore, improvements on the land were continuous, long-standing, and periodic. Improvements meant diverting water from the mountains and sea so that it no longer flooded the plains, and incidents of malaria dwindled. At the same time, fresh water was brought to cultivatable lands on the plains through irrigation. What changed is that with capital formation and development, from the late medieval period onward, a new type of land reclamation emerged to create the ecological conditions for expanded commodity production. In that sense, in historical capitalism land reclamation is a type of commodity frontier.

In this chapter, I explain how land reclamation has been a commodity frontier in the longue durée, over a long period of time during which the point and purpose of reclamation changed slowly and unevenly but distinctly. I argue that there are two pillars of this type of commodity frontier: The first pillar is that the state incentivizes individual men or private entities to reclaim the land, and in doing so, the state gains revenue (and possibly subjects), offsets the costs of reclamation (onto that grantee), and builds political allegiances. The first pillar long preceded the capitalist mode of production, as I will show, and can be considered a pillar of state power. The second pillar is rather unique to historical capitalism: The grantee transforms the land so that it is suitable for the extraction or production and sale of commodities that brings a return on investment. What differs across space and in the centuries

The Frontiers of Corporate Food in Egypt. Marion W. Dixon, Oxford University Press.
© Marion W. Dixon (2023). DOI: 10.1093/oso/9780192842985.003.0004

of capitalist development is the type of land that was reclaimed, how it was reclaimed (i.e., the labor force, the property regime), and how the land was made productive (e.g., via irrigation). However, the types of land that have been brought into the circuits of capital through reclamation have continuously expanded—from coastal and riverine lands to hilltops to semi-arid and then arid lands.

Land Reclamation as a Commodity Frontier

The frontier is a ubiquitous concept, and it may be thought of in two ways in the social sciences and humanities: as a space and as a place. As a space, a frontier often refers to an opportunity or an avenue yet to be explored (as in knowledge production, for example). As a place, a frontier is often understood in the most general sense as a territory, people/s, and so on that are not yet governed (e.g., Rogan 1999; Richards 2003; Barbier 2011). Combining both place and space is Anna Tsing's (2005) concept of resource frontier: an imaginative space and place of conquest and extraction, and yet, a type of wildness (yet to be conquered). A resource frontier is a "zone of not yet—not yet mapped, not yet regulated" (Cons and Eilenberg 2019: 12).

In this book, I am rather concerned theoretically with frontiers as places for capital accumulation. In Jason W. Moore (2010a, 2010b, 2011, 2015) terms, these places are commodity frontiers. More specifically, for Moore a commodity frontier is a place of accelerated commodification in the face of growing inter-state and inter-capitalist competition in the capitalist world-ecology. This process of accelerated commodification involves combinations of appropriation and exploitation. Appropriation refers to bringing in unpaid work/energy into the circuits of capital, and exploitation of labor power refers, in the Marxist sense, to the laborer producing greater value than the wage received (Moore 2015: 15–17). In Moore's commodity frontier, nature's "free gifts"—soil, water, forests, etc.—are appropriated with a small amount of capital (Marx 1967 cited in Moore 2010b: 4). In contrast, in the frontiers of reclaimed lands, significant time, energy, and resources are required. Hence, the two pillars of this frontier of capital:[1] The state incentivizes a person (or private entity) to bare the cost of reclaiming the land, and the grantee transforms the local ecosystem to maximize the output of commodities for sale so as to get more money than what was put in.

In the longue durée, land that is reclaimed is by definition land that is not being used for any of the four general purposes: cultivation, pasturage, extraction, and settlement. There are many reasons why land is uncultivated, unsettled, not used for pasture nor for the extraction of resources. The land may be left fallow for a growing season or more. The land may be partially or wholly submerged under water. The land may be degraded—through soil erosion, extreme weather, and the like. The land may be abandoned—due to war, tax evasion, and the like. The land may be distant from other settlements, transportation routes, and/or irrigation. For the purposes of this chapter, it is useful to think additionally of two categories of land that are reclaimed: unused land or land that has not been used recently, and used land but not used in the four ways identified. This second category of land is generally thought of as common property; land held in common for grazing, foraging, fallowing, transit, and so on. Various types of non-sedentary groups, who are not involved in fixed-field grain agriculture, are often associated with this category of land.

When and where states and fixed-field grain agriculture emerged, land reclamation became tied to state building through the general practice of conferring some version of land rights to the grantee to bring that land under cultivation. The incentives to get the grantees to reclaim the land have varied by state. This practice should be considered basic to territorial control and expansion: By bestowing the right to land (and wealth), the state is wielding obligations from that individual grantee (in the form of taxes, services, political allegiances, and so on). By expanding fixed-field grain agriculture and, thereby, the peasantry—the state is not only expanding the tax revenue base but is also developing land and population registries, property rights, and the like to administer tax collection and other state services (Scott 2009 cited in Herman 2018: 94–95). That is why for James C. Scott (2009) fixed-field agriculture was the foundation of state power. Fixed-field agriculture is also inherently expansionary as it leads to population growth, and a new generation without enough land, if not checked.

From the state's perspective, land that is not used in one of the four general ways would be considered waste or even empty land (*tabula rasa*). There is a considerable body of literature on the designation of common property as waste in proto-capitalist and modern capitalist states—say, in England in the early modern period during the enclosure of the commons (e.g., Goldstein 2012), or during European colonization of the Americas (e.g., Hodge 2007) or of arid lands and nomadic peoples (e.g., Davis 2016), or in the so-called Western frontier of the United States (e.g., Pisani 1992, 2002). This way of seeing is not particularly unique to the proto-/capitalist states of western Europe, though. Rather, the practice of transforming uncultivated land, whether used or not, into cultivated land (or pasture) should be understood as a state practice. At the same time, with the development of the capitalist mode of production, there is a qualitative shift in what is done with reclaimed land, either directly in the cases where states became proto-capitalist states or indirectly where trade relationships changed and territorial integrity was increasingly threatened.[2] In his influential book on the early modern period, John F. Richards (2003) argued that states were being built through a so-called unending frontier—from intensified human land use along settlement frontiers to biological invasions. However, Richards (2003) failed to acknowledge a new type of frontier that emerged at this time—what may be generally referred to as a commodity frontier. He was then unable to meaningfully distinguish between, say, the plantations in the New World from the settler frontiers of the Qing empire. Moreover, he did not account for how states, even pre-capitalist states, and inter-state competition changed with the drive for ever more commodities in an increasingly coordinated world-economy.

Theorizing land reclamation as a commodity frontier provides a nuanced understanding of the original conditions for capital accumulation that Karl Marx (1979) theorized as so-called primitive accumulation. Given that lands that are reclaimed may not be used, or used recently, or even if used may be marginal to livelihoods (e.g., marginal common property), this frontier of capital does not necessarily involve dispossession in any direct sense. Plus, no a priori radical legal property changes may be necessary. Both tendencies point to why land reclamation not only is a commodity frontier in the longue durée of historical capitalism but also can provide the initial conditions for capital formation and development in land.

Land Reclamation in the World-Economies of the Twelfth to Fifteenth Centuries

Land reclamation intensified in the late medieval period in various parts of the world as empires and city-states proliferated and trade networks extended from China to the coasts of Western Europe, reaching South Asia, the Middle East, North Africa, and beyond. By the fourteenth century, the large continental-mass—from Asia through Europe—consisted of what Eric Mielants (2007: 41) called "interconnected regional economies" and an international trade that was becoming more important.[3] The Mongolian Empire's expansion, from 1200 to 1350, connected the Eurasian landmass to China, making the links between the regional economies stronger and international trade more possible.[4] The regional economies are considered world-economies in that their economic activities extended beyond territorial boundaries (Wallerstein 2011a). The trade was in luxuries (spices, especially) but also in grains, manufactured goods (textiles, for example), and bullion (Abu-Lughod 1989; Mielants 2007). And the trade was competitive, as empires and city-states sought to gain control over trade routes. For example, in the twelfth and thirteenth centuries, there was competition between the textile industry of Mamluk Egypt, which was exporting throughout the Mediterranean, and the Flemish and Italian textile industries, which were exporting to parts of the Mediterranean (as well as the Black Sea area and Eastern Europe) (Mielants 2007: 138, 150).

Immanuel Wallerstein (2011a: 37–38) referred to the first part of this period (c. 1150–1300) as a period of expansion of the European world-economy, geographically, commercially, and demographically.[5] This expansion corresponded with the Medieval Warm Period (c. 950–1250) when the climate got warmer in parts of the world including in Europe (Patel and Moore 2017: 8). Given the corresponding growth of cities, warfare (for territorial expansion and/or control), populations, and markets in all the regional economies, this expansionary dynamic is likely to have been experienced throughout the interconnected world-economies of this period, albeit unevenly. The kind of markets that were prevalent at the time can be thought of generally as economies in which market exchange and the use of money (and credit) go together and, in Erica Schoenberger's (2008) terms, are normal and widespread enough to be unremarkable yet are not central to the dominant mode of production. In other words, most social classes in these respective class societies would not have been dependent on the market. The markets would have been concentrated in the centers of empires and in city-states, with merchants playing an important role in trade.

Markets were in existence when the first Islamic empire was founded, and within the first century of the empire, the legal infrastructure for the creation of rent-yielding property was established. This legal infrastructure was in the form of the tenancy contract (*ijara*), which was based on "the idea that use of land does not engender the obligation to pay rent, unless it is preceded by a valid or voidable contract of tenancy or share-cropping" (Johansen 1988: 39). The possession of arable lands then could by legally transformed into rent-yielding property. This legal foundation became relevant when what is often referred to as a type of tax-farming system began to develop during the Fatimid period, from the late tenth through the twelfth centuries. Nazih Ayubi (1995) argued that this system should be referred to not as taxes or involving taxation but rather as tribute.[6] The Fatimid empire no longer paid army officers from the public treasury and, instead, appointed them districts from which the officers would collect tribute from the peasantry as renumeration for their services.[7] This practice essentially obscured the distinction between rent and taxes as only a small percentage of the tax went to the public treasury, whereas most of the tribute went to the officer as his private revenue, effectively like a landlord would collect rent from tenants (Johansen 1988: 80). These changes occurred as the domain of state (*miri*) land expanded through the Mamluk period (c. twelfth to fourteenth centuries) and the early Ottoman period (c. fourteenth to seventeenth centuries) (Johansen 1988: 80–81).

The slow development of this particular tributary system in the consecutive Islamic empires can be understood as a way to manage resources over an expanding territorial state over time. At the very least, how was the imperial state going to maintain troops not only during battle but also after the conquest of new territory and people? The military lords—i.e., the army officers who were appointed districts from which to collect tribute—would be the source of food, men, armor, horses, and so on. In other words, direct provisions could come from nearer districts rather than from the distant center. This tributary mode of production represents a move away from private landed property and, in turn, the development of markets in land, as will be explained below. At the same time, the tribute could be exchanged in the market; therefore, this system strengthened the integration of the trade networks within the empire and the broader interconnected world economies.

Further, for Johansen (1988) the tributary system represented a decline in the position of peasants. In the early years of the Islamic state, the cultivator of the land was considered the owner when he paid a tax on private landed property (*kharaj*).[8] This early legal doctrine served the empire's purpose of agricultural expansion through the development and extension of irrigation and the reclamation of land. As market towns grew, the state encouraged the development of irrigation systems not only to expand agriculture but also to extend water to the towns (Watson 1983). The qanat system was the main irrigation system, which had ancient roots, and involved gravity-flow tunnel wells that transported water great distances with little loss from evaporation (Burke 2009: 85–86). This system was disseminated throughout the empire. Edmund Burke (2009: 88–89) further pointed out that this system as well as other water-management techniques were later adopted in the Iberian peninsula and informed the reclamation of land in the lowlands and marshlands of the Po river estuary in western Europe, as will be discussed in the sub-section on capital formation in land.

As with other empires at the time like the Byzantines, the Islamic empire also encouraged land reclamation. The state did so through laws that gave ownership rights to those who converted degraded or abandoned land into arable land and cultivated it. Also, this land was taxed at lower rates (Watson 1983: 116). Reclaimed (*mawat*) lands became private property in the sense that the cultivator became the proprietor. Conversely, the state discouraged abandoning land through laws that allowed the state ownership of lands that had not been cultivated for two or three years, and taxes were levied on any uncultivated land with access to water (Watson 1983: 116). With greater state ownership of land and the development of the new tributary system, though, the peasant ceased to be an owner of landed property and was, instead, considered a sharecropper on largely state land (Johansen 1988: 69, 81).

Greater state ownership of land also supported policies of provision, in which a town or city had reserves on food and other crops produced in the vicinities.[9] In Mamluk Egypt, the two major industries, textiles and sugar refining and confections, depended on the raw materials from the vicinities. According to Janet Abu-Lughod (1989: 231–232),

> the state controlled "the lands on which the raw materials were grown, owned many of the factories in which the goods were processed, and ultimately bought large quantities of the finished product, either to consume or to re-sell to the Italian merchants."

For Ayubi (1995: 48), the two main features of pre-capitalist modes of production were the absence or weakness of private land ownership and the powerful role of the state. Further, in the consecutive Islamic empires, the so-called nomadic kin-ordered mode of production routinely disrupted the dominant tributary mode of production (Ayubi 1995: 49). The Islamic state's efforts to end this disruption through sedentarization will be explored further in the next section on Land Reclamation in the Early Modern Period.

The move toward greater state control over land and production in the Islamic states from the twelfth century onward should be understood within the growing competition of the world-economies at this time. The Mamluk state was competing with the Italian city-states to establish monopolies in trade (Abu-Lughod 1989: 215), and during the 1250–1345 period, Mamluk Egypt's position in trade was slowly deteriorating as the Italian city-states developed strong maritime skills and gained advantages in various parts of the Mediterranean trade (Mielants 2007: 138–139). Does the growing competitive strength of the European city-states mean that the European world-economy was already a dominant force in this period of expansion? No, it does not. Following Abu-Lughod (1989), a more reasonable conclusion to make about this period of expansion is that there was no power center.

More importantly, for the purposes of this chapter, this expansionary period created the conditions for a new type of market—a capitalist market—to develop in the European inter-city-state system (Mielants 2007). With the slow and uneven development of capital, a new type of land reclamation emerged. The new capitalist market is often confused with the market economies of the time and the wealth that they created.[10] To clear this confusion, I start with Mielants's (2007) inquiry: I ask how much the merchants were oriented toward capital accumulation to ascertain the emergence of two modes of production, a feudal mode and a capitalist mode, that co-existed and impacted one another.

Capital Formation in Land

The urban nexus that developed during the expansion of the late medieval period up and down western Europe—Northern Italy, parts of France and Germany, the Low Countries, Southern England—was made up of a large number of industrial activities such as mining, textile production, minting, glass making, ship building, and so on (Mielants 2007: 44). This nexus created the demand for food for merchants, artisans, and workers, and city-states were importing food from increasingly greater distances, from Eastern Europe in particular (Mielants 2007: 42). The urban industries also often depended on long-distance trade for their raw materials (wool, cotton, silk, alum, and dyestuffs), and deepened interregional trade networks (Mielants 2007: 44–45).

The continuing threats from the vast empires to the East and South worked to the advantage of the merchants. In the East, the Mongolian Empire expanded into parts of Eastern Europe and was a constant threat and weakened the trading partners in the region. At the same time, the Mongolians eased overland trade for western European merchants (Anievas and Nişancıoğlu 2015: 72–73), including the Italian city-state's so-called steady colonization of the Byzantine Empire for cotton and alkali ashes (for the soap and glass industries) (Mielants 2007: 27–28). In the South, the Crusades waged centuries earlier likely contributed to marketization and the early development of this urban nexus.[11] The Christian Reconquista, the centuries-long military campaigns against the Islamic empires, as well as constant conflicts between the rival city-states, also led the Italian city-states to build sizable navies and militaries. Instead of standing armies, though, they relied on mercenaries. To pay the mercenaries, the city-states began to seek financing from private individuals; Genoa was first, floating municipal debt in 1149 (Roos 2019: 86).[12] The development of a complex system of public credit during this expansionary period constitutes an embryonic stage of the capitalist state's development, during which merchants were greatly empowered and a banking class was born.[13] This process had a regional dynamic, as proto-capitalist states in the region appear to have developed together, with the system of public credit also involving sovereign debt, i.e., governments borrowing across borders. In this case, most significantly, the Iberian aristocracy (Portugal and Castile) became dependent over time on the Italian bankers for war financing (Patel and Moore 2017: 13–14).

The urban nexus also depended on what Wallerstein (2011a: 38) referred to as a "classic internal frontier of forest, swamp, marsh, moor, and fen for fuel, land, food, and other raw materials." This internal frontier centrally involved the reclamation of land from the sea and river estuaries, particularly in the low countries and along the Po River in Northern Italy (Mielants 2007: 27). Why was land reclamation so important? Mielants (2007: 27) claimed, but did not develop the argument, that massive land reclamation at this time became an important aspect of capital formation in the European world-economy. This claim deserves further development, and I attempt to do so by, first, detailing land reclamation in the low countries of Flanders, Holland, and the North Sea coast of the Netherlands.[14]

In Flanders, Holland, and the North Sea coast, the point and purpose of land reclamation began to differ from the reclaimed lands that individual peasant landholders could maintain and had maintained. This change was an important part of what Petra J. E. M. van Dam (2001) called the ecological transformation of what is today the Netherlands between 1350 and 1550. In the fourteenth century, small-scale subsistence peat digging "developed into large-scale peat mining" (van Dam 2001: 35). Merchants and others central to this urban nexus (such as guild masters, officials, and the like), in particular, were involved in reclaiming the land. Energy (in the form of peat soil), salt, and other resources that they needed for their industries, or that they could trade, could be mined or cultivated on the coasts and along waterways. They put time and effort—mobilizing labor, acquiring technologies (sluices, etc.), receiving official permissions, and so on—to reclaim the land. Much of the reclamation was in the form of polders, i.e., dikes built on the shores that made possible the creation of arable or pasture lands. Although the data on land ownership is incomplete in the late medieval period, trends show how peasant landholdings declined as land ownership of absentee landlords increased. In Zeeland, Flanders, for example, peasant ownership in coastal areas had been in decline since the late thirteenth century (van Tielhof 2015). By the 1400s, in various areas of the south-west Netherlands, town-dwellers, who were absentee landlords, were owning roughly 20–30% of the land, while peasants still owned the majority in most places (van Cruyningen 2014: 248). These new absentee landlords would rent the reclaimed land to peasants to produce and sell the commodities. This shift in the reclaimed coastal lands represents a shift away from the feudal land tenure system to what Wallerstein (2011a: 110) called a "money rent" system.[15]

The new point and purpose of land reclamation is also clear from the soil degradation, land subsidence, and declining yields throughout the Netherlands. These lands were peat lands, made of carbon-rich soil.

> When these soils were drained for use as arable farmland, the level of the land subsided through shrinkage and oxidation of the peat. This made the area vulnerable to flooding and obstructed the disposal of excess water, a situation that was made worse by the digging of peat for fuel and salt production.
>
> (van Cruyningen 2014: 245–246)[16]

Inland land subsidence led to the creation of freshwater lakes (van Dam 2001). These cascading effects from the sinking of surface levels illustrate in part that absentee landlords were unwilling or unable to invest in the upkeep of the polders, drains, and the rest (van Cruyningen 2014; van Tielhof 2015). The fact that land/water maintenance rested with absentee landlords reflects a process of communalization of maintenance—a process that shifted the responsibility for upkeep from the individual cultivators of the land to the community (van Tielhof 2015; Xu and Blussé 2019). In Zeeland, for example, there emerged a water management board (van de Ven 1996: 89–90). As the scale and scope of reclamation increased, no longer could individual farmers handle the maintenance.[17]

Massive land reclamation in the Netherlands should not be viewed singularly as an initial process of undermining subsistence producers' access to their subsistence for the accumulation of capital in land. Although as percentages of total land ownership, peasant ownership declined as absentee landlord ownership increased over centuries, this outcome was not simply the result of land privatization—a peasant's loss was a private landlord's gain. How do we know? First of all, the total area of arable and pasture land increased multifold during (and before) this period,[18] so that the increase in landholdings of absentee landlords would likely also reflect this overall increase in the total land area through reclamation. Also, given the type of land that was privatized, land that was partially or entirely submerged under water, it is likely that much of this land was marginal land (land that was not central to peasant livelihoods, even if it was common property). That likelihood is important because it means that radical transformations in property and social relations were not needed initially to reclaim the land for commodity production. If there were minimal conflicts regarding claims to this land, then it was possible to make these lands larger than existing land parcels. Even if the lands were not very large, this larger size is important as reclamation was costly. Getting back more than what they put in the land would be important, imperative really, and given the size, devoting the land to commodity production would make this return on investment more likely. Also, because the land was in some way restored, diminishing returns to more intensive production and/or extraction would be delayed.

Who would rent this land if there were not yet generalized capitalist social relations and people were not dependent on the market? Let us assume that there were peasants who needed land for subsistence purposes given the expansionary tendencies of the feudal land tenure system and the apparent need for more land given the widespread participation of peasants in land reclamation. If they rented the land, they would need to produce/mine commodities that they would not consume or that would not be central to their own subsistence. They would produce those commodities as their rent. It is likely that they would not only be producing their rent and that they would also produce for their own needs. Over time landlords began asking for rent in cash, which meant that the renters would need to sell their commodities for cash to then give to their landlord, hence the term "money rent" system.[19] Having to pay rent in cash further meant that renters would become increasingly dependent on the market. Since they could not control the price that they got on the market, they would be inclined to produce more commodities for sale. The more that they devoted to commodity production for sale, the less that they would devote for subsistence production.

In these ways, land reclamation was amenable to capital formation, of transforming these lands into a commodity—something to be acquired, improved upon, and profited from (van de Ven 1996: 60). Because land reclamation was amenable to capital formation in some areas does not imply that land reclamation led to capital formation in all areas, however. Peasants continued to be engaged in land reclamation for the purpose of preserving or expanding their subsistence base. But the gradual penetration of capitalist social relations, as peasants moved away from subsistence production, accelerated during the contraction (c. 1300–1450) that followed the expansion of the world-economies (Wallerstein 2011a: 37–38). During the contraction, peasants continued to be involved in land reclamation—and in ways that undermined the feudal social order.

In Abu-Lughod's (1989) terms, the contraction meant that the world-system of the thirteenth century was dead by the fifteenth century. The Warm Period had ended and was replaced by the Little Ice Age (after 1250). This climatic shift in Europe contributed to lower yields, malnutrition, and famine, making the region more vulnerable to disease (Patel and Moore 2017: 9–10). The Mongolian Empire collapsed in the wake of the Black Death, which spread all along the fourteenth-century trade routes (Abu-Lughod 1989: 19). The European inter-city-state system, and the concomitant development of private property in reclaimed lands, had already undermined the feudal social order, and the Black Death weakened it even more. The population declined, wages rose, and peasants migrated to towns and cities. Over all, peasants were now in a better position to take land and bargain for wages. Peasant revolts were widespread (Wallerstein 2011a: 24–25; Patel and Moore 2017: 10–13). Those leading the revolts were likely the better-off peasants who were in a position to expand cultivation into new land and improve it (Dobb 1967: 11 cited in Wallerstein 2011a: 24–25). In the North Sea areas of Friesland and Groningen, peasant-led land reclamation stimulated the growth of independent peasant republics (van de Ven 1996: 60–61).

The empires that formed and (some of which) would carry us into the modern era—from the Habsburg, Ming, and Ottoman (in the 1300s) to the Portuguese and (Habsburg) Spanish (in the 1400s) to the British, Dutch, Mughal, Salavaid (in the 1500s)—emerged out of this crisis. The Ottomans gained from European retreat in the Black Sea and in Constantinople, and the Portuguese and Spanish were partially propelled to the Atlantic as Ottoman advances cut off supplies of bullion coming from Sudan and Central Europe (Wallerstein 2011a: 42).[20] The territorial expansion of the European city-states turned nation-states beginning in the early-1400s was more than just what empires do, however.[21] When have empires before gone to all corners of the globe within a matter of three centuries and, in doing so, radically transformed ecosystems and social relations along the way?

Land Reclamation in the Early Modern Period, circa Fifteenth to Seventeenth Centuries

The contraction following the expansion of the late medieval period caused a crisis for the ruling elites (Wallerstein 2011a), and what was unique about the European inter-city-state system was that the ruling elites of western Europe could attempt to resolve the crisis in part by jumping on the proverbial capitalist ship that was already sailing.[22] In short, the states, the nobility, and the church attempted to reinvent themselves through territorial expansion, and within about one hundred years, from the mid-1400s to the mid-1500s, first the Portuguese and the Spanish, and soon after the Dutch, English, and French, had set up trade stations (and later coastal city-states) throughout Asia and in parts of the North Sea and plantations on islands in the Atlantic and Caribbean and along the coasts of the Americas, and began the transatlantic slave trade to support this growth.[23] Genoese finance enabled this type of proto-capitalist development: According to Roos (2019: 92), this creditors cartel—the top ten Genoese banking families accounted for 70% of all loans—exercised market discipline on King Philip II, whose rule extended from Spain to Portugal to the Netherlands and throughout the coasts of the New World. The beginning of market discipline of international lending was important to the growth of a capitalist world-economy.

In world systems scholarship, the designation of a capitalist world-economy in the long sixteenth century (c. 1450–1640) should not be meant to imply that capitalist social relations had become generalized around the world by this time nor that capital accumulation happened in a linear process from Europe and then spread around the world. Rather, this designation implies that the drive to accumulate capital changed subsistence livelihoods, patterns of consumption, trade routes, and market competition in ways that in some cases solidified, and in other cases created new, divisions of labor between regions. In so doing, imperial state building in the early modern period was directly and indirectly impacted.

The nexus of reclamation, irrigation, and urban water-supply systems of many empires and city-states of the late medieval period continued in the early modern period.[24] States developed and dispersed new technologies (water-lifting, irrigation, river-control, etc.) that enabled the expansion of reclamation into new lands internally. The Ottomans, Ming and Qing, Tokugawa Shogunate, western European states, among other early modern states, reclaimed not only coastal lands but also land from inland lakes and river estuaries (such as moors, swamps, and marshes),[25] hills, and still more types of uncultivated lands. This expansion led to settlement in these new lands (Richards 2003). In the Mediterranean region, where pastoral and nomadic populations were significant, this practice was tied to policies of sedentarization as the state sought to incorporate nomadic and pastoral populations into the state (Braudel 1972; İnalcık 1994). Competition for territory between states and political contestations within states spurred this conquering of ever new lands, and the proto-capitalist states' extension of various types of territorial control far and wide exacerbated this competition. Perhaps more importantly, but more difficult to discern, is the influence of expanded commodity production in Asia and especially in the New World. In some cases, the introduction of crops from the New World shaped the possibilities of internal frontiers in other regions.[26] In other cases, there was a direct change in what was grown either because of political power relations[27] or because of market dynamics in which new crops displaced existing ones in trade networks.[28]

More significantly for the purposes of this chapter, in the early modern (capitalist and non-capitalist) states, the practice of designating prominent men (at the upper echelons of the social order and/or local elites) to reclaim land and then confer privileges to them became a prominent practice. This practice was a way to gain allegiances while centralizing power (Diaz Alejandro 1970: 37; Richards 2003: 106). It became more relevant as states confronted growing revenue deficits due to the changing monetary system from the influx and adoption of silver from the New World. Because reclamation was expensive, conferring rights to private entities/persons to make investments to improve the land became imperative. In addition, the state then was able to tax the grantees.

In the proto-capitalist states, reclamation continued to be for the expansion of agriculture and state revenue and for the conferring of privileges to political allies. However, instead of expanding peasant production (that involved necessarily their own reproduction), the point and purpose was to extract and/or produce commodities for sale, thereby, directly and indirectly undermining subsistence livelihoods. The conquering of new lands abroad syncopated with the continued internal frontier: These western European imperial states very quickly reclaimed lands for maritime settlement and ports—to build port cities for the transport of commodities in conquered territories (Hudson 1996).[29] Internally, these states undertook large-scale reclamation projects, which were just one type of large-scale project for capitalist development that the European early-modern states carried out—others being mines, shipyards, foundries, harbors, forts, and so on (Ash 2017: 10). Below, large-scale state projects will be detailed and then contrasted with land reclamation in the early years of the Ottoman Empire to highlight what is distinct about land reclamation as a commodity frontier.

Large-Scale State Reclamation Projects

The collapse of coastal defenses in the Netherlands that was discussed in the previous section led to massive intermittent flooding starting in the fifteenth century. This flooding turned out to be a windfall for the capitalist classes and greatly accelerated capitalist development in land. This contingent outcome was based in part on the type of soil that replaced the peat after decades of mining and flooding: fertile marine soil. This fertile soil, in turn, drastically changed the cost-benefit calculus of reclamation (van de Ven 1996; van Cruyningen 2014). Plus, those who could not incur the costs of reclamation—most peasants, the Church, some of the nobility—lost land. Those who could—namely, the various capitalist classes—then acquired huge swaths of land.[30]

The capitalist classes' capture of submerged lands accelerated the process that began in the late medieval period—of declining common property and Church property and its replacement with private property.[31] Large commercial farms had, in turn, emerged, characterized by (primarily or solely) the production of cash crops on private property by largely agricultural laborers. In Flanders, for example, these farms were not necessarily the property of capitalists in the towns as there had already been the development of rich peasants through differentiation and the development of a "living land and lease market" (van Cruyningen 2014: 254).

It was not only the flooded coastal areas of present-day Netherlands that experienced the consolidation of capitalist social relations in the countryside. In the long sixteenth century, in the northern Mediterranean, for example, the rich and powerful landowners had an essential role to play as small-scale reclamation projects were abandoned in favor of extensive, longer-term schemes (Braudel 1972: 75).[32] These developments in land, from ditches to trenches to canals to low-powered pumps, in turn, corresponded with a type of social stratification: peasants were pushed to poor land in the hills and large estates "remained the rule in the plains" (Braudel 1972: 77). As in the late medieval period, this reclamation was in response to the needs of the towns, whose population in the fifteenth and sixteenth centuries was steadily increasing (Braudel 1972: 69–70).

As peasants lost land, they often became wage laborers and town dwellers, and this meant that increasingly the labor force that was mobilized for reclamation projects was wage labor. Milja van Tielhof (2015: 331) makes this very point about the North Sea Coast: In one area (Honsbossche), in the 1420s, repair work was ordered in kind among a group of villages. By the 1470s, work for repairs was given in cash. Also, two cases of large-scale water management in the region in the sixteenth century demonstrate the large number of dike workers who could be hired in Holland at the time: In one project, in 1505, 15,000 workers were recruited in the province of Frisia. Five years later, major repair works at another site were carried out by about 1,000 dike workers, mostly recruited from the northern part of Holland (van Tielhof 2015: 331–332). Van Tielhof (2015) is not claiming that all repair projects were dependent on wage labor in this way, but the use of wage labor for water/coastal management appears to have been common throughout the North Sea region by the long sixteenth century.

The center of finance had moved from Genoa to Antwerp and then to Amsterdam by the seventeenth century (Roos 2019). Following the Italian city-states, a public credit system had already developed under Habsburg rule, and by the time of the Dutch Republic, international lending became highly coordinated by a handful of private banks (Roos 2019: 93–14). Public credit funded states' territorial expansion (along with the other state-led projects), and the invention of the joint stock company made it possible to organize large numbers of private investments—both abroad and in drainage and land reclamation projects at home. Those who invested in reclamation in the Netherlands were merchants, who traded in the North Sea area, the Baltics, the Caribbean, the South American coast, and beyond (van Cruyningen 2014: 257–258). When the East and West India Companies were founded, many of the initial shareholders became investors in reclamation projects.[33] These merchants were often landowners in the towns. Many were also officials; for example, Jacob Boreel, Master of Zeeland Mint and Mayor of Middleburg, invested in shipping in the Dutch East India Company (VOC) and also in several drainage projects in Zeeland and Flanders from 1595 (van Cruyningen 2014: 258). Zeeland merchants began to organize new companies for land reclamation that resembled the VOC: The investors needed to first obtain a charter or exclusive right from the provincial government or the national government (the States General). Then, they would set up a drainage consortium to reclaim the land. They had to compensate the previous owners of the submerged land and would receive a period of tax exemption. Each investor would then own a portion of the reclaimed land (Xu and Blussé 2019: 438).

These companies invested in improved windmills, which could pump out entire lake basins and develop them into polders (Xu and Blussé 2019: 428). The wind-powered drainage mill was introduced in 1408 (van Dam 2001: 42), and through the support of the central Water Authority became widely adopted after 1600. This new technology provided thousands of acres of new fertile land and moved the wheels and saws of factories (van Veen 1962: 42–43).

This technical development in land for (largely) expanded commodity production was also possible with the development of a professional class of so-called experts and the accompanying development and institutionalization of the sciences and relevant technologies. The Dutch were sending hydraulic engineers across Europe (Zanetti 2017: 352). Many of these professionals would come out of the engineering school that Leiden University opened in 1600 to teach land surveyors in Dutch (rather than in Latin) (Xu and Blussé 2019: 434–435).

One of the largest drainage and reclamation projects that Dutch engineers became involved in was the English Fenlands, a marshy landmass along the North Sea coast that had largely been held in common. Throughout much of Queen Elizabeth's reign, between 1570 and 1600, numerous patents were awarded granting exclusive rights to Englishmen and foreigners to drain a designated area of the Fens or to use a new technology for drainage (Ash 2017: 53). Before the mid-1500s, the Crown did not have the resources to undertake such a project. Then, in the early 1600s, King James met with the special ambassador for the United Netherlands to discuss the Dutch East India Company and other trade matters, and this ambassador's brother-in-law was Cornelius Vermuyden, a known Dutch hydraulic engineer (Korthals-Altes 1925). However, the Crown did not commission Vermuyden to drain the Fens until the reign of King Charles. The charter that the Crown issued to Vermuyden is noteworthy: Most of the land that would be drained and reclaimed was the Crown's. The Crown needed revenue. Vermuyden was named the projector, who was responsible for securing the investors for the project.[34] In return, the Crown made the import of materials for the project duty free. In addition to securing the investors, the projector would need to compensate any owners in and around the drainage works who lost their homes. Upon completion of the project, the reclaimed land would be divided into thirds: a third going to the projector, a third to the Crown, and a third to the commoners.[35] The point and purpose of draining the Fens was to increase the area of the pasture land and arable land for "marketable crops" (in contrast to, in one pro-ponent's words, the "ludicrous overevaluation of eels, reeds and peet turves that the poor fenlenders claimed to make a decent living from") (Ash 2017: 3).[36]

The draining of the Fens was possible because property relations had already been legally transformed in England as they had in the Netherlands. This project and other large-scale reclamation schemes in the Kingdom followed the English Parliament's passage of the General Draining Act in 1600 that provided the legal framework for the reclamation of "wastes, commons, marshes, and fenny groups there subject to surrounding [flooding]" in the hope of "recovering many hundred thousand Acres of marshes" (Richards 2003: 214). The fact that there was already a radical legal change of property relations does not imply that there was minimal opposition to the schemes. The opposition was recurring and well-documented: Common fen-lenders, (some) nobility and local sewers commissions engaged in various forms of resistance, both sporadic and prolonged, using legal and extralegal means, to pro-tect the commons and the livelihoods it maintained. At the same time, this massive enclosure of common property was also a response to the changed property relations. One of the justifications for the enclosure was to accommodate the surplus popula-tion of neighboring regions (Lindley 1982: 4). Poorer commoners had migrated to the region to use the common property of the Fens (Ash 2017: 147)—an indication that enclosures elsewhere were creating, or at the very least contributing to, this surplus population.

These so-called public works projects required experts to design and build them as well as some level of centralized public governance—to mediate the local oppo-sition to them, to manage their upkeep, and so on. In the Fens, the medieval-era sewers commissions were "broken, co-opted, or supplanted so that the local interests of fenland commoners and smallholders could be subordinated to the more market-oriented interests of drainage projectors" (Ash 2017: 8). In the terms of the charter with the projector, Vermuyden, a corporation was to be created once the drainage was complete to continue the maintenance. Vermuyden would nominate the mem-bers of the corporation and set aside sufficient lands to pay for it through the rents earned (Ash 2017: 153). In the Netherlands, the communalization of water main-tenance (including coastal defenses) continued from the medieval period through the seventeenth century, gradually shifting the responsibilities of upkeep from the regional water boards to the state. Officials from the powerful cities dominated the provincial governments, and these officials were also often landowners, so it was more likely that the provincial governments would support polders that were at risk of flooding when requested (van Cruyningen 2014: 258). In Amsterdam, for example, the city was directly involved in water maintenance in the surrounding regions and was compensated via taxation in Holland (van Tielhof 2015: 339). The centralization of water maintenance went hand-in-hand with professionalization and monetization of maintenance of dikes and polders. When the state was not involved, profession-ally trained and licensed land surveyors were in charge via water boards, and they would tax landowners to carry out maintenance (Xu and Blussé 2019: 434–435; also van Tielhof 2015).

The early modern European states were able to accomplish these large-scale technical projects for revenue generation via capital accumulation by quantifying, rationalizing, and exploiting the natural environment (Ash 2017: 5), or in Candiani's (2014: 3) terms, regarding the basin in the Valley of Mexico, by transforming a fluid landscape into "one amenable to Spanish patterns of production." These state reclamation projects are a form of intensive production of nature (Goldstein 2012: 360) and reflect radical changes in the European elite's views of nature including the land itself—as a commodity that they could acquire, improve, and profit from (Mielants 2007: 27). In Carolyn Merchant's (1980) terms, these large-scale reclamation schemes of the early modern period required the death of an organismic view of nature— in the example of the Fens, of turning the marsh lands from a vibrant ecosystem that provides to a "wasted natural resource for the good of the commonwealth" (Ash 2017: 5).

More than this, as Merchant (1980) showed, there was public opposition to these elite views of wild nature to be controlled and conquered. The long ecological transformations of the vast wetlands of much of the Netherlands had, in van Dam's (2001) terms, dug the roots of the Republic of the United Netherlands. In the case of the Fenlands, the opposition was successful in making its way to debates in Parliament and the mounting political opposition to King Charles I, culminating in the English Revolution (Lindley 1982). These large-scale reclamation (and other) projects of the proto-capitalist states that required centralized governance were also in a sense the beginnings of public governance. And they differed fundamentally from the large-scale projects that non-capitalist early modern states like the Ottoman state carried out.

Early Ottoman Years

Much of the territorial expansion of the Ottoman state occurred in the 1400s and 1500s when the Ottomans captured territories throughout Anatolia, the Balkans, the Mamluk Empire and other parts of the Mediterranean. As with earlier Islamic empires, a tributary system suited this territorial expansion. Under the Ottomans, the tributary system was referred to as the *tımar* system—*tımars* being military fiefs or areas of land that the Sultan allocated to army officers in the ruling elite upon them gaining an imperial diploma.[37] The two institutional bases of the *tımar* system were that the cultivator was legally bound to the soil and that the state had eminent domain, by right of conquest, over most of the cultivated land.[38]

As Huri İslamoğlu-İnan (1994) argued, state ownership of land should be understood as a negotiated process of rules that governed the relationships between peasants and the *tımar* and between peasants and the *tımar* holder (and others who could claim revenue from peasant production). Cavalrymen were granted *tımars* and collected both a grain-tithe (1/10th of grain production) and a land tax in return for the delivery of local cavalry (mounted soldiers who would join the imperial army when called upon). Higher-level authorities—for example, provincial governors—were also able to collect tax from the *tımars* but indirectly. They lived in the towns and had an income as officials. Peasants were independent in this system in that they had secure tenure; there were state rules limiting what the *tımar* holder could do to peasants in terms of the requirement of labor services, the payment of taxes, and so on. It was the higher-level officials, and the local judge, who enforced these protections.

The *tımar* system was the dominant system of organizing territories and peoples within the Ottoman empire during the early years (c. 1300–1600), but it was not the only one. The state adapted as territories were conquered and incorporated. In one such region, North Central Anatolia, for example, local elites maintained their ownership of land (İslamoğlu-İnan 1994). The *tımar* system was flexible in accommodating the competing groups within a growing military-administrative class, including local elites. Also, the system was flexible enough to assist (to varying degrees) the state in its efforts to sedentarize nomads. The trade that nomads engaged in within the *tımars* began to be taxed (İslamoğlu-İnan 1994: 148–149).

As I noted in the section on land reclamation in the world-economies of the twelfth to fifteenth centuries, the tributary system worked well serving not only territorial expansion but the market expansion that accompanied it. In the sixteenth century, at least in parts of Anatolia, there was exponential growth in market towns. This growth was likely caused by displaced people coming into towns due to warfare, the trade that was associated with the provisioning of troops, and overall population growth. In İslamoğlu-İnan's (1994) case study of sixteenth-century North Central Anatolia, the growth in towns did not correspond with the greater involvement of peasants in the market or with an increase in the division of labor between regions.[39] Those who benefited most from the accompanying increase in prices during this market growth were the *tımar* holders who sold in the market about two-thirds of their grain tithes—and that two-thirds was about 13% of the total grain yields from the districts. The *tımar* holders needed to sell their tithe in order to provide for their cavalry.

Land reclamation was part of the empire's territorial and agricultural expansion especially given the high level of land desertion (due to banditry, famine, taxes, and so on) in the early years (İnalcık 1994). The Ottoman state provided incentives to cultivate unused lands by granting tenure to individuals who paid taxes for ten years (Keyder 1991: 7). Most reclamation appears to have been undertaken by peasants, but there were also bigger farms and ranches that were formed out of reclaimed lands (İnalcık 1994: 170).

As with other early modern states, a focus of reclamation of the Ottomans in Egypt (1516–1798) was on the Nile Delta. On the Nile River, in early summer, the two river tributaries, the White Nile and the Blue Nile, would reach the flood stage. By early August, the water would arrive in Egypt where it would inundate the valley. By the end of the month, the water would retreat in time for fall planting, leaving a deposit of silt coating the fields (Burke 2009: 84). This inundation had irrigated the fields along the Nile since ancient times and before, and made agriculture very productive. But to be productive, this irrigation system required constant maintenance, especially in the Delta where the river's flow ends and empties into the Mediterranean Sea. Rivers shift, and as they do, the surface area changes. As Alan Mikhail (2011: ch. 1) details, under the Ottomans, new canals were built, new fields reclaimed, and peasants recruited to settle on and cultivate the land and maintain the canals. The cities—one on the coast of the Delta (Alexandria), the other near to the Delta's opening (Cairo)—continued to grow through reclamation.[40]

The expansion of water canals to the cities as well as the expansion of their surface areas was essential as the êntrepot trade was re-established during the Ottoman era, connecting Asia and Africa on the one hand and the Mediterranean on the other hand. This time coffee replaced spices as the mainstay of this trade: Coffee was grown in Yemen and exported via Egypt to (primarily) the rest of the Ottoman Empire and (secondarily) to Europe. The zenith of the coffee trade lasted between 1690 and 1725, declining after that, as Europeans began to set up coffee plantations in the Caribbean. Also, after 1730, Egyptian cloth exports to France fell. Both of these factors contributed to a growing trade deficit in the Ottoman province of Egypt by the end of the eighteenth century (Richards 1987). The growing trade deficit in Egypt reflects a broader process by which the long-distance trade in luxuries that passed westward through Egypt from the this period gradually dwindled and was replaced by an interregional trade in staples grown in Ottoman provinces—grain, animal hides, and animal fibers in the sixteenth and seventeenth centuries, cotton and tobacco in the eighteenth century (McGowan 1981: 3).

The period of what Rifa'at 'Ali Abou-El-Haj (2005: 48) called "major upheavals" within the Ottoman Empire beginning in the seventeenth century likely played a role in the enveloping asymmetrical trading relationships with western Europe.[41] This period led to a system of what is often referred to as (a new type of) tax farming (or *iltizam*) that replaced the *tımar* system. The *iltizam* system grew rapidly in Ottoman Egypt after the mid-1600s (Abbas and El-Dessouky 2011: 4–5). Instead of army officers, many of the tax-farmers were high- and middle-level Istanbul-based officials. They had agents in the districts who supervised the sources of revenue and ensured the delivery of taxes. The central state had switched from a cavalry to an infantry army with fire arms so that the district officials no longer needed to maintain troops. Declining terms of trade compounded with a decline in revenue due to the switch to a monetized form of tribute (in silver) put pressure on the Ottoman state to seek more tax revenues. The state (along with the Ming and the Habsburg Spanish empires) had converted tax receipts to a fixed quantity of silver when there was an influx of silver from the New World during what Dennis O. Flynn and Arturo Giráldez (2002) called the Potosi cycle of silver (1540s-1640s), during which the value of silver slowly declined. The *iltizam* system ensured that larger shares of grain production could be taxed than did the *tımar* system. The Ottoman state was also abdicating part of its involvement in district governance; therefore, the tax farmers had more autonomy. With more autonomy and larger revenue, the *iltizam* system was a way of alleviating the intensifying competition between the various claimants of revenue in the *tımars* that developed with the growth of market towns. Wallerstein et al. (1987: 90–91) claimed that greater autonomy also led to greater abuse of peasants—forceful appropriation, usury, and so on—that paved the way for the growth in the size of land units.

In conclusion, land reclamation in the early Ottoman years, and large-scale recla-mation projects under the Ottomans in Egypt, were for the production of state revenue through peasant production. During the course of the early modern period, the peasant position appears to have declined over all, in part because of changes in trade and consequently in state revenue with the growth of a capitalist world-economy. Nonetheless, the growth of state ownership of land and market towns in the Ottoman state through the early modern period did not undermine in any signif-icant way peasant subsistence livelihoods as peasants did not appear to be dependent on these markets, near or far. In contrast, land reclamation in western Europe in the late medieval period, and the large-scale reclamation projects in England in the early modern period, were fundamentally for state revenue through the extraction and/or production of commodities that directly and indirectly undermined subsis-tence livelihoods. These projects were one part of a general process well underway of making the masses dependent on the capitalist market that was built through the division of and trade between world regions.

Conclusions

In this chapter, I argue that land reclamation was important in the long durée of his-torical capitalism. First, I establish the long relationship between land reclamation and state building: Land reclamation should be understood as foundational to ter-ritorial control and expansion. Then, I show how and why this relationship began to change with the role reclamation played in capital formation and development within the European inter city-state system of the late medieval period. As a capitalist world-economy developed, a dominant trend among early modern states (capitalist and non-capitalist) was the state granting rights to individual men who would reclaim the land.

The point and purpose of land reclamation differed between proto-capitalist and non-capitalist early modern states. In the early years of the Ottoman empire (c. 1300–1600), the state granted tenure to anyone who paid taxes for a given time period on land that they reclaimed. In contrast, the proto-capitalist city-states and empires of western Europe incentivized land reclamation for the extraction and/or production and sale of commodities at scale through the privatization of land, the legal and insti-tutional protection of investment, and so on. In the low-lying coastal and riverine lands of the Netherlands, the incentives to reclaim land took at least three general forms: The first was communalization of management of the polders and the like, which was increasingly carried out at a regional level. This process meant that indi-vidual responsibilities for absentee landlords were minimized. Second, in the case of peat mining, capitalists in the towns acquired land and received the Count's permis-sion to dig peat (van de Ven 1996: 125). There were permits for given amounts of peat, but these limits were rarely observed given that local authorities had an incentive to maximize peat mining for tax revenue (van de Ven 1996: 125). The lack of regula-tion led to the rapid depletion of peat. Third, the creation of joint stock companies minimized risks as capitalists pulled capital together for large-scale reclamation projects.

By the early modern period, land reclamation in the proto-capitalist states increasingly took the form of large-scale state projects involving planning, expertise, technologies, legal property changes, negotiating competing claims on land and resources, and on and on. These so-called technical projects can be understood as planting the seeds of state agricultural development and extension services that became prominent from the long nineteenth century onward.

Also, the contingent processes that made possible capital formation and development in land in the low countries of western Europe from the late medieval period to the early modern period will become relevant in the discussion and analysis of early capitalist development in the Ottoman province of Egypt in the next chapter. These processes, in the context of high military conflict, included a merchant class developing an orientation to accumulate capital and a state developing mercenary forces and borrowing from the merchants, in part, to pay the forces.

Notes

1. Thanks to Jason W. Moore for suggesting this name to distinguish reclaimed land as a frontier from his concept of commodity frontier.
2. Goldstein (2012) gets at the qualitative shift in this state practice in his discussion of how the designation of wastes shifted during the long enclosure movement in England. Common wastes in medieval England were marginal lands or lands not central to livelihoods that were held in common. With capitalist development, the entirety of common property came to be designated as the wasted commons—a wasted potential.
3. On these world-economies (or world-system) of the late medieval period, see also Abu-Lughod (1989).
4. On the influence of Pax Mongolica of the late medieval period, see Anievas and Nişancıoğlu (2015: ch. 3).
5. This periodization is rough but consistent. For example, van de Ven (1996: 49) claimed that in the Netherlands there was an enormous expansion of agrarian society through reclamation and the intensification of agriculture from 1000 to 1250.
6. Barkey (2008: 229) also referred to this tax farming as a tributary system that can be found in other states and empires since antiquity.
7. It was not only this tributary system that took centuries to develop; endowed (*waqf*) land too developed later (Watson 1983: 142). Endowed land was for the benefit of religious and educational institutions.
8. Johansen (1988: 19) acknowledged that the classical Hanafite doctrine that recognized peasant ownership of land did not protect peasants from exploitation, say, from onerous taxation.
9. For a description of this policy of provision in the Ottoman empire, see McGowan (1981: 11).
10. In prevalent comparisons of wealth between empires and city-states, even in different time periods, there is often a failure to recognize different forms of wealth or to mistake capital and even capitalism with various combinations of markets, commodities,

and money that likely had nothing to do with capital. Hypothetically, a merchant may "buy low and sell high" and use that income for tribute and/or other political obligations and/or for consumption of fine apparel and palatial residences to maintain his family's social status. Furthermore, depending on the social arrangements in a market economy, there may be no incentive or need to have more money than one had before to maintain one's market share.

11. Patel and Moore (2017: 8–9) discuss the level of commercialization involved in the Crusades, and Schoenberger (2008) hypothesized the role of the Crusades in the development of a market economy in western Europe.

12. Genoa was followed by Venice in 1164 and Florence in 1166. "In subsequent decades and centuries, cities like Siena, Arras, Bremen, Cologne, and Barcelona all developed their own systems of public credit" (Roos 2019: 86).

13. The world's first chartered bank, Casa di San Giorgio, was founded in 1407 in Genoa. This bank was essentially a consortium of private bondholders, who established direct control over the management of public finances (Roos 2019: 88).

14. The main references on land reclamation in the Netherlands in the late-medieval and early modern periods, include: Korthals-Altes (1925); van Veen (1962); van de Ven (1996); van Dam (2001); van Cruyningen (2014); van Tielhof (2015); Xu and Blussé (2019).

15. The periodization is in the fifteenth century in Wallerstein's account, but clearly this shift happened unevenly from the late medieval period onward.

16. See also Van de Ven (1996: 53, 56) and van Dam (2001).

17. Such processes of communalization of land-water management were happening elsewhere within the European world-economy of the late medieval period. For example, in England, in the thirteenth century, the first formal commissions of what they called sewers were formed—reflecting, institutionalizing, and building on "what were long-standing practices in England's wetlands" (Ash 2017: 7).

18. Patel and Moore (2017: 9) cite a sixfold increase in agricultural land from roughly the tenth century to the fourteenth century.

19. See, for example, Mielants' (2007: 158) discussion of urban residents demanding payment in cash.

20. For more on how the threat of the Ottomans in the Mediterranean in the 1400s pushed the Iberian aristocracy to the Atlantic, see Anievas and Nişancıoğlu (2015).

21. A question like, "What if China had reached the Americas first?", as Anievas and Nişancıoğlu (2015: 72–73) raise, is a counterfactual that begs the question of why the Chinese would go to the Americas in the first place. This common counterfactual falsely assumes that any expansionist empire would expand territory as far as it could given its technological and other capabilities.

22. Literally, it was the younger sons of noble families, who had no land, whom Wallerstein (2011a: 47) suggested offered the initial motivation for Iberian explorations. The role of nobility in Dutch explorations, the stock exchange, and land reclamation will also be suggested in this section.

23. Intense competition over trade routes and territories during roughly this first hundred years led to the establishment of the monopoly charter companies by the turn of the seventeenth century (Austen 2017).

24. Cristiano Zanetti (2017: 338) identifies the Renaissance water-lifting technologies as dealing mainly with this nexus of problems, and my point in the previous section on the late medieval period is that states dealt with these problems in an earlier period.

25. Xu and Blussé (2019) make this point about the new types of land that began to be reclaimed in the early modern period in their comparison of the Rhine and Yangzi Deltas.
26. There are a number of examples from Richards (2003) that demonstrate this relationship. For example, in the transition from Ming to Qing rule in China in the seventeenth century, the Qing pushed for rapid agricultural expansion, which took the form of migrants and workers settling in and cultivating thinly populated tracts in hilly uplands (Richards 2003: 114–115). The imperial Qing policy of rapid agricultural expansion could be expected given war and land abandonment, but the form that this expansion took should not be assumed. As Richards noted, the introduction of New World crops, corn, and sweet potato, made this possible as these crops could be planted in hilly uplands without cultivation. Yet, Richards interpreted this "internal settlement frontier" to a particular type of state-making rather than to the participation of the state in the development of a capitalist world-economy.
27. See, for example, Richards (2003) and Austen (2017) on how early on the Dutch were able to use various coercive mechanisms in their trading stations-turned-colonies in Asia to get locals to trade and produce commodities on demand—through settlement, treaties, etc.
28. See Watson (1983) on how the introduction of New World crops quite quickly disrupted Mediterranean markets.
29. See, for example, Marriam Dossal's (2010) magisterial work on the drawn-out reclamation of the islands of Bombay under Portuguese rule in the long sixteenth century and then under British rule. It should be noted, though, that if looking at the long sixteenth century alone, not all of the cities that the European empires built were port cities. Most significantly, the Spanish undertook in New Spain, in Vera S. Candiani's (2014:4) terms, "one of the most ambitious early modern projects undertaken by Europeans anywhere," in which the lakes surrounding Mexico City were drained. This century-long project of the Habsburg Spanish Crown should be understood as an outcome of a more systematic public and private effort in reclaiming so-called swamp lands within the Empire following the Peace of Carteau-Cambresis (Zanetti 2017: 338). (The Peace ended more than a 60-year conflict between the French Monarchy and the Spanish Habsburgs for control over Italy, and the Habsburgs were victorious.)
30. For example, on the Island of Zuid-Beveland, after the floods in the 1530s and 1550s, wealthy merchants and dignitaries from the cities Antwerp and Malines invested in drainage as the island had been submerged (van Cruyningen 2014: 249–250).
31. For example, in Zeeland, the Church's land was reduced from as much as 35–40% of the total land area around 1550 to only 7% of the total area by 1665 (van Cruyningen 2014: 250–251).
32. Here Braudel overstated the uniqueness of the role of the rich and powerful in reclamation in the Mediterranean (as opposed to northern Europe). Reclamation projects along coastal and riverine lands were generally costly.
33. For example, wealthy merchant brothers, Dirck and Hendrik van Os, were co-founders of the Dutch East India company and among the first investors in the Beemster Polder, 'the biggest and best-known reclamation project in the province of North Holland in the early-1600s' (Xu and Blussé 2019: 431–432).
34. In England, projector was the name given to so-called experts. By the turn of the seventeenth century, Henry IV of France had already created the position of dike-master of the kingdom, who was Dutch (Clout 1977).

35. It is noteworthy to briefly compare the English charter for the main drainage project of the Fens with the Habsburg's arrangement for its comparably large drainage project in New Spain. The Habsburg Crown required the viceroy to secure the funds, which largely came from taxation (Candiani 2014: 56).
36. The increased revenue for the Crown was estimated to at least £6,000 annually in rents (Ash 2017: 152).
37. The main references on the *tımar* system of the early Ottoman years (c. 1300–1600) include: Wallerstein et al. (1987); Johansen (1988); İnalcık (1991, 1994); Keyder (1991); İslamoğlu-İnan (1994); Abou-El-Haj (2005); Anievas and Nişancıoğlu (2015).
38. McGowan (1981: 105) pointed out that the first institutional base was a new one, in the sense that it had not been fully developed previously, while the second institutional base was already established in the previous empires.
39. For the full case study, see İslamoğlu-İnan (1994: Chapter 3), and for a summary, p. 205.
40. Mikhail (2011: 73–74) details a reclamation project of the Mamluk leader 'Ali Bey al-Kabir in 1771 and 1772 to expand the commercial district of Cairo.
41. See also Pamuk (2000) on the downturn of the Ottoman economy and state finances at this time, which also led to various rebellions within the empire.

5

The Frontier and Export Plantation Economy of the Long Nineteenth Century

In the long nineteenth century (c. 1780s–1914), the world center of finance shifted from Amsterdam to London and lending became international as some of the most powerful governments, along with independent, nominally independent, and colonial states, borrowed (Roos 2019: ch. 6). Prices of commodities exchanged became tied to a world market price, set in the commodity exchanges in London, with sterling as the international currency (Friedmann and McMichael 1989: 99; see also Davis 2001). The European imperial states deepened and extended their territories and rule, and with the charter companies no longer being relevant, began to administer their colonies from home. In this colonial-era food regime, new territories began to produce or to expand production of raw materials and food stuffs for the metropolitan centers, and, in time, became markets for metropolitan manufactured goods and so-called expertise.

In this chapter, I place commodity frontiers of reclaimed lands centrally in the colonial-era food regime. I argue that a frontier of reclaimed lands in the Ottoman province of Egypt—and, then, the colonial state—was a condition for the growing integration of the state and society into the colonial-era food regime of the long nineteenth century. When the old order of the Ottoman state, a type of tributary system highlighted in the last chapter, began to break down, agroexport estates began to develop throughout the empire—and especially in reclaimed lands. The Ottoman state increasingly relied on offsetting the costs of reclamation onto prominent men, who would seek a return on investment by producing commodities for sale—and often in distant markets. In Egypt, these agroexport estates turned into plantations by the end of the nineteenth century and were a main avenue for the state's integration into an increasingly integrated capitalist world economy. This integration, in turn, rapidly developed capitalist social relations domestically.

Why did the reclamation of land—and into new types of land—continue to be important in the longue durée of historical capitalism? The continual or at least episodic frontier making is necessary given the ecological conditions of commodity production. As I demonstrate in this chapter on nineteenth-century Egypt, if and where monocultures are planted, defenses against pest infestations are lowered and top soil is degraded. If and where perennial irrigation is involved, the natural regeneration of soil is thwarted and waterlogging and erosion a greater risk without

The Frontiers of Corporate Food in Egypt. Marion W. Dixon, Oxford University Press.
© Marion W. Dixon (2023). DOI: 10.1093/oso/9780192842985.003.0005

adequate drainage. The introduction of seed varieties that allow for the intensification of production leads to genetic erosion as the genetic diversity within species dwindles. Any of the above can further lead to the elimination of friendly pathogens for crops. Theoretically, these ecological conditions of commodity production show that capital accumulates in agriculture, not only by affecting the environment (degrading the soil, cutting down the trees, draining the lakes, etc.), but through and in nature (Moore 2015).

Food Regimes and Frontiers

Food regime analysis emerged to explain the role of agriculture and food in processes of capital accumulation and the building of the modern state system (McMichael 2009). In Bill Winders' (2009: 132–133) terms, a food regime is an international order shaping the world economy through complementary state policies that affect agricultural prices (relative to other prices) as well as patterns of specialization and of trade and consumption. The hegemon, or the most powerful state where finance is centered, constructs the parameters for this complementary set of policies, thereby, bolstering its own economic position (Winders 2009: 132–133).

In the long nineteenth century, the first such international order emerged as the imperial capitalist states, with Britain taking the lead, offshored the production of grains and livestock to the settler states. The extension of colonial rule, as well as indirect rule, further raised the production and export to Europe of raw materials (e.g., cotton, indigo) and food stuffs (e.g., sugar, tea). Both the offshoring of production (largely via family farming) in the settler states and the plantation economies in the colonies were a type of subsidy for industry in the metropolitan centers by providing wage foods—cheap foods for the industrial working classes—and cheap raw materials for the manufacturers (Friedmann and McMichael 1989; Araghi 2003; McMichael 2013). This trade made possible rapid industrialization in western Europe and the northern United States and may be understood within the growing wealth and power of the new capitalist class of manufacturers.[1] The production of grains and livestock in the settler states for the metropolitan centers bolstered national agricultural sectors within these states, and national agricultures and national industries in the imperial states were brought together in a tight web (McMichael 2009: 141). The industrial working classes in the metropolitan centers and the various wage and non-waged labor forces in the colonies came to depend on one another in a reconfigured international division of labor, a skill/technological hierarchy of world regions (Araghi 2003).[2] Growing competition within the international division of labor led colonial producers to intensify the exploitation of labor, which laid the foundations for the decolonization movement (Friedmann and McMichael 1989: 100–101).

There were four trends in frontier making that are relevant to analyses of the colonial-era food regime: The first trend is that deltas, and other lands partially or wholly submerged under water (e.g., marshes), continued to be reclaimed—and in even more extensive ways with the development of dam technologies.[3] The second trend is the extension of irrigation in so-called dry regions (hot climate and low rain-fall). Irrigated agriculture extended to the Mediterranean basin and to arid lands in various parts of South America, Australia, South Asia, and beyond.[4] The significance of irrigation for the expansion of agroexport production has led a number of scholars to highlight the significance of the control of water to colonial rule.[5] Not only was irrigation extended into dry climates, but a new agricultural field called dry farming emerged at this time. Dry farming involved agriculture in dry climates but with no irrigation.[6] Both of these developments in dry climates meant that uncultivated, used lands were increasingly being reclaimed; therefore, non-sedentary peoples' claims on these lands became compromised. Notably, many arid lands were the home to pastoral peoples and used as pasture, so by the long nineteenth century, pasture lands then also became subject to so-called improvements for the other three land uses—cultivation, extraction, and settlement.

Scientific fields and state extension and services developed considerably to extend irrigation, including through the construction of dams, to reclaim new types of land, and to manage the many contradictions of single-crop ecology (Stoll 1998: 94–95) as well as perennial agriculture in coastal and riverine lands. With the extension of irrigation and monoculture production came the embryonic stages of biological control in agriculture (Tyrell 1999: 12)—to protect capital from pests, declining yields due to genetic erosion, soil salinity, and on and on.[7] These multiplying contradictions signal what Jason W. Moore (2011, 2015) refers to as relative exhaustion—of costs of production rising relative to other places due to the degradation of the conditions of production—that propels frontier making in new places. When the costs of production in one commodity frontier rise due to the degradation of the conditions of production, then a new commodity frontier is built.

Export Plantations within the Ottoman Empire

By the mid-eighteenth century, the first phases of industrial capitalism in Western Europe grew the demand for cotton, grains, corn, cattle and tobacco, spawning new granaries in the American Midwest, Russia, India, and the Balkans as well as other parts of the Ottoman Empire (Wallerstein et al. 1987). The European states pressed the Ottoman state to further commercial concessions within the empire, and the Ottomans extended the capitulations, which were initially privileges granted to non-Muslim foreign nationals but were then extended to non-Muslim Ottoman subjects (Wallerstein 1979). Then, these capitulations were converted into bilateral treaties. For example, the Treaty of Küçük Kaynarcca in 1774 ended the Ottoman monopoly in the Black Sea trade.

The expansion of agro-exports within the Ottoman provinces depended on the expansion of large estates (*çiftliks*).[8] *Çiftliks* can be thought of as plantation agriculture or, more precisely, in Huri İnalcık's (1991: 19) terms, "large agricultural lands organized as a production unit under a single ownership and management and usually produced for the market." *Çiftlik* agriculture entailed the enserfment of labor and sharecropping relations.[9] It emerged slowly and unevenly in the Ottoman provinces, beginning in the sixteenth century, so *çiftliks* existed alongside the *tımar* system in some regions, chipping away at the old order, and emerged out of the *iltizam* system in other regions. Also, agro-export production did not happen only via *çiftliks* within the empire, but *çiftliks* were a main avenue for greater integration of the empire into the colonial-era food regime.

Before the eighteenth century, it was usually the higher echelons of the ruling elite, including the military and clerical classes, who built *çiftliks*. Even through the eighteenth century, merchants and urban guild masters were rarely found being the proprietors of such lands (İnalcık 1991). After the eighteenth century, there emerged a class of provincial notables (*ayans*), who became the so-called tax-farmers of the *çiftliks*. The provincial notables tried to maximize the revenue from the estates due to pressures coming from two directions: the expanding external market and the central government's tax revenue requirements to sustain their positions (İnalcık 1991: 23).

Both Caglar Keyder and Huri İnalcık agreed that reclamation of uncultivated land led to the development of *çiftliks*—and under the internal and external conditions that eroded the *tımar* system in the first place (İnalcık 1991; Keyder 1991). As was discussed in Chapter 4, reclamation is costly, and it was generally only those in the highest echelons of the social class order who could afford to reclaim the land. Also, as in previous eras, the state provided incentives to individuals to reclaim land, and this time to gain the Sultan's permission grantees were required to introduce "substantial improvements" to the land through, for example, the construction of water canals (İnalcık 1991: 19–20). The new provision to substantially improve the land suggests a new point and purpose of land reclamation—i.e., a level of intensive production of nature.

Much debate has surrounded *çiftlik* agriculture: Do *çiftliks* represent the transition from a tributary mode of production to a capitalist mode of production, or do they represent changing trade opportunities, or do they represent the internal restructuring of the Ottoman empire (Veinstein 1991)? Correspondingly, the accounts of *çiftliks* are mixed: Some argue that they were geared toward agroexports, others argue that they weren't. Some point to the growing power and wealth of the provincial notables, others point to the notables' other (non-*çiftlik*) sources of wealth. This confusion is understandable given that these estates developed over centuries and unevenly within the empire. Thus, they were bound to look and act differently depending on the circumstances. As *çiftliks* developed, they combined the tributary mode of production with the capitalist mode of production in contingent ways.[10]

There do seem to be general trends concerning the development of *çiftlik* agriculture that can be pointed to. The first trend is that *çiftliks* on largely reclaimed lands producing staple crops for Europe concentrated on irrigated plains near trade routes—the plains of the Balkans, Egypt, Syria, the coastal plains of southern and western Anatolia, and the like (İnalcık 1991: 25). Most *çiftliks* were larger than the average peasant landholding but smaller than eastern European estates or New World plantations. Keyder (1991: 7–8) attributed the average size of *çiftliks* to labor shortages and the fact that *çiftliks* on reclaimed land remained the legal property of the state. Also, similar to many New World plantations, most *çiftliks* were characterized not singularly by monocultures but also by diversified subsistence crop production (of mainly wheat, barley, cotton, and corn) (İnalcık 1991: 28). Even though there was a concentration of agroexport production in certain regions, over all the development of *çiftlik* agriculture did not lead to a significant increase in agroexports until after the capitulations and treaties from the mid-eighteenth century onward. McGowan (1981: 170) highlighted that during the seventeenth and eighteenth centuries the Ottoman export trade as a percentage of total world trade was modest and grew little. It was not until the last decades of the eighteenth century and later that a noticeable upward trend in trade began; for example, from 1775 to 1789, cotton exports from Turkey to Great Britain alone more than doubled (Kurmuş 1987).

The Frontier in the Egyptian State

In Egypt, the decline in the coffee trade, as discussed in Chapter 4, corresponded with a shift in the ruling class during the eighteenth century. By the 1760s, the Mamluks had come to rule the province, beating their rivals, the Janissaries and other tributary-based military groups, who lost wealth in the declining trade (Gran 1979). The change in who ruled was expectedly characterized by ongoing internecine struggles between the Mamluks and their rivals and between the Mamluk leaders (emirs) themselves. Unlike the previous military rulers, the Mamluk emirs were warriors who hired mercenaries. The need to pay their mercenaries as well as to import weapons (and various luxuries) from Europe led them to borrow from the merchant elite, who were largely minorities who traded most closely with Europe (Gran 1979). According to Peter Gran (1979: 20–21), it is likely that one of the reasons why the *iltizam* system began to break down during Mamluk beylicate rule is because the emirs seemed to have paid back merchants by giving them their *iltizam*. Also, both the Mamluks and the merchants were investing in land in response to an increase in demand for rice and other crops largely from France.[11] Gran's (1979) analysis supports the conclusion that a merchant class that was increasingly directed to accumulating capital emerged during this time period as did the burgconing stages of a capitalist state that borrowed from this class to expand commodity production for revenue.

Napoleon's incursion into Alexandria in 1798 precipitated a new set of struggles over power, and in those struggles over several years emerged a Mamluk emir, Muhammed 'Ali, who arrested control from the French and then from the British and the Ottomans. 'Ali's reign would accelerate capitalist development. Seeking autonomy from the Ottomans, and facing Ottoman and European aggressions, 'Ali (the Pasha) built what Khaled Fahmy (2004) called a personal empire. In doing so, he was essentially no longer a Mamluk (Gran 1979). The Mamluk era was over; however, 'Ali continued his predecessors' trade relationships with Europe. Instead of building on the alliance with the merchant elite, however, he sought to replace the merchants with government officials and foreign merchants of his choosing (Gran 1979: 114). The Pasha's personal empire would expand raw material and primary commodity production and exports to Europe. With the revenue earned, weapons and other technologies would be imported and European experts hired to build a type of war economy.

Rapid capitalist development in Egypt via the state's integration into the world economy depended on three waves of frontier making: the first being during the second half of 'Ali's reign (c. 1820s–1840s); the second during and in the immediate aftermath of the U.S. Civil War (c. 1860s–1870s); and the third during direct British colonial rule (c. 1880s–1914). Each wave represents an expansion of land reclamation in response to an increase in the price of agricultural commodities on the world market. This bubble led to a commodity boom—an increase in the overall production and export of commodities. The focus in this section is on the cotton commodity booms, which happened in part through the expanding Nile Delta (Figure 5.1). There was cotton and other commodity production elsewhere, along the Nile Valley and especially in Upper Egypt where sugar plantations concentrated. However, much of the frontier making at this time was for cotton and in Lower Egypt (in and around the Delta, Alexandria, and Cairo). The uneven development of capitalist social relations geographically, between Upper and Lower Egypt, is also important to frontier making in the long nineteenth century, as will be discussed below.

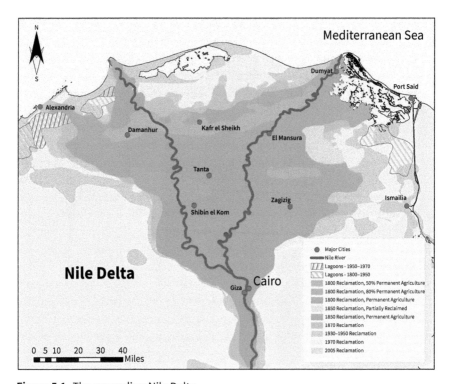

Figure 5.1 The expanding Nile Delta.

Source: Johannes Plambeck.

Wave of Frontier Making (i): Muhammed 'Ali's Reign, 1820s–1840s

The expansion of cotton production for export to Europe occurred rapidly during the second half of Muhammed 'Ali's reign (1820s–1840s), transforming the Nile Delta into cotton fields. This shift to cotton began in the 1820s when production changed to long-staple cotton because of its higher market price; already in 1823, approximately 76% of Egyptian exports were going to Europe (Richards 1987: 215). Cotton exports, which began to rise sharply in 1822–1823, contributed between 10 and 25% of the revenues of the Egyptian state during the following two decades (Beckert 2014: 132).[12]

The rapid increase in cotton production and exports to build the Pasha's war economy depended on agrarian restructuring on a massive scale. The Pasha abolished the *iltizam* when he took power in 1805 (Abbas and El-Dessouky 2011: 8). Doing so allowed him to increase taxes on the peasantry, who was the main source of revenue for the war economy (Cuno 1999). Forced conscription into the army[13] and agricultural mandates also led to the desertion of peasants from the land and dispossession (from not being able to pay taxes). Also, the government began to seize and reassign the land from indebted peasants to rural notables.[14]

The government of 'Ali instituted a number of overlapping property regimes to replace the *iltizam* and to facilitate the upward distribution of land (Table 5.1). The two most significant property regimes for the purposes of this chapter were firstly the *çiftliks*, which in Egypt were essentially seized lands for the Pasha and his family members (Abbas and El-Dessouky 2011). The *çiftliks* existed alongside a new category of uncultivated state land (*ab 'adiyah*) that 'Ali used to extend the area of cultivation.[15] In 1830, he began leasing *ab 'adiyah* lands to prominent men—his employees, foreigners, Bedouin sheiks, and the like—who promised to reclaim them. The lands tended to be uncultivated and untaxed. Sometimes the Pasha gave tax breaks for the first three to seven years of bringing the land under cultivation. He and his successors began to grant title to lands that became developed. However, Bedouins were not given land titles. Rather, they were released from corvée labor obligations and military conscription. In summary, these legal property changes granted all types of uncultivated lands to the Pasha's political allies (or potential allies) to reclaim the lands for cash crop production.

These property changes were possible with the development of a new hydrological system in the Nile Delta, where much of the cotton and other cash crop production was concentrated. 'Ali built the first barrages where the Nile divides into the Damietta and Rosetta branches, just north of Cairo (Figure 5.1). Barrages were built to retain water and direct the water to the secondary and tertiary irrigation networks. By 1833, 144 kilometers of new canals had been constructed, notably the Mahmudiya canal (Waterbury 1979: 31–33 cited in Burke 2009: 101). The Mahmudiya (originally known as Ashrafiyya) was reconstructed in the 1820s to provide drinking water for

Table 5.1 Frontiers in Egypt: Long nineteenth century to early twenty-first century

Frontiers	Characteristics	
Frontier of capital I *i. and ii.* Ottoman (autonomous) province (c. 1820s–1880s)	Property regimes:	*çiftliks, ab 'adiyah,* among others—uncultivated state lands granted to private individuals to reclaim for (largely) the production of agricultural commodities for export
	incl. social relations:	Class of rural notables (the Pasha's family members, the Pasha's employees, Bedouin sheikhs, etc.); and forced (corvée) labor for large-scale canal (and other) projects
	Geography:	Concentrated in the northern Nile Delta—the Damanhur-Kafr el-Sheikh-Mansura strip
	Type of land:	deserted, flooded and/or fallow land in existing villages and on outskirts of villages
	Type of production:	Irrigation through a growing system of canal networks; mechanization involving pumping stations
iii. British colony and quasi-independence (c. 1880s–1950s)	Property regimes:	*'izba system*—plantations with groups of villages in the custody of individual officials (rural notables, European merchants, etc.
	incl. social relations:	Bifurcated system of labor with wage-laborers (who may have had subsistence plots or sharecropping arrangements) and migrant laborers who were employed seasonally
	Geography:	Expansion of the Nile Delta including in coastal areas and wetlands
	Type of land:	Farther from existing villages
	Type of production:	Perennial irrigation; intensified mechanization (imported chemical inputs, state breeding of seeds, etc.)
State frontier (c. 1940s–1970s)	Property regimes:	Mixed—state farms and small-scale family farms for sustenance as well as the production of luxury goods for the domestic urban market
	Incl. social relations:	Agricultural workers on state farms and settlers (landless among others) on small private plots (3–5 acres)
	Geography:	Concentration in the west of the Delta
	Type of land:	Large areas for reclamation communities/villages including fields
	Type of production:	Irrigation through tertiary canals; mechanization and industrialization (via Green Revolution technologies) on collectivized/state farms

Frontier of capital II (Desert frontier) (c. 1980s–present)	Property regimes:	Agribusiness, state and informal reclamation communities/villages (largely small private plots), military land, and customary land for both sustenance and the production and processing of agricultural commodities for corporate food markets at home and abroad
	Incl. social relations:	Bedouin stewardship on customary land; Capital-wage labor relations via agribusiness; a trifurcated system of wage labor—permanent (managerial, supervisory) employees, regular wage labor (from nearby reclamation communities and Delta provinces), and seasonal labor (brought to farms through contractors, mostly female)
	Geography:	Great expansion: concentrations remain in the west of the Delta; expansions to the east of the Delta, in and around the Sinai peninsula, along the Valley to Upper Egypt
	Type of land:	Both irrigated lands (through the system of canals) and non-irrigated lands (customary) that require wells to reach the aquifer
	Type of production:	Biosecure production—including distance between farms and between farms and residential areas; the extensive use of plastics, drip-irrigation, and other environmental controls to keep out the unwanted and unanticipated

Alexandria (Mikhail 2011: chapter 6). Existing canals were also deepened so that they would be below the level of the river.

Early on, the Pasha relied on so-called experts from western Europe for the construction of this new hydrological system and the founding of engineering schools. He commissioned Charles Lambert, a graduate of the École in Paris, to establish an Ecole Polytechnique in Egypt, and with the development of these schools the title of engineer (*muhandis*) began to be elevated to a type of honorific (Burke 2009: 99). With French assistance, 'Ali also planned to construct a dam on the Nile at Aswan in 1834—a plan that did not take shape until the end of the nineteenth century under British rule (Burke 2009: 100). In short, these large-scale irrigation projects facilitated the development of a professional class of engineers.[16]

At the same time, these technical projects required the large-scale mobilization of labor. As Alan Mikhail (2011) argues, they prompted a shift in the use of corvée labor—a system of shared labor among peasants for local irrigation and other infrastructure projects became a system of forced labor for large-scale irrigation projects on a province-wide scale. Concerning the reconstruction of the Mahmudiyya, peasants

> were no longer villagers of a certain area fulfilling a repair function directly bene-
> ficial to themselves and to the irrigation network of Egypt as a whole. They were
> stripped of this local identity and made part of a massive faceless pool of labour
> brought to work on projects throughout the countryside.
>
> (Mikhail 2011: 255)

The new irrigation systems of the Delta and Nile Valley allowed for large-scale reclamation. Ghislaine Alleaume (1999) identified three broad categories of land that was reclaimed: land that was left uncultivated due partially to faults in the hydraulic system (*matruk*); land too elevated or distant from water to be irrigated (*ab 'adiyah*); and flooded land from the river alluvium (*ziyada*). These lands were essentially an outcome of the old hydrological system that was incompatible with the expansion of commodity production. As Figure 5.1 shows, most of these lands during the first wave of frontier making were in the northern Delta—the Damanhur-Kafr el-Sheikh-Mansura strip.

As Alleaume (1999: 338) pointed out, the new irrigation networks were designed for larger units of production: At the center was the pumping station and the irrigation network extending from the center covered a large surface area. The larger units were imperative for the individual title holders to invest in reclaiming the land. The ecology of the Delta—the largely saline soil in the northern areas, in particular, with the water table lying close to the land surface—'determined that land reclamation was a slow process and also an expensive one' (Allan 1983: 476). Given the expense and delayed returns, cash crops (cotton, sugar cane and, to a lesser extent, rice and tobacco) were invariably cultivated on these lands (Alleaume 1999: 338). Allan (1983: 475) argued that, more than incentivizing commodity production, the effort to reclaim the northern strip of the Delta led 'Ali to grant title to land, which in turn led to land transactions and mortgage credit, as the following sub-sections detail. By granting elites and (potential) political allies the rights and responsibilities to reclaim land that had been deserted, degraded, and/or uncultivated, the regime was not only able to offset the costs of frontier making but also to build a system of patronage. These reclaimed lands then became the private estates of agroexport production, which diverted the first irrigation water and able-bodied male laborers from neighboring villages (Rivlin 1961)[17]—a main source of revenue for the war economy and the center of capital formation and development in land.

Wave of Frontier Making (ii): U.S. Civil War and Its Aftermath

The Ottoman *tanzimat* reforms and shift in British imperial policy informed the policies of 'Ali's successor, Muhammed Saïd (1854–63). Nearly a decade of 'Ali's policies of accelerating trade to, and technology transfer from, Europe, in effect, paved the way for the second wave of frontier making that began during the U.S. Civil War (1861–1865). The British were focusing on India, and with developments in steam shipping, put pressure on the Pasha to commit to the Suez Company, which would build the Suez Canal. The Canal would serve as a more direct trading route between India and Europe. Foreign merchants had been permitted to trade directly with landowners and peasants in the provinces, and they tried to organize joint-stock commercial banks, usually with British interests (Landes 1958: 61–62). Saïd borrowed from these commercial banks, at exorbitant rates, to fund the Suez Company, which began construction of the Canal in 1859—just one year after the imposition of direct British rule in India.

The U.S. Civil War had further prompted the proliferation of commercial banks in Egypt. During the war, metropolitan finance began to look increasingly to territories that if not colonized would soon be colonized. By the end of 1865, two-thirds of the credit companies, discount banks and finance corporations in the London market aimed "to exploit and develop colonial and foreign enterprise" (Landes 1958: 60). The banks were certainly responding in part to the precipitous rise in cotton prices during the war, and high cotton prices coupled with the Suez Canal construction, which lasted a decade, led to a type of "Klondike" in Egypt (Landes 1958: 57). Alexandria, in particular, like other non-metropolitan financial centers at the time such as Bombay and Constantinople, attracted European and other bankers and merchants because of their higher interest rates (Landes 1958: 57). Cotton production quintupled during the war years alone—rising from 50.1 million pounds in 1860 to 250.7 million pounds in 1865—and in the post-Civil War period, cotton output in Egypt was two and a half times larger than it had been before the war (Beckert 2014: 293–294). Virtually overnight the Alexandria port had risen from the eleventh to the fourth most important port in the Mediterranean (Owen 1969: 142–143).

This expansion of cotton production depended on a path to private property—from the granting of land titles to land transactions to mortgage credit (Baer 1969)—paving the way for the private agroexport estates to consolidate into large landed estates ('izab) or plantations. From 1863 to 1875, the landed estates doubled in cultivated land area—from one-seventh to two-sevenths of the total cultivated land area of Egypt (Mitchell 2002: 70 cited in Beckert 2014: 298). As the private property of large landowners, peasants on the estates were subject to the landowners' whims. Peasants who did not follow were expelled from the estates and joined "the ever-growing ranks of the landless agricultural proletariat" (Beckert 2014: 298). Subsistence livelihoods of peasants were compromised as land was being converted from production for consumption to production of cotton for export. Given the compromise in subsistence production, by the end of the war (from mid-1864 to early-1866), a ban was placed on the export of grain and flour in order to prevent famine (Landes 1958: 190).

Cotton production continued despite falling prices after the war and, with it, mounting debts at multiple scales: Debts of the provincial government to foreign creditors (for building irrigation canals, railroads, etc.) and debts of peasants and other landholders to local merchants (for the working capital to produce cotton) (Beckert 2014: 298–299). By the time that the global recession set in in 1873, debts, sovereign and personal, were spiraling. Spiraling sovereign debts compounded with a global El Niño drought beginning in 1876, when Saïd's successor, Isma'il (c. 1863–1879) declared his government's inability to pay the debt-servicing. This default was part of a wave of sovereign debt defaults:

> Within the space of several years, the Ottoman Empire, Egypt, Tunisia, Greece, Spain, Bolivia, Costa Rica, Ecuador, Honduras, Mexico, Paraguay, Peru, Santo Domingo, Uruguay, and Venezuela had suspended debt servicing or reduced interest payments on their outstanding obligations, leaving 54 percent of bonds issued in London in arrears by 1883.
>
> (Roos 2019: 99–100)[18]

As Roos (2019: 100) points out, in this wave of defaults, there were few consequences for the borrowers with the exception of the Ottoman Empire and Egypt, for which the defaults were the most consequential politically. In Egypt, Franco-British Dual Control was set up almost immediately to gain control over the Egyptian budget (Cole 1993: 14). Mixed Courts were established to introduce European property laws; thereafter, mortgaging land began (Owen 1969: 271). Landowners were mortgaging their land as collateral for money borrowed from banks, and these mortgage or land companies would become heavily involved in land reclamation (Abbas and El-Dessouky 2011: 46).[19] Some owners of mortgage companies were also large landowners, and they continually petitioned the government to undertake land reclamation projects (Abbas and El-Dessouky 2011: 47).

The creditors' management of Egypt's finances led not only to an influx of European capital, especially mortgage companies, but also to various austerity measures like raising taxes and reducing bureaucratic and military positions (Cole 1993: 273–274). Also, money lenders grew in their power and reach, especially in the countryside. As Mike Davis (2001: 103–105) has shown, this rule of creditors exacerbated the impacts of the El Niño in the countryside, leading to recurring semi-famine and famine in 1877–1879. Khedive Isma'il was removed from power under pressure from the British in 1879 after he invaded and occupied Sudan.[20] It is in this context that the 'Urabi movement and uprising (1879–1882) may be placed—a broad multiclass coalition against the dual elite, the Ottoman-Egyptian landed classes and the European investor class (Cole 1993). As the uprising reached revolutionary potential in 1882, the British invaded Egypt and instituted direct colonial rule.

Wave of Frontier Making (iii): British Colonial Rule, 1882–1922

The third wave of frontier making began during the regime of Lord Cromer (1883–1907), who built what Robert Vitalis (1995) referred to as a highly oligopolistic private market economy that underwrote a massive transfer of ownership rights in land as well as state-owned enterprises.[21] Those who were grantees of state land and/or had made early investments in cultivating that land—a new class of local or Egyptian capitalists—built a more fully developed capitalist economy, including large-scale capitalist institutions, during this period.[22] By World War I, this class, who was organized in rival investor coalitions or family business groups, were running this economy largely through public contracts. Family business groups often partnered with European investors, and began investing in early import-substitution industries (ISI) (food processing, textiles, construction) (Vitalis 1995: 15–16; Beckert 2014: ch. 13 on the effort to build a cottage industry).[23]

These developments were possible because of a decade-long financial boom: "the capital that arrived from abroad between 1897 and 1907 exceeded the total amount from the previous fifty years" (Jakes 2020: 85). Most of this capital went to the establishment of banks and mortgage companies, which were both responding to and precipitating the rapid increase in land prices, which spurred a great expansion of reclaimed land (Owen 1969: 242). And the National Bank of Egypt was founded in 1898 to facilitate the proliferation of credit arrangements. As Aaron Jakes (2020: 89) argues, this Belle époque boom signaled land becoming a financial asset, treated "as one among any number of revenue-generating assets through which capital in search of higher returns might circulate."

In one way or another, the financial boom aimed to increase cotton production. Between 1885–1890 and 1905–1909 alone, cotton production more than doubled, from just over 11.8 million pounds a year to 2.6 billion in 1905–1906, and the annual value tripled, from EGP 8.9 to 24.4 million (Owen 2006: 84).[24] The annual average of land for cotton cultivation rose from 850,000 acres in Lower Egypt in 1885/86–1887/88 to nearly 1.3 million acres in 1907 (Owen 2006: 84). This wave rested on the continued expansion of plantations and growing landlessness among peasants as land was consolidated. By 1894, 42.5% of the land in private ownership was held in estates of 50 acres and above, while medium-size land parcels (of 5–50 acres) accounted for 37.7% of the land, and subsistence-size parcels of five acres and under 19.8% of the land (Owen 1969: 289). To put it differently: By 1901, the estate owners controlled 50% of the cultivated land area of Egypt (Mitchell 2002: 70 in Beckert 2014: 298). The large landed estates emerged out of the expansion of cultivated land and the creation of private estates during the earlier periods (Baer 1969; Alleaume 1999). Estimates of land consolidation during the expansion of the plantations include cultivated land that had been reclaimed in the earlier periods.

The consolidation of this plantation economy, in turn, depended on the upgrading and expansion of the hydrological systems of the Nile Delta and Valley. William Willcocks, the British-appointed state engineer, restored the Delta barrages from 1883 to 1896 (Beinart and Hughes 2007: 141). The annual flood cycle continued to inundate the Delta, which meant that deposits of silt were left in the soil, salts flushed out, and water and sediment moved to the sea (Stanley and Warne 1998: 808). Because much of the silt was on reclaimed lands in the northern Delta, the floods rather led to waterlogging. The restoration of the barrages would have helped correct that temporarily, but only with the construction of the Aswan Dam at the turn of the twentieth century did the annual flood cycle cease. With the end of flooding, perennial irrigation fully replaced the so-called basin irrigation system, the implications of which will be discussed below.

In addition to a growing percentage of cultivated land in Lower Egypt being devoted to cotton, the total area of cultivated land grew exponentially to make this expansion possible. When the British re-invaded Sudan in 1898 to gain control of the Nile, the colonial administration was able to complete the construction of the Aswan Dam in 1902. As Jennifer L. Derr (2011: 146) notes, the colonial irrigation engineers' explicit objective in the construction of the Aswan Dam was to expand the area of cultivation through land reclamation. And the Dam was successful: Between 1893 and 1914, mortgage companies reclaimed well over 100,000 acres (Owen 1969: 292–293; Figure 5.1).[25] So significant was land reclamation that by the end of WWI the capitalization of mortgage companies amounted to 45% of the total capitalization of joint-stock companies in Egypt (Derr 2011: 146). In addition, the introduction of the Mit Afifi seed enabled about half the cotton area to switch from a three- to a two-year rotation, making cotton cultivation even more profitable (Owen 2006: 84).

How did the plantations differ from the private estates for agroexport production that initially developed under the reign of Mohammed 'Ali? They were organized as personal estates and resembled plantations, with groups of villages in the custody of individual officials (i.e., members of the rural family, European merchants, etc.) (Table 5.1). When the British ended the forced labor system, a bifurcated system of labor developed: wage-laborers (*tamalliya*) were hired on an annual basis and some-times were given subsistence plots and other times sharecropping arrangements, and migrant laborers (*tarahil*) were seasonally employed, usually through contractors. According to Roger Owen (1969), there appears to have been a shift within the estates, at least partially—from a sharecropping system into a kind of third-party tenancy mixed with migrant labor. Wage-laborers were pulled from villages, and the migrant laborers came from Upper Egypt. Even as early as 1888–1889, seasonal labor migra-tion from Upper Egypt involved between half a million and 800,000 men and boys for the annual cleaning of the Delta canals and for work in the cotton fields (Owen 2006: 93).

As a result of the development and growth of the plantation economy, there was large-scale rural out-migration (Mitchell 1991). Most rural families had barely enough to satisfy their needs and a growing percentage had no land: In 1907, an esti-mate is that only just a little more than "one-twelfth owned sufficient land to secure an adequate living for themselves, another two-thirds possessed some property but not enough to satisfy their needs, while a quarter had no land at all" (Owen 1969: 240). And the number of landless continued to increase: By 1917, 53% of the rural popula-tion was landless in Upper Egypt, 40% in Middle Egypt and 36% in the Delta (Owen 1969: 240). As Joel Beinin and Zackary Lockman (1987) argued, the landless joined urban artisans and workers as well as foreign immigrants to make up an emerging working class. This working class engaged in small-scale handicraft industries as well as relatively large-scale industrial and transportation capitalist enterprises.

The rapid expansion of the frontier quickly reached a point of relative exhaustion. The commodity bubble burst in 1909. The cotton crop failed in part from genetic erosion (Owens 2006: 85–86). Even before the failure, by the turn of the twentieth century, there were signs of exhaustion from intensive monoculture production and perennial irrigation. For example, the wetlands of the northern Delta, an integral part of delta systems and fisherfolk livelihoods, had been seriously compromised (Figure 5.1). The wetlands were widespread in the early nineteenth century, but by the end of the century, Lake Maryut was flooded and drained and reduced in size and Abu Qir Lagoon disappeared due to draining as part of the reclamation of the land (Stanley and Warne 1998: 817). Also, disease became endemic, as the perennial irrigation system without adequate drainage spread bilharzia, malaria, and other diseases (Farley 1991).[26]

The relative exhaustion of the frontier in Egypt corresponded with the making of a frontier in what was then Anglo-Egyptian Sudan. The Gezira Scheme, a large-scale irrigation project for the creation of a mega cotton plantation at the confluence of the Blue and White Niles, was discussed within the British government by the turn of the twentieth century (Tvedt 2004). However, it was not until 1914 that the government officially supported the scheme. This was following the 1909 cotton crop failure in Egypt, when "the semi-famine conditions that prevailed on the Blue and White Niles" assured promoters of the Scheme that the supply of labor would not be difficult to secure (Tvedt 2004: 93). With a fading Nile Delta frontier and heightened tensions with the Egyptian government and nationalists, in part over control over Sudan, Britain terminated direct colonial rule in 1922. As it did so, though, the imperial state tightened its control over the fronter in Sudan: The Gezira Scheme was fully underway after the completion of the Sennar Dam in 1925.

At the time of the Sennar Dam's construction, the degradation of the Nile Delta was readily apparent: "by 1920–4 the yield of every major Egyptian crop, with the exception of maize, was well below its 1913 level" (Owen 1969: 254–255). The degradation of the Delta ecosystem precipitated the import of ever more chemical fertilizers. The Khedival Agricultural Society, which was formed at the turn of the twentieth century by landlord-capitalists, had introduced chemical fertilizers as well as new seed varieties and the like. The application of fertilizers became a necessity as the soil rapidly exhausted with perennial irrigation (Issawi 1963: 136). This cycle of exhaustion-application became chronic: Between 1920 and 1937, there was a 400% rise in total fertilizer imports (Vitalis 1995: 79), and by the end of the 1930s, 600,000 tons of fertilizer were being consumed per year—at the highest rate per cultivated area in the world (Mitchell 2002: 20). When fertilizer imports were cut-off during World War II, one of the wealthiest Egyptian capitalists, Aḥmad ʿAbbud, founded a fertilizer industry, the first large-scale import-substitution project of the post-war era (Vitalis 1995; Mitchell 2002).

Conclusions

In this chapter, I argue that the reclamation of land was important, if not central, to capital formation and development in land in Egypt and to the integration of the state and society into the colonial-era food regime. Throughout the long nineteenth century, agrarian restructuring happened on a massive scale to enable the rapid production and export of key commodities (cotton, sugar, and indigo especially) to the metropolitan centers of Europe. This integration into the food regime led specifically to the expansion of the Nile Delta and its subsequent ecological transformation.

The Egyptian state (autonomous Ottoman province and then colonial state) gained revenue via the export plantation economy, built state institutions and services (e.g., engineering schools for the expansion of irrigation canals), and borrowed from international lenders to pay for manufactured goods and services from Europe (for example, to pay for the construction of the Suez Canal). Capitalist social relations rapidly formed as more and more people became dependent on a capitalist market: a landholding class and a class of sharecroppers and seasonal migrants from Upper Egypt; a merchant class (devoted to accumulating capital); a capitalist class (of finance and family business, both of which often invested in land reclamation) and a (small) working class (industrial and artisanal); and a surplus population of the landless and unemployed. As a capitalist market began to grow, the market co-existed with the old order and the two informed one another. The particular character of the frontier of reclaimed lands is a case in point: One form that reclamation would take was patrimonial; the Pasha gave land to his family members, who would often devote their holdings to agroexports. Also, the gradual but steady erosion of peasant rights over the centuries of property regime change (within the Islamic and Ottoman empires) set the stage for the rapid growth of plantations during the long nineteenth century. Yet, the important role of land reclamation meant that subsistence production was not completely undermined. During the three waves of frontier making identified in this chapter, plantations were built in part on new lands that were not cultivated and may have been used only marginally.

It is noteworthy here to highlight the three social formations of capitalist development that I identify in this book that structure the Egyptian state and society's integration into an expanded world economy—and that are most relevant to the making of a corporate agri-food system. The first social formation is highlighted in this chapter: the frontier of capital, i.e., the reclamation of land for expanded commodity production and sale. The second and third—diversified family business groups and finance—are explored in Chapters 6 and 7. These three social formations faded as the colonial-era food regime contracted, beginning in the interwar period and continuing through the 1970s, when a new food aid regime replaced the old regime. The food aid regime was short-lived, and by the 1980s, a new regime began to emerge, a corporate food regime. In Egypt, the three social formations of the colonial-era food regime re-emerged in full force, with variations, as a corporate agri-food system developed. In this way, the frontier of capital, family business groups, and finance should be understood not as colonial legacies. They do not simply represent a continuity from the colonial past. They are rather constitutive of the uneven and combined development of the Egyptian state and society into a broader world economy in the era of so-called globalization. The expanded world economy can be understood as not a thing but as a set of relations and structures born out of the interaction of societies; as

Egyptian society interacts, these social formations develop and shape that economy as they develop.

Notes

1. See, for example, Beckert (2014) on the wealth and power of the merchant and manufacturing classes in building an empire of cotton at this time. Also, see my work on the importance of commodity frontiers in the chemical industries, which enabled economies of scale and scope in industrial production (Dixon 2018, 2021).

2. For Araghi (2003), the production of absolute surplus value (the prolongation or intensification of the working day) is tied directly to the production of relative surplus value (the decline of the value of labor power under conditions in which the working day is regulated). A decline in the value of labor power occurs through a rise in technical efficiency or by expanding the production of absolute surplus value in wage goods producing industries. Free and unfree labor thus became tied together through a regime of global value relations. In Araghi's concept of the regime of global value relations, free and unfree labor are combined but without a determined causal relationship between them.

3. The Nile Delta's transformation in the long nineteenth century will be highlighted in this chapter. See also, for example, Adas (1974) on the rapid growth of the rice industry in the Burma Delta during the period 1852–1907; and Federico (2005: 44–52) and Pisani (2002: 275) on the draining of marshes throughout the southern and western United States in the nuneteenth century.

4. For a summary of the extension of irrigation to dry regions, see Federico (2005: 44). For the extension of irrigation, land reclamation, and settlement in the canal colonies in western Punjab, in India, see Battacharya (1995), Agnihotri (1996), and Gilmartin (2006). For the western US, see Stoll (1998), Tyrell (1999), Pisani (2002), Nash (2006).

5. See, for example, Tvedt (2004) on how and why control over the Nile River was central to British imperial ambitions in the region. When Beinart and Hughes (2007: 130) argued that "Irrigation became a major enterprise in the British Empire," they were making a similar argument but seem to be confusing the means with the ends of imperial rule.

6. See Pisani (2002) for discussions of the two types of agriculture in the western United States.

7. For agricultural research and extension services in various states, see, for example, Feeny (1982) on Thailand and Hayami and Yamada (1991) on Japan during the Meiji Restoration.

8. The main references on the *çiftliks* of the later Ottoman years (c. 1600–1800) include: McGowan (1981); Kurmuş (1987); Wallerstein et al. (1987); İnalcık (1991); Keyder (1991); Veinstein (1991).

9. Wallerstein et al. (1987: 91) argued that this class order developed through usury. Landlords extended loans to peasants at high interest rates, and repayment of debts took the form of produce to be delivered at the harvest time at rates much lower than the market price. These combined pressures left many indebted peasants to lose their land, and without land many were forced into share-cropping tenancies. "Although small peasant property was not completely destroyed, usury mediated the accumulation of capital in the hands of the new powerful landlords."

10. McGowan's (1981) detailed case study of the development of *çiftliks* in western Macedonia from 1620 to 1830 is illustrative of how the *çiftliks* replaced the *tımars*. In this region, a new legal system developed gradually through various means of undermining the *tımar* system—for example, usurping land from the state treasury (by designating state land as endowed land, for example) and displacing certain cavalrymen from their *tımars*. This gradual attempt to break the old order was possible after the mid-seventeenth century epidemic of indebtedness and flight from land. The abandoned land worked in favor of the *çiftlik* holders. The new legal system created and transferred quasi-property rights over reclaimed land, which the title holder or proprietor need not cultivate himself. While there were some larger agroexporting estates in the seventeenth and eighteenth centuries that were concentrated in exporting zones, most *çiftliks* in western Macedonia were still smaller-scale (but larger than an average peasant holding). McGowan explained that the *çiftliks* existed alongside the *tımars*, and slowly chipped away at them. During the time period covered, they were not isolated developments nor was foreign demand dominating property relations. Further, the Ottoman judicial system worked both for and against the old order, but seemingly mostly against it as *çiftliks* developed and grew.

11. Gran (1979) argued that France began looking to secure food and other raw materials from closer territories after losing colonies in its war with England (1758–1768).

12. The main references on Mohammad 'Ali's reign include: Rivlin (1961); Baer (1969); Gran (1979); Richards (1987); Brown (1991); Alleaume (1999); Cuno (1999); Fahmy (2004); Burke (2009); Abbas and El-Dessouky (2011); Mikhail (2011); Beckert (2014).

13. Conscription for 'Ali's army is estimated to have involved an average of 100,000 male peasants or 4% of a population estimated at 2,500,000 (Rivlin (1961) cited in Brown (1991: 241)). Brown (1991) admitted that the percentage from Rivlin was probably over-stated as the population estimates are low. Clearly, though, conscription was considerable in villages. Reports of intentional mutilation of children to avoid conscription were not uncommon (Rivlin 1961 cited in Brown 1991: 215).

14. The most prominent among the rural notables were the village headmen (Cuno 1999).

15. The main references for the *ab 'adiya* lands are Rivlin (1961) and Abbas and El-Dessuky (2011). See also Baer (1969: 77) for references to "uncultivated state land."

16. By 1882, most irrigation engineers were Egyptian nationals (Burke 2009: 99).

17. According to Rivlin (1961), it was the village headman (*shaykhs*) who were enlisted to funnel these productive resources to the private estates.

18. According to Roos (2019: Chapter 6), this wave of 1877 was the second of three waves of sovereign debt defaults in the age of High Imperialism; the first was in the 1820s and the third was in 1933.

19. These companies are referred to as both mortgage companies and land companies. Here, I will stick with the designation of them as mortgage companies.

20. From 1867, the Ottoman governor of Egypt became known as the Khedive. The post had already become hereditary, and succession was arranged on the basis of primogeniture, or inheritance of the firstborn son (Cole 1993: 14).

21. One example of many that Vitalis (1995) offered of the massive transfer of ownership rights under the Cromer government is of the state-owned Tura–Helwan railway. The railway was sold to private investors, who were also given permission to extend the railway line. They built the last segments of the railway line in partnership with a German joint-stock bank, Berlin Handels Gesellschaft, and after the line was built, they leased the line back to the Egyptian State Railways.

22. The designation of this class is mostly meant to distinguish them from both the old guard (the Pasha's family, notables, and so on) and European merchants and companies. See Owen (1969: 282–283) on how these three classes began to mix. Also, note that Beinin and Lockman (1987: 24) referred to them as the "new class of indigenous large landowners."

23. The main references on British rule in Egypt, direct and indirect, include: Owen (1969, 2006), Beinin and Lockman (1987), Mitchell (1991, 2002), Cole (1993), Vitalis (1995), Derr (2011), Beckert (2014), Jakes (2020).

24. Here, I converted *cantars* to pounds, and as before, I equate *feddans* with acres.

25. Owen (1969: 184) noted that the area devoted to cotton cultivation did not increase during the 1880s and early 1890s due in part to the 'Urabi rebellion, during which canals were blocked and the personal security of European merchants threatened.

26. Charles Issawi (1963) argued that it wasn't until after WWI that drainage began to be constructed in the Delta.

6
Post-Colonial Frontier Making?

State Land Reclamation and the Desert Frontier

The drastic changes to the international order that ended the colonial-era food regime began during World War I and continued through the interwar period. Two main, intertwining forces were at play: the Great Depression and the bourgeoning Global Politics of Decolonization. The Great Depression led the Northern imperial states to begin regulating their agriculture sectors more actively and looking for substitutes to colonial crops. The politics of decolonization led nominally independent and independent states to likewise regulate their agriculture sectors in an attempt to halt the declining terms of trade with the Northern imperial states as the export market contracted and commodity prices fell.

National agricultures were regulated in this new era of economic nationalism in the colonies and former colonies (the global South) and of social welfarism in the imperial Northern states (the global North).[1] Furthermore, the Bretton Woods system that kept the U.S. dollar convertible to gold and the Cold War helped reconfigure the international division of labor. The United States, and later Europe, became the so-called breadbasket of the world and the former colonies became the recipients of U.S. food aid.

In this chapter, I show that in this new era, in post-1922 Egypt, frontier making developed a distinct character. The development and expansion of reclaimed lands became a way to resolve, in Hegel's (1967) terms, the inherent tension of capitalist society (cited in Harvey 2001: 286). To diffuse the tension from the growing polarization between the wealth and power of the ruling class and the immiserated rural masses, land reclamation began to be used as a policy to redistribute land to the landless (and other surplus populations) and to create a new peasant subject. The state frontier became institutionalized, and was greatly expanded, after the 1952 independence, becoming a pillar of the economic nationalist policies of the Gamal Abdel Nasser administration during the next two decades. The Nasser administration's agrarian reforms in the Nile Valley and Delta justified the continued expansion of the state frontier, which, in turn, contributed to the limitations of agrarian reform. U.S. food aid further worked in tandem and in tension with these economic nationalist policies.

When the Bretton Woods system collapsed in the 1970s, and U.S. food aid began to unravel, the food aid regime declined and a new regime developed. Under this corporate food regime, a re-emerging frontier of capital in Egypt began to replace

The Frontiers of Corporate Food in Egypt. Marion W. Dixon, Oxford University Press.
© Marion W. Dixon (2023). DOI: 10.1093/oso/9780192842985.003.0006

the state frontier. But the state frontier informed the character of this second frontier of capital—what I refer in shorthand to as the desert frontier. The desert frontier is technically not in the desert but in arid lands. These lands began to be reclaimed that are farther from existing settlement and irrigation canals. Land reclamation for re-distribution—i.e., state reclamation—as well as other state development projects continued and existed alongside the selling of state reclaimed lands and state farms (on reclaimed lands) to investors, beginning with the Anwar Sadat administration in the 1970s and continuing under Hosni Mubarak's administration from the 1980s onward. Unlike the frontier of capital of the long nineteenth century, the desert frontier at the turn of the twenty-first century combines a premise of economic nationalism with the drive to accumulate capital via the production of agricultural commodities for both the corporate market domestically and the export market abroad.

Food Aid Regime

U.S. food aid was a pillar of the agriculture supply management policy of the United States—a policy that many countries replicated in various ways from the interwar period onward. In the context of falling prices, the U.S. government passed the Agriculture Adjustment Act in 1933, which became the basis of U.S. supply management, a policy that expanded and contracted throughout the twentieth century (Winders 2009). Although many countries followed the United States in building and/or expanding such policies, agriculture supply management generally can be considered a fundamental policy apparatus of capitalist states. If prices of key crops drop, farmers may not plant that crop or will be disincentivized to plant it. In order to avoid a food shortage, governments offer incentives to keep planting (e.g., price supports, supply mandates) and/or attempt to avoid the fall in prices in the first place.

U.S. supply management rested on price supports and production controls (Winders 2009: 1). Doing so increased farm income but also encouraged overproduction (too much supply to maintain a desired market price). Acreage restrictions coupled with price supports by volume incentivized farmers to intensify production by producing more crop per land area (Winders 2009: 138). Initially, the United States used the food surpluses from overproduction to regain trading partners via the Marshall Plan. Then, food surpluses began to be used to dominate new markets in former colonies via Public Law (PL) 480, which created so-called food aid. Newly independent governments sought subsidized grains to keep costs for workers down, thereby, lowering the costs of industrialization (Friedmann 2005). Also, the corporate manufacture of colonial crop substitutes (e.g., cotton with synthetic fibers) shrank the international market for key colonial crops (Friedmann and McMichael 1989). The shrinking market meant less revenue for these governments to support the building of domestic industries. With less revenue, governments strapped for cash were more likely to accept low-cost imported food.

PL 480 had three titles: Title I was the core of the legislation, accounting for 50–90% of all funds via PL 480 (Winders 2009: 149). USAID administered these concessional sales of surplus agricultural commodities to so-called friendly nations. Concessional sales means that the recipient government paid for (largely) grains in their national currency. U.S. agencies within the recipient countries would then use these counterpart funds for various development projects, including agribusiness. Title II allowed for disaster relief and similar aid, and Title III covered foreign donations and barter trades.[2]

Sales of U.S. wheat in particular came to dominate PL 480. The U.S. wheat industry faced a competitive world market and pushed for the guaranteed export market via PL 480. As Winders (2009: 150–152) showed, the world wheat market was much more competitive than the world corn market. The U.S. corn industry already dominated the world market; thus, they did not push for food aid. PL 480 was the main export program of the United States in the 1950s and 1960s, accounting for 33% of U.S. wheat exports between 1954 and 1971 (Winders 2009: 150). During these decades, there was a remarkable shift toward imported wheat in countries in Latin America, Africa, and Asia: Before 1954, these countries had imported little wheat, and by 1978, former colonies received 78% of U.S. wheat exports (Winders 2009: 150).[3] In the 1970s, PL 480 declined sharply as the Nixon administration focused on commercial exports. The world price of wheat had risen dramatically, and there was growing competition for export markets as the Soviet Union entered the world wheat trade (Winders 2009: 150–155; González-Esteban 2018: 97–99).

In Egypt, PL 480 began in 1952 and lasted until 1996, although funds were cut off during and after Egypt's war with Israel, from 1967 through 1972. The food aid began with Title II, which lasted until 1989, but Title I, which lasted from 1956 to 1996, made up nearly 90% of all PL 480 funds and totaled $4.76 billion (historical). The funds continually multiplied from the time of the Free Officers coup in 1952 through the 1980s—but at declining rates. The funds increased nearly four times following the first decade (1952–1960), two and a half times after the second decade (1961–1967), and one and one-seventh times after the third decade (1973–1980). They declined sharply after the 1980s.[4]

Of all U.S. economic and military aid to Egypt during this period, PL 480 funds were relatively small, hovering around 7.5% of all aid. Yet, food aid in Egypt can be considered significant. Compared to other importing countries, Egypt had become the largest per capita consumer of U.S. food aid by the early 1960s (Dethier and Funk 1987: 23). Although PL 480 funds as a percentage of total U.S. wheat exports declined significantly in the 1970s, signaling the long-term decline of the food aid regime, the funds to Egypt continued to increase in the 1970s and 1980s. Plus, as will be addressed in this chapter, unlike some recipient countries for which wheat consumption was novel, in Egypt, wheat imports accelerated trends that were already underway to make wheat production and consumption unified across the urban–rural divide.

According to Winders (2009: 149), the primary benefit of PL 480 for the U.S. government was to dispose of surpluses, thereby, averting the crisis of excess stocks that would lead to falling prices. The United States also used food aid as a political weapon to achieve its foreign policy goals, as is exemplified by the cutting off of PL 480 funds to Egypt during and in the aftermath of Egypt's war with Israel in 1967. This regime of US-led food aid and supply management can be considered an international order because other countries were incentivized to adopt the U.S. agricultural model. On the one hand, the U.S. agricultural market protections closed off the U.S market; on the other hand, other countries needed to protect their own farmers from cheap agricultural commodities from the United States (Winders 2009: 145). These countries had to subsidize their exports to make them competitive. Furthermore, PL 480-recipient countries internalized the U.S. agro-industrial model, using the counterpart funds to further the industrialization of agriculture. Agrarian reforms also became a way to penetrate market relations in the countryside by making it possible for a growing number of farmers to buy industrial inputs (McMichael 2009: 141).

The rapid decline of PL 480 as a percentage of total U.S. wheat traded in the 1970s signifies the weakening of the food aid regime. Commodity prices, including wheat prices, rose sharply. The Bretton Woods system of the post-WWII order collapsed when the United States dropped the gold standard and all the Northern countries began to relax capital controls and financial regulations. An increase in capital flows internationally enabled more countries to enter the world agricultural trade that the United States and Europe had dominated under the food aid regime. First, the Soviet Union and satellites entered the trade in the 1970s following détente. Then, in the 1980s, a group of countries primarily in Latin America and South East Asia entered the trade, pushing the price of wheat and corn down. In fact, with the exception of the price hike in the 1970s, world wheat and corn prices had been on a steady decline since 1960: The price of wheat dropped from around $250 per tonne in 1960/61 to around $175 per tonne in 2009/10, and the price of corn fell around $200 per tonne in the early 1960s to around $125 per tonne through the 1990s (FAO 2011a). The new group of agroexporting countries formed a political coalition known as the CAIRNS group.

In the 1980s, the CAIRNS group joined with agrifood corporations to push for the inclusion of food and agriculture in the General Agreement on Tariffs and Trade (GATT) negotiations. This successful push was a driving force behind the emergence and exponential growth of agrifood corporations (national, regional, and transnational) worldwide following the establishment of the World Trade Organization (WTO) in 1995 (Friedmann 2005). This growth is part and parcel of the growth of a corporate agri-food system in Egypt and the concomitant change in frontier making.

Distinct Character of the State Frontier

Bourgeoning economic nationalism within the nominally independent states, notably in Latin America and to a lesser extent in Egypt, should be understood as part of a broader global politics of decolonization of the interwar period. Economic nationalism worked to stop and even reverse the declining terms of trade vis-à-vis the Northern imperial states through industrialization and lessen the growing gap between the rich and the poor via social welfare (see Prebisch 1950). Economic nationalism combined with the international effort of former colonies to build a more just world order beginning in the 1950s—what Vijay Prashad (2007) called the Third World Project and what in Egypt is referred to as Nasserism—can only be understood by examining the decades that preceded the formal era.[5]

There had long been efforts to build a cottage textile industry in Egypt, but it was only after World War I that import-substitution efforts began to take hold (Beckert 2014: 409–410). Ahmad Shokr (2016: 62) describes how an Egyptian parliamentarian traveled to England in the early 1920s to find ways to improve Egypt's position in the cotton trade—say, by cutting out the middlemen. This quest remained a main concern of state officials in the interwar and postwar periods (Shokr 2016: 62).

The living conditions of the rural masses had already deteriorated, as was described in Chapter 5, and were getting worse. Between 1931 and 1950, rental values increased fourfold, access to rural credit was limited, and rural poverty intensified (Bush 2007: 256). The plantation system had a stranglehold on cultivators: 0.1% of landowners owned 20% of the cultivated land area, while 75% of landowners owned less than one acre and cultivated only 13% of the land (Bush 2007: 256). To address these political problems of the countryside (Mitchell 2002: 38), the government made modest efforts to establish land rent controls in the early 1920s. Also, a cooperative section was established in the Agriculture Ministry (Shokr 2016: 45)—a move that can be considered an institutionalization of the cooperative movement.[6] In 1931, the government created the Banque du Credit Agricole d'Egypte to make short-term advances to peasants and agricultural cooperatives to enable them to cultivate their land (Shokr 2016: 66). Ultimately, though, the Banque failed to extend credit to peasants. As living conditions in the countryside continued to deteriorate, a Ministry of Health was created in 1936 (Mitchell 2002: 38).

In the context of rural immiseration and a heightened threat of famine during World War II, the Egyptian government declared a state of siege, which was legislated into the 1923 constitution (Schewe 2017: 51–52).[7] The government also created a Ministry of Supply, which eventually managed the food supply in rural areas. As Eric Schewe (2017: 51–52) explains, the Military Proclamation no. 243 in 1942 made purchases of wheat from every cultivator compulsory for town consumption and for reserves.[8] Out of this procurement policy emerged a subsidized bread loaf made of a mix of wheat, corn, and possibly other grains. For Schewe (2017), this new national loaf became a new national right of all Egyptians—and it transformed the kind of bread consumed. Before the national loaf, there had not been a universal bread, and in many areas, corn predominated as the local grain (Goldberg 2017).

Supply management, rent controls, and the like should not be understood singularly as social protections from the vagaries of the market. As Omnia El Shakry (2007: 91) elucidated, in the quasi-independence period of the 1920s and 1930s, the peasantry became an object of social scientific intervention and engineering. For El Shakry (2007: 91), in the aftermath of the 1919 revolt, which some elites understood as "potential Bolshevism," the peasantry became the central contradiction to an emerging national identity. On the one hand, peasants represented a kind of cultural authenticity, and on the other hand, they represented backwardness. Economic nationalism essentially had twin cores: industrialization and the peasantry as the object of social engineering.

The policies of agrarian reform and land reclamation that emerged in the 1940s were both outcomes of this economic nationalism with industrialization and the social reform of the peasant at its core. Agrarian reform debates, which had emerged by the early 1940s, vacillated between the family farm model and the collectivized farm model. Out of these debates emerged a series of bills in Parliament (between 1944 and 1947) to limit the size of farms, but none of the bills were passed (Mitchell 2002: 40). It is at this time that land reclamation became a pillar of agrarian reform. The Ministry of Social Affairs agreed in 1946 to launch an experiment in collective farming on reclaimed land that the state would rent to farmers, but the project did not get approval from the palace (Shokr 2016: 76). Then, a couple of years later, the government launched a program to distribute reclaimed land in five-acre plots to peasants, who also received so-called hygienic houses grouped in four villages, each with a school, mosque, health facility, and public bath (Mitchell 2002: 40). As will be detailed in the next section, by the early 1950s, the U.S. Truman administration was also pushing for land reform centered on land reclamation, the settling of landless peasants, and regulation of landlord–tenant relations (Vitalis 1995: 172). This state frontier both fueled and diffused agrarian reforms in the existing agricultural lands.

The State Frontier and Agrarian Reforms

> The "basic malady" [...] here considered is the prevalence of institutional monopoly in land-ownership, linked with a monopolistic supply of capital to agriculture. There is nothing peculiar to Middle Eastern countries in this condition. On the contrary, it is a feature of the land systems of many countries in the three agricultural continents which are now conventionally described as "underdeveloped."
>
> (Warriner 1957: 6)[9]

State land reclamation and agrarian reforms of the post-colonial era should be understood as mutually constituted rather than as separate histories as they are often analyzed.[10] The two sets of policies were administered separately under the Gamal Abdel Nasser administration of the 1950s and 1960s. Yet, the agrarian reform model, which was written into the laws of 1952, 1961, and 1969, governed the countryside of the Nile Valley and Delta and informed the character of land reclamation. In this section, I argue that state reclamation was an institutional force behind the limits of agrarian reform, including the degradation and/or deactivation of the agrarian reform lands. These limitations further fueled land reclamation—and well beyond Nasserism.

Land reclamation programs continued immediately after the Free Officers coup of 1952. The main purpose of land reclamation that was articulated in the 1940s remained: to redistribute land and to create a "new rural social order" centering on the peasant (Johnson et al. 1983; El Shakry 2007: 208). Two models of farming prevailed in the state frontier of the Nasser years (roughly until 1967): Most of the reclaimed lands were distributed to settlers in small plots based on a family farm model that the United States promoted, but reclaimed lands were also designated for large, highly mechanized collective farms, especially in the 1960s when the Nasser administration developed closer ties to the Soviet Union. During this two-decade period, there were many state reclamation projects, big and small, involving numerous institutions and political constituencies (El Shakry 2007: 208). Two of the most ambitious projects began right after the Officer's coup and reflect the two farm models: The Egyptian American Rural Improvement Service (EARIS) project was based on the family farm model and would claim to reclaim 37,000 acres and resettle 7,500 families, and Tahrir Province was based on a socialist utopian model (El Shakry 2007) and set out to reclaim 1.2 million acres in 12 districts with 11 villages each (Voll 1980).

The Egyptian American Rural Improvement Service (EARIS) was one of the projects that began before the 1952 coup: A general agreement between Egypt and the United States was signed in 1951.[11] EARIS was then launched in 1952 and lasted until 1963. From the beginning, EARIS was joint funded with Egypt contributing $15 million and the United States funding $10 million. U.S. funding was cut during the 1956–1958 Suez Canal crisis, and even after the project was disbanded in 1964, the Egyptian government continued the project and realized the targets by 1967 (Johnson et al. 1983).

The USAID evaluation of EARIS in 1981 claimed that 13 main villages and 64 satellite villages were built across the three reclamation sites (Johnsen et al. 1983). Each of the 7,500 settlers was supposed to have received a house, 3–5 acres of reclaimed land, and a water buffalo on a 40-year repayment schedule. In their report, USAID claimed that they "launched what remains Egypt's most successful land reclamation project" (Johnsen et al. 1983: v). They supported this claim by arguing that a much higher percentage of EARIS lands remained under cultivation since the launching of the project than the national average of reclaimed lands at the time of the evaluation: more than 80% as opposed to about 57%. At the same time, the report acknowledged the uneven success between the three sites. The site nearest to Alexandria, to the west of the Delta, was by far the most successful in terms of farm income, crop production, irrigation water infrastructure, and the like. The other sites, near to Fayoum, suffered from a lack of irrigation water. They further recognized that they had not appreciated "what a fragile environment they were attempting to create nor the vulnerability of the agreements and institutions which were to guarantee the areas lifeline of water from the Nile" (Johnsen et al. 1983: 11). In 1954, the Permanent Organization for Land Reclamation was established to administer land reclamation and resettlement (El Shakry 2007: 208), and the Irrigation Ministry was affiliated with the agencies in charge of the agrarian reform areas.[12] The different responsibilities between the agency in charge of the EARIS lands and the Irrigation Ministry was a source of this problem.

Tahrir Province, on the other hand, was built on the socialist utopian model of socialized production and reproduction: mechanized farming, social living including nurseries, and (Islamic) socialist education. The lands were also to the south of Alexandria and the west of the Delta. Settlers had to fulfill numerous requirements to qualify for migration. Among these requirements included literacy, being either landless or with less than five acres, having a clear police record, and passing a health test. As El Shakry (2007: 211) described, settlers underwent extensive training. They followed a daily schedule; wore uniform clothing; and placed their children in nurseries during the work day.[13]

From the time of the Suez crisis to the early 1960s, the socialist vision of village life was muddled as Magi Hasanayn, the Free Officer who headed the province, was ousted and replaced by a conservative, Sayed Marei. However, the Leftist faction within the government began to re-gain influence by the early 1960s (El Shakry 2007: 212). The Soviet Premier Nikita Khrushchev visited Tahrir Province in 1964, and the Soviets promised to provide machinery and loans to reclaim 300,000 acres west of the Nubariya Canal—what Springborg (1979) claimed became the only reclamation project following the 1967 Six-Day War. The aim on the state farms was economies of scale through mechanization: In the Second Five Year Plan (1966/70), state farms were designated for mechanized production of high-value crops like citrus and animal protein (Voll 1980). However, Tahrir Province and other state farms began to be dismantled and replaced within roughly a decade, as will be explained in the following section.

The Free Officers had carried out land reclamation in earnest from the early 1950s because there was a state plan to construct the Aswan High Dam, which would greatly expand the dam that the British built. The horizontal expansion of land for cultivation and settlement was only possible through the expansion of hydroelectric power (Springborg 1979; Voll 1980; Alterman 2002). And the construction of the dam was expensive: An estimate is that the dam accounted for more than 60% of the increase in state agriculture expenditure (as a percentage of total public expenditure) from 1952–53 to 1967–68.[14] Land reclamation was also expensive: One estimate is that by the end of the 1970s land reclamation was taking nearly half of the total agriculture expenditure while contributing less than 1% of total agriculture production (Voll 1980).

The Aswan High Dam flooded villages upstream and downstream, making them uninhabitable, and displacing thousands of Nubians. This level of displacement exacerbated the uneven capitalist development that began in the long nineteenth century. Also, both the dam and reclamation accelerated the degradation of the Delta ecosystem. Over the medium term, the dam salinated the soil, eroded the coastline, and damaged the wetlands (Stanley and Warne 1998).[15] Land reclamation had further been draining the northern lagoons, which had a deleterious effect on the livelihoods of fisherfolk (Stanley and Warne 1998; Bush and Sabri 2000). EARIS, in fact, charged itself with reclaiming lake bottom—and that included parts of Lake Maryut. As the USAID report on EARIS admitted, state plans were often made without considering the ecological landscape—the types of soil, the elevations above sea level, the unevenness of the terrain, and so on (see also Voll 1980; Cole and Altorki 1998). Alan Richards (1980: 8–9) argued that soil salination was the result of not enough investment going into drainage. The dam resulted in a dramatic rise in water supply, and without proper drainage systems, soil salinity would inevitably increase. Both reclaimed lands and agrarian reform lands suffered from salination.

The large percentage of state agriculture investment diverted to the dam and land reclamation at the very least dampened the ambitious agenda in the so-called old lands. The agrarian reform laws (of 1952, 1961, and 1969) involved both expropriation and sequestration: Land was expropriated to then be redistributed, and other land was sequestered as a political punishment for families that the Nasser government considered a threat. In line with the parliamentary bills of the 1940s, the reforms mandated a ceiling on privately held land: from over 200 acres to 100 acres in 1961 (Bush 2007: 257). Those who were given land received on average 2.4 acres and had to pay for the land in instalments over a 40-year period. Those who did not receive land were given three-year contracts and rights of inheritance in perpetuity (Bush 2007: 258–259). Furthermore, the reforms steadily took over the endowed (*waqf*) lands: Land endowed for private wealth accumulation was abolished in 1952, and all existing endowed lands were placed under the newly created Waqf Ministry (Pioppi 2004). By 1962, all endowed lands were transferred to the Agrarian Reform Committee.[16]

Agricultural cooperatives became a pillar of the agrarian reforms by the 1960s. Agrarian reform beneficiaries, both title holders and tenants, would be registered in their local cooperative, which became a central conduit to the government's supply management policy and the dissemination of the U.S. agro-industrial model through the provision of industrial farming inputs. Quotas of key crops (especially cotton) were enforced via the cooperatives: peasants would sell the key crops to the cooperatives at state-mandated volumes and prices, and the cooperatives would sell peasants inputs to produce those crops. These crops were then sold to the import-substitution industries (e.g., textile, food processing).[17]

Despite the limitations of the agrarian reforms, as will be discussed below, the agrarian reforms were successful in helping to transform the social class order by elevating the social position of the smallholder (with less than five acres) and breaking the political and economic power of the landed elites (the Pasha's family, the rural notables) and the accompanying elites in manufacturing and finance. That political outcome of destroying the old order, which, in this case, was the plantation economy, was an aim of the Nasser government and most post-colonial states (Westad 2007: 94). This success does not mean that the elites gave up power willfully. Even though there was not a civil war or even a significant counter-revolutionary force in Egypt, a culture of fear—a fear of former landowner retaliation—existed in many villages (Mitchell 1999). Nonetheless, as I explain in Chapter 3, agrarian reforms and state reclamation improved the social position and living standards of the vast majority of peasants by breaking the economic and political power of the landed elites. The vast majority of peasants were no longer being subjected to coercive and intimidating work and living conditions.

By the 1970s, a large number of studies were conducted to assess the impacts of the agrarian reforms.[18] A consensus among them was that the reforms were limited in scope, capturing only roughly 12–13% of arable land, distributed to 9% of the rural population (Bush 2007: 257; Westad 2007: 94). Many exceptions had been applied to the land ceiling—for families with more than two children, for endowed land, for reclaimed land, and so on (Bush 2007: 257).

The impacts of the agrarian reforms have been difficult to assess in part because of the way in which farmers were categorized in the assessments. Three categories were given: the landless; those with less than five acres; and a so-called middle peasantry with 5–50 acres. As Richards (1980: 6) noted, the category of middle peasantry alone is problematic because there is obviously a large difference between owning five acres and owning 50 acres. Richards (1980) chose to refer to that category as "rich peasants," because in Egypt, those with even five acres are considerably better off than the majority of peasants with less, who must work at least part-time as wage laborers.

Using this categorization, a new pattern of social differentiation among the peasantry becomes clear. Rich or better-off peasants (owning 5–50 acres) grew even more than smallholders (with less than five acres). Smallholders, who represented 94% of all landowners in 1952, owned 35% of the cultivated land in 1952 and came to own 52% following the first agrarian reform law (Bush 2007: 258). The middle peasantry, which represented only 3% of all landowners in 1952, came to own 24% of the cultivated area by buying sold lands following the 1952 reforms (Bush 2007: 259).

A second consensus among the 1970s studies was that the agrarian reforms failed to address landlessness. The number of landless laborers actually rose as the plantations broke up and family-based small farms became prevalent (Bush 2007). This problem not only reflects the limited scope of the reforms but also the social relations within villages. In Detlef Müller-Mahn's (1998) case study of the effects of the agrarian reforms in two villages, the social position of the migrants within the plantation system determined whether migrants would become landless laborers or tenants with secure contracts following the reforms. The persistent problem of landlessness also provided justifications for state reclamation as the landless were understood to be among the primary beneficiaries.

A third consensus was that agrarian reforms accelerated the penetration of capitalist social relations in the countryside. Under the cooperative system, and through the black market that developed parallel to it, more households began to buy chemical and mechanized inputs. Estimates of the increase in chemical fertilizer use range anywhere from an increase of more than 100% to up to 300% during the 1950s and 1960s.[19] The cooperatives had also taken over pest control through hired child labor and occasional pesticide use. Because cotton crop rotations were imposed, Kathy Glavanis (1990) argued that these costs of pest control were also imposed on smallholder households. Further, from 1961 to 1976, pest control charges rose as compared to the price of cotton, thereby, increasing the burden of cotton production for smallholders (Glavanis 1990: 152).

The process of agro-industrialization via the cooperative system further exacerbated inequalities among peasants. Better-off peasants were able to afford the costs of inputs, which were subsidized but still beyond the reach of most peasants (Richards 1980: 7). Plus, a number of the input provisioning schemes of the cooperatives were restricted to those with certain assets; for example, the animal insurance schemes of the 1960s were only for those owning at least five work animals (Richards 1980: 8). Better-off peasants could further afford to produce crops outside the cooperative system while smallholders tended to become indebted through the system of pur-chasing inputs to meet crop quotas (Abdel-Fadil 1975; Radwan 1977). Reem Saad's (1988) case study confirmed these findings: In some cases, smallholders were left in debt by meeting the crop quotas, while better-off peasants were able to shift to more profitable, unregulated crops (such as vegetables and fruit).

While peasants did generally come to rely more on the market, directly and indi-rectly, for their livelihoods, this dependence was far from complete. Non-market relations and social cooperation helped mitigate against the trend of social differen-tiation. Glavanis (1990: 150) found that while peasant households were increasingly reliant on bought inputs and consumer goods, non-market relations remained. For example, many households saved seeds, at least seeds of the main subsistence crops (clover, wheat, and corn). If the seeds were not sufficient, they would borrow from a neighbor or relative and repay in kind the following harvest. Other types of seeds were obtained through the cooperatives—namely, high-yielding wheat varieties. Also, regarding irrigation, the state ran the secondary irrigation canals, but villages ran the tertiary canals (Hopkins 1999). Because water from the tertiary canals was below the level of fields, peasants had to draw water from the canals to irrigate the fields. As Hopkins (1999) described, the management of this process took much social organization and cooperation among peasants.

The contradictions of agrarian reforms should be understood in relation to the ongoing development of state reclaimed lands. The state budget under the Nasser administration was directed to the construction and maintenance of the Aswan High Dam, which made possible large-scale land reclamation. Also, state reclamation projects themselves were taking a sizable portion of the state agricultural budget. The state frontier was about not only distributing land to the landless, a problem which the agrarian reforms failed to adequately address, but was also about increasing agri-cultural production via industrialization and collectivization for urban workers and national industries. State reclamation contributed to the degradation of the Delta ecosystem in particular, and the institutionalization of Green Revolution technolo-gies via the agrarian reforms contributed in the long-run to the gross contamination of soil, water, and crops in the Nile Valley and Delta (Abbassy et al. 2003; Anwar 2003; Mansour 2008), thereby, further de-activating agricultural areas. These and other limitations of agrarian reforms, in turn, justified the expansion of the state frontier.

Contradictions of Economic Nationalism and U.S. Food Aid

The historical relationship between agrarian reforms and the state frontier cannot be explained through the agrarian reform and land reclamation laws and policies alone. After all, these laws and policies were pieces of an economic nationalist puzzle and a broader politics of decolonization. From 1952, along with building the state frontier and the agrarian reforms, the Nasser administration immediately undertook a host of additional sequestrations (not just of land but also other assets) as well as nationalizations. A well-known example is the sequestration of Ahmed Abboud's sugar company in 1952. The Nasser government became a major shareholder, paying for the shares of the French investors who dominated the board (Salem 2020: 143). The question of financing the Aswan High Dam had set the stage for the nationalization of the Suez Canal in 1956 (Salem 2020: 138). The United States had canceled its offer to finance the construction of the dam when Nasser accepted a shipment of arms from Czechoslovakia in 1955. By nationalizing the canal, the government could use the revenues to help pay for the dam's construction (Salem 2020: 138). After Britain, France, and Israel invaded Egypt to re-gain control of the canal, and then, withdraw with pressure from the United States, Nasser nationalized foreign oil, tobacco, pharmaceuticals, banking, insurance, among other key economic sectors (Latham 2011: 80). In the first five-year plan of 1960, not only were nearly 300,000 acres slated to be reclaimed, but more state controls were exercised over the economy and social welfare provisions were extended.

Given the threats from Western powers throughout the 1950s and 1960s, the Nasser administration built the Egyptian army: from 80,000 soldiers in the mid-1950s to about 180,000 in the mid-1960s (Abul-Magd 2017: 67). Also, the administration, like most post-colonial states, sought formal industrial growth directed to the national (rather than export) market. The administration attempted to keep agricultural commodity prices low for urban industrial workers and import-substitution industries (Sadowski 1991). At the same time, the world cotton trade contracted, having the immediate and dramatic effect of plummeting the production and export of agricultural commodities ("output in agriculture"), which fell by up to 50% (Westad 2007: 94). Agrarian reforms attempted to reverse this trend by increasing peasant production. And the reforms did succeed in increasing production on agrarian reform lands (Bush 2007: 259). Also, by the late 1950s, the Nasser administration was asking the U.S. Kennedy administration for a large, long-term multiyear commitment of food aid. The Egyptian ambassador to the United States, Mustapha Kamel, argued that the food aid would assist Egyptian economic development planning by allowing the government to divert its limited foreign exchange holdings from food imports to industrial investments (Latham 2011: 79). As was explained above in the section on the Food Aid Regime, PL 480 funds to Egypt multiplied nearly fourfold by the 1960s.[20]

In these ways, food aid aided economic nationalism, of which agrarian reforms were a pillar. Food aid provided wage foods—low-cost food that kept living costs down and wages down. Peasant crops, while also wage foods, were more significantly industrial inputs. Cotton was diverted to the textile industry, sugar to the food processing industry, and so on. A result was formal industrial growth. The state built large industrial areas, largely for import-substitution industries, as well as large infrastructure projects, notably the Aswan High Dam. The state frontier should be considered a part of this formal industrial growth as mechanized farming was directed largely for the production of crops for urban areas. This formal industrial growth went hand-in-hand with the development of a new capitalist class (Sadowski 1991), which will be explored further in Chapter 7.

Formal industrial growth relied on pulling resources and labor from the countryside. While cheap food kept wages down, industrial wages remained higher than agricultural wages, which led rural migrants to take jobs as laborers in infrastructure projects and other industrial activities (Toth 1998). In the 1950s, when the world cotton price declined, state research for cotton seed development also declined. The result was that the cotton crop became vulnerable (yet again) to plant diseases. The cotton leaf worm (*S. littoralis*) developed a resistance to insecticides, the application of which had become widespread on cotton fields by the early 1950s (Mansour 2008). The result was the cotton leaf worm attack of 1961, which devastated the cotton harvest and lead swiftly to the universal establishment of agriculture cooperatives (Richards 1980). Toth (1998) argued that the devastation from the cotton leaf worm in 1961 was the result of not having enough workers for the labor-intensive process of protecting the crop from the worm. Workers in Aswan were being paid three times the rate of agricultural work.

Agrarian reforms and food aid worked to complementary ends to fuel urban industrial growth, but they were also contradictory. For one, PL 480 had the uneven effect of increasing peasant dependence on the consumer market. In Glavanis's (1990: 156) case study of an Egyptian village in the late 1970s–early 1980s, the introduction of subsidized American wheat flour did not divorce peasants from the cultivation and processing of wheat. However, patterns of consumption began to change as peasant households increasingly ate the subsidized bread loaf rather than their own wheat loaf.

These combined developments fueled long-term processes that would grow considerably with time: rural outmigration and the concomitant growth of an informal economy.[21] While formal Cairo grew considerably during these decades with the building of industrial zones and massive public housing projects, at the same time, there was the nascent expansion of unplanned, unlegislated neighborhoods, often on agricultural land. As was hinted at above, a considerable number of agricultural activities existed outside the cooperative system. Not only were better-off peasants selling higher-value crops outside the system, but the landless, smallholders, and others were also involved in food peddling and vending (see Waterbury 1983: 159–161).

The Collapse of Bretton Woods

When the U.S. Nixon administration suspended the gold standard, the convertibility of the dollar into gold in 1971, the immediate effect was currency trading, which led to the volatility of currencies. Then, in 1973, commodity prices began to rise sharply when the oil companies increased the price of oil as a response to OPEC (Mitchell 2011). With rising prices and currency volatility, Western governments began to lift their capital controls and financial regulations, and a so-called lending binge (including from the global North to the global South) followed (Roos 2019: 122). The overseas profits of the seven largest U.S. banks rose from 22–60% of their total profits from 1973 to 1982 (McMichael 2017: 103). Newly independent governments had borrowed to build and expand their public sphere: State enterprises across the global South enlarged their share of their country's GDP by almost 50% (McMichael 2017: 105). As McMichael (2017: 103) highlights, for the borrowing governments this meant a rather rapid shift from multilateral lending to private debt: In the early 1970s, bank loans amounted to only 13% of Southern debt, while multilateral loans made up more than 33%. At the end of the decade, there was a reversal: Private banks held 66% of the debt (McMichael 2017: 103).

In Egypt, the rise in oil prices was experienced as a type of regional oil boom. Oil rents as a percentage of GDP in Egypt rose from 1.5% in 1973 to 32.6% in 1980.[22] Revenue from crude oil exports rose as did the revenue from the Suez Canal. Not only did GDP increase steadily, but there was a type of inclusive growth with national earnings, per-capita income, domestic savings, and investment rates all increasing (Schechter 2019: 52). Skilled urban workers were permitted to work in the Gulf states. These emigrants then sent their earnings home to buy land, build informal housing, and/or start informal businesses.[23] According to Ahmed Soliman (2004 cited in Davis 2006: 58), this type of spending led to the biggest upsurge in informal urbanization in Egypt since independence. This effect was characteristic of the general effects of the oil boom regionally (Abu-Lughod 1996 cited in Davis 2006: 85). One estimate is that informal housing construction rose from 72% of total housing during the 1960–1970 period to 89% during the 1971–1976 period (Schechter 2019: 104). This informal urbanization meant the accelerated loss of agricultural lands: According to a 1982 National Urban Policy study, which compared Landsat images taken in 1972 to images in 1978, approximately 120 km^2 of agricultural land was lost (Kishk 1986).

Growing government revenue, in turn, led to more government spending. The spending responded in part to a growing middle class (who benefitted from informal urbanization) plus a growing population of rural migrants and young people. Between 1960 and 1987, the population nearly doubled, rising from 26 million to 48 million (Schechter 2019: 18). Spending on social and welfare services, especially education, rose exponentially. Food and oil subsidies rose rapidly. As was discussed in the section on the Distinct Character of the State Frontier, bread subsidies began during World War II, but during the 1950s and 1960s, subsidies for bread and other basic commodities remained low and included only a few consumer goods. But as world prices rose, so did government subsidies: By 1974, consumer subsidies (both food and oil) reached 16.5% of government expenditure and remained at this level until the aftermath of the oil boom (Schechter 2019: 87). Rulli Schechter (2019: 87) argues that the growth of subsidies can be understood as part of securing a government safety net for the expanding middle class given that most consumer subsidies were designated for urban areas. The middle class also had changing consumption patterns—toward milk, meat, and other high-income luxury goods—and this demand contributed to an increase in imports (Mitchell 1998; Schechter 2019).

Imports rose and production of staples fell, and in 1974, Egypt became a net importer of agricultural commodities for the first time (Richards 1980: 3). As was discussed in Chapter 2, the U.S. Carter administration and the IMF pressured the Sadat administration to cut food subsidies in half, leading to the January 1977 riots. Because the policy response to the growing deficit was to cut subsidies of staple foods, it is often assumed that Egypt's food import dependency was the main culprit of government expenditure exceeding revenue. As I show in Chapter 2, this assumption is wrong. In the case of the 1970s, PL 480 continued and even multiplied, allowing food subsidies to grow exponentially, thereby, contributing greatly to the country's food import dependency. Given that food aid was paid for in Egyptian currency, however, subsidized food imports were a significantly smaller burden on government expenditure than oil subsidies. In 1979, energy subsidies were estimated to be three times higher than expenditure on food subsidies (Schechter 2019: 89). Egypt was experiencing an oil boom from the explosive growth in earnings from the export of crude oil. But crude oil is not consumed directly; it needs to be refined to be used in industry and transportation. While Egypt was exporting crude oil, it was importing refined oil, the cost of which was rising exponentially, as Raúl Prebisch's (1950) doctrine of unequal exchange would predict, as the price of manufactured goods rises at faster rates than the price of primary goods.[24]

In essence, the collapse of Bretton Woods in the 1970s presaged, what the Paris Club called, the debt crisis of the 1980s. In 1980, the U.S. Federal Reserve Board, under the chairmanship of Paul Volcker, reduced dollars in circulation, to save the value of the dollar, and this so-called Volcker shock led to a rapid increase in interest rates (McMichael 2017: 113). Mexico, an oil-exporting country, was the first country to go into default a couple of years later. Egypt went into sovereign default a couple of years after that, in 1984 (Borensztein and Panizza 2008; Erce and Mallucci 2018). Debt servicing on external debt rose from $518.5 million in 1979 to $2.8 billion in 1985.[25] Existing debt multiplied as did new debt—and, in particular, debt from military aid. The Defense Minister under the Sadat administration, Abu Ghazala, had secured military aid from the United States, which began in 1978 (USAID n.d.). As Abul-Magd (2017: 80) shows, under Mubarak, Abu Ghazala continued as Minister and secured a fixed annual amount of $1.3 billion in military aid. For Abul-Magd (2017: 80–81), the 1980s were the "golden age" for Egypt's arms industry as the military budget reached 22% of government expenditure in 1982–83 and continued roughly at that figure until 1987–88.

Debt rescheduling began in Egypt in 1986, which, in Samer Soliman's (2011: 44) terms, marked a turning point for the Egyptian treasury. Military spending as a percentage of total public expenditure declined (Soliman 2011: 62). Also, food aid began to decline precipitously; the United States began to demand market prices for wheat (Mitchell 1998). In response, the Egyptian Ministry of Supply increased the price of subsidized bread and decreased the availability and quality of both the bread and flour. By 1987, the government also supposedly ended its control of crop areas, quotas, and prices—except for rice, cotton, and sugarcane (Mitchell 1998). But as Timothy Mitchell (1998, 2002) has pointed out, bread and other food subsidies did not end; therefore, the government had to maintain some regulations of wheat and the other key crops that remained subsidized. By the tenth anniversary of the Camp David Accord in 1989, Egypt was also slated to start paying back the military debt to the United States; this $4.5 billion was out of a total foreign debt of $44 billion (Abul-Magd 2017: 87).

Debt rescheduling compounded with declining petroleum prices (yet again), which further led to declining Suez Canal revenue (Soliman 2011: 44). Plus, a US-centered economic downturn, from the late 1980s to the early 1990s, compounded the sovereign debt default.[26] This long debt crisis, beginning in the 1970s and culminating in the 1991 rescheduling, marked the end of the state frontier and the beginning of a new frontier of capital.

The Desert Frontier

In the 1970s, government expenditure, including on social and welfare services, rose at the same time that the Sadat administration pursued the Open Door Policy (*Infitah*) that would slowly undo the Nasserist project, including especially the agrarian reform institutions. The two seemingly contradictory set of policies are rather commensurate as the Open Door Policy was extremely controversial and growing government expenditure would serve to mollify the impacts of releasing capital and price controls. This relationship was apparent when the subsidies of staple foods were cut, leading to the urban revolts in 1977.

The twin forces of increasing government spending and declining capital controls under the Sadat administration also transformed frontier making. Beginning in the early 1970s, the agency responsible for the reclaimed lands, the Egyptian Authority for the Utilization and Development of Reclaimed Land, began to slowly sell and distribute its roughly 330,000 acres under cultivation—to various groups for their political support, including the Syndicate of Agricultural Engineers, peasants, private investors, survivors of the heroes of the 1973 War, and oasis dwellers in the New Valley (Springborg 1979).[27] Then, in 1978, Sadat announced the launching of the Green Revolution, which would reclaim lands for secondary and college graduates as well as private investors and would privatize state farms. The Egypt–Israel Peace Treaty the following year further pushed forward Sadat's Green Revolution as the treaty led to sustained exchange on agriculture in arid lands between the two countries (Adriansen 2015). For nearly two decades, until the second Palestinian intifada, Egyptian farmers attended training courses in Israel, Israeli experts stayed in the reclaimed lands, and drip and other irrigation technologies were transferred from Israel to Egypt (Adriansen 2015).

These initiatives under the Sadat administration show the beginnings of a new type of frontier: on the one hand, a frontier that continued state land reclamation for redistribution, and on the other hand, one that enabled investors to build farms and processing facilities at economies of scale. After Sadat's assassination in 1981 and Hosni Mubarak gaining the presidency, the new frontier of capital became more concrete as land reclamation became tied to a larger state program of desert development. The Mubarak administration built waves of industrial cities in reclaimed areas to the west and east of the Delta: 6th of October, 10th of Ramadan, Sadat City, and Borg Al Arab. The Inland Investment Law (no. 8/1997 and no. 159/1981) set up industrial zones in these cities and offered investors various incentives like no export minimums and a ten-year tax exemption for land cultivation and production activities related to livestock, poultry, and fish. These zones, where much food processing came to be concentrated, became connected to both agribusiness farms and facilities as well as state (and informal) reclamation communities via the extension of two main highways that surround the Delta vertically—the Alexandria-desert road to the west and the Ismailia-desert road to the east. These highways connect the expanding frontier to Cairo (and Middle and Upper Egypt) in the south and to Alexandria and the Mediterranean ports in the north (see Figure 6.1).

As Abul-Magd (2017) shows in her groundbreaking book on the Egyptian military, desert development was significantly for the military industrial complex as well. New laws allowed the military to acquire hundreds of thousands of reclaimed land for apartment complexes, agribusiness farms, social clubs, toll highways, and other revenue-generating activities (Abul-Magd 2017: 137). And the role of the military in the desert frontier would increase over time: For example, law no. 7 of 1991 dictates that the state authorities responsible for the new lands should "coordinate with the [Ministry of Defense] first before making decisions and observe the rules and conditions that the latter sets" (Abul-Magd 2017: 138). Many of the military's factories and apartment complexes were built in the new industrial cities to the west and east of the Delta.

The second frontier of capital—what I call in shorthand the desert frontier—both builds on and departs from the state frontier of the post-independence years. Not only does redistribution continue, but the character or ethos of state reclamation communities reflect in some ways the social engineering project of both farming models under Nasserism, with the peasant subject at the center. Also, state reclamation, both the development of existing reclaimed lands and farms and the reclaiming of new lands, concentrated to the west of the Delta, at least initially, where the state frontier had concentrated.

At the same time, many new actors have been involved in building and expanding the desert frontier, including the military, medium-sized agricultural entrepreneurs, migrant day laborers, state agencies, international development agencies, investors, and more. The focus here is on investors and reclamation communities near to areas concentrated with agribusiness—and the relationship between the two. By investor, I am referring to any entity that invests in reclamation for the purposes of settlement and/or cultivation. Prominent among the investors are the agricultural investment arm of wealthy family business groups, regional and transnational corporations, and financial firms. Together, in so far as they are devoted to agricultural production and/or processing, they are referred to generally as agribusiness. Agribusiness has been drawing workers, crops, and other resources from nearby reclamation communities. These communities are both formal and informal.

For example, the Mubarak Resettlement Scheme (MRS) was to reclaim land to the west of the Delta for graduates. From 1987 to 2003, the project claimed to have distributed 230,000 acres to more than 45,000 graduates (Adriansen 2009). That was on average 4–5 acres per recipient. The administration even attempted to use state reclamation to legitimate the counter agrarian reforms of the 1990s by offering evicted tenant farmers the opportunity to apply for compensation in the form of plots of reclaimed land. According to 2003 MALR figures, only 16,727 evicted tenants were given 43,000 acres (Adriansen 2009). During the building of MRS, workers and others created a reclamation community themselves near Wadi Natrun, which at the time of research was in a concentrated area of agribusiness.

Agribusiness was primarily concerned with establishing horticulture farms, seed farms, food processing facilities, and industrial animal facilities (of poultry, dairy, and fish) for both the national market and export market. Why did agribusiness move to the reclaimed lands and reclaim new lands? State farms and large plots of state-owned reclaimed land were sold at bargain prices compared to rising land prices in the Nile Valley and Delta.[28] Interviews with agribusiness executives reveal that some family businesses moved from the Delta into reclaimed land with rents from, or the sales of, newly valuable land in the Delta, acquiring much larger plots of land. Any one landholding in the desert frontier is immense compared to holdings in the Delta, where a farm of 50 or more acres is considered large. In horticulture, investors claimed farm holdings from 930 to as much as 20,000 acres. The total holdings of any one investor were often spread out in different locations.

Agribusiness developed two types of reclaimed land: irrigated land from the Nile River that is in or near to state and informal reclamation communities; and non-irrigated land that is outward from these communities (and most other infrastructure) and is irrigated by digging wells to the aquifer. The government had been leasing the irrigated land for a period of seven years, and then, selling the land to the leasee if a required percentage of the land was cultivated. As agribusiness moved farther from reclamation communities, they gained usufruct rights to the non-irrigated land that Bedouin hold under *wad' yad* (squatters' rights), a type of customary land right.[29] They paid local Bedouin to "lift the hand," which allowed them to develop the land and provide their farms with Bedouin protection. Encroachment into these more remote lands also led to greater interaction between investors and illegal trade routes (see, for example, Wahid 2012). When I visited non-irrigated farms in 2011, in the aftermath of the January 25 uprising, guards were armed with AK-47s and farm employees' movements were restricted outside of the farm after dark.

In horticulture, the labor force is gendered and trifurcated with well-paid male managers and supervisors, who live weekly or monthly on farms and who may or may not be from Egypt, daily laborers who come from nearby reclamation communities, and young female migrant, seasonal (*tarahil*) laborers, who are also pooled from nearby Delta governorates by contractors. Most of the seasonal laborers are unmarried girls, who are brought to the farms for half a day (so they return home before dark). A foreign agribusiness manager confided during a farm visit that contractors would routinely bring children to work, and even though employing children violates the retail certifications, he felt morally obliged to accept them and at times had them do menial tasks for a wage so that, in his words, they did not face punishment at home or a meal-less evening if he turned them away.[30] At the time of my farm visits, agribusinesses were even enjoying the free labor of local high-school students through the USAID-funded Agriculture Exports and Rural Incomes (AERI) program, which was intended to train the students to become farm supervisors upon graduation.

Further, the presence and expansion of agribusiness in and near to state reclamation communities impacted the livelihood strategies of smallholders by changing what smallholders produced and sold. The agribusiness managers and executives whom I interviewed all admitted to regularly overcoming supply shortages for both the agroexport market and the domestic corporate food market from crops that smallholders from nearby reclamation communities would supply. Smallholders would bring their crops to the pack house (processing center), and agribusiness managers claimed to follow up with them to ensure the quality standards of their crops. However, any such arrangement would have been non-contractual.

These arrangements were informal, and as I explain in Chapter 3, many of the ways in which smallholders have been incorporated into corporate commodity chains are non-contractual. However, there are also formal contracts that international development agencies arranged. In the following sub-section, I highlight one such arrangement that was part of a broader development project for rural livelihoods in a state reclamation community that I visited in September 2011.

West Noubariya Rural Development Project

The West Noubariya Rural Development Project (WNRD) was a joint funded project between the Ministry of Agriculture and Land Reclamation, the Italian government, and the International Fund for Agricultural Development (IFAD) that ended in 2014. The objective was to improve the livelihoods of the West Noubariya state reclamation community, which the Mubarak Resettlement Scheme founded. West Noubariya is about 20 kilometers from Alexandria, along the Alexandria-desert road. By the time of my visit, the project was less than 10 years old, having launched in 2002. There was a total of 19 villages and 36,185 families who were claimed to be the beneficiaries. These families were families of graduates, the landless, and former local government officials. Many of these families were not the original settlers, who had been granted land in 1984. The redistributed plots had changed hands often, and the project administrators claimed that they were successful in attracting and retaining new settlers. They claimed that in 2002 the villages were at only a 25% capacity and by 2009 they were at 98%.

Similar to the state frontier, the focus of WNRD was not just on livelihoods but on the peasant subject. Now such efforts are called community development. The project built schools, mosques, and numerous other facilities to assist the villages. So-called improvement was now about smallholders better positioning themselves in the market, to increase their earnings by what they grow, how they grow it, and the markets that they sell in.

The WNRD technical assistance concerned three areas of production: plant production, livestock production, and water management. The project built two extension training centers, which included training smallholders on "applying modern agricultural techniques." There was also a laboratory for soil, water, and nematode analysis, and an artificial insemination center for breeding. Training services also included farmer-to-farmer exchanges in Upper Egypt and in Italy.

Better positioning in the market as a so-called petty commodity producer involved technical know-how as well as social cooperation. The project registered six marketing associations and 97 agricultural associations with the Ministry to reach buyers and to attain higher prices for the members' crops. Also, WNRD set up a direct market: a farmer's market in downtown Alexandria. Better positioning further involved value-added production, and WNRD established a processing facility for plant-based and dairy products (e.g., dates processed into Tamr Al Din rolls, milk into mozzarella cheese).

Much of this project assistance was offered through credit. The project administrators claimed to have dispersed EGP 118 million in loans between 2002 and 2010. The credit scheme was a type of Grameen bank scheme, whereby a group of borrowers was selected and a credit committee formed. While not all of the assistance was paid for, members did have to pay for the laboratory services at "reasonable prices." And when they went to distant markets to sell, the project had bed trucks that they would rent to members to reduce transportation costs.

Smallholders also needed to borrow to participate in the contract arrangements that WNRD secured. Contracts were made with processors, traders, and retail outlets. Some examples include with the tomato processors El Ein, Heinz, and Best; the apricot processor (Al Kahara); and the peach processor (Hero). The main food retailer was the Makro supermarket. One of the significant contracts in operation at the time of my visit was with ACDI-VOCA, an INGO based in Washington, DC, with Agrimatco, a multinational agricultural distribution company based in Cyprus, and Heinz (Figure 6.1).[31] As I explain in Chapter 3, in these formal arrangements, smallholders borrow to purchase the seed and other necessary inputs from the corporate partner. The contract specifies the inputs, volume, and price, among other specifications.

West Noubariya is in several ways distinct from many, if not most, state reclamation communities. If the WNRD project numbers can be accepted, the vast majority

Figure 6.1 Tomato types produced for manufacturing.
Source: WNRD.

of new settlers had chosen to stay in West Noubariya. This level of retention contrasts with the historically high turnover rates in the Mubarak Resettlement Scheme. For example, in one MRS area that Günter Meyer (1998: 345–346) studied in 1991, only about 40% of the graduates were still actively involved in the farms. The others tried to lease or illegally sell their land. Also, as indicated above, the WNRD established extensive contract arrangements, which on the whole are not usual. Many arrangements between agribusiness and smallholders are rather informal. The proximity to Alexandria further made it easier to earn an income from farming in West Noubariya—with access to direct markets in the city, lower transportation costs, and so on. This advantage for West Noubariya was also an advantage for the reclamation community that EARIS built near to Alexandria in the 1950s. The EARIS site near to Alexandria was by far the most successful in providing a livelihood for settlers.

At the same time, there are many ways that West Noubariya is similar to other state reclamation communities. The peasant subject is the object of improvement. In the neoliberal era, this improvement involves what has come to be called community development as well as other development indicators, including especially women's empowerment. As in Tahrir Province under Nasserism, the new lands of the MRS have been a gateway for forging new social norms. In Tahrir, the new social norms that were attempted were akin to socialist feminist norms. Now, the attempt is for women to gain access to assets and decision-making power—i.e., neoliberal feminist norms. As Dina Najjar et al. (2020: 6) explain in their comparative study of the Delta area of Kafr Sheikh and of Noubariya (the entire state reclamation community, not only the western part), the WFP provided food aid to settlers in Noubariya on the condition that women received 20% of distributed land titles. The WFP also required the inclusion of women in leadership positions in the formal land-related committees and associations (Najjar et al. 2020: 6). Over all, Najjar at el. (2020: 7) found that women's land ownership was greater in Noubariya than in Kafr Sheikh. Yet, while some social norms were subject to change in the reclaimed lands in ways that favored women, others were not. For example, women in Noubariya were less likely to get their land inheritance shares than women in the Delta (Najjar et al. 2020: 7).

Plus, in West Noubariya, like in other state reclamation communities, settlers were provided with the basics to sustain themselves. Scholarship on similar development initiatives that seek to improve the market positions of petty commodity producers (for example, contract farming, micro-credit) highlight the neoliberal logic at work in seemingly attempting to turn smallholders and others eeking out a living into entrepreneurs (Elyachar 2005; Bateman 2012). After all, why would WNRD make the settlers pay for the lab services, trucks, seeds, and other resources and services when the project could provide them for free, and in doing so, increase the settlers' income? Why make them go into debt that they will have a difficult time paying off? The WNRD administrators, in fact, admitted to me that they don't claim to help the settlers out of poverty. In line with the ethos of the Grameen bank, they claimed to be providing the basics so that the settler families do not go hungry and destitute. As Julia Elyachar (2005) has argued, this "empowerment debt" is not empowering at all as petty commodity producers find themselves unable to get out of debt and are merely scraping by.

I do not seek to draw conclusions about whether state reclamation is achieving its objectives. There are clearly mixed outcomes and low-bar objectives, and such an assessment is beyond the scope of this chapter. My conclusion is that the trends found in state reclamation communities show a basic contradiction of frontier making as a way to solve the social problems associated with growing economic inequality. The very basic livelihood that state reclamation communities provide involves strategies (of development projects like WNRD as well as households) to earn income through integration into the corporate agri-food system. Whether settlers work as wage laborers for agribusiness or provide crops on demand or crops via contracts, settlers are pushed to do so because their livelihoods depend on it. The corporate agri-food system has, in turn, grown as state desert development integrated state reclamation communities, agribusiness, and corporate (and other) markets.

Conclusions

Under the food aid regime of the post-WWII period, in recipient countries like Egypt, food aid worked in tandem and in tension with agriculture supply management and other economic nationalist policies, broadly defined. The administration of Gamal Abdel Nasser—and what is referred more broadly to as Nasserism—attempted to build state sovereignty in the context of the Cold War and to achieve better terms of trade with Western countries via militarization and industrialization. The Nasser government faced intermittent threats from Western powers throughout the 1950s and 1960s, and, in turn, sought to build the Egyptian army and formal industrial growth directed to the national (rather than export) market. On the one hand, U.S. food aid aided the realization of a World War II-era food security initiative involving a national bread loaf; the expansion of the middle classes; and the building of national industries. On the other hand, food aid quickly led to food import dependency, becoming the basis of popular claims regarding state legitimacy as food prices became more tightly tied to the world market.

The state frontier, which had its beginnings in the interwar period after nominal independence in 1922, was institutionalized during the Nasser years, and can be understood as a key strategy of Nasser's economic nationalism. Reclaimed land was distributed to the landless, among others, and industrial, collective farms were built for the production of largely luxury goods (fruit, meat, etc.) for the middle classes in urban areas. State farms on reclaimed land and state reclamation communities were both concerned with the peasant subject as an object of improvement. The limitations of agrarian reforms in the Nile Valley and Delta justified the continued expansion of reclaimed lands, which, in turn, contributed to agrarian reform limitations.

The state frontier began to transform in the 1970s. The Bretton Woods system of the post-WWII period collapsed and capital from the West became available in former colonies. In the emerging sovereign debt crisis, the new Anwar

Sadat government both continued state reclamation and began to sell to investors reclaimed lands and farms. By the 1980s, under Hosni Mubarak, state and private reclamation became tied to a desert development program. This new frontier of capital differs from the state frontier and the colonial-era frontier of capital in that commodity production in the desert frontier is both for national markets, including the corporate food market, and for export abroad. Similar to the frontier of capital in the long nineteenth century, however, family business groups and finance return, making possible the rapid growth of the corporate agri-food system.

Notes

1. This new era is also referred to as a new global consensus—for example, a global Keynesianism (Borgwardt 2005).
2. For details of the three titles of PL 480, see Winders (2009: 148–149).
3. See González-Esteban (2018) on how decades of the food aid regime set the stage for food import dependency throughout the post-colonial countries.
4. The data on PL 480 to Egypt comes from the USAID (n.d.) greenbook.
5. Salem (2020: 2) argues that "Nasserism as a political project was formed through the radical movements of the 1930s and 1940s, produced in and through the global politics of decolonization, and representative of major shifts in elite nation-building in Egypt and the broader postcolonial world."
6. A leading visionary of the cooperative movement within the Ministry, Ibrahim Rashad (1939), defined a cooperative as an association "which workers themselves form to combat the ill effects of the Industrial Revolution on the working classes." For Rashad, a cooperative was a democratic institution "of the highest order."
7. This law gave the executive "military governors general" powers and was patterned on French and Belgian constitutional law (Schewe 2017: 51–52).
8. Notably, the government made a few private institutions (e.g., Barclay's bank) the legitimate buyers of wheat, and these institutions operated grain storage pits around the country (Schewe 2017: 51).
9. The reference to Middle Eastern countries is to Egypt, Iraq, and Syria (Warriner 1957).
10. Literature that deals with state land reclamation tends to relate it minimally, if at all, to agrarian reforms (e.g., Springborg 1979; Voll 1980; Allan 1983; Meyer 1998; Sowers 2011). Likewise, literature on agrarian reforms often gives little attention to land reclamation (e.g., Harik 1974; Abdel-Fadil 1975; Radwan 1977; Bush 2007).
11. The agreement was the General Agreement for Technical Cooperation under the Point IV Program, which was founded after U.S. President Harry S. Truman's inaugural speech. As Vitalis (1995: 184) described, Point IV was the institution through which the Truman and Eisenhower administrations paid for American business leaders, economists, engineers, and other technical consultants to help design and promote the 1952 Revolution's early industrialization initiatives.
12. By 1966, the Permanent Organization for Land Reclamation was consolidated with other agencies to form the Egyptian Authority for the Utilization and Development of Reclaimed Land (El Shakry 2007: 208).
13. For description and details of Tahrir Province, see El Shakry (2007: 207–212).

14. This estimate comes from Richards (1980: 8): The share of agriculture investment as a percentage of the total public capital expenditure rose from 11.6% in 1952–53 to 15.8% in 1967–68, but this percentage goes up to 25% when the Aswan Dam is included.
15. For the Nile Delta in comparison with other delta systems, see Syvitski (2008) and Syvitski et al. (2009).
16. When I was attending meetings and press releases concerning the counter agrarian reforms during the 2008–2011 period, endowed (*waqf*) lands were often at the center of discussion. In one meeting with a long-time activist, he claimed that most of the endowed lands were transferred as agrarian reform lands that were redistributed to peasants to buy (July 16, 2010, Cairo).
17. See Owen (1999) for an account of how cotton production became directed for national consumption at this time.
18. According to Saad (1988), the main studies refer to Harik (1974), Abdel-Fadil (1975), and Radwan (1977).
19. Glavanis (1990: 151) estimated that fertilizer use rose 300% between 1956 and 1967, and Richards (1980: 8) estimated that fertilizer use rose by 126% between 1952 and 1967.
20. Total PL 480 funds increased from a total of $144.2 million (historical) during the 1952–1960 period to $554.9 million during 1961–1967 (USAID n.d.).
21. On how Nasserism helped fuel the nascent processes of rural outmigration and informalization, see Abdel-Fadil (1975), Radwan (1977), and Bayat and Denis (2000).
22. Oil rents refer to the value of crude oil minus the total costs of production. The oil rent numbers come from the World Bank databank.
23. See Elyachar (2005) and Koptiuch (1999) on Egyptian workers abroad sending remittances home.
24. This misunderstanding about what the oil boom meant in Egypt is exemplified in Schechter (2019: 87), who writes that the rise in expenditure on subsidies (as a percentage of government expenditure) from 1970/71 to 1974 was "even more striking because Egypt was enjoying the windfall of oil-related earnings that were simultaneously increasing its GDP." This assertion fails to account for Egypt's oil imports; therefore, Schechter misses the complete picture of what an oil boom means for oil-exporting countries at the time like Egypt, Iran, and Venezuela.
25. The totals on external debt come from the World Bank databank.
26. See Mitchell (2002) on how the crisis of the mid-to-late 1980s unfolded in Egypt.
27. The New Valley was a name given to the series of depressions in the Western desert where it is punctuated by oases, stretching from Dakhla to Siwa. In the 1960s, the Nasser government launched a 20,000-acre reclamation pilot scheme there (Issawi 1963: 133).
28. Interviews, 10/3/2011, 10/12/2011, 11/29/2011, Cairo. See also Meyer (1998).
29. For more on this customary land right, see Cole and Altorki (1998).
30. Interview, 10/2/2011, Ismailia.
31. This ACDI-VOCA-Agrimatco-Heinz contract was arranged with various villages, not only in the villages in West Noubariya.

7
Ghosts of Finance Pasts

The Return of Finance and Family Business Groups

Before the January 25 uprising, it was common in Egypt to hear or read about someone touting their noble or elite past from pre-1952 independence. These claims of elite
ancestry were not always metaphorical or made in jest; they were also real. Some of
the same families even returned from the long nineteenth century—like ghosts. Family business groups and financial firms, in particular, re-emerged by the 1990s as two
of three structures that pattern capitalist development as Egypt integrates into the
expanded world economy and a type of private oligopoly develops within its borders.

These ostentatious displays were amplified by the close association publicly
between finance and Gamal Mubarak, son of the then President Hosni Mubarak.
The story of finance at the turn of the twenty-first century is, in fact, usually told
from the perspective of Gamal, who had an investment banking career in London
at Bank of America, and then, in 1996, formed an investment banking firm, leading to the formation of EFG-Hermes (MacFarquhar et al. 2011). EFG-Hermes is one
of the largest investment banks in the Middle East today, and Egyptian Financial
Group (EFG), established in 1984, had been a "key player in creating, analyzing and
managing the privatization program for the Government of Egypt" (Ismail 2009: 74).
Gamal Mubarak had risen within the ruling National Democratic Party (NDP) and
became head of the party's Policies Secretariat in 2002, paving the way for private
banks, especially foreign banks and investment banks, to increase their influence
(Roll 2010; Iyer 2011). This influence led to the passage of the 2003 banking law and
the administration of Prime Minister Ahmed Nazif beginning in 2004—an administration overwhelmingly made up of the patriarchs of the country's most powerful
family business groups.

The role of Gamal Mubarak is important to the rise of finance—but provides a
partial explanation at best. Focusing on Gamal Mubarak further obscures a contradiction of finance capital: On the one hand, there were public proclamations of the
righteousness of inherited wealth; on the other hand, there was an elusiveness of this
new capitalist class. Compared to the Central Bank and other banks from the colonial past that are difficult to miss in downtown Cairo, the investment banks, private
equity firms, and other new financial firms were nowhere to be found. During the
2008–2012 period, I attempted multiple times—and unsuccessfully—to meet with,
and interview, representatives of financial firms in Cairo. This apparent contradiction
reflects the constitution of their class power.

The Frontiers of Corporate Food in Egypt. Marion W. Dixon, Oxford University Press.
© Marion W. Dixon (2023). DOI: 10.1093/oso/9780192842985.003.0007

In this chapter, I rather offer a world-historical perspective on the emergence of this new capitalist class to further explain the development and growth of the corporate agri-food system in Egypt. I argue that the class power of finance capital is constituted through two related processes. The first is a basic tension: As they have attempted to cement their class position, doing so they have become a focus of subversive critiques of the arbitrary nature of their wealth and privilege. Hence, they attempted to conceal their wealth. Second, their power is constituted through a continual process of negotiation within a transnational framework of doing business legally and legitimately. Negotiating the many protocols and rules to participate in world trade and international investment—what I call the corporate standard.

I begin this chapter with an explanation of the class power of finance; why the particularly direct transmission of wealth and privilege makes them susceptible to popular critiques. I show how this class first emerged during the colonial-era food regime and went under the radar during the food aid regime of the post-colonial period. Then, I detail how they re-emerged in three stages to highlight the growth of the corporate agri-food system: 1970s–1980s—the rise of an agribusiness political coalition; 1991–2003—corporatization of the agri-food industry; and 2003–2011— financialization of the agri-food industry. Lastly, through participant observation at a consulting firm in Cairo, I show the intertwining of social networks, cultural institutions, kinship, and new types of economic exchange that was central to negotiating the corporate standard.

The Class Power of Finance

In establishing the role of finance in agriculture and food in Egypt, I follow Greta Krippner (2005) in examining long-term structural changes—in this case, to the Egyptian economy. However, rather than adopt an accumulation-centered perspective on where profits are generated, as Krippner (2005: 175–176) advocated, I analyze changes in the organization of economic activity (primarily through family business groups and new financial firms), the substance of those activities (the production of industrial, durable agri-foods), along with the political character of class (re-)formation, that is, the class power of the capitalist class. Further, I heed Krippner's (2011: 4) warning not to reify the distinction between finance and production, or between the speculative and the real economy (see also Fairbairn 2014).

Finance capital is shorthand in this chapter for the mutually reinforcing processes of sectoral financialization, or the growing role of the financial sector (as opposed to production and trade) for capital accumulation, and non-sectoral financialization, that is, the growing reliance on portfolio income among non-financial firms (Krippner 2005: 182). Sectoral financialization involves primarily the emergence of new actors (private equity firms, hedge funds, sovereign wealth funds, etc.) and new products and instruments (for example, so-called securitization) within the financial sector (Lawrence and Smith 2018: 31). Non-sectoral financialization refers to the growing reliance of non-financial firms on their own financial transactions (rather than on banks) as well as the growing reliance of banks on household borrowing (Lawrence and Smith 2018: 31).

In this chapter, the role of finance in the corporate agri-food system in Egypt, and the economy more generally, is placed within trans-Atlantic financialization since the 1970s, which heralded shifts in capital circuits worldwide (including shifts in the forms of capitalist economic enterprise and in class formation) (Arrighi 1994; Konings 2011). The first sovereign defaults of the 1980s led to a decade-long period of recurring banking, currency, and debt crises in Southern indebted countries and nearly two decades of relative economic stability in the Northern core (Figure 7.1).[1]

During the Northern boom–Southern crisis, the trans-Atlantic powers continued to liberalize their financial sectors. The launch of the euro and the liberalization of the European financial system encouraged financial trade within the Eurozone and across the Atlantic (Lane 2012). By the end of the 1990s, there were significant financial liberalization measures in the United States—including the repeal of the Glass-Steagall Act and the Commodity Futures Modernization Act (CFMA). Trans-Atlantic financialization meant not only that transnational and local banks could lend more (and that many banks grew exponentially), but that there was growth in new financial markets (securities and derivatives) (Clapp 2014). It was European banks that were active in purchasing asset-based securities in these markets, which likely accelerated the growth of the asset-based securities markets in the United States (Lane 2012). Concomitant to the securitization of the trans-Atlantic financial markets was the proliferation of private equity, hedge funds, and other financial firms (Clapp 2014).

Paradoxically, in Egypt, this Northern boom–Southern crisis led to record levels of economic growth as family business groups, MNCs, TNCs, and financial firms bought public enterprises and rapidly consolidated the formal economy, including the agri-food industry. Concerning how financialization has shaped the organization

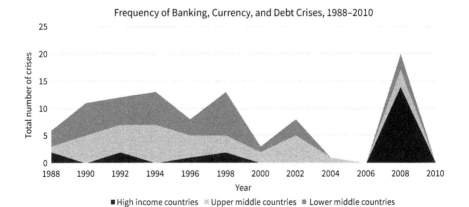

Figure 7.1 Frequency of banking, currency, and debt crises, 1988–2010.

Source: compiled from Broner et al. 2012.

of economic activity, I focus on the (re-)organization of capitalist enterprise into family business groups. Robert Vitalis's (1995: 22) definition of a business group during direct colonial rule and quasi-independence in Egypt is relevant here: First, a business group is defined as a diversity of firms or holdings across different economic sectors. Second, a business group is characterized by what Vitalis (1995: 22) referred to as an ownership–management coalition that often includes several individuals or families, though a single individual is typically identified as the group leader (or mistakenly taken as the sole owner). In contradistinction to the corporate model, which is based on the separation of ownership from management, in today's era of finance, "there is an indelible relation between the accumulation of corporate capital and the production and reproduction of great fortunes" (Carroll 2010: 133). For Vitalis (1995: 22), the third characteristic of a business group is that the core leadership is bound by personal, family, ethnic, or other communal ties.

In today's world, these great fortunes can be understood more specifically to be based on patriarchal kinship social units—or what Maurice Zeitlin and Richard E. Ratcliff (1988) called the kinecon group.[2] In short, the re-emergence of family business groups is not unique to Egypt. Rather, what Vitalis was describing in colonial Egypt became a common type of capitalist enterprise during the long nineteenth century. This type of capitalist enterprise became prominent around the world again by the 1990s—and has re-shaped social class systems (and social inequality).[3]

Finance capital as a political class is made up of the executives and owners (shareholders) of financial firms and of family business groups—and the networks or interlocks among them through family, education, and economic interests. In Bourdieu's (1986) terms, their power is exercised through their ability to convert various capitals (economic, social, cultural) into profits and future profits, and to use these capitals for accumulating even greater advantage through institutional mechanisms.[4] While this class is connected tightly to the centers of finance globally, and may accumulate capital primarily through global capital circuits (e.g., FDI and mergers and acquisitions across borders), they are indelibly tied to a country or region politically, socially, and culturally. In Carroll's (2010: 35) words, there is a certain disjuncture between class formation as a sociocultural process and the economic process of capital accumulation. Furthermore, both finance (M-M+) and kinship-based economic units as ways to accumulate wealth and privilege are the most direct, with few disruptions in the transmittal of forms of capital (Bourdieu 1986), and at the same time, defy most clearly any notions of meritocracy. Therein lies a tension in the constitution of their class power: Through socio-cultural practices and economic re-organization, they have attempted to cement their class position (Montgomerie 2008; Carroll 2010), but in doing so, they have become a focus of subversive critiques that bring to light the arbitrariness of their entitlement (Bourdieu 1986).

Cementing their class position through the growth and consolidation of the agriculture and food sectors, in particular, has been fraught. This is because of the double entendre of what McMichael (2000) called the power of food: Given food's material and symbolic functions that link nature, human survival, livelihoods, culture, and health, food becomes subject to greater capital concentrations, while also fostering resistance to growing corporate power. Although there are studies that implicate agrifood financialization in the explosion of trading on the commodity futures markets (Crotty 2005; Clapp 2014), literature on the financialization of agriculture and food largely misses this power.[5] It is through food that finance capital cements class power, while simultaneously and paradoxically undermining its class position.

Ghosts of Finance Pasts

One of the most ostentatious displays of wealth and privilege among the upper classes in Egypt before the 2011 uprising was Pashawi-ism, or identification among members of the upper class with being descendants of the former Pashas (colloquial for the upper class of the Ottoman and colonial eras). This self-identification was a way to claim rights to regain what was stolen under Nasserism in the 1950s and the 1960s. During my research in Egypt, it was not uncommon to hear, and to read commentary, about the losses of the colonial-era elites, who during the first half of the twentieth century built capitalist enterprises, which were later nationalized under Gamal Abdel Nasser.[6] The term pashawi-ism comes from a meeting that I had in Cairo with the head of one of the elite social networks, who was a self-proclaimed Pashawi.[7] There are well-known figures like Ahmad 'Abbud, the wealthiest and most politically influential Egyptian capitalist during the late colonial period, and the Bigio family, who owned the manufacturing facilities of Coca-Cola Egypt, who were put under house arrest following the 1952 coup and whose companies were later sequestered by the Nasser government—and who then went into life-long exile. However, the resurgence of Pashawi-ism indicates that at least some capitalists of the colonial and nominally independent eras were also able to retain assets during the nationalizations, as it is their descendants who were making such claims to privilege at the beginning of the twenty-first century.[8]

Conversely, there are stories of well-known capitalists coming back and recovering after the nationalizations. Perhaps most notably is Onsi Sawiris, who came from a landholding family and purportedly started a construction company that was nationalized in the 1960s. The Sawiris family is today's wealthiest billionaire family in Egypt. There is the Mansour family, also among the wealthiest billionaire families. Lofty Mansour is said to have founded a textile factory, which was later sequestered. One of Lofty's sons, Mohamed Mansour, became Minister of Transport under the Nazif administration in 2004.

There are prominent members of today's capitalist class who claim to be the direct descendants of elite families of the colonial and quasi-independence eras. For example, the former prime minister Ahmad Nazif is the grandson of the former undersecretary of the Ministry of Health under King Farouk of the quasi-independence era, and the Al Alfi family of Americana, one of the most significant agrifood MNCs, came from a landholding family during the colonial period. Yasser

El Mallawany, former CEO of EFG-Hermes, one of the largest investment banks in the Middle East, claimed to be the descendant of colonial-era industrialists. Also, widely disseminated are rags-to-riches stories of small-scale entrepreneurs like Uthman Ahmed uthman, who began accumulating capital in the colonial era and grew increasingly wealthy through the post-1952 independence era.

These so-called ghosts of finance pasts may be understood within the system of private oligopoly of the interwar period (Vitalis 1995). By the First World War, the local capitalist class had cross-sectoral holdings in banking, trade, urban real estate, cotton export, manufacturing and land reclamation companies, as well as plantations. Importantly, these capitalist enterprises were mostly organized as family-based investor coalitions (Vitalis 1995)—similar to today's family business groups. The investment strategies of the business groups that Vitalis (1995: 54) detailed are reflected in today's family business groups: They are highly diversified, with holdings in multiple economic sectors; tied deeply to foreign capital (namely, North American, European, and Gulf/Levant); and heavily reliant on public contracts, state subsidies, and other state supports. The oligopolistic character of the domestic economy today resembles the private oligopoly of the interwar period: Of the largest agribusinesses in Egypt during the 1970–2010 period, a handful of these corporations were established in the interwar period as private companies and were later nationalized under Nasser (e.g., Bisco Misr, Coca-Cola Egypt).[9] When these state-owned companies were privatized in the 1990s, most were not sold as privately held companies but were made public (IPO'd). These large public corporations are now controlled by their largest shareholders.

This trend in the agriculture and food sectors is part of a broader trend of privatizing state-owned enterprises (whether from the pre-1952 independence era or not), which generated considerable public opposition.[10] The sale of large-scale public assets to private owners or shareholders greatly expanded the market share of those investors who already had large shares, thereby, contributing to the waves of corporate consolidation of the Egyptian economy in the 1990s and 2000s.[11]

The character of the colonial-era political economy was consequential for how postcolonial developments and policies affected this small group of capitalists. For instance, studies of Nasser-era agrarian reforms confirm that, although they ended the landed estates, they ultimately failed to break the landlord class.[12] As was explained in Chapter 6, many loopholes remained in the mandated ceiling on privately held land (Bush 2007). Also, the government compensated the landlords for their sequestered land and property. Given that this class was largely organized as business groups, it is then imaginable how they would have been able to hold on to some of their assets even if one property (land or company) was sequestered. In short, those who stayed in Egypt, or left temporarily and returned, were well-connected and/or had enough wealth to send their children to elite educational institutions in order to be able to take advantage of the economic transformations during the three phases of the growth of the corporate agri-food system, from the 1970s onward.

1970s–1980s: Rise of the Agribusiness Political Coalition

Rising debt levels in the 1970s that spawned the first set of liberalization and privatization measures under the Anwar Sadat administration also bore an agribusiness coalition. This coalition was mostly made up of the Pasha landlord class, public contractors who grew under the Nasser government (i.e. those who built businesses via import substitution), rich peasants, and a new class of agricultural capitalists. Among the agricultural capitalists were former government officials and military officers who bought privatized state enterprises and/or reclaimed land. This class was also made of Egyptian investors who joined public firms and (to a lesser extent) foreign firms to invest within the agri-food industry. Public contractors, who perhaps benefited the most from import substitution during the Nasser years, were among the first investors to diversify their portfolios—and into agriculture and food.[13]

During this phase of the corporate agri-food system's development, the agribusiness political coalition benefited from, and helped push through, policies that relaxed trade barriers, tax regulations, and bank credit; liberalized the land, especially reclaimed land; and promoted investments in industrial agriculture on reclaimed land. For instance, in 1981, Sadat decreed Public Law 143, containing a number of investor incentives including the right of joint-venture companies to own thousands of acres of reclaimed land (Springborg 1990).

Also, USAID instituted a number of projects with the Egyptian government, namely, to support the growth of industrial agriculture (horticulture and animal husbandry) and the agroexport market. For example, the California Project (1979–1983) developed seed varieties and production technologies for various horticulture crops. Immediately following the California Project was USAID's Egypt Major Cereals Improvement Project (EMCIP), which focused on the seed development of crops that are used largely for animal feed (corn, sorghum, soybean) (Finkner 1983; Harwig 1983). Moreover, the Overseas Private Investment Corporation (OPIC) of the U.S. government, the International Finance Corporation (IFC) of the World Bank, and the Egyptian Agricultural Credit Bank all heavily financed the development of the poultry industry (Freivalds 1982; see Chapter 8 for more details).

According to Robert Springborg (1990), by the early-mid 1980s, horticulture crop production was dominated by large-scale capitalist farmers in the old lands and a new class of agricultural capitalists in the desert frontier. The agricultural capitalists in the desert frontier were also heavily involved in animal agriculture. In 1982, there were 35 companies, public and private, with holdings in excess of 50 acres, totaling about 347,000 acres of agricultural land. By the end of 1982, of the joint-venture agri-industrial projects, the Egyptian government provided 29–40% of the total investment capital, private Egyptian investors 40%, and foreign individuals and companies 20% (Springborg 1990: 454–455). There were only a few dozen joint ventures between Egyptian firms and foreign firms; one example is Vitrac, a manufacturer of fruit preserves owned by French and Egyptian private investors (Springborg 1990: 454–455).

A number of the largest agribusinesses at the turn of the twenty-first century started at this time. One well-known example is the agricultural capitalist who is considered the father of the agroexport market in Egypt and who later formed one of the largest family business groups in the country: the Diab family's PICO group. The father Diab was a former state official and got a hold of reclaimed land in the state reclamation community, Tahrir, and became one of the early agroexporters. Another example is Ismailia Misr Poultry, which was one of the largest poultry companies in the country during the 2008–2012 period. A former officer of the state Poultry Company founded Ismailia Misr Poultry in 1977. This officer with a group of other officers expanded production by purchasing 1,380 acres of reclaimed land near to the Suez Canal with a capital advance from the IFC in 1979 (Sjerven 1986).

A second investment trend was of joint ventures: Egyptian investors joined public firms and (to a lesser extent) foreign firms to invest in the agri-food industry. One well-known example is of Americana, a regional agribusiness chaired by the billionaire Kuwaiti Al-Kharafi family and founded by the Egyptian billionaire Moataz Al-Alfi. During the 1970–2010 period, Americana was the fourth largest agribusiness in Egypt.[14] Americana began operations in Egypt in the 1970s, and among other investments opened up a beef factory in the early 1980s. Another example is the Wadi Group: The Wadis are Lebanese capitalists who came to Egypt in the early 1980s during the Lebanese civil war and began with investments in poultry.

A third trend was of public contractors diversifying their portfolios in agriculture and food. One well-known example is Uthman Ahmed Uthman, founder of the Arab Contractors Company, who had multiple investments in the agri-food industry— livestock, fish farming, poultry, food retail, and so on (Sadowski 1991). As Yahya Sadowski (1991) detailed, Uthman and his company benefited from state reclamation as the company was granted free land as part of Sadat's Green Revolution.

Agribusiness as a political coalition grew during the 1970s and 1980s not only through the tax, banking, and land laws, but also through a set of social networks and cultural institutions that began to normalize the transmission of wealth and privilege within Egyptian society. In the early-mid 1970s, when the first joint banks (Egyptian-foreign) were created and foreign investors were permitted to invest in Egypt with Egyptian partners, the U.S. government created the Egyptian-American Business Council for Americans and American companies doing business in the country and the Egyptian agents of foreign capital. Then, in 1981, local businessmen, with support from the U.S. Embassy, formed the American Chamber of Commerce, which was independent from government control. The next year the Egyptian Businessmen's Association was formed from meetings between the Egyptian government and the Egyptian-American Businessmen's Association (Sadowski 1991: 194–195). Through the establishment of this new generation of autonomous business organizations, for which the American Chamber of Commerce in Cairo was the model, the class of agricultural capitalists, and more generally capitalist classes, gained political influence (Sadowski 1991).

When Yousef Wali became Minister of Agriculture and Land Reclamation in the early 1980s, the ruling NDP became closely associated with agribusiness, who became particularly influential as lobbyists in the NDP's Agricultural Committee and Economic Committee (Sadowski 1991). Many of these agribusiness groups (e.g., poultry breeders, agroexporters, and others) developed into institutionalized, independent lobbies and their political influence grew substantially. While the presence of foreign agribusiness did not grow in the 1980s (Springborg 1990), nor did the agroexport market appear to have grown much, the political coalition grew as the animal protein complex and food processing grew with the establishment of the industrial zones in the desert frontier beginning in the early 1980s.

These initial social and cultural institutions were important, not only to the growth of political power and influence of agribusiness, but also for the creation of an infrastructure for Egyptian agribusiness to negotiate the growing sets of rules and protocols of corporate retailers and Western states. This so-called corporate standard would increasingly come to govern the growth of the corporate agri-food system, particularly by the turn of the twenty-first century.

1991–2003: Corporatization of the Agri-food Industry

The second phase—of corporatization of family business groups and non-sectoral financialization—is tied directly to the Economic Reform and Structural Adjustment Programme (ERSAP) of 1991, which was passed to resolve Egypt's sovereign debt crisis. ERSAP led to a rapid increase in liquidity, which enabled family business groups to expand. The stock exchange re-opened and the exchange rate was floated, leading to interest rates on the Egyptian pound being higher than on the U.S. dollar to attract capital inflows (Berthélemy and Bentahar 2004; Roll 2010). ERSAP also paved the way for the (re-)entry of TNCs and MNCs and the country joining the WTO in 1995 (along with the bi- and multi-lateral trade agreements that followed).

Growing competition led to both the corporatization of family business groups and non-sectoral financialization. Corporatization refers to companies being bought and sold through a legal framework of mergers and acquisitions; separating (to some extent) ownership and management with the establishment of a Board of Directors; instituting legally binding regulatory and accounting procedures; and (possibly) becoming a publicly traded company on the stock exchange through a set of reviews, value assessments, and so on. Corporatization also refers to the general process by which a transnational framework of doing business legally and legitimately increasingly governs Egyptian family business groups.

Concerning non-sectoral financialization, family business groups began to set up their own investment firms. For example, the Mansour family (the two heads, Mohamed and Yasseen), joined their cousins in the Maghraby family in 1996 to form Mansour-Maghraby Investment and Development (MMID). In 2001, MMID became an important shareholder in EFG-Hermes, the investment firm connected to the Mubaraks. In 2004, Rashid Mohamed Rashid, who at the time was the head of Unilever Mashreq (a Middle East Foods and the Home and Personal Care Division of the Unilever Group International), also bought into the investment bank. That same year Ahmed Nazif became Prime Minister, and Rashid Mohamed Rashid, Mohamed Mansour, and Ahmed Maghraby all became ministers in the newly formed Nazif administration.

In agriculture and food, these policy shifts led to a handful of TNCs and MNCs re-entering the country and existing agri-food companies expanding their market shares. Family business groups diversified into and within agribusiness either vertically or horizontally, in competition as well as in cooperation with TNCs and MNCs. For example, family business groups bought into state-held food companies. Under the Public Enterprise Law of 1991, about 13 publicly owned agribusinesses were privatized. Family business groups also began to buy into fast food franchises. A handful of agribusiness executives and representatives that I interviewed in 2011 had captured a significant share of the poultry industry before moving into the agroexport market and/or food processing.

Also, after Egypt joined the WTO in 1995 and the Common Market for Eastern and Southern Africa (COMESA) in 1998, and signed bi- and multi-lateral trade agreements, the country became a trading hub of agri-food corporations. Corporations began: importing food (and other) inputs into the country, or buying crops produced in the country; packaging/processing them; and then selling them to super/hypermarkets in the Middle East, the European Union, and/or North America. For example, the EU-Egypt Association Agreement of 2004 stipulates that Egyptian industrial products enter the EU with no tariffs or quotas and that Egypt liberalizes trade and tariff barriers over twelve years to allow the entry of European products.

The political coalition that formed during this second phase is often referred to as the business lobby. Immediately after Parliament pushed through ERSAP in 1991, family business groups and others promoting greater financialization formed the Egyptian Centre for Economic Research, a think tank which became the "conceptual and ideological mastermind behind the second phase of economic reforms [beginning in 2003]" (Roll 2010: 363). Groups with investments in the agri-food industry, in particular, yielded considerable political influence. For example, beginning in the mid-1990s, Americana was the largest contributor to the NDP. And Americana spread its social influence through interlocking directorates: The chairman, Moataz Al Alfi, was also a member of the Board of Directors of the Centre for Economic Research, the director of the Cairo Poultry Company (one of the largest poultry companies in Egypt), the CEO of Egypt Kuwait Holding (a private equity firm) and the vice chairman of the Board of Trustees at American University in Cairo, among other titles. The brother of Moataz, Sayed Al Alfi, was the former treasurer of the NDP. According to one interviewee within the Ministry of Trade and Industry, once Sayed became treasurer of the NDP, Americana Group contributions to the party rose considerably.[15]

The rise of this so-called business lobby by the 1990s should also be placed in the context of the growing military business. By the mid-1980s, the Egyptian military lost revenue and aid, as was discussed in Chapter 6. Abul-Magd (2017: 116) argues that this structural loss led Egyptian officers to "covert the military industrial complex into the production of civilian goods," including food (and especially bread).

2003–2011: Financialization of the Agrifood Industry

The economic boom in the trans-Atlantic world from roughly 2003–04 to 2007–08 was short-lived but in many ways far surpassed the economic boom of the 1990s in its reach and depth (see Figure 7.1 on the steep decline in crises globally between these years). Because the proliferation of cheap debt financing characterized this upswing, it is often referred to as a securitization boom (Lane 2012; Clapp 2014). Financial liberalization measures were being implemented around the world. Global private equity alone grew threefold: from $141.7 billion in 2004 to $445 billion in 2008 (Ismail 2009: 13). In the MENA region, financial liberalization—as measured in terms of the level of stock market capitalization, the level of competition in banking, and so on (El Safti 2007)—was uneven and comparatively significant. The extent of financialization in the region prior to 2003 was low compared to East and Southeast Asia and Latin America (Kaminsky and Schmukler 2003; Creane et al. 2004: 13).

What spawned this global economic boom? Merely one year after record global FDI levels in 2000 (UNCTAD 2001: 1), the economic bubble (of the 1990s) burst as the United States became embroiled in large-scale corporate accounting fraud scandals and the ensuing dot-com crash (as well as the September 11, 2001 terrorist attacks). The US-centered economic downturn was short-lived: Gross capital flows in the United States increased markedly between 2002 and 2004 (Broner et al. 2012) as the government attacked and occupied Afghanistan and then Iraq. Furthermore, the U.S. government's response was weak in terms of placing controls on financial market expansion through stricter accounting measures and the like.[16] During the economic upswing, capital flows were increasingly, and on an unprecedented scale, directed to so-called emerging markets, especially the east-Asian region as it recovered from the 1997–98 sovereign debt crisis (UNCTAD 2004; Lane 2012). Nonetheless, most capital flows remained transatlantic, between the United States and Europe (Tooze 2018).[17]

Countries in the MENA region responded to the increase in global capital flows by passing increasingly potent financial liberalization measures. In Egypt, banking reform was passed in 2003, and in the Gulf Cooperation Council a series of financial liberalization measures were passed in 2004 alone (UNCTAD 2005: 282). While a Wall Street-led campaign against financial regulation had pointed to this growth in capital inflows outside the Triad—North America, the European Union, and Japan—as evidence that regulations were scaring away investment in the United States (Stoltenberg et al. 2011), growing investments in the MENA region (and other regions) is said to have helped fuel the economic boom in the United States and Europe (see Lane 2012).

The US-centered economic downturn and political scandals of 2001–02 spawned an economic downturn in Egypt, and the 2003 Unified Banking Law was justified as a means to stabilize prices in the context of growing inflation (Iyer 2011). The 2003 United Banking Law departed significantly from previous finance reforms because it expanded the Central Bank's authority and authorized the selling of public banks (via joint mergers) and the mergers of private banks. These policy measures led to significant foreign capital penetration: transnational banks (such as Barclays, Credit Agricole, Société Générale) and regional banks (including Greek bank Piraeus, Lebanese bank BLOM, Abu Dhabi Islamic Bank, and the National Bank of Kuwait) played a key role in consolidation of the banking sector. Also, select private Egyptian banks bought existing (private/public) banks—and these banks were largely investment banks, like MMID (Global Investment House 2008). In terms of market capitalization, the capitalization to GDP ratio rose significantly: from $28 billion in 2002 (29% of GDP) to $82 billion in 2010 (40% of GDP) (Diwan and Chekir 2014: 12). Accompanying the exponential increase in the value of newly formed publicly traded corporations was a sharp increase in FDI from 2003–04, and FDI, with the largest sources from the United States and United Arab Emirates, continued to go upward only dipping slightly after 2007–08 (Kapadia 2011: 47).

The 2003 law also precipitated the rapid growth of private equity funds, which rose from $533 million in 2004 to $6.4 billion in 2008 (Ismail 2009: 16, 61). Most private equity funds in Egypt are created with private co-investors (generally sovereign wealth funds, institutional funds (such as pension funds), and Gulf investors with the firm's managers, who generally commit 10–20% of the funds, and institutional investors like the IFC. In fact, the IFC and other institutional lenders have been major guarantors of private equity activity in so-called emerging markets like Egypt (Daniel 2012: 722).

From roughly 2003 to 2011, the corporate agri-food system underwent a third wave of growth and consolidation, as financial firms (especially private equity) began to invest in the agrifood industry—and in the formal economy, more generally. Financial firms' mergers and acquisitions in the agri-food industry followed from the 2003 banking law and grew exponentially after the 2007–08 crisis (and until 2011), when food prices rose and were expected to continue to rise in the long term (Table 7.1). The primary activity of private equity is acquiring large companies (including formerly state-owned ones) in order to make them more competitive

Table 7.1 Sample of mergers and acquisitions within the Egyptian agri-food industry

1993	Coca-Cola (re-)acquires Coca-Cola Egypt
1997	Cadbury buys Bim
2000	Best foods/Unilever partly acquires Rashidi El-Mizan
2000	Bongrain partly acquires Rachid Mashreq[a]
2001	Ajwa acquires Safola Oil[b]

Continued

Table 7.1 *Continued*

2001	Tasty Foods/Pepsico acquires Chipsy[c]
2002	Ajwa acquires Basma[d]
2002	Heineken acquires Al-ahram beverages[e]
2002	Hero acquires Vitrac[f]
2003	Kraft foods acquires Family Nutrition[g]
2003	Unilever partly acquires Fine Foods[h]
2003	Danone joins Rachid Mashreq
2003	Cadbury Schweppes acquires SONUT[i]
2003	Actis acquires Rashidi El-Mizan from Unilever
2004	Americana acquires Greenland
2005	Haykala acquires Enjoy
2005	Concord International Investments acquires majority stake in Bisco Misr[j]
2006	Haykala acquires Honeywell
2007	Citadel Capital's Gozour acquires Dina Farms
2007	EFG-Hermes acquires Al Misrieen
2007	EFG-Hermes acquires minority stake in Adita
2008	Actis acquires minority stake in Mo'men Group[k]
2008	Gozour acquires Rashidi El-Mizan from Actis
2008	Gozour acquires Al-Misrieen from EFG-Hermes
2008	Gozour acquires minority stake in National Company for Maize Products
2008	Gozour acquires majority stake in Mom's Food
2008	Gozour acquires Al Aguizy Farms
2009	Gozour acquires Enjoy from Haykala
2009	EFG-Hermes acquires minority stake in Wadi Foods
2009	EFG-Hermes acquires Sokhna Beef
2009	Almarai and Pepsi acquire Beyti[l]
2015	Kellogg acquires Bisco Misr
2015	Hagag Group acquires El Misrieen
2015	Olayan Financing Co. (Saudi) acquires Rashidi El-Mizan

[a] Bongrain is a French food multinational corporation (MNC) and Rachid Mashreq is the consumer goods company of the Rachid family.
[b] Ajwaa Group for Food Industries is a Saudi company.
[c] Chipsy was a leading potato chip producer.
[d] Basmah was a leading frozen fruits and vegetables company.
[e] Al-ahram beverages was the dominant Egyptian alcoholic beverages company.
[f] Hero is a Swiss food MNC and Vitrac was a leading fruit product company.
[g] Family Nutrition was a leading biscuits producer.
[h] Fine Foods was a member of the Rachid group.
[i] SONUT is part of the SONID group, an Egyptian investment group.
[j] Bisco Misr was the leading public company of baked goods and confectionary.
[k] Mo'men Group is a large agro-food family conglomerate.
[l] Almarai is a Saudi food MNC and Beyti is one of the leading dairy and juice companies.
Note: shaded rows indicate financial sector activity
Source: compiled from IMC (2005); Schurgott (2008); HC Brokerage (2009); Ismail (2009); Citadel Capital (2010); EFG-Hermes (2010); Roll (2010); *PR Newswire* (January 15, 2015); *Qalaa Holdings* (November 10, 2015); *Mubasher* (December 10, 2015).

by increasing their size and/or their geographical reach and, then, re-selling them to corporations or other financial firms.

Citadel Capital (aka Qalaa Holdings)

The private equity firm Citadel Capital (CC) (now an investment bank, Qalaa Holdings) created the largest holding company within the agri-food industry, Gozour, during the 2003–2011 period, "with the purpose of creating a vertically integrated regional agriculture and multi-category consumer foods conglomerate with primary lines of business" (Ismail 2009: 178; see also Citadel Capital 2010). Until 2015, when Citadel Capital changed to an investment bank and began divesting from Gozour, the holding company was made up of three integrated parts: agri-foods and dairy (Gozour Agri), fast-moving consumer goods (Gozour Foods), and intermediate industries such as sugar and corn processing (Gozour Intermediate). For example, Gozour first acquired (and then sold) Dina Farms, the largest private farm with nearly 10,000 acres, which supplied the milk of Enjoy, one of the largest producers of packaged milk, juices, and yogurt at the time. Gozour combined the packaging facilities of Mom's Food and Enjoy, and Enjoy was in-line to supply Al Misrieen, a cheese and juice company, with fruit juices. Citadel Capital had plans not only to integrate its companies but to expand them. The history of Rashidi El Mizan, the leading sesame producer in the country, is illustrative: Gozour had been expanding Rashidi El Mizan since buying the company from private equity firm Actis in 2008. Rashidi El Mizan had since gained a near monopoly of the sesame product market, with 60% of the halawa market and 80% of the tahina market. Then, Rashidi El Mizan acquired a majority stake in al Musharraf, one of the largest producers of biscuits and sweets in Sudan.

When world commodity prices rose sharply in 2007, many investors began to invest in agricultural land. Citadel Capital was one of them: In 2007, the firm created the Wafra Portfolio company. In the first years of its founding, Wafra included three agricultural companies (Figure 7.2): the Sabina Company, which held a 30-year lease on 254,000 acres of irrigated land near to Kosti, Sudan, a river port owned by Keer Marine (Citadel Capital's Portfolio Company), on the White Nile and not far from Khartoum. The Concord Company, formerly the Sudanese Egyptian Agricultural Crops Company (SEAC), held a 25-year lease on about 250,000 acres of rain-fed land in the Unity State of South Sudan. The third company, El-Nahda for Integrated Solutions, signed a 30-year lease on 60,000 acres of land in Ed Dueim, on the White Nile and 150 kilometres south of Khartoum. All three agricultural projects were for cash crop production. In 2011, Sabina had harvested over 2,000 acres of wheat. Concord would grow cash crops like rice, corn, mung beans, chickpeas, soybeans, oil seeds and grain legumes. Citadel Capital announced that Concord would seed 4,000 acres for corn by mid-2011. El-Nahda planned to build a large-scale commercial rice farm.

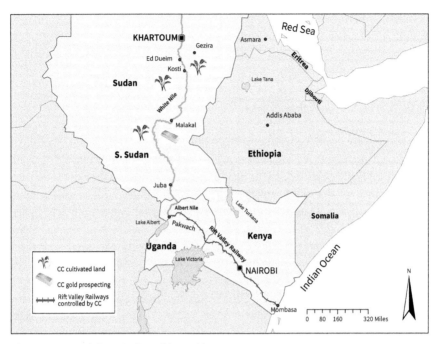

Figure 7.2 Citadel Capital's Gold Corridor.
Source: Johannes Plambeck.

At the same time, Citadel Capital made major investments in so-called green transport in the region largely through its MENA Joint Investment Funds (JIFs), which had been supported by the IFC and other international finance institutions like the European Investment Bank (EIB). In 2009, the IFC made a commitment of up to $25 million in the firm's MENA Joint Investment Funds (IFC 2009). These funds were to invest two U.S. dollars for every dollar Citadel Capital invested. Although the firm was primarily investing with private co-investors, in 2010, institutional investors made "substantial new investments via the JIFs" (Citadel Capital 2010: 65). That year Citadel Capital acquired a 51% stake in Rift Valley Railways, which held a 25-year concession to operate more than 2,300 kilometers of railway built by the British colonial state from the port of Mombasa into Kenya and Uganda. In 2011, institutional investors committed $164 million for the restructuring of Rift Valley Railways. Also, the firm's Green Transport platform, of which its Nile Logistics platform was a shareholder, received institutional investor support ($21 million) from the German Development Finance Institution (DEG) and the EIB. Nile Logistics invests in river transport via barrages along the Nile in Egypt (via its Nile Cargo company) and the White Nile in Sudan and South Sudan (via its Keer Marine company).

The acquisition of Rift Valley Railways coupled with the Nile Logistics companies would theoretically enable the firm to control the movement of commodities (and people) from the Mediterranean Sea to the port of Mombasa on the Indian Ocean (what I call the Gold Corridor, Figure 7.2). Facing criticism (see Sadek 2012), Citadel

Capital asserted that they would cultivate and control only a portion of the Sabina land, as Sabina was a joint development project with the area's residents, who would be allotted part of the land over the next decade (potentially over 20,000 acres by the end of 2019) (HC Brokerage 2009). Also, Citadel Capital insisted that production of cash crops at both Sabina and Concord would be for local markets in apparent accordance with Sudanese law. However, the law stated that only 30% of agricultural output needs to be sold locally (HC Brokerage 2009). The firm stated that it had expected returns of 15–20% and had already sold its first Sabina wheat harvest at rates 25–30% higher than international prices. These high returns can be explained in part by Keer Marine's contract renewal with the UN World Food Programme to transport food aid throughout Sudan. Concord announced that it would sell its crops to the UN as well as the South Sudanese army, in a region where millions faced hunger and starvation (Laessing 2012).

Citadel Capital's cereal production was not only for local markets, however. It was also likely for export markets (in the Gulf primarily) and for its own food processing companies (in Sudan and Egypt and potentially other neighboring countries). The firm had already been expanding its agri-food companies regionally, and after acquiring a majority stake in Rift Valley Railways, the firm was trying to buy Kenyan agri-food companies and arable land for wheat and rice farming (Irungu 2010).

A year after the 2011 uprising, the firm reported that between 2010 and 2012, its investments in Egypt dropped by 7% points while they doubled in South Sudan (from 2% to 4%) and rose by a third in Sudan (from 9% to 12%). The firm was transitioning from a private equity firm to an investment firm that acts as a long-term principal investor. Their investments toward integration responded to other investors (especially Gulf states) seeking to secure food offshore with the looming threat of political unrest at home (Arnold and al Sayegh 2013), and to rising oil prices, with the expansion of markets for alternative forms of transport (river, rail) and alternative forms of energy. More than this, their investments anticipated and precipitated the growth of corporate agri-food industries throughout the COMESA trading bloc. Wheat, corn, and sugar production would largely be designated for animal protein and food processing for the consumer market of the middle and upper classes, while the poor and displaced would remain chronically food insecure. As the manager of Concord said, regarding the South Kordofan refugees who were camped next to the farm, "They will need to be fed" (Laessing 2012).

The Corporate Standard

The growth of finance in Egypt—and the corporatization of the formal economy, more generally—occurred not only through policy changes that increased capital flows, but also through the intertwining of types of economic exchange (e.g., mergers and acquisitions) with social networks, cultural institutions, and kinship. This intertwining enabled both the growth of the corporate agri-food system and greater class cohesion among this so-called business lobby. Greater class cohesion was important to being able to take advantage of the structural shifts in the Egyptian economy via membership in the WTO, bi- and multi-lateral trade agreements, and continued structural adjustments. The local business associations and think tanks that formed in the 1980s and 1990s set the foundations for these social networks and cultural institutions.

The social networks were made up not only of the CEOs and managers of family business groups, financial firms, and other corporations, but also government officials, ambassadors, and other embassy officials, NGO leaders, among others. One of the most well-known elite gatherings was the American Chamber of Commerce's monthly luncheon, which usually featured a keynote address by a prominent member of the government with business members, embassy officials, and others present. These kinds of meet-n-greets, which had been a cornerstone of American aid in the region (Dixon 2011), were usually on the theme of business development, social entrepreneurship, education, and youth leadership.

One of the new think tanks representing the interests of the financial firms was Global Trade Matters (GTM), which described itself as an organization concerned with "economic policy and reform." GTM organized conferences, seminars, and award ceremonies among the who's who of the economic elite. In 2010, GTM hosted the Egyptian Business Oscars—and all the familiar actors within finance were there: Best CEO Under 40—Hisham El Khazindar, CEO of Citadel Capital; Best Company Overall—Commercial International Bank; and Best Investment Bank—CIB's CI Capital Holding. As a member of the GTM network said, "We are one big family."[18]

EFG-Hermes was at the center of this emerging class of finance. Many of the heads of private equity firms worked for EFG-Hermes at some point (Figure 7.3). Hassan Heikal, the former CEO of EFG-Hermes, is the brother of Ahmed Heikal, the co-founder of Citadel Capital. Ahmed Heikal was former Managing Director of EFG-Hermes Private Equity, and the other co-founder of Citadel Capital, Hisham El-Khazindar, was an Executive Director of Investment Banking at EFG-Hermes. Those associated with EFG-Hermes often have backgrounds in the world centers of finance: for example, Aladdin Saba and Aly El-Tahry, the co-founders of Beltone Financial, "one of the fastest growing financial services firms in the region" (Ismail 2009: 78) during the 2008–2011 period, both worked on Wall Street before returning to Egypt to form Hermes Financial. When Hermes Financial merged with EFG, Saba and El-Tahry became managers of EFG-Hermes.

From November 2009 to July 2010, while I was conducting participant observation at a consulting firm in the commercial district of Mohandiseen, social networking events were constant. Meet-and-greets, award ceremonies, and the like were hosted not only by local associations and think tanks but foreign ones as well. For example, during that time period, the Qatar Foundation hosted the 2010 World Innovation Summit for Education (WISE) in Doha, bringing together business leaders, educators, state officials, civil society members and others to discuss so-called innovations within the education sector. Also, in 2010, the British Council launched its International Young Creative Entrepreneur programme in Egypt and a host of other former

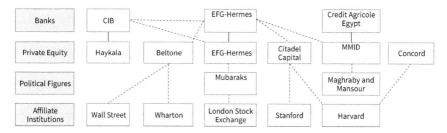

Figure 7.3 EFG-Hermes at the Center of Finance: sample of financial institutions and their affiliate ties.

Note: dotted lines indicate informal ties through individual work, family, or education.

colonies that sought to "showcase international business innovation in the field of interactive entertainment and media using the UK as the nexus for cultural, creative and commercial exchange."

This social networking occurred among individuals who, in Bourdieu's (1986) terms, had acquired dispositions through upbringing or embodied cultural capital. Embodied cultural capital was more apparent among the younger generations of CEOs and sons of family business groups as well as the political elite and military elite. It was not uncommon for the sons and daughters of those in the power elite—i.e., the highest echelons of the corporations, state, and military—to get their undergraduate degrees from the American University in Cairo or the American University in Beirut. Graduates of either one of the American universities, or one of the new private business and technical universities that sprung up in the desert frontier since the 1990s (e.g., German University of Egypt), may also be considered to make up the new cadres of managers and professionals. If the younger executives did not get a degree from an English-medium university, they were likely to obtain a second degree from the centers of knowledge production globally. Returning to the finance capitalists, many were educated at elite business schools. Beltone's Saba has an MBA from Wharton. The founder of Concord Investments International Group, Mohamed Younis, and Citadel's El-Khazindar both have MBAs from Harvard Business School (Figure 7.3).

For Bourdieu (1986), embodied capital is not just habitus, or acquired perception, thought, and action, but can also be of a scientific or technical type and can be in person or by proxy. In other words, members of the power elite may have educational qualifications and may also have access to managers, experts and others who have needed skills to carry out the day-to-day operations. For example, although most agribusinesses in the agroexport market are corporatized family business groups with family members running parts of the group, they hire managers with experience in the agroexport market to run their farms.

Social capital and cultural capital (through schooling, for example) work together in any exchange that presupposes and produces mutual knowledge and recognition (Bourdieu 1986: 250). The interlocking directorates, which are common in the formal economy, are also important to producing this mutual knowledge and recognition.[19]

And mutual knowledge and recognition are at the heart of what I am referring to as the corporate standard, or the set of rules, protocols, ideologies through which Egyptian actors and institutions participate in the world economy.

The head of the consultancy in Mohandiseen, "the doctor," was a trained medical doctor and member of a business family.[20] The doctor would meet on a weekly basis, sometimes several times a week, with people occupying high-level positions within universities, multinational corporations, embassies, the Egyptian government, Egyptian NGOs, INGOs, and foundations. He would hold the meetings in his large office with marble floors, a finely polished wooden desk and glass doors leading to a balcony facing the lush side streets of Mohandiseen's commercial district. In one such meeting, in February 2010, the doctor was meeting with a British professor of business, who was heading a new private university in Egypt. We sat on upholstered leather couch and chairs; to our side was a large ornate Quran resting on a tall wooden stand and a large bookshelf with a row or two of the latest management guru books. The doctor, dressed in a signature polo shirt, introduced himself to the professor in clear, articulate English as the son of a medical doctor, raised in the United Kingdom, educated in medical school at Cairo University and trained in New York. The British professor told us his story of promoting social entrepreneurship in Egypt and quickly spoke in earnest of the problems that he has faced. In this meeting, and in all the meetings in which I was present, there was mutual recognition that those in the exchange were not part of the problem. Not only did mutual knowledge and recognition make these kinds of meetings intelligible, but the new types of economic exchange in this restructured economy also depended on mutual knowledge and recognition.

For every meeting, talk, and event that the doctor was invited to there were announcements of competitive bids for private companies to perform a service for the state or for another private company, or there were foreign universities, embassies, and companies looking for local partners to co-invest. All these potential business opportunities were institutionalized via so-called best practice contracts. For example, there were regular public announcements of public private partnerships (PPPs); within a three-month period, I read more than six PPP bid announcements from the Egyptian government. The announcements were international bids to assess, plan, construct, or upgrade, and possibly run infrastructure or other large-scale projects (e.g., a wastewater facility). The contracts were issued by, say, the Ministry of Health, the Ministry of Housing, the Ministry of Aviation, or the Ministry of Public Works and often in partnership with institutional investors (e.g., the European Development Bank). The investor would loan the private contractor money to fulfill the contract and the investor often had some role in overseeing the competitive bid process. The contractor then issued a lease to the government for use of the infrastructure or the provision of a service, or the government would buy (full) rights from the contractor.

The biggest corporations were often the only bidders who could meet the contract expectations. For example, in one bid to consult on the conception of the implementation of a Medical City in 6th of October city (a project of the Ministry of Health and a consortium of British investors), to even be considered for the competition, there had to be a three-member consultancy team: an Egyptian firm, a firm that focuses in the medical field, and most importantly, one of the Big Five auditing and financial consultancy TNCs. The doctor's firm was unable to win this or any other PPP contract, because public–private contracts are really a reserve of the Big Five TNC contractors, the largest TNC construction contractors, and their local partners, who are among the most capitalized firms.

The set of expectations that standardized the competitive process of these best practice contracts exist in virtuality (Deleuze 1990 cited in Braun 2007), not in the sense that the standards (against which the expectations are made) do not exist but that they are known and not realizable. Thus, their effects are real. A corporate body or two set the standards, and in this way, they appear Western. An Egyptian agribusiness that wants to supply a European food retailer, for example, produces according to the retailer standards. Not only are these standards not actually realized as such (there may be practices that violate the retailers' codes, for example), but they then reproduce the group's limits (the few elite agribusinesses that actually supply to European retailers), as is detailed in Chapter 8. This economy of appearances (Tsing 2005) appears as the continual production of a false image of the standard. A manager of an Egyptian agribusiness that has acquired all the retailer certifications (e.g., Global Gap) confided to me that in the weeks and days leading up to the visit by the certifiers they would frantically put together an image of compliance. In that year, in which he finally felt that they could claim that they were complying with the certifier, continually there were issues that arose—such as contractors bringing child labor to the farm—a direct violation of the certification. Another Egyptian firm that I visited was located in a dilapidated building; the offices were disheveled with desks crammed together and papers and boxes piled on top of the desks. That same firm produced glossy brochures with pictures of the firm's director sitting in an office with a Persian rug and a large work of art hanging on a wallpapered wall. In the brochures, the director appeared to be in his own office but was actually sitting in a lobby of the Four Seasons Hotel. The thin veneer of the gloss and glitter of the doctor's consulting firm revealed itself easily and forcefully. The firm's former clientele were supposedly the largest corporations and banks operating in the region, but the firm never had working relationships with most of these corporations.

Rather than think of this merely as a false image of the standard, I suggest that the production of the image is part of the standard itself. The rules, protocols, ideologies are institutionalized by definite corporate and even multilateral entities but they are constituted historically in the translocal interstices of exchange. Moreover, it is the work of meeting the expectations that symbolic capital, or the production of legitimate competence or authority, is created (Bourdieu 1986). In Aihwa Ong's (1999: 36) terms, national and local processes "negotiate new relations to capital"— a negotiation "within local frameworks of the East-West divide." In other words, Egyptian family business groups and financial firms negotiate within these local institutions and networks the transnational rules and protocols that enable them to, and limit the extent to which they, participate.

Conclusions

The role of finance capital was important to the development of what Vitalis (1995) called a private oligopoly that characterized the political economy of colonial and quasi-independent Egypt. Local business groups that diversified, tied tightly to foreign capital (especially finance), and relied heavily on the state drove this period of capital accumulation via heightened integration into the world economy. In the post-1952 period of independence, a period during which the world economy contracted, the Egyptian political economy transformed. It was not until the 1990s when the private oligopolistic character of the political economy returned as Egypt re-integrated into an expanding world economy. During this second period of globalization, some of the same families even returned to form and/or expand their business groups. This time family business groups, TNCs, MNCs, and financial firms worked in cooperation and competition to build a corporate agri-food system—and more generally, a corporatized formal economy.

I argue that what is unique about this current period of globalization is the set of rules, protocols, and ideologies that corporate actors, often with the help of multilateral institutions, set up to govern participation in the world economy. This set of rules, protocols, and ideologies is what I refer to as the corporate standard, and the corporate standard shapes the character of today's private oligopoly. I show that Egyptian family business groups and financial firms are able to diversify their holdings, develop ties to foreign capital, and gain from state resources through the intertwining of kinship, broader social networks (especially through business associations), cultural institutions (especially English-language schooling), and new types of economic exchange (for example, mergers and acquisitions). Egyptian family business groups and financial firms have been able to grow the corporate agri-food system to the extent that they have been able to negotiate this corporate standard—and this negotiation constitutes the standard itself.

Notes

1. According to Broner et al. (2012), there are 38 high-income countries (examples are Australia, Austria, Canada, Denmark, Finland, France, Germany, Greece, Italy, Japan, Netherlands, New Zealand, Norway, Spain, Sweden, United Kingdom, and United States). There are 26 upper-middle-income countries (including Argentina, Brazil, Chile, Costa Rica, Croatia, Iran, Libya, Malaysia, Mexico, Russian Federation, South Africa, Turkey, Venezuela). There are 38 lower-middle-income (including Albania, Algeria, Angola, Bolivia, China, Ecuador, Egypt, India, Indonesia, Jamaica, Morocco, Namibia, Nicaragua, Thailand, Tunisia, Ukraine, and Vietnam).
2. In Zeitlin and Ratcliff's (1998: 7) terms, this group refers to the social unit that inextricably ties common economic interests to close kinship relationships.

3. See Credit Suisse (2011) on family business groups in South and East Asia. For histories of family business groups, see Zeitlin and Ratcliff (1988) on Chile, Janelli (1993) on South Korea, Yanagisako (2002) on Italy, and Mayer (2016) on the United States.

4. For Bourdieu (1986: 243), economic capital is immediately and directly convertible into money and may be institutionalized in the form of property rights; cultural capital may be institutionalized in the form of educational qualifications; social capital may be institutionalized in the form of titles; and both cultural capital and social capital may be convertible into economic capital in certain conditions.

5. See Isakson (2014) for a comprehensive literature review.

6. See Mowafi (2009) and Moukheiber (2011) for examples.

7. Interview, 8/13/2010, Cairo.

8. The family histories summarized in this section are publicly known through business websites (e.g., Forbes, Bloomberg) and/or their families' own websites (of their companies or foundations).

9. This information is based on a General Authority for Investment and Free Zones (GAFI) internally distributed document listing the top agribusinesses in Egypt based on the total issued capital between January 1970 and May 2010.

10. See Sfakianakis (2004) and El-Naggar (2009) for examples of this opposition.

11. The privatization of large-scale state industries since the 1980s has informed the oligopolistic character of the economies of many countries in the global North and South. See Klein (2007) for various country examples and the World Economic Forum (2008) on the UK in the 1980s.

12. See Saad (1988) for a summary of the agrarian reform limitations.

13. This summary description of the composition of a so-called agribusiness political coalition is based on the following references: Zaalouk (1989), Springborg (1990), Henry (1997), and El-Naggar (2009).

14. This ranking is based on total issued capital between January 1970 and May 2010 (GAFI internally distributed document).

15. Interview, 7/25/2010, Cairo.

16. It should be noted that re-regulation, in the form of new accounting measures with the Sarbones Oxley Act (SOX) in 2002, applied only to publicly traded companies.

17. In 2007, "roughly twice as much money flowed from the UK to the United States as from China" (Tooze 2018: 76).

18. Interview, 8/13/2010, Cairo.

19. Carroll (2010) points out that interlocking directorates are a common characteristic of transnational corporations.

20. I was not able to confirm if the doctor's family was a family business group with multiple holdings.

8
Biosecurity and the Ending of Frontiers?

During the first months of 2006, a highly pathogenic strain of the Avian flu (H5N1 HPAI) spread rapidly from Asia to Europe and Africa. In February, in Egypt, the first infected domestic bird was reported and a month later the first human case of infection and death. By early 2009, the human cases of avian influenza had occurred in 15 countries, and Egypt had the highest number of confirmed human cases worldwide (Tseng et al. 2010: 453). The virus had spread rapidly among the country's poultry population and became endemic, recurring and transmitting frequently to humans. On the heels of H5N1's endemic spread was an outbreak of the swine flu (H1N1). In frenzied anticipation of the highly contagious flu's global march, the Egyptian government ordered the culling of the pig population. But by 2014, the Ministry of Health announced death and illness from the swine flu. H1N1 had returned. Not only was there the new threat of swine flu, but a new strain of foot-and-mouth disease ravaged cattle and other hooved animals in the Nile Delta in 2012 (*Reuters*, March 22, 2012; Garrett and Cook 2012). And human infection rates from endemic Avian flu were still rising, reaching 175 infections with 63 deaths in 2014 (Arafa et al. 2016: 2).

Threats to the animal protein complex—and to public health—have multiplied as globally transmitted pathogens grow and become more virulent. While animal agriculture is particularly susceptible to these threats, pathogens and the other unwanted and unanticipated also regularly threaten cash crop production. There remains not a single sub-industry of commercial agriculture that is unaffected by multiple threats at any given moment. The expansion of the desert frontier—new and existing reclaimed arid lands—has been necessary for the protection of profitable commercial agriculture and public health. The desert frontier has allowed for distance between farms and from populated residential areas as well as production in a dry climate and in soil that had not previously been cultivated intensively. Farm organization and on farm practice in the desert frontier are built and organized around ever stricter demarcations between what is marked as the inside and the outside of production zones to exert greater control over the production environment. In these ways, frontier making in the neoliberal period reflects a process of biosecuratization—of more clearly delineating zones of production to protect them from agricultural pests and other threats to production. These biosecure measures, institutionalized through the World Trade Organization (WTO), have become ever more elaborate, even at the molecular level of plant cells. At the same time, agriculture and food has been beset with growing and increasingly virulent pests and pathogens. At the time of my research in Egypt, there were a series of so-called monsters that shook the agroexport market (of fresh

The Frontiers of Corporate Food in Egypt. Marion W. Dixon, Oxford University Press.
© Marion W. Dixon (2023). DOI: 10.1093/oso/9780192842985.003.0008

fruits and vegetables) and the animal protein complex, including the dramatic entry and endemic spread of the Avian flu in 2006.

In this chapter, the transformation of biosecure protocols and technologies from a marginal practice to an agrifood industry standard since the 1970s is co-constitutive of two movements: the spread of industrial agriculture from the Northern temperate zone to Southern regions on a worldwide scale, and the movement of industrial horticulture (fruits and vegetables) and industrial poultry from existing agricultural lands into the expanding desert frontier in Egypt. I argue that the corporate agri-food system in Egypt grew and consolidated through emergent and recurrent zoonotic and plant diseases, the management of which has been governed in part by biosecure institutions, protocols, and technologies. The desert frontier became crucial to this management.

I substantiate this argument by detailing the organization and on-farm practice of industrial horticulture (largely for export) and industrial poultry (for the domestic market). By looking at the extensive use of plastics as a biosecure technology in industrial horticulture and the value chain of industrial poultry in the spread of the Avian flu, following Jason W. Moore (2015), I am able to theorize capital accumulating in agriculture not only by degrading the environment but through nature—in the interaction of capital, arid soils, the wind, parasites, and the other unwanted and unanticipated.

Biosecurity

Biosecure agriculture systems have historically been referred to as controlled environment agriculture (CEA) that organizes farm organization and on farm practice in ways that attempt to delineate the inside and outside of the production zone. Today, biosecurity is an umbrella term for the technologies, governance mechanisms, institutions, and discourses that have emerged during the last couple of decades to manage and explain the knowns and unknowns (e.g., invasive species, zoonotic diseases, etc.) that are impacting and potentially threaten economy and society. Biosecurity can be understood as one significant branch of the corporate standard that I outline in Chapter 7. Steve Hinchliffe and Nick Bingham (2007) noted three different uses of the term biosecurity: attempts to manage the movement of agricultural pests and diseases (exemplified by quarantine); attempts to reduce the effects of invasive species on so-called indigenous flora and fauna (e.g., border controls); and attempts to protect against the dangers of purposeful and inadvertent spreading of biological agents. While biosecurity as a general practice of securitization based on distinctions between inside and outside (Nerlich et al. 2009) may be considered a defining technology of the modern era, the onset of global governance and corporate dominance coupled with the biological turn in the War on Terror (Cooper 2006) has turned biosecurity into a hegemonic technology in the twenty-first century (Enticott 2008).

How is biosecurity hegemonic? The space of overlap between biosecurity and the corporate food regime has been institutionalized through the WTO. The WTO created a regulatory framework made up of corporate food retailers' private standards and their third party certifications (e.g., Codex standards, Good Agricultural Practices (GAP)) and the WTO's Agreement on the Application of Sanitary and Phytosanitary Measures ("SPS Agreement") and the resulting International Standards for Phytosanitary Measures (ISPMs) which outline biosecurity protocols for a broad range of species categorized as pests (Phillips 2013; Potter 2013). These standards and certifications—what is referred to as private governance or quality governance—determine the conditions of participation of countries and local suppliers in global agri-food trade by attempting to standardize what is grown (i.e., what varieties of fruits and vegetables), how it is grown (i.e., what kinds of inputs and how much of each input) and how it is processed (i.e., specifications of when and how it is moved from the field to the processing plant to (and out of) transport) (Busch and Bain 2004; McMichael 2013). These interventions are a hegemonic technology (Enticott 2008) not only because they govern global agri-food trade and national agri-food industries in WTO member countries, but because they dictate a process of biological simplification.

WTO-sanctioned private governance benefits the most capitalized firms and the largest agroexporting countries: corporate food retailers set the standards, and agribusinesses with the most capital and large agroexporting states that offer sizable subsidies are able to invest in the required certifications and capital-intensive technologies (Gibbon and Ponte 2005). Thus, in John Law's (2006) terms, private governance helps explain how the corporate food regime has resulted in a "disease free" bubble of wealthy countries that use the WTO trade rules to maintain their privilege. The particular character of these changes—toward ever more elaborate conditions of participation in global agri-food trade, through which corporations have consolidated national agri-food industries and world trade—cannot be explained through a political economy analysis alone, however. A political economy analysis tends to explain these changes as a strategy (of corporations, the largest agroexporting states) and/or a privileging of certain consumers (for example, consumer preferences for the near perfect fruit) (Goodman and Watts, eds. 1997; Busch and Bain 2004; Friedmann 2005). Such a perspective tends to conflate the effects of this system with the causes. Rather than offer a purely political economy perspective, I offer a perspective that marries a political economy perspective with an analysis of nature–society relations.

A common concern within the social scientific literature on biosecurity is to avoid conceptual and material boundaries between nature and society in accounts of the nonhuman, thus, highlighting nonhuman mobility and indeterminacy (see Barker 2008). Biosecurity has been theorized by its premise and organizing principles—that is, of a direct positive relationship between biosecuritization and protection. Greater biosecuratization (i.e., more clearly delineated zones of production between the inside and outside) leads to greater protection of the inside zone of production. As such, biosecurity is theorized as an attempt to protect established and valued life from emergent, transgressive, and undesirable life (Clark 2013: 18; see also Braun 2013). Such theorizations draw either explicitly or implicitly on Michel Foucault's (2008) concept of biopolitics, the modern technology of power that regulates and controls populations, increasingly to intimate spheres of life (Braun 2007).[1] Greater biose-curitization may lead to greater protection in time and space; for example, through the regular application of antibiotics, most livestock in factory farms are saved from illness and death from pathogens. Therefore, in an immediate and perpetual sense, valuable lives are saved at the expense of undesirable lives. However, across time and space, there is not a direct relationship between biosecuritization and protection; for example, the Avian flu virus in one production site can end up in another site. The concept of biopolitics, in effect, fails to capture a central problematic: biosecure protocols, practices, and ideologies proceed on a false premise.

In case after case of the application of biosecure measures, a resounding conclu-sion is that biosecure systems are in fact negotiated and indeterminate. In these case studies, biosecurity is characterized by its inability to create definable, impenetrable borders between zones of production (human control) and outside zones (the Wild) (Bingham and Hinchliffe 2008; Maye et al. 2012; Hinchliffe and Ward 2014). Charles Mather and Amy Marshall (2011) refer to this inability as the impossibility of "bio-containment" and "bio-exclusion"—i.e., the building of physical barriers between clean and diseased spaces. Biosecurity boundaries are understood as reformed through socio-ecological processes (Phillips 2013), and biosecurity is characterized by a spatial duality of prescription (disease flows tightly constrained) and negotiation (flows loosely ordered) (Murdoch 1998 cited in Enticott 2008). According to Gareth Enticott (2008), despite numerous efforts in the United Kingdom to eradicate bovine tuberculosis (bTB) in cattle and badgers since the late nineteenth century, the dis-ease has re-emerged and increased in prevalence. In Kezia Barker's (2008) account of the campaign to control gorse in New Zealand, gorse grew back despite an inten-sive government-subsidized herbicide-spraying campaign in the 1970s and 1980s. In South Africa, the mass culling of infected ostriches as part of the government's eradication program against H5N1 in 2004 led to a new outbreak of the disease that same year (Mather and Marshall 2011). Australia's Fruit Fly Exclusion Zone (FFEZ), an 18.5 million hectare biosecure area to protect against the Queensland fruit fly (Qfly), generally maintained a pest-free status following its creation in 1996, but there has been an explosion of Qfly within the FFEZ in recent years (Phillips 2013). For instance, in the state of Victoria, outbreak numbers jumped from seven in 2007 to more than 130 in 2010 (Phillips 2013: 1690).

There are subtle but important differences in how the unintended consequences of biosecure measures are interpreted. The interpretation of a failure of biosecurity (Mather and Marshall 2011) or a management problem (Phillips 2013; Shaw et al. 2013) produces an image of nonhumans arresting human control. While this inter-pretation may highlight nonhuman mobility and indeterminacy, it fails to avoid the conceptual and material boundaries between nature and society. Case studies that, in contrast, move beyond this dualism are illustrative. In Enticott's (2008) case study, the U.K. bTB eradication program led to a new bovine tuberculosis (bTB) outbreak not because bTB or its hosts simply evaded capture but, rather, because the program led to a new ecology among badger populations that created new flows of disease. Similarly, Barker (2008) argued that the century-long attempt to eradicate gorse, an invasive species, in New Zealand is inseparable from gorse's extensive spread into most ecological niches. In short, gorse has had "mutually constitutive effects on biosecurity approaches" as gorse is "a product of exchanges and adaptations between the plant, environment, and human actions" (Barker 2008: 1611). Rather than conclude that biosecurity measures fail to create impenetrable borders between the inside and the outside due to nonhuman mobility, these case studies show that biosecurity develops and changes in direct relation to changes not only in the unwanted life (bTB, gorse, etc.) but in the hosts (badgers, ostriches, mosquitos, etc.), the wider environment, and so on. In short, the multiplication of crises (new outbreaks, the spread of invasive species, etc.) is seen not as a reality today *despite* biosecurity measures. Rather, the crises are a characteristic effect of, and a determinant factor in, biosecurity as a changing set of protocols, technologies and institutions.

Bruno Latour's (1993) relational concept of the work of translation—the creation and proliferation of new types of beings, hybrids of nature and culture—and the work of purification—the creation (and re-creation) of two distinct ontological zones, that of humans and that of nonhumans—captures well this problematic in the biosecurity literature. The effort of creating distinct boundaries between zones of human creation and control and the so-called Wild is inseparable then in *and* across time and space from the growth of monsters, for example, growing populations of ostriches infected with H5N1 and orchards infested with Qfly. The work of purification makes possible the work of translation, but as Latour (1993) pointed out, this relationship can work both ways. In the effort to value certain lives at the expense of other lives, those other lives change, maybe subtly or dramatically. In turn, the effort to protect certain lives changes, often intensifying through more comprehensive demarcations of the outside and the inside of production zones. The double movement of biosecure agriculture explored in this chapter embodies this tension: The movement from the Northern temperate zone to Southern regions, and from existing agricultural areas to reclaimed lands in Egypt, reflects how the creation of ever more clearly delineated zones of production precipitates and responds to the creation and proliferation of threats to production—the very blurring of those zones.

Plastics and Horticulture

In Egypt, the ever-present image of the country's population squeezed into a thin strip of arable land surrounded by a vast desert has long promoted the reclamation of land. Reclamation has held the promise of expanding the total area of arable land—and permanently, through cultivation and settlement. And on a global stage, a version of these greening the desert narratives re-surfaced following the 2007–2009 financial-food-energy crises: water-efficient (and even water-less) agriculture production in arid areas was presented as a sustainable solution to the problem of food insecurity in a warming, water-scarce planet.[2] Drip irrigation, hydroponics or soil-less cultivation, and solar-powered irrigation systems with desalinated water were among the technical feats touted in the face of re-ignited fears of ecological limits to production under the specter of overpopulation, climate change, and peak oil.

These greening the desert narratives come at a time of growing public attention to the water crises that have been intensifying in arid regions from industrial agriculture production. Attention in the United States was particularly striking in 2015 as the state of California, the largest horticulture region in the country, if not the world, announced mandatory water restrictions in the face of a four-year drought (Boxall 2015; Gillis and Richtel 2015). Other examples abound: Facing rapid depletion of fossil aquifers, Saudi Arabia imposed limits on the extraction of groundwater—a restriction that compelled Saudi investors and agribusinesses to acquire agricultural land in neighboring countries since the 2007–2009 crises (GRAIN 2008; Pearce 2012). In 2010, the Royal Academy of Engineering produced a report warning that British demand for fresh fruits and vegetables was exacerbating water scarcity in producing countries in the global South (Lawrence 2010). Greening the desert narratives at a time of multiplying water crises seem contradictory: Arid regions that have long been turned into sites of intensive agriculture production are now drying up, and yet, these narratives promote the same set of processes that created the present-day crises, just in new lands and with the latest agri-technologies and practices.

Nonetheless, strands of the alternative food movement joined state development planning in touting the sustainability of the agri-technologies and on-farm practices that make greening the desert possible.[3] Greening the desert narratives have re-gained traction following the 2007–2009 crises through explanations of the crises as a management or governance problem—e.g., a tragedy of the commons or water thirsty crops irresponsibly planted in dry lands (*The Economist,* October 7, 2010; Gillis and Richtel 2015). As such, in these narratives, the latest technical feats, coupled with proper management, hold the promise of solving the problem of food production in the face of imminent ecological crises as a result of desertification, depleted aquifers, soil salination, and on and on.

Greening the desert narratives and policies have played a role historically in the development of global horticulture—that is, places of specialization for the production of fruits and vegetables (as well as ornamentals like flowers), destined for the supermarket shelves of the global consumer class, largely in Northern countries. Global horticulture and the global consumer class have, in effect, reproduced one another: those with the means are now able to consume fruits and vegetables year-round, regardless of the season (McMichael 2013). The role of greening the desert was pronounced following the price hikes of 1972–73 and the inflation of the 1970s, when similar fears of ecological "limits to growth" emerged (e.g., Meadows et al. 1972). And the reclamation of land in arid regions in the global North and South made the global spread of industrial horticulture possible. The development of two of the largest horticulture regions, the state of California's Central Valley and northeast Brazil's São Francisco River Valley, and a horticulture region of lesser significance, Peru's western coast, in fact, share common characteristics with the development of industrial horticulture for export in Egypt.[4] Frontier making in all four regions has a long lineage that precedes the neoliberal period, with the Central Valley in many ways setting a precedent for the other regions, as will be discussed below. The state was a central actor in claiming the land by force or cooptation from those who had been using the land through, for example, extensive water works, leveling of the land, and development of electricity lines and transport routes. In their common histories, both small-scale agriculturalists and capitalized investors developed the land, but these regions are sites of extensive capitalization. What is more obscured in the literature on these frontier regions, and what this analysis of the desert frontier in Egypt seeks to highlight, are the ways in which frontier making and farm organization and on-farm practice in the frontier regions represent a movement to protect working capital from multiplying threats to production.[5]

By detailing how Egypt became a node in global horticulture, I show that the problems of water scarcity today reflect, rather than contradict, the social and ecological relations of agriculture production in arid regions and will not be resolved through better management practices or the next technical fix. Egypt became an agroexporter of fruits and vegetables not only through the expansion of reclaimed lands farther into arid regions, largely to the west and east of the Delta, but also through the continual adoption of the WTO-enforced biosecure agri-technologies and protocols, which have become increasingly coercive and capital-intensive. In horticulture, these agri-technologies and protocols fall under the classification of plasticulture, a system that organizes production through the extensive use of plastics.

All that Wilts under the Sun

In interviews in 2011, agribusiness directors and managers repeatedly cited the ecology of the desert frontier as ideal for horticulture production. The soils are largely virgin soils, not having been cultivated intensively previously or recently. The distance between farms and from residential areas is great enough to offer some protections from traveling pathogens. The arid climate was cited as the best protection from molds; as one manager said, "This area is paradise for agriculture. There is water, it is dry and there are no funguses [sic]."[6] This manager was referring not to just any type of agriculture, but to a particular type—one that has become increasingly vulnerable and highly volatile.

It is not only the geography of farms but also plasticulture that seeks to control contact of the unwanted, the unruly Wild, with the inside of the production zone while simultaneously increasing labor productivity (i.e., the efficiency of production including the use of water, inputs, and the like). Plasticulture is usually defined as drip/spray irrigation (made of plastics) coupled with plastic mulches, greenhouses, and other plastic applications (such as tents and tarps). Plasticulture may involve soilless cultivation (in greenhouses) and often includes fertigation, or treated irrigation water (filtered and applied with fertilizers and other inputs) (Lament 1993). Plastics were functional in all the fields that I visited, either placed directly on fields (as

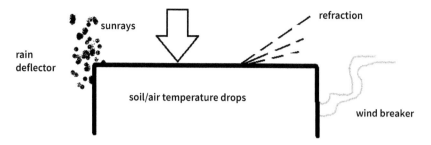

sunrays

refraction

rain
deflector

soil/air temperature drops

wind breaker

Figure 8.1 Silver low-density polyethylene (LDP).

mulches) or above crops (as in greenhouses or with tarps) and weaving throughout fields in the form of irrigation hoses and tubes. The main plastic in these farms is low-density polyethylene (LDP), which is used extensively in industrial horticulture production worldwide.

There are different colors of LDP, and LDP regulates the soil and air temperature depending on the color (Figure 8.1). Opaque LDP sheets increase the soil temperature, while silver lowers slightly and white lowers the temperature. Often greenhouses are in white and beds are covered in silver. Plastic mulch also reduces soil water evaporation, which is critical to intensive cultivation in arid areas, and other plastics are used as wind and sun breakers.

Plasticulture is considered a biosecure agriculture system in that it seeks to manage insect pests and soilborne disease pathogens while reducing weeding and enabling intensification (double/triple cropping) (Schrader 2000; Jensen 2011). As a result, plasticulture contributes to higher and quicker crop yields: In one study, the combined application of plastic mulch, drip irrigation, and fertigation was reported to increase yields by as much as two to three times and quickened growth by as much as 21 days (Lament 1993). The desert frontier also renders plasticulture more effective by reducing the risk of humidity in enclosure that can lead to molds and wilting. While plasticulture and greening the desert agri-technologies and practices are not synonymous as plasticulture is used in other environments, plasticulture broadly understood has heavily shaped greening the desert agri-technologies and practices in industrial horticulture. Today, plasticulture is found throughout the NACs—with a vast majority of plastic greenhouses (based on total area) in China and to a much lesser extent in the Mediterranean region (Jensen 2011). Estimated world consumption of LDP has more than doubled from 1985 to 1999 (Levin et al. 2007: 184). In 1999, the estimated worldwide area of plasticulture included 121,300 km² of plastic mulch (Levin et al. 2007: 184). Industrial horticulture production in arid regions is attributed to plastic technologies. For instance, an Agriculture Minister of Israel said that the country's plastics industry has been able to "make the desert bloom" (Udasin 2012).

Consistent with greening the desert narratives, plasticulture is touted as sustainable in terms of more efficient water and fertilizer use (Schrader 2000; Jensen 2011). However, such a claim belies the fact that plastics are energy intensive, produced by petroleum and imported over long distances. Further, plasticulture's set of controls—of water and nutrient flows, soil moisture, and the like—operates through other imports, including most importantly corporate-approved, high-yielding seed varieties. The seeds in essence respond to the conditions of production within this system, but it is no easy feat to create such a harmonious relationship. The imported seeds are tested and retested on the farms. Nearly all the farms that I visited had at least one field devoted to seed testing. Agribusiness managers reported to travel regularly through the Horticultural Export Improvement Association (HEIA) to learn about new varieties, often at U.S. and European universities. The continual development of seed varieties should not be interpreted singularly as negotiations or translations of international standards by local actors to attain a certain aesthetic. Rather, the trials and errors are necessarily involved in the high volatility of agro-industrial production, and in the case of the seed varieties, continual experimentation are essential in order to avoid genetic erosion, as present-day horticulture crops represent a small genetic pool and are extremely susceptible to pathogens (Marsden et al. 1996; Weis 2010).

The high volatility of production is an overlooked driver in the development of increasingly coercive agri-technologies and practices—toward the creation of ever more distinct ontological zones of humans and nonhumans. In industrial horticulture, even the wind and the sun potentially spell disaster. Plastic mulches and sheets act as a cover to block out and eliminate not just pests but the wind and the sun. On one banana farm, the banana bunches that were being harvested were wrapped in plastic so as to slow ripening. On another farm, a field was left fallow and the beds were covered with opaque LDP. The farm manager told me that the plastic mulch sterilizes the beds by raising the temperature of the soil above a certain threshold above which all organisms die. Once the soil is sterilized, the beds are replanted (a process called solarization). The greenhouses in which they were breeding the plants (the breeding rooms) are supposed to be controlled. Before entering the breeding rooms for strawberries, I stepped into a sanitizer pool in front of the entrance and then again in the holding room (between the entrance and the plant area of the greenhouse). There I covered my shoes with plastic and sprayed my hands with Dettol (an antibiotic sanitizer). In the breeding rooms, the strawberry plants were in artificial (or soilless) soil, the soil-medium's temperature and moisture measured regularly. The air temperature was supposed to be kept cool and constant.

These multiple, overlapping controls over production represent biophysical overrides, in Weis's (2010) terms, agri-technologies and on-farm practices designed to minimize the damage caused by intensive cultivation, monocultures, genetic erosion, global warming, among other threats. However, in attempting to create separate ontological zones of humans and nonhumans, these overrides amplify the monsters of industrial agriculture. Seed varieties are constantly vulnerable. On one 30-acre greenhouse of sweet peppers, not one pepper survived from an infestation. On another short visit to a farm, there was an emergency as a plant pest (tomato leaf miner) that had been traveling regionally through southern Africa had begun to infest one tomato variety. The managers had to act quickly as in monoculture fields pests like tomato leaf miner can move easily, potentially infecting all crops in a field.

The high volatility of production illustrates that the work of separating controlled and uncontrolled zones leads to their blurring. The citrus becomes easily parched from the sun. On one farm, nearly 250 acres of grape vines collapsed in an unusual rain storm one year. When it rained, the plastic sheet over the orchard filled with water and broke, collapsing the vines underneath. Many farms that were built from the 1940s through roughly the 1980s in state reclaimed lands are today lined with tall pine trees to serve as windbreakers, but in many of the newer farms, there is no cover from common winds and agribusiness managers described the wind as one of the farms' biggest enemies.

While Egyptian agribusiness representatives commonly referred to reclaimed lands as ideal for horticulture during field research—in terms of the dry climate, virgin soil, distance between farms and human settlements, and so on—it is clear that only the most capitalized firms have been able to invest in the years of trial and error involved in frontier making. In terms of certification alone, it took one agribusiness seven years, another 15 years, to attain the common certifications for agroexporters (e.g., Tesco Natural Choice, Global Gap, Field 2 Fork, Leaf and Tesco Natural Soil). Given the high-levels of capitalization of production, however, the desert frontier can be ideal for industrial horticulture only through a historically specific constellation of forces and conditions that is detailed in Chapter 6: The state's facilitation of a cheap market in reclaimed lands and the combination of a feminized, contingent labor force and an institutional infrastructure (through which LDP and other agri-technologies became more accessible).

Greening the desert narratives that tout land reclamation as a solution to water and food insecurity in the country further contribute to the relative exhaustion (Moore 2011, 2015) of existing agricultural areas. Because drip or spray irrigation (as part of plasticulture) uses water more efficiently than flood irrigation, production via drip or spray irrigation in reclaimed lands is touted as sustainable by increasing the country's arable land with less water. As this section has demonstrated, this assumption fails to account for what is being grown, by whom and for whom. By the turn of the twenty-first century, just a few years after Egypt joined the WTO, the development and expansion of the desert frontier was already leading to the rapid depletion of the water table that irrigates a portion of reclaimed lands to the west of the Delta—at a rate of about one meter per year.[7] To explain the exhaustion of underground fresh water sources, proponents of greening the desert point to a recurring problem of water-thirsty crops like banana and cotton being planted in arid regions. Although the production of thirsty crops was cited as a problem during research in Egypt, this governance problem does not explain the exhaustion of irrigation water sources in arid regions.[8] The region of western Peru, for example, has been facing a water crisis from the large-scale production of asparagus, a so-called colonizing crop that is bred to survive in sand with little water (Glover and Kusterer 1990; Lawrence 2010). Large-scale commodity production, even if it is production of water-efficient crops using water-efficient technologies, requires considerable water if crops are to grow quickly and abundantly. As one agribusiness executive in Egypt put it, an olive tree may need water once a month if it is for local consumption, but an olive tree that produces lots of olives needs water every other day![9]

In conclusion, making the desert ideal for industrial horticulture (and plasticulture an industry standard) was not a mere design of state planners and corporations to expand capital accumulation in agriculture, but rather avenues for expanded capital accumulation in the desert were forged through the degradation of the ecological conditions of production, including (but not limited to) the volatility of production and the depletion of irrigation water sources. The relative exhaustion (Moore 2011, 2015) of existing agricultural areas propelled the development and expansion of the desert frontier not only for the agroexport market of fresh fruits and vegetables but also for industrial animal agriculture. The growing capitalization of horticulture—as CEA has moved toward more comprehensive controls over "air and root temperatures, light, water, humidity, carbon dioxide, and plant nutrition" (Jensen 2011)—also characterizes industrial poultry.

Industrial Animal Agriculture and Parasite Ecology

The revolutionary transformation in the production and consumption of poultry took place in Egypt in just two decades: From the early 1980s to the turn of the twenty-first century, the country transformed from a net importer of poultry into a producer with a full-scale corporate poultry industry. During this transformation, poultry production underwent processes of corporate consolidation. When the Avian flu hit Egypt in 2006, the industry was facing massive losses: an estimated $1 billion in 2009–10 (Abdelwhab and Hafez 2011: 911). In response, they went further into the desert and underwent yet another wave of consolidation.

This outcome is consistent with other analyses in the social sciences of the Avian flu that conclude that the flu has had the effect of further consolidating the poultry industry in countries where it has hit and become recurrent (Davis 2005; Hinchliffe and Bingham 2007; Chuengsatiansup 2008; Wallace 2009). This literature argues that the primary force behind the growth of industrial poultry and the decline of cottage poultry is state-class alliances, or a form of biopolitics (Foucault 2008), technologies of power that privilege some lives over others. States have responded to the crisis in ways that bolster the capitalist classes and undermine small-scale producers and distributors. In their analysis of the H5N1 event in Egypt, Hinchliffe and Bingham (2007) and Bingham and Hinchliffe (2008) explain a similar outcome through Foucault's concept of biopolitics. In response to the massive losses facing corporate poultry, the government initiated a vaccination campaign in the corporate biosecure facilities and a mass culling campaign of cottage poultry. Live bird markets were temporarily closed, and slaughtering was moved to designated slaughter houses. This response, in effect, secured the lives of corporate birds while sacrificing the lives of birds in live bird markets (and the livelihoods of small-scale operators).

While state intervention clearly benefited some lives over others, this analysis offers only a partial explanation for the spread of the disease and the wave of consolidation. In this analysis, the two forms of production (and thus the two types of birds) are assumed to be distinct. In fact, at the time of the outbreak, corporate poultry was inseparable from smaller-scale operations and live bird markets. In response to (human and non-human) risks to production, the industry had built a value chain of concentration and control at the top (over breeders) and of sub-contracting (of broilers) to other operators at the bottom.[10] This value chain and what Hinchliffe (2013) refers to as "ecologies of production"—the relations between parasites, hosts, and the (production) environment that constitutes the chain—explain how biosecure poultry within Egypt and beyond acted as a vector of the virus and, yet, was largely saved from the virus's global march.

What is enigmatic about the Avian flu pandemic is that human and bird illness and death from the flu have concentrated in cottage poultry and live bird markets (van Kerkhove et al. 2011; Cowling et al. 2013). Yet, the evidence has suggested (even at the time of the outbreak) that the intensification of production of, and trade in, poultry contributed to the increasing virulence of the virus (Bingham and Hinchliffe 2008; FAO 2011b). The global Livestock Revolution, coupled with rapid Southern urbanization, expanded the zoonotic pool, or the available set of possible diseases that could cross between nonhuman and human populations (Hinchliffe 2013: 200). In the context of an enlarged zoonotic pool, the Avian flu predictably reappeared and with greater virulence from the decades of relative dormancy.[11] There was an outbreak in Hong Kong in 1997, and then the virus re-emerged in 2003, with the Pearl River Delta in China thought to be its regional incubator (Davis 2005; Wallace 2009). From the Pearl River Delta, the virus spread globally by 2005–06. So how was industrial poultry in the context of a Planet of Slums both a vector of H5N1 and, at the same time, relatively unscathed?

The first piece of the puzzle is the direct relationship between parasite ecology and industrial agriculture. In industrial animal facilities, parasite populations follow life cycles of rapid growth followed by drastic decline (either from the slaughtering of hosts or drug treatment), thus favoring faster life-histories (or virulence) of parasites (Mennerat et al. 2010). The global Livestock Revolution has standardized poultry production so that the birds (hosts) and parasites grow quickly: industrial poultry facilities keep thousands of birds in confined spaces, and rely on a single bird breed, which for broilers (the Cornish Cross) has been bred to reach market weight in seven weeks. Standardized production also leads to drastic declines in parasite populations: frequent culling of birds shortens host lifespan and anti-parasite applications, which are widespread, cause high direct mortality (Mennerat et al. 2010). In short, these facilities favor virulence. However, because the life cycles are short, adult survival of parasites is lower within them as parasites focus on "current reproductive effort" (Mennerat et al. 2010: 62). The focus on current reproductive effort means that the pathogen is more likely to develop drug-resistance and virulence but is less likely to reach adult lethality in the facilities. Rather, lethal adult parasites are carried out through air pathways, the transport of birds, or waste disposal. The case study of

Egypt suggests that lethal adult parasites ended up with smaller-scale operators, in part, through industrial poultry's value chain.

When the Avian flu struck Egypt, the industry was characterized by three types of production: integrated (large-scale with high biosecurity, in-house processing and feedmills), commercial (medium- to large-scale, with low to high biosecurity) and cottage or household (see FAO 2006b). Approximately one out of four birds was kept by households (Abdelwhab and Hafez 2011: 647); most of these household birds were layers (for eggs), as households have come to rely heavily on eggs for their livelihoods. The industry was heavily concentrated: five corporations dominated broiler production (for poultry meat), and there was some level of concentration within layer production. By 2006, only a handful of broiler farms were integrated, while a vast majority were medium- to large-scale non-integrated farms. Annual production on the farms ranged from about a half million to 10 million, and the largest corporations may have produced 90 million chickens per year on their farms combined.[12]

Corporations dominate broiler production by controlling the grandparent and parent breeding (Figure 8.2). As part of the non-integrated value chain, they sell broiler chicks to sub-contractors (medium- to large-scale farms), who then sell the adult birds in live bird markets. At that time, more than 70% of broilers were sold in live birds markets (FAO 2006b), the rest being processed for the corporate food sector from the few integrated farms or exported or consumed within households.

During the industry's growth and consolidation, instead of moving toward greater integration of production, the industry moved toward sub-contracting to

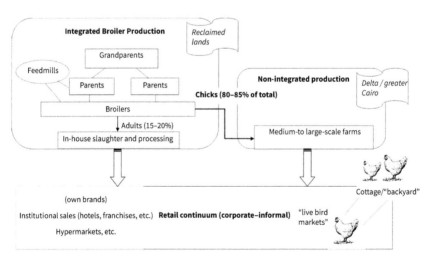

Figure 8.2 Egyptian poultry industry's value chain (at the time of the 2006 Avian flu outbreak).

Note: the estimate of the percentage of broiler chicks sold comes from an interview with a corporate executive in Cairo on August 16, 2011.

non-integrated farms, which then sold adult birds in live bird markets. This type of value chain—contracting out risk and responsibility to smaller-scale operators—has become common in the poultry industry globally in anticipation of known and unknown threats (Hinchliffe and Ward 2014: 137). In Egypt, the industry decoupled production from the costs of raising broilers into adult birds to be slaughtered in live bird markets. The costs were calculated based on the risk of broilers carrying adult pathogens as they grow to market weight and the difference in retail price between wholesale and value added. The retail price of both was anticipated to fall following bilateral and multilateral trade agreements.[13] Even before the Avian flu outbreak, the corporate strategy was essentially to build what was referred to as fortresses for their breeders and broiler chicks in the desert frontier. An agribusiness executive stated the reasons for this strategy: "The bigger farms [like ours] are less susceptible as they have institutional protections and are out in the desert."[14]

While the few biosecure poultry facilities were in reclaimed lands when the Avian flu struck, most poultry production (broiler and layer, small-scale to large-scale) was concentrated in the Delta: more than 60% of production was in the five governorates of Lower Egypt/Delta in 2005 (FAO 2006b). In Davis's (2005: 59) terms, the Delta is an Avian flu epicenter: a breeding ground for influenza, with dense human and animal populations, regular contact between different animal species, and chronic respiratory or immune disorders. Not only have processes of urbanization in the Delta shrunk the distance between animal and human population centers, but there has been the emergence and resurgence of epidemic diseases—including, but not limited to, lung diseases (Anwar 2003), trachoma (Watts and El Katsha 1995), hepatitis C (Lehman and Wilson 2009), early onset of cancer (Soliman et al. 1999, 2006), and obesity (Nahmias 2010). During the outbreak, then, most birds were sold in live bird markets in the Delta, where contact between cottage poultry and industrial poultry and between diseased birds and people with compromised immune systems was regular. In essence, in the Avian flu epicenter, quick transmission of the virus was assured. Most human infections were reported in live bird markets and back-yards (although significantly the source of the infection in 15% of reported cases is unknown) (Tseng et al. 2010). By 2010, Egypt was the only other country besides for Indonesia with endemic H5N1 HPAI (Kim et al. 2010). The country had the highest number of confirmed human avian influenza cases worldwide: By March 4, 2010, there were a total of 104 human cases, including 30 fatalities (Tseng et al. 2010: 453).

While it appeared that small-scale poultry was the vector, the H5N1 pathogen had actually moved from industrial farms to industrial farms to households (I-I-H) on a global scale. In the span of a few years, the Pearl River Delta Avian flu epicenter in China connected to the Nile Delta, where biosecure poultry acted as vectors of the H5N1 virus (Abdelwhab and Hafez 2011; Kayali et al. 2011). Biosecurity poultry is implicated in the growing crisis and, yet, left the industry relatively unscathed.

Biosecure Poultry

Within the poultry industry, biosecurity means that poultry do not have any access outside of the so-called controlled environment and movement within poultry factory farms is restricted and sanitized. This is how an agribusiness executive excitedly explained their new biosecure poultry facility (paraphrase):

> There is a red area and a yellow area within the facility and vicinity. In the red area, movement is restricted and regulated, and in the yellow area, movement is not as restricted. No one can enter the facility without a 24-hour quarantine. All outside effects are kept and left in this quarantined space. Any effects that are brought into the room where the birds are must be first placed in a fumigation room. The feeding is mechanized and stays within the facility. All the crates and other equipment used inside and outside of the facility are also disinfected. The idea is to create a seal.[15]

In the executive's words, "This is how harsh biosafety needs to be for the breeders."[16] Biosecure poultry facilities look like sealed warehouses. Due to the quarantine procedures (and the long distances of the farms from the Delta), workers generally come and stay on the farm for five months during the flu season and then take the rest of the year off.

Biosecure poultry facilities are designed to prevent the introduction of pests and diseases into the birds' environment. However, there are "environmental pathways by which pathogens can spread across and out of large confined animal feedlot operations" (Wallace 2009: 938) (Figure 8.3). In order to keep the birds alive, ventilation and circulation of air are essential. This ventilation also allows for the movement of rodents, wild birds, and insects in and out of the factories (M. F. Davis et al. 2011). Biosecure procedures often do not include the management of animal waste, and broiler farms like the one described above transport chicks to other farms, which raise the chicks and sell the adult birds to retailers. The seal is, in fact, impossible to create.

Biosecurity measures effectively secure the inside of factory farms via the continual application of antibiotics and vaccinations and the short life cycle of birds. At the same time, parasite populations develop virulence and drug resistance within the farms (M. F. Davis et al. 2011). Poultry production is maintained while the environmental pathways of the farms spread outside pathogen virulence and antimicrobial resistance.

At the time of the H5N1 outbreak in Egypt, birds across the industry were affected, although production facilities with lax biosecurity measures were much more vulnerable to the virus than those with strict biosecurity measures (Abdelwhab and Hafez 2011: 654). The Egyptian government followed a standard retinue of measures: The government immediately began a vaccination program for all industrial farms and not including backyards, under pressure from the poultry industry (Abdelwhab and Hafez 2011). Given how quickly the virus could spread in the confined production environment of their facilities, the industry was potentially facing even

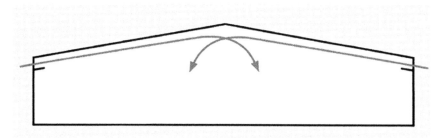

(a) Inlet setting and air flow during minimum and transitional ventilation to keep air movement off the birds.

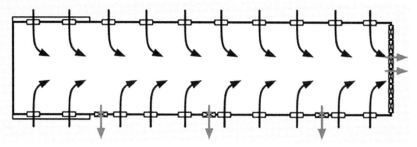

(b) Transitional ventilation utilizing a combination of side wall and tunnel fans, introducing air through side wall inlets.

Figure 8.3 Environmental pathways of biosecure poultry.

Source: Image courtesy of Aviagen.

greater losses in the immediate term. Further, in order for vaccinations to be effective in the short term, transmission of the virus to vaccinated birds needed to be eliminated. Confinement of vaccinated poultry in live bird markets and backyards was (and still is) considered impossible, in contrast to vaccinated industrial poultry. Thus, the government immediately initiated a mass culling campaign: In 2006, more than 40 million cottage birds were culled (FAO 2006b: 29). The government further mandated the temporary closing of live bird markets and the slaughtering of birds in slaughterhouses. Although these combined measures clearly had the effect of saving agribusiness and decimating informal markets, the value given to industrial birds' lives reflects not only the value of commodity production but also the knowledge production embedded in international standards of emergency bio-containment. International protocols assume that biosecurity prevents birds inside industrial facilities from being in contact with birds (and other potential hosts) outside. Official responses, in effect, proceed on the premise of biosecurity—that biosecure facilities can prevent pathogens from infecting vaccinated birds given the adoption of certain capital-intensive practices and agri-technologies.

Pathways of H5N1 transmission between hosts remained, however, and the combined measures of mass culling (of household birds) and mass vaccinations (of industrial ones) did not control the pathogen. The mass culling and (to a certain extent) the vaccinations led to drastic declines in the pathogen's life cycle; however, rates of the pathogen's transmission remained high. Many householders and small-scale operators were not compensated for the loss of their birds; therefore, they did not notify authorities about a sick bird for fear of losing their flock (Meleigy 2007). Further, the vaccines proved to be ineffective (Kayali et al. 2011) because biosecurity measures do not completely prevent pathogens from entering and exiting farms, and the vaccines were not properly tested or stored prior to their widespread application (Abdelwhab and Hafez 2011). Drug resistance has further impeded any subsequent efforts to contain the flu. Along with several other countries, Egypt is now home to an oseltamivir-resistant strain of H5N1 ("tamiflu oseltamivir" being the main commercial vaccine for the flu) (Tseng et al. 2010: 458). This deadly combination of virulence and drug resistance within the virus population has established the pathogen-host relationship, following the initial outbreak. Every influenza season, the virus reappears and damages its host, making the Avian flu endemic in the country.

Industry producers have largely responded to this new reality by continuing to move production from the Delta into the desert, especially in reclaimed land in Middle and Upper Egypt, and by building biosecure systems. The government instituted a regulation that poultry facilities be at least two kilometers apart and outside of agricultural areas, so even the facilities that were already in reclaimed areas were moved farther into the desert. As one agribusiness executive confided, the loss of nearly all of their broilers (500,000) from the Avian flu, close to their entire working capital at the time, compelled them to build biosecure facilities farther into the desert.[17] An outcome of H5N1's endemic spread is, in an agribusiness manager's words, "Poultry is gold in Egypt." Industry producers with the capital to expand the desert frontier and build biosecure production systems have grown. For instance, the long-term assets of one of the dominant poultry producers, Cairo Poultry Company, jumped 77% in 2006 alone. At the same time, cottage poultry has been damaged, compromising the rural livelihoods of millions who rely heavily on poultry and endangering local breeds (e.g., Fayoumi) (FAO 2006b; Eltanany and Distl 2010).

The path to expanded capital accumulation in agriculture is paved by the multiplication of crises. Even before the official responses, at the time of the outbreak, corporate poultry faired far better than birds in live bird markets and backyards. In Egypt and worldwide, corporate industrial poultry has remained relatively safe in the face of emergent and recurrent viruses in part by transmitting pathogens to sub-contracting farms and/or live bird markets. Sub-contracting has historically been part of, rather than contradictory to, processes of biosecuritization during the neoliberal period. Emergency bio-containment measures following the outbreak further created new hybrids through the pathways of transmission that are necessarily part of biosecure poultry. In other words, this outcome is not a failure of biosecurity but rather reflects the practice of biosecurity. Even if all poultry in Egypt was produced in an integrated biosecure production system, as WTO protocols and industry leaders promote, transmission of viruses would remain possible within and across national borders, as long as there are production zones that promote virulence.

Historicizing the Double Movement of Industrial Agriculture

The industrialization of horticulture and poultry production in the global North began long before the standardization of agri-technologies and practices and their concomitant spread to Southern regions. The high commodity prices of the 1970s precipitated a shift: The development of U.S. patents of controlled environment agri-technologies coupled with the beginnings of structural adjustment policies throughout the indebted South spawned a second green revolution, or transfer of privately owned agri-technologies for the production of high-value foods (animal protein and fresh fruits and vegetables) from the core agroexporting countries to the New Agricultural Countries (NACs) for a global consumer class (McMichael 2009, 2012). The second green revolution gave birth not only to year-round fresh fruits and vegetables in hyper/supermarket shelves around the world but to a global Livestock Revolution that spread industrial animal agriculture throughout the NACs.

Animal agriculture has been a site of extensive work of purification and work of translation (Latour 1993) throughout much of the twentieth century. Farms have been transformed into units of production progressively organized toward containment (with fewer access points to and contact with the outside of factories), restricted movements (of animals and workers), biological simplification (through animal breeding), and pharmacological intervention (e.g., antibiotics, vaccines) (BC Poultry 2006; ISA Poultry 2010; Weis 2013). Weis (2013) interprets this long transformation as a consequence of capital's dictates of efficiency. Chickens were at the center of industrial agriculture due in part to their genetic specialization into meat "broilers" and egg "layers," which made automation and various forms of animal confinement easier, leading to the use of the so-called battery cage in layer production in the United States in the 1930s. However, the global "fowl plague"—recurrent outbreaks of Highly Pathogenic Avian Influenza (HPAI) in poultry in the industrializing and colonized worlds at the time (Alexander and Capua 2008)—also likely played a role in this early work of purification. And HPAI was likely an adaptation to the transnational breeding and trade in poultry combined with rapid processes of urbanization during the latter part of the nineteenth century and the first decades of the twentieth century. The first known influenza subtype that jumped the species barrier from birds to humans—H5N1—was identified in 1959 and recurred in apparently isolated incidents in the industrialized North during the next few decades (Alexander and Capua 2008). During this time, animal agriculture became increasingly industrialized in the North, with the development of Concentrated Animal Feeding Operations (CAFOs). Animals respond to change and other stresses in ways that undermine or complicate their growth and production over all, and influenza as a system of host-parasite interaction is a "constantly emerging disease" that undergoes mutations based on changes in the host and the wider environment (Davis 2005: 11). Given this host-parasite dynamic, animal agriculture has been at the center of industrial agriculture (cf. Weis 2013).

The industrialization of horticulture, including the extensive use of plastics, occurred in part through the strength of the chemical industries and the development of state infrastructures—the U.S. state infrastructure, in particular—for the creation, promotion, and dissemination of agri-technologies and protocols. At the turn of the twentieth century, the petrochemical industry found a way to create ethylene from petroleum; ethylene is a gas that contains a manufactured plant compound responsible for plant development, i.e. the ripening of fruit, the opening of flowers, and the shedding of leaves. Then, in the 1930s, Imperial Chemical Industries, one of the largest manufacturers of the British Empire, developed polyethylene, the type of plastic used in agriculture, which is the product of an energy-intensive manufacturing process that breaks down petroleum into smaller molecules. By the 1970s, plastics were used in greenhouses throughout the Northern temperate zone, including U.S. Southern states (White 1979).

Rising oil prices of the 1970s meant not only declining profits but growing fears of limits to the expansion of production within given conditions (of land, labor, technologies). With oil prices high, costs rose to maintain the production environment in temperate regions where greenhouses and CAFOs were used extensively. Further, in the United States, there was growing recognition among agriculture extension and industry that frontiers for industrial horticulture were ending with the deactivation of agricultural lands (through real estate development, soil erosion, etc.), representing, in Moore's terms, limits to the appropriation of nature's "free gifts" (Marx 1967 cited in Moore 2010b: 4). Transnational corporations and the agricultural sciences in the global North began touting controlled environment agriculture (CEA) as a sustainable solution to the so-called limits to production. Sustainable here has a double meaning: production that uses less energy and that is kept profitable relative to other regions. In horticulture, the promise of CEA technologies was in their ability to retain heat while preventing condensation/humidity. Thus, they conserve energy use (from heating, irrigation) and are even more effective in arid regions that are drier and hotter. The development and patenting of CEA technologies proliferated beginning in the 1970s (White 1979; McGrath 1981). At the same time, these developments anticipated the expanding frontier of industrial horticulture. Among proponents of CEA technologies within the U.S. agricultural sciences, there was an expressed inevitability of not only the development of increasingly coercive agri-technologies but also the spread of these innovations to new regions south of the Northern temperate zone. As one scientist proclaimed at the time:

> The question is not one of whether we will have environmental controls, but rather, what types of controls and how much and where to practice the controls with the least cost in supplying the desired products. Fortunately, it is possible to practice environmental controls anywhere.
>
> (White 1979: 158)

The spread of U.S. patented agri-technologies and on-farm practices to growing and emerging agroexport regions at home and abroad was not inevitable but, rather, was realized through a marriage between the U.S. land grant university system (including agricultural extension services) and international development agencies (USAID, in particular) (McMichael 2012: 74).

This state-facilitated and corporate-led revolution enabled the spatial center of industrial horticulture and animal agriculture to move from the industrialized core to NACs, and CEA to transform from a marginal practice to an industry standard in global agri-food trade. This movement on a global scale co-constituted the movement of industrial horticulture (for export) and industrial poultry (for the national market) in Egypt from the Delta to reclaimed lands. Agribusiness managers and executives routinely pointed to the greater accessibility of agri-technologies—namely, polyethylene—since the passage of ERSAP in 1991 and Egypt joining the WTO in 1995 as an enabling factor in agroexport growth.[18] As is detailed in Chapter 7, the institutional infrastructure through which the corporate agri-food system grew— the state agencies (e.g. Export Council), professional associations (e.g. HEIA, the Chamber of Food Industries), and international development projects like the AERI program—further helped agribusiness negotiate the growing set of standards and certifications of corporate retailers and WTO protocols. During farm visits and interviews in 2011, agribusiness directors and managers uniformly affirmed the importance for agribusiness growth of funding and institutional support from state and international development agencies and professional associations. Farm management regularly attended trainings, study tours (often at U.S. universities), and international trade shows under the auspices of, for example, the Export Council or a USAID-funded initiative. In official terms, as was articulated at a Food Safety Conference at American University in Cairo in 2011, this institutional infrastructure was designed for Egyptian agribusiness to adopt "good agricultural practices" for food safety, part of the SPS Agreement's goal of harmonizing agricultural practice. From the point of view of on-farm practice, however, an overriding concern of agribusiness in attaining the certifications of corporate retailers (e.g., Global Gap) and achieving so-called best practices of the SPS Agreement is dealing effectively with emergent and recurrent diseases in ways that both conform with industry standards and save working capital.

Conclusions

Emergent and recurrent diseases have become increasingly virulent during the last couple of decades and have affected not only animal agriculture in Egypt but the country's agriculture and food system generally, with real and potential consequences for public health. During farm visits and interviews in 2010 and 2011, attention and resources on farms and in business operations were devoted overwhelmingly to threatening situations due to the blurring of the inside and outside of the production zone. For example, colleagues of an agribusiness manager were on a trip to a breeding station in Morocco to breed the predators of the pests destroying their crops.[19] For the poultry industry, aside from U.S. corn and soy feed, the import bill came from the continual rounds of vaccinations for viral infections (H5N1 being one among many infections).[20] These visits and interviews made me take seriously the unwanted and unanticipated in processes of planned change.

Through a lens on the relations between nature and society, the desert frontier embodies a tension: While biosecure agri-technologies and protocols attempt to control the inside of the production zone, even at the level of biological material, attention and resources on farms and in business operations are devoted overwhelmingly to threatening situations due to the very blurring of the inside and the outside. Across time and space the work of translation (Latour 1993)—the growing monsters of agriculture and food—relates directly to biosecurity as a changing set of governance mechanisms, agri-technologies, and institutions that constitute the corporate food regime and WTO members' corporate agri-food systems. From the movement to reclaimed lands to the extensive use of plastics to the Cornish Cross breed, this work of purification (Latour 1993) has become increasingly capital intensive and coercive.

This chapter demonstrates that biosecurity measures proceed on their premise— of a direct positive relationship between demarcating the inside of a production zone and effectively keeping out the unwanted, unexpected, and unintended. Yet, paths of disease transmission and the other unwanted exist between the inside and the outside in biosecure systems. Biosecurity is, in effect, based on a false premise. At the same time, the Avian flu outbreak and the flu's spread on a world stage since 2006 seem to have lent further support for biosecurity. Although at the time of the outbreak in Egypt not a single type of production unit was left unaffected, corporate biosecure poultry was relatively unharmed while birds in so-called backyards and live bird markets were most vulnerable. This outcome gave the appearance that non-biosecure or informal poultry was the vector of the virus. And developments in the poultry industry that followed reflect the great promise of biosecurity, as the agribusinesses with the most capital moved production farther into the desert and to the south of the country. Corporate poultry was responding by attempting to build greater "fortresses of gold," including a massive integrated poultry complex in Middle Egypt.[21]

The biosecurity regime has further been greenwashed since 2007–2009 with growing food and energy security fears given rising world prices. In the wake of the financial-food-energy crises, the food industry, policy makers, and environmentalists alike began embracing biosecure agri-technologies and protocols that make the expansion of commodity production in arid regions possible. Greening the desert has been framed as a novel response to the technical problem of food production under conditions of water and arable land scarcity due to desertification and fresh water depletion. According to these narratives, the dissemination of the latest technological innovations (e.g., on-farm desalinization plants) will enable this greening on a global scale. As this chapter shows, these greening the desert narratives re-emerged from an earlier era of rising fears of ecological limits to production— during the 1970s inflation. And these earlier narratives, in fact, coincided with the growth of existing, and the development of new arid regions for the intensification of horticulture production, in part through the development, patenting, and dissemination of biosecure agri-technologies and practices, especially plasticulture. Decades later, not only has the birth of global horticulture not overcome the proposed ecological limits to production, but in fact, the socio-ecological contradictions of industrial horticulture are now being expressed through the current heightening water insecurity and accelerating volatility of production.

As I write, threats to agriculture multiply: the latest swine flu is killing pigs throughout China, south-east Asia and elsewhere (S. Moore 2019; Philpott 2019). This threat and other threats raise the question of whether frontiers are coming to an end. Or more precisely: Does the frontier of capital represent the end of frontiers in the medium term? There are plenty of arid lands and even hyper-arid lands, but can any combination of factors in frontier making be reproduced, over and over, given the energy and capital intensity of the technologies and protocols? Given the questionable water-saving potential of the technologies? Given the rapid depletion of underground fresh water sources? Given the multiplying threats to production from increasingly virulent pests and pathogens?

In theoretical terms, the development and expansion of the desert frontier reflects the relative exhaustion of existing places of production (Moore 2011, 2015): Given the degradation of the ecological conditions of production in the global North and in the Delta in Egypt, frontier making in arid regions enabled profitable commodity expansion. Do rising prices since 2007–2008 represent a point of absolute exhaustion in the medium-term, though, in which levels of appropriation—of bringing the work/energy of the wind, sun, and so on into the circuits of capital—can no longer offset capitalization to maintain profitability (Moore 2011, 2015)? In the short term, no. But in the medium term, yes, likely so. The frontier continues to expand, but only in a perpetual, short-term sense by offsetting the risks from agricultural industrialization. Fears of limits to expanded capitalist development in the desert frontier in Egypt have animated imaginations of a west corridor, an underground waterway discovered in the 1960s by Occidental Petroleum, running 90% perpendicular to the Nile and cutting across the western desert.[22] And in the aftermath of the January 25 uprising, when the long-held promise of desert development to solve a host of the country's social and environmental problems needed to be evoked, public discussions of the underground waterway surfaced (*Egypt Independent*, June 20, 2011; Werr 2015).

Notes

1. See also Lorimer and Driessen (2013) on the biopolitics of biosecurity and Major (2008) on the biopolitics of labor.
2. Water-less agriculture refers to irrigation via desalinized water. For recent examples of these narratives, see Holden (2012), Margolis (2012), and Finley (2015).

3. On the alternative food movement, see Holden (2012) and Margolis (2012). For Israel, see Siegel (2015). For Egypt, see Sims (2018).
4. For the Central Valley, see Stoll (1998) and Nash (2006). For the São Francisco River Valley, see Marsden et al. (1996), Damiani (1999), and Selwyn (2007). For the western coast of Peru, see Glover and Kusterer (1990) and USDA (2010b).
5. A notable exception is Marsden et al. (1996): The similarity of their observations in the horticulture region in Brazil to my own in Egypt compelled me to research further the São Francisco River Valley as well as the other horticulture regions.
6. Farm visit and interview, 10/20/11, Alex-desert road (near to Sadat City).
7. In order to save the farms that rely on the aquifer, the World Bank loaned Egypt over $200 million for the West Delta Water Conservation and Irrigation Rehabilitation Project, which would essentially build a western extension of the Nile Delta branches to irrigate 190,000 acres, despite protests among farmer groups in the Delta (Barnes 2012: 530). This massive infrastructure project was closed after the World Bank determined in 2011 that the Egyptian government had not spent the loan money for the project. For details, see Sims (2018).
8. Interview, 8/5/2011, Cairo: In some cases, production of water-thirsty crops was illegal, as in the case of a government ban on rice cultivation in parts of the Delta. In a banned area of the Delta (Borg el Arab), smallholders had waged a campaign against wealthy farmers who had illegally planted rice.
9. Interview, 8/15/2011, Cairo.
10. By operators, I refer to poultry producers who may own medium- to large-scale farms but whose total production is much smaller than the dominating corporations within the poultry industry.
11. From 1959 to 2003, only 21 outbreaks occurred worldwide, mainly in the Americas and Europe (WHO 2004).
12. Interview, 8/16/2011, Cairo.
13. Interview, 11/16/2011, Cairo.
14. Interview, 8/16/2011, Cairo.
15. In interviews, as in this excerpt here, production sites were often referred to as farms or houses. Given that they are industrial and look like warehouses, the sites are referred to here as facilities.
16. Interview, 10/3/2011, Cairo.
17. Interview, 10/3/2011, Cairo.
18. Interview, 10/12/2011, Cairo. Farm visit, 10/18/2011, South Tahrir.
19. Farm visit, 10/2/2011, Ismailia.
20. Interview, 8/16/2011, Cairo.
21. Farm visit, 10/2/2011, Ismailia.
22. Interview, 1/18/2011, Cairo.

9
Conclusion

Frontiers and Corporate Food

When food and other prices rose sharply in 2007–2008 and the Northern financial sector nearly collapsed a year later, agricultural land suddenly became a valuable asset for investors. Large-scale investments in agricultural land, especially in countries where land was sold or leased at low prices, were heralded as a solution to food and energy insecurity (Allan et al. 2013; Woertz 2013). Analyses of these developments have tended to focus on the past decade of land contestations as the latest wave of accumulation by dispossession—of dispossessing people from land that they depend on for their livelihoods (Allan et al. 2013; McMichael 2013). Less attention has been given to the renewed promise of land frontiers in the wake of the food and financial crises.

Commercial agriculture has long developed through various types of frontiers, and today frontiers that "green the desert"—turning arid regions into centers of food production—have surfaced as a sustainable answer to the problem of food insecurity (Holden 2012; Margolis 2012; Finley 2015). In the face of global warming, soil degradation, genetic erosion, and fresh water depletion, highly capitalized production zones in arid lands are being developed and existing lands expanded.[1] This book shows that in Egypt corporate food has grown not only by various forms of dispossession including by degrading the environment—but also by remaking local and regional ecosystems for the expansion of cash crop production.

I argue that the continual expansion of the frontier of reclaimed lands has been necessary, but not sufficient, for the development of a corporate agri-food system in Egypt. The price of land mattered: The Egyptian state incentivized investors (and others) to buy reclaimed land (or arid land for reclamation) by selling the land at lower prices than agricultural land in the Delta and Nile Valley. The state also pro vided additional supports to agribusiness to incentivize production on reclaimed land. The ecology of commercial agriculture also mattered: Cash crop production necessarily leads to vulnerabilities from the loss of biological defenses for plants and animals—vulnerabilities from multiplying and increasingly virulent pests and pathogens, especially. These threats to capital, in turn, have led to ever greater controls over the production environment. By the turn of the twenty-first century, controlled environment protocols and agri-technologies fell under the broad umbrella of biosecurity, i.e., protections of society and economy from the unwanted and/or unknown. The movement of horticulture farms and poultry facilities to more

The Frontiers of Corporate Food in Egypt. Marion W. Dixon, Oxford University Press.
© Marion W. Dixon (2023). DOI: 10.1093/oso/9780192842985.003.0009

arid lands during the neoliberal period that I detail in Chapter 8 was a process of biosecuritization; as threats have increased, ever stricter production zones, even at the molecular level, have been delineated. Biosecuritization is coupled with multiple threats to production from global warming (for example, extreme weather in the arid regions) and persistent social problems in the Delta and Nile Valley, including land-lessness and un/underemployment. These multiple forces have pushed and pulled investors, smallholders, and other settlers from the Delta and Nile Valley into the expanding desert frontier.

I also show in Chapters 4, 5, and 6 the importance of a longue durée analysis of land reclamation—an analysis of land reclamation over a long period of time, under-going subtle but qualitatively distinct transformations and unevenly across regions. In historical capitalism, land reclamation became a distinct commodity frontier: the state incentivizes individual men or private entities to bear the cost of reclaiming the land and the grantee transforms the local ecosystem for the extraction/production of commodities for profit. Further, I show that land reclamation can provide the ini-tial conditions for capital formation and development in land. Why? Land that is reclaimed may not be used or used recently, or even if used, may be marginal to liveli-hoods. This historical fact means that land reclamation does not necessarily involve dispossession in any direct sense, and no a priori radical legal property changes may be necessary for land to be reclaimed. If there are minimal conflicts regarding claims to the land, which is more likely given these conditions, larger (than existing) land parcels will be reclaimed. Given that reclamation is costly, larger-size land parcels and the extraction/production and sale of commodities on this land would be imperative to get a return on investment.

The production and/or extraction of commodities for sale (in often distant mar-kets) concentrated on reclaimed lands in parts of western Europe from the late medieval period onward. Also, extended commodity production was concentrated in reclaimed lands in various regions of the Ottoman empire by the eighteenth cen-tury. In modern-era Egypt, during what I call the first wave of frontier making, during the second half of Mohammed 'Ali's reign, 'Ali granted land titles to prominent men in exchange for them reclaiming and cultivating the land, which led to the develop-ment of a market in land (land transactions and mortgage credit). This development occurred throughout the subsequent waves of frontier making in the long nineteenth century. In both cases, in late medieval western Europe and in nineteenth-century Egypt, land reclamation as a commodity frontier was a dynamic response to demand from distant markets and involved a merchant class devoted to accumulating capital and a state borrowing to pay for mercenary forces (in the face of growing inter-state and inter-capitalist competition).

Stating that land reclamation provided the initial conditions for capital forma-tion and development in land in late medieval western Europe and in the early-nineteenth-century Ottoman province of Egypt is not a statement that one happened because of the other. I am not arguing that this practice or social formation occurred in Egypt because it occurred in western Europe. Rather, I am arguing that these prac-tices constitute initial conditions for capital formation and development—and are born out of a contingent process. These conditions are by no means the only conditions for capital formation and development in land historically. At the same time, the time sequence matters: Land reclamation as a commodity frontier developed in western Europe in the late medieval period, creating a reinforcing dynamic between an external frontier in the New World and Asia and an internal frontier, centuries before the Ottoman state. Rapid capitalist development led to the ascendence of western European states within an emerging world-system, divided into world regions that specialize and trade in certain commodities ordered by a value hierarchy. By the time of rapid capitalist development in Egypt, this development led to the state's participation in a transforming system—but in a less powerful position, toward the bottom of this hierarchy.

I am hardly stating that what the Egyptian state has done or does doesn't matter. Rather, my point is that state (and other) decisions are structured and, thereby, limited. This point takes me back to the present-day, which is overwhelmed with commentary and analyses of the failures and mistakes of the Egyptian government from scholars, development officials, and bureaucrats alike. What this singular focus misses is that the corporate food regime, or global food economy, structures decisions that impact agriculture and food in Egypt, as I have tried to show in this book. Up to this point, this book has referenced little about the country's corporate agri-food system following the time period (2008–2012) of my research in Egypt. In the following section, I offer brief reflections on developments related to the corporate agri-food system since the start of the Abdel Fattah El-Sisi administration in 2014.

Frontier Making under the Sisi Administration

Mounting sovereign debts coupled with declines in revenues from the Suez canal, oil, and gas, and tourism in the aftermath of the 2011 popular uprising culminated in forming a type of military-civilian economy (Adly 2020: 20) or hybrid economy (Kandil 2016: 7)—with major state projects being run by the military since 2014. Gulf money poured into Egypt during and in the aftermath of the popular uprising to bolster counter-revolutionary, anti-democratic forces (Hinnebusch 2018: 47).[2] This funding dried up by 2015 (Kandil 2016; Mossallem 2017). However, the discovery of the Zohr gas fields in the Mediterranean Sea opened up a new line of credit. By 2018–2019, annual natural gas production exceeded consumption, and the government was claiming "energy independence" (EIA 2022).[3]

What does the development of a hybrid economy mean for the desert frontier? The Sisi administration has pushed forward, at least on paper, a number of mega projects, including projects to greatly expand the desert frontier. One of them was the 1.5 Million Feddan Project for the 2014–2017 period, and according to Sims (2018: xlv–xlvix), as of 2017, little had come of the project. The administration also announced the expansion of the Toshka project despite Toshka's failure during the 1997–2011 period and the subsequent withdrawal of the main external funder, El-Wahid bin Talal of Kingdom Investments (Sims 2018: li). Because GCC funding (as well as funding from Russia and China) began to dwindle, the administration relied on the family business groups and financial firms that grew powerful under Mubarak to help fund these projects (Kandil 2016: 20). In short, many of those who grew wealthy during the Mubarak years have continued to reproduce their wealth and privilege in the post-revolutionary era.

Also, the model of prioritizing investors in industrial plots and on reclaimed lands (or lands to be reclaimed) in the desert frontier has continued (Sims 2018: 235). In Saker El Nour's (2020: 8, 11) recent study of the state reclamation project Wadi Al Nukra, an estimated 77% of the total official project lands were allocated to investors, although most of this land was not devoted to agriculture.

According to Sims (2018: lii), there has also been a government campaign to seize informal land claims since 2010, presumably so that the government can then sell/lease this land to investors. In 2017, the then Prime Minister Sherif Ismail announced that over 919,000 acres had been seized between 2010 and 2017 (Sims 2018: lii). During my research in Egypt, through 2011, I did not observe or hear about any such seizure. Seizures of squatters' lands could have gained momentum after the transitional period between 2011 and 2013, when a second uprising and military coup in 2013 followed the 2011 popular uprising.

Also, significant to the desert frontier is the changing hydropolitics of the Nile— the politics between Egypt and the country's riparian neighbors along the three river systems of the region, the White Nile, Blue Nile, and Atbara. The Ethiopian government built the Grand Renaissance Dam, the continent's biggest dam, measuring 1800 meters long, 155 meters high with a capacity of 74 billion cubic meters of water (Ayeb and Bush 2019: 39). The 2010 Entebbe Agreement nulled the 1959 Nile Agreement, which had given Egypt 55.5 in cubic meters of water per year as opposed to Sudan's 18.5 cubic meters. Following the 2010 agreement, Egypt's share of the Nile water for irrigation, electrification, and the like remains uncertain. As I conclude in Chapter 8, the frontier of capital in reclaimed arid lands is likely coming to an end in the medium term. A west corridor will not appear magically to provide an endless supply of irrigation water for commercial agriculture.

Comfort Foods in Uncertain Times

Despite the delays of the mega projects and what appears to be a slowdown of agribusiness expansion in the desert frontier, the country's corporate agri-food system, and food processing in particular, has continued to grow since 2011. Food processing averaged a compound annual growth rate of 12% during the 2010– 2014 period (USDA 2015). In terms of agricultural ingredients for food processing, $1.89 billion were imported in 2014 alone (USDA 2015). The food processing sector with the largest revenue in 2014 was the impulse and indulgence sectors (including tobacco, alcohol, soft drinks, and confectionary). The two highest grossing TNCs in this sector were Cadbury ($388 million) and Nestlé ($366.85 million). Even instant noodles have been growing in popularity, like in India as I explore in Chapter 3.

According to the 2015 USDA report, Egypt flour mills were expanding lines in their bakeries for instant noodle production. Also, a so-called cupcake craze was rapidly expanding the bakery industry.

The corporate poultry industry also did well. In 2020, there were 25,000 licensed poultry facilities with investment reaching $4.15 billion (USDA 2021). The industry recorded producing 1.4 billion chickens (i.e. broilers) and 13 billion table eggs. Industry projections were that production would continue to rise to 2 billion broiler chickens and a doubling of table eggs by 2030 (USDA 2021).[4]

During the high levels of political and economic uncertainty, with high rates of inflation, following the 2011 uprising, it is not surprising that there was a surge in foods/drinks high in unhealthy sugars, fats, and sodium. Although it is still early to conclude how food consumption habits changed, if at all, during the COVID-19 global pandemic, predictably eating out went down significantly during the 2020 lockdown (Ali et al. 2021). But by February 2021, the Supply Ministry announced a threefold increase in total food consumption since the start of the pandemic (*Middle East Monitor*, February 9, 2021). Given that cravings for sugary, salty, and fatty foods are associated with stress (Moss 2013; Yau and Potenza 2013), I would predict that similar trends in food processing (type 2 and type 3) and animal protein continued during the pandemic, explaining at least in part this increase in total food consumption.[5]

The continued growth of the country's corporate agri-food system, including food processing and poultry, depends on and shapes the expanding desert frontier. The ongoing COVID-19 pandemic, the ongoing avian flu pandemic, and the multiple unknowns and unwanted that intersect directly and indirectly with the corporate food regime—all create uncertainty, risks to capital and to public health. Zoonotic diseases, in particular, will continue to push agribusiness farther from residential areas and other production facilities, and relative exhaustion will be reached as costs of production rise. The first global pandemic in 100 years raises these doubts as well as questions about what the COVID-19 virus will evolve into and what and when the next global pandemic will strike.

The Right to Food

Each citizen has the right to healthy and sufficient food and clean water. The State shall ensure food resources to all citizens. The State shall also ensure sustainable food sovereignty and maintain agricultural biological diversity and types of local plants in order to safeguard the rights of future generations.

The Constitution of Egypt, Article 27 (2014)

By the end of the 2010s, studies emerged highlighting the role of the rural poor in the popular uprisings in Egypt. These studies have pointed out that while protests in 2011 began in Tahrir square in Cairo, protests quickly spread to other provinces. Plus, many participants in Tahrir came from other provinces (El Nour 2015; Ayeb and

Bush 2019). Smallholders demonstrated on the streets, rebuilt houses that they have been evicted from, formed independent farmer unions, and more (De Lellis 2020). According to a 2012 LCHR report, smallholders carried out 158 protests, with 74 sit-ins and 84 demonstrations) (cited in El Nour 2015: 204). The momentum that began when an independent farmers' union was formed in 2010, as I describe in Chapter 3, continued during and after the uprising. Four organizations representing the rural poor in total were established after the fall of Mubarak. One of them, the Egyptian Federation of Small Farmers, had a membership of more than 70,000 (El Nour 2015: 203).

These mobilizations could be argued to have won a victory in the inclusion of the Right to Food article in the 2014 constitution, as El Nour (2015) argues. This right is for the state to guarantee food sovereignty, "healthy and sufficient" food and water to citizens. However, the Right to Food has become a mainstream agenda of the multilateral organizations. Multilaterals have been pushing the Right to Food at the very same time that they have been pushing to end universal food subsidies in Egypt and elsewhere (see Jakobsen 2018 on the Right to Food in India).

As was discussed in Chapter 2, the Sisi administration replaced universal bread subsidies with a type of dietary regime, limiting the number of loaves for each recipient. The food (non-bread) subsidy was turned into cash transfers (for certain population groups) and the Tamween conditional system for others, with registered recipients using ration cards in designated shops for food and non-food items. Those who were covered through the Tamween began to be chipped away at: about 75% of the population was registered in 2015 and that percentage dropped to about 65% in 2019 (Breisinger et al. 2021). Registration is not simple and is costly, and the declining coverage would be expected especially among poorer households.[6]

The Right to Food—and the so-called hybrid economy more generally—represent the heightened contradictions between the expansions of the market and protections from the market in the post-2007–08 period. Universal bread subsidies are turned into targeted assistance at the same time as government mandates continue to increase wheat production. Since the price hikes of 2007–08, the Egyptian government has continually been committed to increasing wheat (and other cereal) production: A three-year mandate increased yields in 2010–11 and 2011–12 (FAO 2012). Successive Ministers of Agriculture under Sisi, Essam Fayed and Abdel Moneim al Banna, affirmed the importance of reducing dependence on imported strategic crops (Ayeb and Bush 2019: 85). Yet, as I argue in Chapter 2, by turning food subsidies into a rationing system, the government is weakening the very mechanism for buying domestic wheat, to ensure that all Egyptians don't go hungry.

Addressing the "right to healthy and sufficient food" should start with asking which foods are subsidized. Rather than focusing on *baladi* bread, which is more nutritious than processed white bread, the focus should be on the non-bread foods under the Tamween system. At the very least, the inclusion of animal protein should be evaluated: one-fourth of the main food items are animal protein—poultry and red meat.[7] Adding poultry and red meat to the Tamween was undoubtedly intended to make animal protein more available to lower-income households. However, their inclusion is also a subsidy for the corporate poultry industry and the red meat producers and importers. Plus, the most vulnerable are already excluded from the Tamween, as it is a conditional system.

Maintaining "agricultural biological diversity and types of local plants in order to safeguard the rights of future generations" would entail lessening the subsidy on animal protein and increasing the producer and consumer subsidy on a local, protein-rich plant food: fava beans. Fava beans, a legume and natural fertilizer that fixes nitrogen from the atmosphere, is an Egyptian staple that has long been cultivated in the country. Fava beans remain subsidized, but most fava beans for the Tamween (about 64%) were imported in 2021.[8] As Louise Sarant (2020) has recently pointed out, Egypt used to be self-sufficient in fava beans, but under debt management in the 1980s, the crop rotation system that included fava beans ended. A renewed producer subsidy on fava beans could replace animal feed, and an expanded consumer subsidy could substitute animal protein, contributing to greater protein diversity for most Egyptians.[9]

The Specter of Debt

Any gains for the rural poor will further be stunted by mounting sovereign (and other) debts. In Hinnebusch's (2018: 48) terms, the uprisings

> in disrupting economic growth and actually deepening dependence on the Western-centered international financial system, further locked Tunisia and Egypt, the two states with the best prospects for democratization, into neoliberal practices and made it impossible to address inequality and poverty.

At the time of the uprising, Hassan Heikal, one of the bankers who was targeted after the uprising along with the Mubaraks and has since left the country, proposed a one-time wealth tax of 10–20% in an op-ed piece in the *Financial Times* (Heikal 2011 cited in Mossallem 2017). This so-called Tahrir Square Tax was to impose a one-off global wealth tax on individuals with a net worth in excess of $10 million with tax receipts going to their country of citizenship. Heikal was recognizing that political instability, and disruptions to economic growth, would continue unless there was an effort toward more redistribution.

Instead, the economic recovery under the Sisi administration has been debt driven, in Amr Adly's (2020) terms: Foreign debt rose from $55 billion on the evening of adopting the $12 billion IMF deal in 2016 to more than $100 billion by the beginning of the third quarter of 2019. The ratio of foreign debt service to exports rose consistently from 7.7% in 2013 to 37.7% in 2017–18 (Adly 2020: 14).

Given the tendency within the capitalist world-system toward oligopoly—in short, winners winning more over time—redistributive measures like debt relief and progressive taxation will help militate against this tendency, at least temporarily. Relief from the onerous debt of the Mubarak administration and a wealth tax, as Egyptian social movements have called for, will better secure food futures—the ability of the masses, including the rural poor, to have adequate and nutritious food—as long as such measures are applied nearly universally, in most countries and transnationally, in ways that undermine the structural power of global finance. Governments and their ruling coalitions will become more politically stable, ending or at least pacifying the past decade of historically significant global protest.

Such redistributive measures, even if ambitious, will weaken corporate power but will not end corporate rule. As I show in this book, there is a type of symbiotic relationship between global, regional, and national capital. There is competition—but TNCs, MNCs, financial firms, and family business groups have worked in concert to limit that competition, forming quasi-monopolies throughout the formal economy, including in agriculture and food. There would still be the drive to lower costs to the extent that labor and other inputs can be reliable for expanded commodity production. As long as the capitalist mode of production is the dominant mode, the basic class system would remain—and the rural poor would remain poor (but less immiserated). There would still be a hierarchy of world regions, however the hierarchy changes, and debt would return, as was the experience in post-1952 independence. Only a transformation in value on a worldwide scale could radically change the system of agriculture and food so that the universal right to nutritious and adequate food and water is realized.

Notes

1. On the promise of new arid lands, see Holden (2012). On the expansion of production on arid lands and the resulting ecological limitations, see Lawrence (2010) on the arid regions in Peru. See Boxall (2015) and Gillis and Richtel (2015) on the Central Valley in California.
2. Funding from the GCC for the fiscal year 2013–14 amounted to $20 billion (Mossallem 2017).
3. See also the description of the Zohr gas fields on the website of ENI, the oil company to initially develop the fields for extraction. For more recent proclamations of energy independence from President Sisi, see *Zawya*, October 24, 2022.
4. More social scientific research on aquaculture would also be warranted: Egypt remained one of the world's largest fish farming countries (USDA 2021).
5. In the United States, where I was during the first two years of the pandemic (2020–2022), fast food chain sales grew rapidly, taking more than 70% of all eating out sales (Russ 2021).
6. The WFP (2008) predicted these problems in their report defending food subsidies in Egypt.
7. This percentage (two out of eight) is based on 2021 data from the Ministry of Supply and Internal Trade's website.
8. This 2021 data also comes from the Ministry of Supply and Internal Trade's website.
9. On the potential of fava beans to be central to protein diverse diets in a warming planet, especially in countries like Egypt where the bean is already grown, see Multari, Stewart, and Russell 2015.

Epilogue

> The General Assembly is meeting at a time of great peril.
> **UN Secretary-General António Guterres, September 2022**[1]

Skipping Queen Elizabeth's funeral, the Secretary-General António Guterres headed to the United Nations to preside over an emergency meeting in September 2022. It had been more than seven months since Russia invaded Ukraine. There were palpable fears of continued and growing conflict and bloodshed in Ukraine and around the world, of millions going hungry as food prices soared. An agreement between Russia and Ukraine with Turkey and the United Nations had been made to allow for grain, other food stuffs, and fertilizers to be exported out of Ukraine. But calls of Russian foul play remained—not least of which were #FoodIsNotAWeapon being tweeted in the Twitter echo chamber.

Food prices had been rising steadily in 2021, following a year of the onset of the COVID-19 pandemic. Then, in February 2022, Russia invaded Ukraine. World food prices hit a new record high in March (FAO 2022; Whiting 2022). World food prices are tied tightly to oil prices, which rose by 50% from 2021 to 2022 (UN 2022a). In Egypt, by October, food prices reached a four-year high (*English Al Arabiya*, November 10, 2022). Annual inflation rose to 15.3% compared to 6.4% the same month the previous year (*Arab News*, September 8, 2022).

As world food prices soared, the number of people facing acute food insecurity more than doubled between 2019 and 2022 (Whiting 2022). In 2022 alone, the number of people who are acutely food insecure or at high risk reached a record high of 345 million people in 82 countries—an increase of almost 200 million people compared to pre-pandemic levels (WFP 2022). In Egypt, warnings of food insecurity have been less dire; nonetheless, food insecurity has predictably increased. Those covered by the Tamween food (non-bread) subsidy system had steadily declined in the years leading up to the pandemic: The percentage of the population covered dropped from about three-fourths of households in 2015 to 65% of households in 2019 (Breisinger et al. 2021: 3). The poor were much less likely to register for a SMART card, which meant that lower-income households were even more vulnerable as food prices rose again in 2021 and 2022.

The WFP (2022: 5) has warned that this world food price shock is significantly worse than the shock of 2007–08 and 2010–11:

> In those years, there were no pandemic-related shocks, no massive income loss, no record inflation, no supply chain disruptions, and no major record debt burden.

The Frontiers of Corporate Food in Egypt. Marion W. Dixon, Oxford University Press.
© Marion W. Dixon (2023). DOI: 10.1093/oso/9780192842985.003.0010

There was no war in Syria, Yemen, Nigeria or Ethiopia. There were less frequent and less intense climate-related shocks.

As with the previous price shocks, there was a confluence of forces behind this shock—namely, conflict, climate shocks, and COVID-19 (Husain 2022). This confluence has created what Adam Tooze (2022) and others are calling a polycrisis—disparate shocks that appear to interact and "to add up to more than their sum."[2] The UN Secretary-General's declaration above refers after all not only to world hunger or Russia's war of aggression. Rather, this "time of great peril" refers to any number of problems, immediate and unforeseen.

The conjuncture of the 2021-2022 food price shock emerged out of the previous food and related crises. Extreme weather events played a role in each of these price hikes—and these events have become more severe and more frequent. Soaring heat in Canada and throughout Europe, drought in India, in 2021–22 alone, contributed to rising world food prices (Rennison 2022). Climate shocks have further contributed to the past decade of political instability. As I show in Chapter 2, the 2011 popular uprisings in the MENA region spawned a decade of historically significant popular protest worldwide, including regime change. Because counter-revolutionary forces emerged, among other reasons, protests have also intersected with a rise in violent conflicts within and between countries. State-based armed conflicts nearly doubled between 2010 and 2020, and the number of people forced to flee their homes rose from 43 million to more than 200 million in 2022 alone (Husain 2022).

As food prices rise to new historical highs, fears mount of greater political unrest, especially in the MENA region (Egypt, Tunisia, and Lebanon, in addition to Yemen and Sudan) (Osterlund 2022; *New York Times*, September 20, 2022). In response, the United States provided $9.8 billion in international food assistance in 2022; $1.8 billion of this package was emergency food aid for the MENA region (Laff 2022).[3] Gulf states also pledged more than $22 billion in investments in Egypt (*New York Times*, September 20, 2022).

Further, zoonotic, infectious diseases have grown in frequency and virulence with the industrialization of animal agriculture and rapid urbanization leading to crowded and unsanitary living conditions, as I show in Chapter 8. The emergence and endemic spread of the Avian flu has been devastating for animal welfare and has endangered agricultural sectors and public health. COVID-19 was the latest in the succession of zoonotic disease outbreaks—and was uniquely able to grow into a global pandemic in part because of its ability to spread quickly among humans. The COVID-19 pandemic has not entirely abated nearly three years since it began. And warning signs are already being issued that another zoonotic monster like a mutated Avian flu loom in the near future.[4] Global warming, the ever-growing intensification and scale of animal agriculture, and the continued shrinking of distances between animals and human living quarters make these threats real and alarming.

The idea of a developing polycrisis warns at the very least of a return to some combination of banking, currency, and debt crises in the global South. The Northern boom–Southern crisis ended with the near U.S. financial crash of 2008–09 (see Chapter 7), followed five years later by the European financial crash (Tooze 2018). This financial crisis and recession immediately affected the transatlantic world, but with the COVID-19 shutdown and economic contraction, effects are now rippling throughout the global South. Warnings abound of an impending debt crisis in low-income and middle-income countries as import bills grow—and calls for debt forgiveness even grow among the mainstream (Summers and Ahmed 2022; iPES-Food 2022).

Contributing to this polycrisis is the fact that two main converging forces driving the 2007–2008 and 2011 price shocks—the growth of both commodity futures markets and the agrofuels market during the decade prior—have since become structural features of the corporate food regime. Efforts to regulate commodity futures trading after 2007–2009 largely failed (see Chapter 7; also iPES-Food 2022). Similarly, efforts to curtail agrofuels have largely been unsuccessful.[5]

The structures of the corporate food regime contributing to the last two food price spikes, outlined in Chapter 2, have also largely remained intact: including de-regulated agricultural sectors, industrialized agriculture (especially animal agriculture) and a heavy reliance on fossilized energy, and capital concentration (Clapp 2022; ETC Group 2022). One exception are public grain reserves, which import-dependent, indebted countries began to re-establish in the intercrisis period, between 2008 and 2011(FAO 2014; iPES-food 2022). This anti-austerity politics gained traction, having been embraced by the multilaterals, and has been a mechanism governments have had at their disposal to try to weather this latest shock. The Egyptian General Authority for Supply Commodities (GASC) keeps a four-to-six month supply of stocks (including wheat) in the "import pipeline" with an additional one-month supply of wheat in transit to the country (USDA 2021). The Sisi administration was even boasting about the establishment of modern wheat silos that have supposedly increased the storage capacity to nearly four million tons (Mahmoud 2022). Clearly, this anti-austerity policy measure in Egypt and elsewhere is here to stay for the medium to long term.

Russia's Invasion of Ukraine and Structural Weaknesses of the Corporate Food Regime

The particular features of the corporate food regime that help explain why Russia's invasion of Ukraine had such an immediately dramatic impact on world food prices are that a small number of staple grains dominate the global grain trade and a small number of "breadbasket" regions export these grains—and both Russia and Ukraine are among them (Clapp 2022). Together the two countries account for over 25% of world wheat exports, 15% of world corn exports, and over 60% of sunflower oil exports (iPES-Food 2022).[6] Over 30 countries depend on both countries for at least 30% of their wheat import needs, and at least 20 countries get over 50% of wheat imports from Russia and Ukraine combined (iPES-Food 2022).

Egypt is one of the countries that has come to rely heavily on both Russian and Ukrainian food imports, as is illustrated in Chapters 1 and 2. An estimated 20% of wheat imports came from Ukraine and nearly 65% came from Russia in 2021 (*APK-Inform*, August 30, 2021). Egypt's top supplier of corn was Ukraine in 2019/2020 (USDA 2021), and 73% of the country's sunflower oil came from Russia and Ukraine (Tanchum 2022). When the Black Sea Grain Initiative was signed—the agreement between Russia and Ukraine, with Turkey and the United Nations, allowing exports from Ukraine—9% of the grains through the initiative were being exported to Egypt (UN 2022b).

A third characteristic of the global grain trade that is important is the role of commodity futures markets in the trade (Clapp 2022). After all, world grain prices did not rise after Russia's invasion of Ukraine because of a drop in supply. The harvesting of grains and sunflower oil had already occurred in both countries. Rather, the invasion triggered trading on the futures markets. Given the fact that both Russia and Ukraine are major exporting countries, traders predicted price increases for the next harvest. The invasion and war will impact supply—but over a 12-month period. Projections are that there will be more than a 46% drop of wheat exports from Ukraine (Rennison 2022). And if world food prices continue to rise by 8.5% within five years, more than 13 million people are expected to be pushed into malnourishment (Patel 2022).

Further characteristic of these structural weaknesses, and not captured in Jennifer Clapp's (2022) typology of the global grain trade, is what the grains are for. There are fewer types of grains being traded and a smaller number of regions exporting grains—and for what are these grains being used? For whom? It is often assumed, as with the coverage of the Black Sea Grain Initiative, that the grain is used to feed people. As I show in Chapters 2 and 3, grain is rather increasingly being used as animal feed and as agrofuels rather than for direct human consumption. According to one 2015 estimate, only about 55% of the world's crop calories feed people directly (Foley 2015). Russia and Ukraine jointly produced 254 tons of grain in 2019; only 41% of that grain was wheat for direct human consumption (*The Economist*, June 25, 2022). All the corn exported from Ukraine to Egypt will go to the feed mills—not for the food insecure.

This latest world food price shock not only confirms the instability of the corporate food regime but the acceleration of its de-stabilization. As Clapp (2022) points out, the three price shocks in just 15 years—2007–08, 2010–11, and 2021–2022—are more shocks than there had been in the previous 80 or more years. However, this latest price shock is not merely an intensification of the contradictions of the post-2011 period that I highlight in Chapter 9. I highlight signs of a heightened contradiction between the deepening of the gains of corporate-led globalization and a retreat through greater social protections. This 2021-2022 crisis demonstrates rather more clearly a retreat from globalization—a messy and protracted retreat but, nonetheless, a retreat.

The 2021–2022 Crisis and Authoritarian (Economic) Nationalism

This retreat from globalization is quite unlike the rapid and solidaristic retreat of the post-WWII period. I call it a twenty-first-century authoritarian pseudo-economic nationalist retreat. The instability of the world order has ushered in both a tide toward global authoritarianism and mass popular resistance to it at every step. In that tussle has emerged a significant bloc of low-income, middle-income, and even high-income countries engulfed in this twenty-first-century version of authoritarianism. It is pseudo-economic nationalist in that most states' abilities to direct economic planning are greatly hindered by the remaining power of finance and corporations. Yet, Egypt and other states in this bloc strive for protections from the world market, and they strive to do so in ways that minimize popular participation.

The Sisi administration's attempt to increase public grain reserves while cutting food subsidies is a case in point: While the re-establishment of public grain reserves have been embraced, the austerity politics of blaming subsidies (food and fuel) for import bills remains. Blaming food subsidies continues even though the bread ration (of 150 loaves per month per recipient) stayed the same during the pandemic, while demand for wheat for industrial uses rose by 2.5% (USDA 2021).[7] During the latest negotiations with the IMF for another loan, the Ministry of Supply and Internal Trade announced that it was studying the potential of switching to a conditional cash bread subsidy for subsidized bread—something similar to the Tamween card system (USDA 2021). Then, in 2022, in response to inflation and in an effort to thwart a black market from forming, the government increased the cost of eight essential goods offered through the Tamween system, but the value of the ration cards had remained the same since 2017 (Kassab 2022). This latest policy measure will undoubtedly contribute to a rise in food insecurity nationwide in 2022.

The Sisi administration will have greater control over food prices through the re-establishment of grain reserves while at the same time cutting off public entitlements (and in turn, channels for expressing public demands or discontent). However, given the limitations of shielding the Egyptian population from the vagaries of the world market, the administration is focusing on large national projects whose economic significance are less clear—for example, the new administrative capital and the new Egyptian Museum. With the recently discovered Zohr gas fields, the Sisi administration can engage in a kind of anti-austerity politics with large-scale projects with national purpose.

It would be a mistake to assume that this long, protracted retreat from the corporate-led globalization project, and by extension, the corporate food regime, is confined to the authoritarian pseudo-economic nationalist bloc. The broader efforts to circumvent the WTO rules that began after 2008 continue. Calls for debt forgiveness and a new role for the multilaterals in debt management are still heard.

Efforts to regulate the financial markets are being renewed. But how this transitional phase turns out is yet to be written.

Notes

1. Lederer 2022
2. On the WTO chief Ngozi Okonjo-Iweala's use of the term, see Blenkinsop and Farge 2022. On Larry Summers, see Summers and Ahmed 2022.
3. The concern is not confined to the MENA region. For example, the Asia Development Bank also devoted $14 billion through 2025 "to help ease a worsening food crisis in the Asia-Pacific" (*Associated Press*, September 27, 2022).
4. On the dangers of a mutated Avian flu that can more easily move from birds to humans, see Miller 2022.
5. The palm oil divestment campaign led by Friends of the Earth and other environmental groups has had some successes. For the latest on this campaign, see the Palm Oil Detectives website.
6. As Chapter 3 shows, vegetable oils are central to dietary changes around the world as food processing has grown in importance.
7. The USDA refers to this use as food, seed, and industrial (FSI) consumption.

Appendix

Calling the years that I conducted research in Egypt, between 2008 and 2012, as politically tumultuous seems like a euphemism. During this so-called inter-crisis period, there was heightened popular resistance and activity, but government authorities responded to this resistance with intimidation, arrest, imprisonment, the threat of violence and/or violence. Generally, the environment was politically repressive. And specifically, the research topic that I began with during the first phase of this research—on the dispossession of smallholders from land—was politically sensitive and parts of the countryside were unstable and potentially violent. The Egyptian government further created obstacles for foreign researchers. Research permissions were rarely granted, and movement of foreigners outside of the main cities of Cairo and Alexandria and the major tourist destinations was limited. These restrictions help explain why there is a paucity of contemporary literature in English on agrarian change in the country—and much of the rest of the region (Deeb and Winegar 2012 cited in Rignall 2021: 206).

This dangerous research setting is one in which "social relationships and cultural realities are critically modified by the pervasion of fear, threat of violence, or (ir)regular application of violence" (Kovats-Bernat 2002: 208–209). Additional methodological and ethical considerations are required when conducting research in this type of setting (Wynn 2007). Practically, if I stayed in Cairo, I remained anonymous, and most of my research activities remained in Cairo. If I were to take visits outside of Cairo, especially to the countryside in the Delta and Nile Valley, I kept them brief, to day trips if possible, so as not to attract the attention of the Egyptian authorities. I followed other foreign researchers who had done similarly, like Kamran Ali (2002), who took short but repeated trips to a village and to an urban industrial neighborhood during his two-sited ethnography in the 1990s. I was not so much concerned at the time for my personal safety; rather, I was primarily concerned for the personal safety and other risks of the Egyptians with whom I met.

Many people at the lower end of the social hierarchy seemed to recognize a level of risk in meeting with me, even in Cairo. While I was able to meet with people, it took years—and often was only possible through direct contacts. For interviews, I nearly exclusively used snowball sampling, which is often used when interviewees are few in number, are hidden, or where some degree of trust is required to initiate contact (Clark 2006: 419).

Beyond the practicalities of the methods used, the various risks involved in this research required me to be flexible and reflexive about my research questions and how I would go about answering them. In dangerous settings, methodology needs to be redefined from a "rigid or fixed framework" to an "elastic, incorporative, integrative, and malleable practice" (Kovats-Bernat 2002: 210). Further, in Nancy Scheper-Hughes's (1995: 419) terms, dangerous settings dictate the primacy of the ethical: responsibility, accountability, and answerability.

Exemplifying these ethical and methodological considerations is the research collaboration that I began to develop with a local NGO in Middle Egypt devoted to improving the livelihoods of smallholders in the area. When I began preliminary research in Egypt, my first informant made it clear to me that she would not help facilitate my research if I had a conventional research agenda. I had insisted to her that I wanted to do research that was relevant to the so-called subjects of research, and over the next couple of years I found this local partner to potentially carry out such a collaborative research project. I met with the director of the NGO on a number of occasions, and in 2010, he invited me to a two-day farmer-to-farmer exchange in the local area. The NGO had to purchase my train ticket as foreigners were not allowed to buy tickets to Middle Egypt. When I was at this farmer-to-farmer exchange, with a group of other researchers and a representative of the main foreign funding body, I learned that the NGO was facing continual problems with the authorities. Foreign funds to NGOs had to be approved by the Ministry of Social Affairs, and the Ministry had held up the funds. Finally, the Ministry released the funds, and the NGO was able to host the workshop.

In the preceding months, I went ahead and created informational materials (in Modern Standard Arabic) as well as a presentation (in Egyptian Arabic) on participatory action research—on a small-scale project carried out by smallholders themselves in some capacity to address a social issue of their concern. The NGO again invited me to Middle Egypt to meet with them and present the proposal. I proceeded, despite having the knowledge that the authorities were surveilling the organization. On this trip and in previous meetings, we had discussed how we would carry out this project; perhaps I would stay only for short visits, changing hotels each time. After this second visit, however, I finally began to question this project pragmatically and ethically. Having received a train ticket from them, I arrived on my own this time. To even get from the train station to my hotel on that trip, I had to pass security guards at the station. Thankfully, that time I passed them with ease, but on each visit, I would need to pass them. I think what took me so long to reflect clearly on this part of my research is that my local partner was willing to collaborate with me. However, as the literature on research in dangerous settings highlights, the risk involved needs to be assessed primarily by the outside researcher, who often has more power than the local partner. Just because the local partner was willing to take the risk does not mean that I should have. I could not ensure that the association with me would not in any way harm the safety, dignity, or privacy of the people involved (see Kovats-Bernat 2002).

It became apparent that continuing with this collaboration was unethical. Because of the restrictions on my movements outside of Cairo, however, the methodological flexibility that I had adopted had already led me to start asking questions about corporate food. By taking this research out of a particular site or sites even, I was able to ask important questions about forces and structures shaping rural livelihoods in ways that may not be readily apparent to smallholders, their advocates, or the funders. Plus, there was little likelihood that any association with me among those higher up in the corporate agri-food system would in any way harm their personal safety, dignity, or privacy.

About a year after my second and last visit to Middle Egypt, in two separate interviews with agribusiness, I learned of "one of the largest corporate poultry facilities" being planned in Middle Egypt.[1] Immediately, I contacted the NGO and the funding body, raising questions well beyond the immediate and directly relevant: What impact would this facility have on local poultry breeds? On the water supply? On the labor and land markets? And that is exactly what I attempt to do in this book: Using the tools of the social sciences, I raise questions to take the discussion farther than the apparent.

Note

1. Farm visit, 10/2/11, Ismailia; Interview, 10/3/11, Cairo.

References

"Can bread subsidies continue in their present form?," *IRIN*, April 10, 2008.

"Deep waters, slowly drying up," *Economist*, October 7, 2010.

"Egypt says Juhayna, others violate competition law," *Reuters*, March 14, 2011.

"Study reveals further details about Western Desert underground waterway," *Egypt Independent*, June 20, 2011.

"New foot and mouth disease strain hits Egypt: FAO," *Reuters*, March 22, 2012.

"Kellogg company completes acquisition of majority stake in Bisco Misr," *PR Newswire*, January 15, 2015.

"Qalaa holdings signs sale & purchase agreement for Rashidi El-Mizan," *Qalaa Holdings*, November 10, 2015.

"Pharos closes the sale of 100% of Qalaa's unit," *Mubasher*, December 10, 2015.

"Food subsidies to increase by marginal 5% in upcoming state budget as austerity measures continue," *Mada Masr*, April 19, 2018.

"Egypt: food consumption increases threefold during pandemic," *Middle East Monitor* (MEMO), February 9, 2021.

"Ukraine and Russia cover 85% of Egypt's wheat demand," *APK-Inform*, August 30, 2021.

"Against the grain; world food," *The Economist*, June 25, 2022.

"Egypt's inflation hits 4-year high amid surge in food prices," *Arab News*, September 8, 2022.

"Egypt feels pain of global disruptions wrought by war and pandemic," *New York Times*, September 20, 2022.

"ADB to devote $14B to help ease food crisis in Asia-Pacific," *Associated Press*, September 27, 2022.

"Zohr field enabled Egypt to become self-sufficient in natural gas: El-Sisi," *Zawya*, October 24, 2022.

"Egypt's urban inflation accelerates on surging food prices," *English Al Arabiya*, November 10, 2022.

Abbas, Raouf and Assem El-Dessouky. 2011. *The Large Landowning Class and the Peasantry in Egypt, 1837–1952*. Syracuse, NY: Syracuse University Press.

Abbassy, M. S., H. Z. Ibrahim, and H. M. Abdel-Kader. 2003. "Persistent organochlorine pollutants in the aquatic ecosystem of Lake Manzala, Egypt," *Bulletin of Environmental Contamination and Toxicology* 70(6): 1158–1164.

Abdalla, Moustafa and Sherine Al-Shawarby. 2017. "The Tamween food subsidy system in Egypt: Evolution and recent implementation reforms." In *The 1.5 Billion People Question: Food, Vouchers, or Cash Transfers?*, edited by Harold Alderman, Ugo Gentilini, and Ruslan Yemtzov, pp. 107–150. Washington, DC: World Bank.

Abdel-Fadil, Mahmoud. 1975. *Development, Income Distribution and Social Change in Rural Egypt (1952–1970)*. Cambridge: Cambridge University Press.

Abdel-Latif, Abla and Hubert Schmitz. 2011. "The politics of investment and growth in Egypt: Experimenting with a new approach," *Development Policy Review* 29(4): 433–458.

Abdelrahman, Maha. 2014. *Egypt's Long Revolution: Protest Movements and Uprisings*. London and New York: Routledge.

Abdelwhab, El-Sayed M. and Hafez M. Hafez. 2011. "An overview of the epidemic of highly pathogenic H5N1 avian influenza virus in Egypt: Epidemiology and control challenges," *Epidemiology and Infection* 139(5): 647–657.

Abou-El-Haj, Rifa'at 'Ali. 2005. *Formation of the Modern State: The Ottoman Empire Sixteenth to Eighteenth Centuries* (2nd ed). Syracuse, NY: Syracuse University Press.

Abu-Lughod, Janet L. 1989. *Before European Hegemony: The World System A.D. 1250–1350.* New York and Oxford: Oxford University Press.

Abu-Lughod, Janet L. 1996. "Urbanization in the Arab World and the International System." In *The Urban Transformation of the Developing World*, edited by Josef Gugler, pp. 185–210. Oxford: Oxford University Press.

Abul-Magd, Zeinab. 2017. *Militarizing the Nation: The Army, Business, and Revolution in Egypt.* New York: Columbia University Press.

Achcar, Gilbert. 2021. "On the 'Arab Inequality Puzzle': The Case of Egypt," *Development and Change* 51(3): 746–770.

Adas, Michael. 1974. *The Burma Delta: Economic Development and Social Change on an Asian Rice Frontier, 1852–1941.* Madison, WI: University of Wisconsin Press.

Adesina, Jimi O. 2020. "Policy merchandising and social assistance in Africa: Don't call dog monkey for me," *Development and Change* 51(2): 561–582.

Adly, Amr. 2020. "Unwarranted suffering: The IMF and Egypt's illusory economic recovery." In *The Impact and Influence of International Financial Institutions on the Economies of the Middle East and North Africa*, edited by Tarek Radwan, pp. 12–25. Tunis: Friedrich Ebert Stiftung Regional Project.

Adriansen, Hanne K. 2009. "Land reclamation in Egypt: A study of life in the new lands," *Geoforum* 40(4): 664–674.

Adriansen, Hanne K. 2015. *The Geography of Peace: Egyptian Land Reclamation and Agricultural Cooperation with Israel.* Aarhus University, Denmark.

Agnihotri, Indu. 1996. "Ecology, land use and colonisation: The canal colonies of the Punjab," *Indian Economic and Social History Review* 33(1): 37–58.

Ahmed, Akhter U., Tamar Gutner, H. Lofgren, and Howarth E. Bouis. 2001. "The Egyptian food subsidy system: Structure, performance, and options for reform," *IFPRI Research Report* 119.

Alebshehy, Raouf, Nura M. Shuaib, Jato D. Mbako, Dina Barffo, and Roland Kuuzagr Nuotol. 2016. "Determinant analysis of obesity among adult females in Egypt," *The Egyptian Journal of Hospital Medicine* 65 (October): 662–669.

Alexander, D. J. and I. Capua. 2008. "Avian influenza in poultry," *World's Poultry Science Journal* 64: 513–531.

Ali, Kamran A. 2002. *Planning the Family in Egypt: New Bodies, New Selves.* Austin: University of Texas.

Ali, Samar Abd El Mohsen, Maged Ossama Aly, and Nessrin Ahmed El-Nimr. 2021. "Dietary practices of adult Egyptians before and during the COVID-19 lockdown," *Nutrire* 46(10): 10.

Allan, J. Anthony. 1983. "Some phases in extending the cultivated area in the nineteenth and twentieth centuries in Egypt," *Middle Eastern Studies* 19(4): 470–481.

Allan, John Anthony, Martin Keulertz, Suvi Sojamo and Jeroen Warner, eds. 2013. *Handbook of Land and Water Grabs in Africa.* London and New York: Routledge.

Alleaume, Ghislaine. 1999. "An industrial revolution in agriculture? Some observations on the evolution of rural Egypt in the nineteenth century." In *Agriculture in Egypt: From Pharaonic to Modern Times*, edited by Alan K. Bowman and Eugene Rogan, pp. 331–345. Oxford: Oxford University Press.

Allinson, Jamie. 2016. *The Struggle for the State in Jordan: The Social Origins of Alliances in the Middle East.* London and New York: I.B. Tauris.

Alterman, Jon B. 2002. *Egypt and American Foreign Assistance, 1952–1956: Hopes Dashed.* New York: Palgrave Macmillan.

Amable, Bruno. 2011. "Morals and politics in the ideology of neo-liberalism," *Socio-Economic Review* 9(1): 3–30.

Anievas, Alexander and Karem Nişancıoğlu. 2015. *How the West Came to Rule: The Geopolitical Origins of Capitalism.* London: Pluto Press.

Anwar, Wagida A. 2003. "Environmental health in Egypt," *International Journal of Hygiene and Environmental Health* 206(4–5): 339–350.

Arafa, Abdelsatar, Ihab El-Masry Shereen Kholosy, Mohammed K. Hassan, Gwenaelle Dauphin, Juan Lubroth, and Yilma J. Makonnen. 2016. "Phylodynamics of avian influenza clade 2.2.1 H5N1 viruses in Egypt," *Virology Journal* 13(49): 1–11.

Araghi, Farshad A. 2003. "Food regimes and the production of value: Some methodological issues," *Journal of Peasant Studies* 30(2): 41–70.

Araghi, Farshad A. 2016. "The rise and fall of the agrarian welfare state: Peasants, globalisation, and the privatization of development." In *Peasant Poverty and Persistence in the Twenty-first Century: Theories, Debates, Realities and Policies*, edited by Julio Boltvinik and Susan Archer Mann, pp. 315–344. London: Zed Books.

Arnold, Tom and Hadeel al Sayegh. 2013. "Arab world urged to close food supply gap," *The National*, April 3.

Arrighi, Giovanni. 1994. *The Long Twentieth Century: Money, Power and the Origins of Our Times.* London and New York: Verso.

Ash, Eric H. 2017. *The Draining of the Fens: Projectors, Popular Politics, and State Building in Early Modern England.* Baltimore: Johns Hopkins University Press.

Ashmawi, Sayyid. n.d. *Peasants and Authority in the Light of Egyptian Peasant Movements 1919–1999* [Al-falahun wal-Sulta 'ala Daw' al-Harakat al-Falahiyya al-Misriyya 1919–1999]. Cairo: Merit.

Atasoy, Yıldız. 2017. *Commodification of Global Agrifood Systems and Agro-Ecology: Convergence, Divergence and Beyond in Turkey.* London and New York: Routledge.

Austen, Ralph A. 2017. "Monsters of protocolonial economic enterprise: East India companies and slave plantations," *Critical Historical Studies* 4(2): 139–177.

Ayeb, Habib and Ray Bush. 2019. *Food Insecurity and Revolution in the Middle East and North Africa: Agrarian Questions in Egypt and Tunisia.* London and New York: Anthem Press.

Ayubi, Nazih N. 1995. *Over-stating the Arab Sate: Politics and Society in the Middle East.* London and New York: I.B. Tauris Publishers.

Baer, Gabriel. 1969. *Studies in the Social History of Modern Egypt.* Chicago: University of Chicago Press.

Barbier, Edward B. 2011. *Scarcity and Frontiers: How Economies Have Developed Through Natural Resource Exploitation.* Cambridge: Cambridge University Press.

Barker, Kezia. 2008. "Flexible boundaries in biosecurity: Accommodating gorse in Aotearoa New Zealand," *Environment and Planning A* 40: 1598–1614.

Barkey, Karen. 2008. *Empire of Difference: The Ottomans in Comparative Perspective.* New York: Cambridge University Press.

Barnes, Jessica. 2012. "Pumping possibility: Agricultural expansion through desert reclamation in Egypt," *Social Studies of Science* 42(4): 517–538.

Barnes, Louis B. and Simon A. Hershon. 1976. "Transferring power in the family business," *Harvard Business Review*, July.

Barrett, Christopher B. 2013. "Food or consequences: Food security and its implications for global sociopolitical stability." In *Food Security and Sociopolitical Stability*, edited by Christopher B. Barrett, pp. 1–34. Oxford: Oxford University Press.

Bateman, Milford. 2012. "How lending to the poor began, grew and almost destroyed a generation in India," *Development and Change* 43(6): 1385–1402.

Battacharya, Neeladri. 1995. "Pastoralists in a colonial world." In *Nature, Culture, Imperialism: Essays on the Environmental History of South Asia*, edited by David Arnold and Ramachandra Guha, pp. 49–85. Delhi: Oxford University Press.

Baviskar, Amita. 2018. "Consumer citizenship: Instant noodles in India," *Gastronomica: The Journal of Critical Food Studies* 18(2): 1–10.

Bayat, Asef and Eric Denis. 2000. "Who is afraid of ashwaiyyat? Urban change and politics in Egypt," *Environment and Urbanization* 12(2): 185–199.

BC Poultry. 2006. *BC Poultry Biosecurity Reference Guide*. British Columbia Poultry Association, November.

Beckert, Sven. 2014. *Empire of Cotton: A Global History*. New York: Alfred A. Knopf.

Beinart, William and Lotte Hughes. 2007. *Environment and Empire*. New York: Oxford University Press.

Beinin, Joel. 2008. "Egypt: Bread riots and mill strikes," *Le Monde Diplomatique*, May 8.

Beinin, Joel and Zackary Lockman. 1987. *Workers on the Nile: Nationalism, Communism, Islam and the Egyptian Working Class, 1882–1954*. Princeton: Princeton University Press.

Berthélemy, Jean-Claude and Nawel Bentahar. 2004. "Financial reforms and financial development in Arab countries." Paper presented at the International Conference on Institutions and Development Performance, Cairo.

Bingham, Nick and Steve Hinchliffe. 2008. "Mapping the multiplicities of biosecurity." In *Biosecurity Interventions: Global Health and Security in Question*, edited by Andrew Lakoff and Stephen J. Collier, pp. 173–193. New York: Columbia University Press.

Bisoka, Aymar N. and An Ansoms. 2020. "State and local authorities in land grabbing in Rwanda: Governmentality and capitalist accumulation," *Canadian Journal of Development Studies /Revue canadienne d'études du développement* 41(2): 243–259.

Bjørkhaug, Hilde, André Magnan, and Geoffrey Lawrence. 2018. "Introduction: the financialization of agri-food." In *The Financialization of Agri-food Systems: Contested Transformations*, edited by Hilde Bjørkhaug, André Magnan, and Geoffrey Lawrence, pp. 1–19. London and New York: Routledge.

Björnberg, Åsa, Heinz-Peter Elstrodt, and Vivek Pandi. 2014. "The family-business factor in emerging markets," *McKinsey Quarterly*, December 1.

Blenkinsop, Philip and Emma Farge. 2022. "WTO chief warns of rocky road to deals amid 'polycrisis,'" *Reuters*, June 13.

Bogaert, Koenraad. 2013. "Contextualizing the Arab revolts: The politics behind three decades of neoliberalism in the Arab world," *Middle East Critique* 22(3): 213–234.

Boltvinik, Julio. 2016. "Poverty and persistence of the peasantry: Background paper." In *Peasant Poverty and Persistence in the Twenty-first Century: Theories, Debates, Realities and Policies*, edited by Julio Boltvinik and Susan Archer Mann, pp. 45–91. London: Zed Books.

Borensztein, Eduardo and Ugo Panizza. 2008. "The costs of sovereign default." IMF Working Paper 08/238, October.

Borgwardt, Elizabeth. 2005. *A New Deal for the World: America's Vision for Human Rights*. Cambridge, MA: The Belknap Press of Harvard University Press.

Borras Jr., Saturnino M., Cristóbal Kay, and A. Haroon Akram-Lodhi. 2007. "Agrarian reform and rural development: Historical overview and current issues." In *Land, Poverty and Livelihoods in an Era of Globalization: Perspectives from Developing and Transition Countries*, edited by A. Haroon Akram-Lodhi, Saturnino M. Borras Jr., and Cristóbal Kay, pp. 1–40. London and New York: Routledge.

Bourdieu, Pierre. 1986. "The forms of capital." In *Handbook of Theory and Research for the Sociology of Education*, edited by J. Richardson, pp. 241–258. Westport, CT: Greenwood Press.

Boxall, Bettina. 2015. "Overpumping of Central Valley groundwater creating a crisis, experts say," *Los Angeles Times*, March 18.

Braudel, Fernand. 1972. *The Mediterranean and the Mediterranean World in the Age of Philip II, vol 1*. New York: Harper & Row.

Braun, Bruce. 2007. "Biopolitics and the molecularization of life," *Cultural Geographies* 14: 6–28.

Braun, Bruce. 2013. "Power over life: Biosecurity as biopolitics." In *Biosecurity: The Sociopolitics of Invasive Species and Infectious Diseases*, edited by Andrew Dobson, Kezia Barker, and Sarah L. Taylor, pp. 45–57. London and New York: Routledge.

Breisinger, Clemens, Yumna Kassim, Sikandra Kurdi, Josee Randriamamonjy, and James Thurlow. 2021. "Food subsidies and cash transfers in Egypt: Evaluating general equilibrium benefits and trade-offs," *IFPRI Regional Program Working Paper* 34, June.

Broner, Fernando, Titiana Didier, Aitor Erce, and Sergio Schmukler. 2012. "Gross capital flows: Dynamics and crises," *Journal of Monetary Economics* 60(1): 113–133.

Brown, Nathan. 1991. "The ignorance and inscrutability of the Egyptian peasantry." In *Peasants and Politics in the Modern Middle East*, edited by Farhad Kazemi and John Waterbury, pp. 203–221. Miami: Florida International University.

Bruff, Ian. 2014. "The rise of authoritarian neoliberalism," *Rethinking Marxism* 26(1): 113–129.

Bruff, Ian and Cemal B. Tansel. 2018. "Authoritarian neoliberalism: Trajectories of knowledge production and praxis," *Globalizations* 16(3): 233–244.

Burawoy, Michael, ed. 2000. *Global Ethnography: Forces, Connections, and Imaginations in a Postmodern World*. Berkeley: University of California Press.

Burch, Jr., Philip H. 1972. *The Managerial Revolution Reassessed: Family Control in America's Large Corporations*. Lexington, MA: D.C. Heath.

Burch, David and Geoffrey A. Lawrence, eds. 2007. *Supermarkets and Agri-Food Supply Chains: Transformations in the Production and Consumption of Foods*. Cheltenham, UK: Edward Elgar.

Burke III, Edmund. 2009. "The transformation of the Middle Eastern environment, 1500 B.C.E.–2000 C.E." In *The Environment and World History*, edited by Edmund Burke III and Kenneth Pomeranz, pp. 81–117. Berkeley: University of California Press.

Busch, Lawrence and Carmen Bain. 2004. "New! Improved? The transformation of the global agrifood system." *Rural Sociology* 69(3): 321–346.

Bush, Ray. 2007. "Mubarak's legacy for Egypt's rural poor: Returning land to the landlords." In *Land, Poverty and Livelihoods in an Era of Globalization: Perspectives from Developing and Transition Countries*, edited by S. M. Borras Jr., C. Kay and A. H. Akram-Lodhi, pp. 254–283. London and New York: Routledge.

Bush, Ray. 2009. "The land and the people." In *Egypt: Moment of Change*, edited by R. El-Mahdi and P. Marfleet, pp. 51–67. Cairo: The American University in Cairo Press.

Bush, Ray. 2011. "Coalitions for dispossession and networks of resistance? Land, politics and agrarian reform in Egypt." *British Journal of Middle East Studies* 38(3): 391–405.

Bush, Ray and Habib Ayeb, eds. 2012. *Marginality and Exclusion in Egypt*. New York: Zed Books.

Bush, Ray and Amal Sabri. 2000. "Mining for fish: Privatization of the "Commons" along Egypt's northern coastline," *Middle East Report* 216: 20–23, 45.

Business Monitor. 2011. *Egypt Food and Drink Report Q3 2011*. Business Monitor International Ltd.

Candiani, Vera S. 2014. *Dreaming of Dry Land: Environmental Transformation in Colonial Mexico City*. Stanford: Stanford University Press.

Carroll, William K. 2010. *The Making of a Transnational Capitalist Class: Corporate Power in the 21st Century*. London and New York: Zed Books.

Chancel, Lucas, Thomas Piketty, Emmanuel Saez, Gabriel Zucman, et al. 2022. *World Inequality Report 2022*. World Inequality Lab.

Charbel, Jano. 2016. "Parliament stacked against labor interests?," *Mada Masr*, February 17.

Chatterjee, Partha. 2004. *The Politics of the Governed: Reflections on Popular Politics in Most of the World*. New York: Columbia University Press.

Chuengsatiansup, Komatra. 2008. "Ethnography of epidemiologic transition: Avian flu, global health politics and agro-industrial capitalism in Thailand," *Anthropology & Medicine* 15(1): 53–59.

Citadel Capital. 2010. *Annual Report 2010*. Citadel Capital, Cairo.

Clapp, Jennifer. 2009. "Food price volatility and vulnerability in the global South: Considering the global economic context," *Third World Quarterly* 30(6): 1183–1196.

Clapp, Jennifer. 2014. "Financialization, distance and global food politics," *Journal of Peasant Studies* 41(5): 797–814.

Clapp, Jennifer. 2022. "Concentration and crisis: Exploring the deep roots of vulnerability in the global industrial food system," *The Journal of Peasant Studies*, early access.

Clapp, Jennifer and Doris Fuchs. 2009. "Agrifood corporations, global governance, and sustainability: A framework for analysis." In *Corporate Power in Global Agrifood Governance*, edited by Jennifer Clapp and Doris Fuchs, pp. 1–25. Cambridge, MA: The MIT Press.

Clark, Janine A. 2006. "Field research methods in the Middle East," *Political Science and Politics* 39: 417–423.

Clark, Nigel. 2013. "Mobile life: Biosecurity practices and insect globalization," *Science as Culture* 22(1): 16–37.

Clout, Hugh D. 1977. "Reclamation of coastal marshland." In *Themes in the Historical Geography of France*, edited by Hugh D. Clout, pp. 185–213. London: Academic Press.

Cole, Juan R. I. 1993. *Colonialism and Revolution in the Middle East: Social and Cultural Origins of Egypt's 'Urabi Movement*. Princeton: Princeton University Press.

Cole, Donald P. and Soraya Altorki. 1998. *Bedouin, Settlers, and Holiday-Makers: Egypt's Changing Northwest Coast*. Cairo: American University at Cairo Press.

Collier, Stephen J. and Aihwa Ong, eds. 2005. *Global Assemblages: Technology, Politics, and Ethics as Anthropological Problems*. Malden, MA: Blackwell.

Cons, Jason and Michael Eilenberg. 2019. "Introduction: On the new politics of margins in Asia mapping frontier assemblages." In *Frontier Assemblages: The Emergent Politics of Resource Frontiers in Asia*, edited by Jason Cons and Michael Eilenberg, pp. 1–18. Oxford: John Wiley & Sons Ltd.

Cooper, Melinda 2006. "Pre-empting emergence: The biological turn in the war on terror," *Theory, Culture & Society* 23(4): 113–135.

Cooper, Melinda. 2017. *Family Values: Between Neoliberalism and the New Social Conservatism*. Brooklyn: Zone Books/MIT Press.

Cowling, Benjamin J., Lianmei Jin, Eric H. Y. Lau, Qiaohong Liao, Peng Wu, Hui Jiang, Tim K. Tsang, Jiandong Zheng, Viky J. Fang, Zhaorui Chang, Michael Y. Ni, Qian Zhang, Dennis K.M. Ip, Jianxing Yu, Yu Li, Liping Wang, Wenxiao Tu, Ling Meng, Joseph T. Wu, Huiming Luo, Qun Li, Yuelong Shu, Zhongjie Li, Zijian Feng, Wiezhong Yang, Yu Wang, Gabriel M. Leung, and Hongjie Yu. 2013. "Comparative epidemiology of human infections with avian influenza A H7N9 and H5N1 viruses in China: A population-based study of laboratory-confirmed cases," *Lancet* 382: 129–137.

Creane, Susan, Rishi Goyal, A. Mushfiq Mobarak, and Randa Sab. 2004. "Evaluating financial sector development in the Middle East and North Africa: New methodology and some new results." *Topics in Middle Eastern and North African Economies* 6: 1–27.

Credit Suisse. 2011. *Asian Family Business Report 2011*. Credit Suisse.

Crotty, James. 2005. "The neoliberal paradox: The impact of destructive product market competition and 'modern' financial markets on nonfinancial corporation performance in the neoliberal era." In *Financialization and the World Economy*, edited by Gerald A. Epstein, pp. 77–110. Cheltenham, UK: Edward Elgar.

Cuno, Kenneth M. 1999. "A tale of two villages: Family, property, and economic activity in rural Egypt in the 1840s." In *Agriculture in Egypt: From Pharaonic to Modern Times*, edited by Alan K. Bowman and Eugene Rogan, pp. 301–329. Oxford: Oxford University Press.

DAI. 2002. "Assessment of Egypt's agricultural sector competitiveness. Volume II: Analysis, principal findings, and recommendations." Prepared for the U.S. Agency for International Development/Egypt under the Rural and Agricultural Incomes with a Sustainable Environment (RAISE) IQC, Development Alternatives, Inc., Bethesda, Maryland.

Damiani, Octavio. 1999. "Beyond market failures: Irrigation, the state, and non-traditional agriculture in northeast Brazil." PhD: Massachusetts Institute of Technology.

Daniel, Shepard. 2012. "Situating private equity capital in the land grab debate." *Journal of Peasant Studies* 39(3–4): 703–729.

Davis, Diana K. 2016. *The Arid Lands: History, Power, Knowledge*. Cambridge, MA and London: The MIT Press.

Davis, Mike. 2001. *Late Victorian Holocausts: El Niño Famines and the Making of the Third World*. London and New York: Verso.

Davis, Mike. 2005. *The Monster at Our Door: The Global Threat of Avian Flu*. New York: Henry Holt and Company.

Davis, Mike. 2006. *Planet of slums*. London: Verso.

Davis, Meghan F., Lance B. Price, Cindy M-H Liu, and Ellen K. Silbergeld. 2011. "An ecological perspective on U.S. industrial poultry production: The role of anthropogenic ecosystems on the emergence of drug-resistant bacteria from agricultural environments." *Current Opinion in Microbiology* 14(3): 244–250.

De Lellis, Francesco. 2020. "Peasants, dispossession and resistance in Egypt: An analysis of protest movements and organizations before and after the 2011 uprising." *Review of African Political Economy* 46(162): 582–598.

De Schutter, Olivier. 2010. "Food commodities speculation and food price crises: Regulation to reduce the risks of price volatility." UN Special Rapporteur on the Right to Food Briefing Note 02, September.

De Smet, Brecht. 2016. *Gramsci on Tahrir: Revolution and Counter-Revolution in Egypt*. London: Pluto Press.

Deeb, Lara and Jessica Winegar. 2012. "Anthropologies of Arab-majority societies." *Annual Review of Anthropology* 41 (Oct): 537–558.

Deleuze, Gilles. 1990. *Expressionism in Philosophy: Spinoza*. New York: Zone.

Derr, Jennifer L. 2011. "Drafting a map of colonial Egypt: The 1902 Aswan Dam, historical imagination, and the production of agricultural geography." In *Environmental Imaginaries of the Middle East and North Africa*, edited by Diana K. Davis and Edmund Burke III, pp. 136–157. Athens: Ohio University Press.

Dethier, Jean-Jacques and Kathy Funk. 1987. "The language of food: PL 480 in Egypt." *Middle East Report* March–April: 22–28.

Diaz Alejandro, Carlos F. 1970. *Essays on the Economic History of the Argentine Republic*. New Haven and London: Yale University Press.

Diwan, Ishac and Hamouda Chekir. 2014. "Crony capitalism in Egypt," *Journal of Globalization and Development* 5(2): 177–211.

Dixon, Marion W. 2011. "An Arab Spring." *Review of African Political Economy* 38(128): 309–316.

Dixon, Marion W. 2014. "The land grab, finance capital, and food regime restructuring: The case of Egypt." *Review of African Political Economy* 41(140): 232–248.

Dixon, Marion W. 2015. "Biosecurity and the multiplication of crises in the Egyptian agri-food industry." *Geoforum* 61: 90–100.

Dixon, Marion W. 2017. "Plastics and agriculture in the desert frontier." *Comparative Studies of South Asia, Africa, and the Middle East* 37(1): 86–102.

Dixon, Marion W. 2018. "Chemical fertilizer in transformations in world agriculture and the state system, 1870 to the interwar period." *Journal of Agrarian Change* 18(4): 768–786.

Dixon, Marion W. 2020. "Agrarian question revisited: Smallholders and corporate food in Egypt." *Canadian Journal of Development Studies* 41(2): 279–295.

Dixon, Marion W. 2021. "Phosphate rock frontiers: Nature, labor, and imperial states, 1870–WWI." *Critical Historical Studies* 8(2): 271–303.

Dobb, Maurice. 1967. *Papers on Capitalism, Development, and Planning*. New York: International Publishers.

Dossal, Mariam. 2010. *Theatre of Conflict, City of Hope: Mumbai, 1660 to Present Times*. New Delhi: Oxford University Press.

Dunn, Stephanie and James Holloway. 2012. "The pricing of crude oil." *Reserve Bank of Australia Bulletin*, September.

Edelman, Marc. 2003. "Transnational peasant and farmer movements and networks." In *Global Civil Society 2003*, edited by Mary Kaldor, Helmut Anheier, and Marlies Glasius, pp. 185–220. Oxford: Oxford University Press.

EDF. 2011. "Agricultural Crops Program of the Export Development Fund [Sunduq Tanmia Alsawdarat Bernamag Alhasallat Alzaray'a]," Export Development Fund, Egypt.

EFG-Hermes. 2010. "Juhayna Food Industries." *EFG-Hermes Buy Rating*, July 29.

EIA. 2022. "Egypt," U.S. Energy Information Administration, April 4.

El-Fiqi, Mona. 2014. "Subsidy-less," *Al-Ahram Weekly*, December 18.

El-Naggar, Ahmad E. 2009. "Economic policy: From state control to decay and corruption." In *Egypt: Moment of Change*, edited by Rabab El-Mahdi and Philip Marfleet, pp. 34–50. London: Zed Books.

El Nour, Saker. 2015. 'Small farmers and the revolution in Egypt: the forgotten actors'. *Contemporary Arab Affairs* 8(2): 198–211.

El Nour, Saker. 2020. "Grabbing from below: A study of land reclamation in Egypt." *Review of African Political Economy* 46(162): 549–566.

El Safti, Ahmed. 2007. "Financial sector reforms in the Arab countries." Arab Monetary Fund, *AMF Economic Studies* no. 8.

El Shakry, Omnia. 2007. *The Great Social Laboratory: Subjects of Knowledge in Colonial and Postcolonial Egypt*. Stanford: Stanford University Press.

Eltanany, M. and O. Distl. 2010. "Genetic diversity and genealogical origins of domestic chicken." *World's Poultry Science Journal* 66(04): 715–726.

Elyachar, Julia. 2005. *Markets of Dispossession: NGOs, Economic Development and the State in Cairo*. Durham, NC: Duke University Press.

Enticott, Gareth. 2008. "The spaces of biosecurity: Prescribing and negotiating solutions to bovine tuberculosis." *Environment and Planning A* 40: 1568–1582.

Erce, Aitor and Enrico Mallucci. 2018. "Selective sovereign defaults." Board of Governors of the Federal Reserve System, International Finance Discussion Papers 1239.

ETC Group. 2005. "Oligopoly, Inc. 2005," *Communiqué* 91, November/December.

ETC Group. 2022. *Food Barons 2022: Crisis Profiteering, Digitalization and Shifting Power*. ETC Group Collective, September 20.

Fahmy, Khaled. 2004. *All the Pasha's Men: Mehmed Ali, His Army and the Making of Modern Egypt*. Cairo: The American University in Cairo Press.

Fairbairn, Madeline. 2014. "'Like gold with yield': Evolving intersections between farmland and finance." *Journal of Peasant Studies* 41(5): 777–795.

FAO. n.d. "WTO agreement on agriculture: The implementation experience—Egypt." *FAO Corporate Document Repository*. Rome: Food and Agriculture Organization of the United Nations.

FAO. 2006a. "The double burden of malnutrition: Case studies from six developing countries." *FAO Food and Nutrition Paper* 84.

FAO. 2006b. "Poultry sector country review: Egypt," Rome: Food and Agriculture Organization of the United Nations.

FAO. 2010. *The State of World Fisheries and Aquaculture*. Rome: Food and Agriculture Organization of the United Nations.

FAO. 2011a. *The State of Food Insecurity in the World: How Does International Price Volatility Affect Domestic Economics and Food Security?* Rome: Food and Agriculture Organization of the United Nations.

FAO. 2011b. "Approaches to controlling, preventing and eliminating H5N1 highly pathogenic avian influenza in endemic countries." FAO Animal Production and Health Paper 171.

FAO. 2012. "FAO Food Price Index," World Food Situation. Rome: Food and Agriculture Organization of the United Nations.

FAO. 2014. *Food and Agriculture Policy Decisions: Trends, Emerging Issues and Policy Alignments since the 2007/08 Food Security Crisis*. Rome: Food and Agriculture Organization of the United Nations.

FAO. 2022. FAO cereal supply and demand brief. World Food Situation, FAO, February 9.

FAO STAT. n.d. "Country profile: Egypt—top imports—2011." Rome: Food and Agriculture Organization of the United Nations.

Farley, John. 1991. *Bilharzia: A History of Imperial Tropical Medicine*. Cambridge: Cambridge University Press.

Federico, Giovanni. 2005. *Feeding the World: An Economic History of Agriculture, 1800–2000*. Princeton and Oxford: Princeton University Press.

Feeny, David. 1982. *The Political Economy of Productivity: Thai Agricultural Development, 1880–1975*. Vancouver and London: University of British Columbia Press.

Finkner, Ralph E. 1983. "TDY Report: Maize, Sorghum & Center Development Programs," EMCIP Publication No. 51, Cairo.

Finley, Allysia. 2015. "How to make a desert bloom," *Wall Street Journal*, October 6.

Fischer, Andrew M. 2020. "The dark sides of social policy: From neoliberalism to resurgent right-wing populism." Special Issue: Social policy under the global shadow of right-wing populism: A debate. *Development and Change* 51(2): 371–397.

Flynn, Dennis O. and Arturo Giráldez. 2002. "Cycles of silver: Global economic unity through the mid-eighteenth century," *Journal of World History* 13(2): 391–427.

Fold, Niels and Bill Pritchard, eds. 2005. *Cross-continental Food Chains*. London and New York: Routledge.

Foley, Jonathan. 2015. "A five-step plan to feed the world," *National Geographic*.

Foucault, Michel. 2008. *The Birth of Biopolitics: Lectures at the Collège de France, 1978–79*. Basingstoke: Palgrave Macmillan.

Fraser, Evan, Alexander Legwegoh, and Krishna KC. 2015. "Food stocks and grain reserves: Evaluating whether storing food creates resilient food systems," *Journal of Environmental Studies and Sciences* 5: 445–458.

Freidberg, Susanne. 2004. *French Beans and Food Scares: Culture and Commerce in an Anxious Age*. New York: Oxford University Press.

Freivalds, J. 1982. "Developing Egypt's poultry industry: opportunity vs. bureaucracy," *Agribusiness Worldwide* Feb/Mar: 48–55.

Friedmann, Harriett. 1993. "The political economy of food : A global crisis," *New Left Review* 197: 29–57.

Friedmann, Harriett. 2005. "From colonialism to green capitalism: Social movements and emergence of food regimes." In *New Directions in the Sociology of Global Development: Research in Rural Sociology and Development* (vol 11), edited by Frederick H. Buttel and Phillip McMichael, pp. 227–264. Bradford: Emerald Group Publishing.

Friedmann, Harriet and Philip McMichael. 1989. "Agriculture and the state system: The rise and decline of national agricultures, 1870 to the present," *Sociologia Ruralis* 29(2): 93–117.

GAFI. 2010. "Invest in Egypt: Retail." General Authority for Investment, Cairo.

Gakpo, Joseph O. 2019. "Egypt poised to again lead Africa in ag biotech innovation," *Alliance for Science*, February 6.

Galal, Osman M. 2002. "The nutrition transition in Egypt: obesity, undernutrition and the food consumption context," *Public Health Nutrition* 5(1A): 141–148.

Garrett, Laurie and Steven A. Cook. 2012. "Egypt's real crisis: The dual epidemics quietly ravaging public health," *The Atlantic*, May 14.

Gengenbach, Heidi. 2020. "From cradle to chain? Gendered struggles for cassava commercialisation in Mozambique," *Canadian Journal of Development Studies/Revue canadienne d'études du développement* 41(2): 224–242.

Gertel, Jörg. 2015. "Spatial orders of hunger: Food insecurity in Cairo." Presented at the workshop "Spatialities of Food – the Urban Case of Cairo," University of Leipzig, Germany, October 15.

Ghoneim, Ahmed F. 2012. "The policy economy of food price policy." UNU-WIDER Working Paper No. 2012/96.

Gibbon, Peter and Stefano Ponte. 2005. *Trading Down: Africa, Value Chains, and the Global Economy*. Philadelphia: Temple University Press.

Gillis, Justin and Matt Richtel. 2015. "Beneath California crops, groundwater crisis grows," *New York Times*, April 5.

Gilmartin, David. 2006. "Imperial rivers: Irrigation and British visions of empire." In Decentering Empire: Britain, India and the Transcolonial World, edited by Durba Ghosh and Dane Kennedy, pp. 76–103. New Delhi: Orient Longman Private Limited.

Glain, Stephen. 2012a. "In Egypt's bread, signs of economic weakness," *Washington Post*, February 20.

Glain, Stephen. 2012b. "Egyptian farmers make themselves heard," *New York Times*, June 27.

Glavanis, Kathy. 1990. "Commoditization and the small peasant household in Egypt." In *The Rural Middle East: Peasant Lives and Modes of Production*, edited by Kathy and Pandeli Glavanis, pp. 142–162. London & New Jersey: Zed Books.

Global Investment House. 2008. *Egypt Banking Sector.*

Glover, David and Ken C. Kusterer. 1990. *Small Farmers, Big Business: Contract Farming and Rural Development*. New York: St. Martin's Press.

Goldberg, Ellis. 2017. "Killing them softly: Dietary deficiencies and food insecurity in twentieth-century Egypt." In *The Food Question in the Middle East*, edited by Malak S. Rouchdy and Iman A. Hamdy, pp. 24–44. *Cairo Papers in Social Science* vol. 34, no. 4.

Goldstein, Jesse. 2012. "*Terra Economica*: Waste and the production of enclosed nature," *Antipode* 45(2): 357–375.

González-Esteban, Ángel L. 2018. "Patterns of world wheat trade, 1945–2010: The long hangover from the second food regime," *Journal of Agrarian Change* 18: 87–111.

Goodman, David and Michael Watts, eds. 1997. *Globalising Food: Agrarian Questions and Global Restructuring*. London and New York: Routledge.

Government of Egypt. 1972. "Law no. 38 of 1972 (re-enacted until 2005)." People's Assembly of Egypt, the Electoral Knowledge Project.

GRAIN. 2008. "Seized! The 2008 land grab for food and financial security," *GRAIN Briefing*, October 24.

GRAIN. 2012. *The Great Food Robbery: How Corporations Control Food, Grab Land and Destroy the Climate*. Cape Town: Pambazuka Press.

Gran, Peter. 1979. *Islamic Roots of Capitalism; Egypt, 1760–1840*. Austin & London: University of Texas Press.

Guthman, Julie. 2011. *Weighing In: Obesity, Food Justice, and the Limits of Capitalism*. Berkeley: University of California Press.

Hanieh, Adam. 2013. *Lineages of Revolt: Issues of Contemporary Capitalism in the Middle East*. Chicago: Haymarket Books.

Harik, Iliya. 1974. *The Political Mobilization of Peasants: A Study of an Egyptian Community*. Bloomington and London: Indiana University Press.

Harrigan, Jane. 2014. *The Political Economy of Arab Food Sovereignty*. New York: Palgrave Macmillan.

Harvey, David. 2001. *Spaces of Capital: Towards a Critical Geography*. New York: Routledge.

Harwig, Edgar E. 1983. "TDY Report: Comments on the Egyptian Soybean Research Program." EMCIP Publication no. 51, Cairo.

Haslam, David W. and W. Philip T. James. 2005. "Obesity," *Lancet* 366: 1197–1209.

Hayami, Yujiro. and Saburo Yamada. 1991. *The Agricultural Development of Japan: A Century's Perspective*. Tokyo: University of Tokyo Press.

HC Brokerage. 2009. "Citadel capital pre-listing company report." HC Brokerage Research Department, November 16.

Hegel, Georg W. F. 1967. *Philosophy of Right*. Translated with Notes by T. M. Knox. Oxford: Clarendon Press.

Heikal, Hassan. 2011. "A tweet from Tahrir Square—time to tax the rich." *Financial Times*, November 21.

Henderson, Christian. 2019. "Gulf capital and Egypt's corporate food system: A region in the third food regime," *Review of African Political Economy* 46(162): 599–614.

Henry, Clement M. 1997. *The Mediterranean Debt Crescent: Money and Power in Algeria, Egypt, Morocco, Tunisia, and Turkey*. Cairo: American University at Cairo Press.

Herman, John E. 2018. "From land reclamation to land grab: Settler colonialism in southwest China, 1680–1735," *Harvard Journal of Asiatic Studies* 78(1): 91–123.

Hinchliffe, Steve. 2013. "The insecurity of biosecurity: Remaking emerging infectious diseases." In *Biosecurity: The Socio-politics of Invasive Species and Infectious Diseases*, edited by Andrew Dobson, Kezia Barker, and Sarah L. Taylor, pp. 199–213. London and New York: Routledge.

Hinchliffe, Steve and Nick Bingham. 2007. "Securing life: The emerging practices of biosecurity," *Environment and Planning A* 40(7): 1534–1551.

Hinchliffe, Steve and Kim J. Ward. 2014. "Geographies of folded life: How immunity reframes biosecurity," *Geoforum* 53: 136–144.

Hinnebusch, Raymond. 2018. "Understanding regime divergence in the post-uprising Arab states," Special Issue: War, revolt and rupture: The historical sociology of the current crisis in the Middle East. *Journal of Historical Sociology* 31: 39–52.

Hlasny, Vladimir and Paolo Verme. 2021. "On the 'Arab Inequality Puzzle: A Comment,'" *Development and Change* 51(3): 1–11.

Hodge, Joseph M. 2007. *Triumph of the Expert: Agrarian Doctrines of Development and the Legacies of British Colonialism*. Athens, Ohio: Ohio University Press.

Holden, Patrick. 2012. "Greening the desert," *Sustainable Food Trust*, March 7.

Holt Gimenez, Eric and Annie Shattuck. 2011. "Food crises, food regimes and food movements: rumblings of reform or tides of transformation?," *Journal of Peasant Studies* 38(1): 109–144.

Hopkins, Nicholas. 1999. "Irrigation in contemporary Egypt." In *Agriculture in Egypt: From Pharaonic to Modern Times*, edited by Alan K. Bowman and Eugene Rogan, pp. 367–385. Oxford: Oxford University Press.

Hossain, Naomi and Devangana Kalita. 2014. "Moral economy in a global era: the politics of provisions during contemporary food price spikes," *Journal of Peasant Studies* 41(5): 815–831.

Hudson, Brian J. 1996. *Cities on the Shore: The Urban Littoral Frontier*. London and New York: Pinter.

Husain, Arif. 2022. "Global food crisis: Fuelled by conflict," Chatham House, *The World Today*, September 30.

Ianchovinchina, Elena I., Josef L. Loening, and Christina A. Wood. 2014. "How vulnerable are Arab countries to global food price shocks?," *The Journal of Development Studies* 50(9): 1302–1319.

Ibrahim, Saad E. and Hans Lofgren. 1996. "Successful adjustment and declining governance? The case of Egypt." World Bank Private Sector Development Department Essays on Governance, Leadership and Communication. Washington, DC: World Bank.

IFAD. n.d. *Egypt: Smallholder Contract Farming for High-Value and Organic Agricultural Exports*. Rome: International Fund for Agricultural Development.

IFC. 2009. "Citadel Cap Fund: Summary of Proposed Investment.' Washington, DC: International Finance Corporation.

IISD. 2014. "Country update: Assessing Egypt's energy subsidy reforms," International Institute for Sustainable Development, Global Subsidies Initiative, August 14.

IMC. 2005. *Egyptian Processed Food Sector Review: Final Report*. Cairo: Industrial Modernisation Centre.

IMF. 2008. *Fuel and Food Price Subsidies: Issues and Reform Options*. Washington, DC: International Monetary Fund.

IMF. 2016. "IMF Executive Board approves us$12 billion extended arrangement under the extended fund facility for Egypt," International Monetary Fund Press Release no. 16/501, November 11.

İnalcık, Halil. 1991. "The emergence of big farms, Çiftliks: State, landlords, and tenants." In *Landholding and Commercial Agriculture in the Middle East*, edited by Caglar Keyder and Faruk Tabak, pp. 17–34. Albany: State University of New York Press.

İnalcık, Halil. 1994. "The Ottoman state: Economy and society, 1300–1600." In *An Economic and Social History of the Ottoman Empire, 1300-1914*, edited by Halil İnalcık and Donald Quataert, pp. 9–409. New York: Cambridge University Press.

iPES-Food. 2022. "Another perfect storm?" International Panel of Experts on Sustainable Food Systems, May.

Irungu, Geoffrey. 2010. "Citadel turns to agriculture in search of investment," *Business Daily* online, April 16.

ISA Poultry. 2010. "Biosecurity requirements for poultry farms." Institut de Sélection Animale AV, European Union.

Isakson, S. Ryan. 2014. "Food and finance: The financial transformation of agro-food supply chains," *Journal of Peasant Studies* 41(5): 749–775.

İslamoğlu-İnan, Huri. 1994. *State and Peasant in the Ottoman Empire: Agrarian Power Relations and Regional Economic Development in Ottoman Anatolia during the Sixteenth Century*. Leiden and New York: E.J. Brill.

Ismail, Ayman. 2009. *Private Equity and Venture Capital in Emerging Markets: A Case Study of Egypt and the MENA Region*. PhD: Massachusetts Institute of Technology.

Issawi, Charles. 1963. *Egypt in Revolution: An Economic Analysis*. London: Oxford University Press.

Iyer, Deepa. 2011. "Building the capacity to regulate: Central bank reform in Egypt, 2003–2009," Princeton University, Innovations for Successful Societies.

Jakes, Aaron J. 2020. *Egypt's Occupation: Colonial Economism and the Crises of Capitalism.* Stanford: Stanford University Press.

Jakobsen, Jostein. 2018. "Neoliberalising the food regime 'amongst its others': the right to food and the state in India," *Journal of Peasant Studies* 46(6): 1219–1239.

Janelli, Roger L. 1993. *Making Capitalism: The Social and Cultural Construction of a South Korean Conglomerate.* Stanford: Stanford University Press.

Jensen, Merle H. 2011. "Controlled environment agriculture in deserts, tropics and temperate regions—a world review." College of Agriculture and Life Sciences, University of Arizona.

Johansen, Baber. 1988. *The Islamic Law on Land Tax and Rent: The Peasants' Loss of Property Rights as Interpreted in the Hanafite Legal Literature of the Mamluk and Ottoman Periods,* London and New York: Croom Helm.

Johnson, Pamela et al. 1983. "Egypt: The Egyptian Rural Improvement Service, A Point Four Project, 1952–1963." AID Project Impact Evaluation Report no. 43. Cairo: USAID/Egypt.

Joya, Angela. 2008. "Egyptian protests: Falling wages, high prices and the failure of an export-oriented economy," *The Bullet*, E-Bulletin No. 111, June 2.

Joya, Angela. 2011. "The Egyptian revolution: Crisis of neoliberalism and the potential for democratic politics," *Review of African Political Economy* 38(129): 367–386.

Kaminsky, Graciela L. and Sergio L. Schmukler. 2003. "Short-run pain, long-run gain: The effects of financial liberalization." *IMF Working Paper*, February.

Kandil, Hazem. 2016. "*Interview*: Sisi's Egypt," *New Left Review* 102 Nov./Dec.: 5–40.

Kapadia, Sana R. 2011. *Egypt's Financial Liberalisation: Why Didn't It Do What It Said It Would on the Box?* MA: International Institute of Social Studies.

Karataşash, Şahan S. 2019. "The twenty-first century revolutions and internationalism: A world historical perspective," *Globalizations* 16(7): 985–997.

Kassab, Beesan. 2022. "Food subsidies for low income households eroded as government hikes food prices to match inflation," *Mada Masr*, October 3.

Kayali, Ghazi, Rabeh El-Shesheny, Mohamed A. Kutkat, Ahmed M. Kandeil, Ahmed Mostafa, Mariette F. Ducatez, Pamela P. McKenzie, Elena A. Govorkova, Mohamed H. Nasraa, Robert G. Webster, Robert J. Webby, and Mohamed A. Ali. 2011. "Continuing threat of influenza (H5N1) virus circulation in Egypt," *Emerging Infectious Diseases* 17(12): 2306–2308.

Keyder, Caglar. 1991. "Introduction: Large-scale commercial agriculture in the Ottoman Empire?" In *Landholding and Commercial Agriculture in the Middle East*, edited by Caglar Keyder and Faruq Tabak, pp. 1–13. Albany: State University of New York Press.

Kim, Soowon and Barry M. Popkin. 2006. "Commentary: Understanding the epidemiology of overweight and obesity—a real global public health concern," *International Journal of Epidemiology* 35: 60–67.

Kim, Jeong Ki, Ghazi Kayali, David Walker, Heather L. Forrest, Ali H. Ellebedy, Yolanda S. Griffin, Adam Rubrum, Mahmoud M. Bahgat, M. A. Kutkat, M. A. A. Ali, Jerry R. Aldridge, Nicholas J. Negovetich, Scott Krauss, Richard J. Webby, and Robert G. Webster. 2010. "Puzzling inefficiency of H5N1 influenza vaccines in Egyptian poultry," *Proceedings of the National Academy of Sciences of the United States of America* 107(24): 11044–11049.

Kindon, Sara L., Rachel. Pain, and Mike Kesby, eds. 2007. *Participatory Action Research Approaches and Methods: Connecting people, participation and place.* London and New York: Routledge.

Kishk, M. A. 1986. "Land degradation in the Nile Valley," *Ambio* 15(4): 226–230.

Klein, Naomi. 2007. *The Shock Doctrine: The Rise of Disaster Capitalism.* New York: Picador.

Konings, Martijn. 2011. *The Development of American Finance.* New York: Cambridge University Press.

Koptiuch, Kristin. 1999. *A Poetics of Political Economy in Egypt*. Minneapolis: University of Minnesota Press.

Korthals-Altes, Jacobus. 1925. *Sir Cornelius Vermuyden: The Lifework of a Great Anglo-Dutchman in Land-Reclamation and Drainage*. London: Williams and Norgate.

Kovats-Bernat, J. Christopher. 2002. "Negotiating dangerous fields: Pragmatic strategies for fieldwork amid violence and terror," *American Anthropologist* 104(1): 208–222.

Kramer, Andrew E. 2010. "Russia, crippled by drought, bans grain exports," *New York Times*, August 5.

Krippner, Greta. 2005. "The financialization of the American economy," *Socio-Economic Review* 3: 173–208.

Krippner, Greta. 2011. *Capitalizing on Crisis: The Political Origins of the Rise of Finance*. Cambridge, MA: Harvard University Press.

Kruseman, Gideon and Wies Vullings. 2007. *Rural Development Policy in Egypt towards 2025: Targeted Conditional Income Support a Suitable Option?* Wageningen: Wageningen – Alterra.

Kurmuş, Orhan. 1987. "The cotton famine and its effects on the Ottoman Empire." In *The Ottoman Empire and the World-Economy*, edited by Huri İslamoğlu-İnan, pp. 160–169. Cambridge: Cambridge University Press.

Laessing, Ulf. 2012. "Egypt's Citadel to grow staple crops in South Sudan," *Reuters*, March 20.

Laff, Michael. 2022. "Assisting farmers in Middle East, North Africa during the food crisis," *ShareAmerica*, October 13.

Lagi, Marco, Karla Z. Bertrand, and Yaneer Bar-Yam. 2011. "The food crises and political instability in North Africa and the Middle East." New England Complex Systems Institute, August 10.

Lament, William J. 1993. "Plastic mulches for the production of vegetable crops," *HortTechnology* 3: 35–39.

Landes, David S. 1958. *Bankers and Pashas: International Finance and Economic Imperialism in Egypt*. Cambridge, MA: Harvard University Press.

Lane, Philip R. 2012. "Financial globalisation and the crisis." Paper presented at the 11th BIS Annual Conference on "The Future of Financial Globalisation," Lucerne, June 21–22.

Latham, Michael E. 2011. *The Right Kind of Revolution: Modernization, Development, and U.S. Foreign Policy from the Cold War to the Present*. Ithaca and London: Cornell University Press.

Latour, Bruno. 1993. *We Have Never Been Modern*. Cambridge, MA: Harvard University Press.

Law, John. 2006. "Disaster in agriculture: Or foot and mouth mobilities," *Environment and Planning A* 38: 227–239.

Lawrence, Felicity. 2010. "How Peru's wells are being sucked dry by British love of asparagus," *Guardian*, September 14.

Lawrence, Geoffrey and Kiah Smith. 2018. "The concept of 'financialization': Criticisms and insights." In *The Financialization of Agri-food Systems: Contested Transformations*, edited by Hilde Bjørkhaug, André Magnan, and Geoffrey Lawrence, pp. 23–41. London and New York: Routledge.

LCHR. 2000. "The impact of implementing the land law in Egypt," *Land and Farmer Series*, no. 10. Land Centre for Human Rights, Cairo.

LCHR. 2006. "Crop Exports—Trade Agreements—Free Market Policies," *Land and Farmer Series*, no. 34. Land Centre for Human Rights, Cairo.

Lederer, Edith M. 2022. "In world beset by turbulence, nations' leaders gather at UN," *Washington Post*, September 18.

Lehman, E. M. and M. L. Wilson. 2009. "Epidemic hepatitis C virus infection in Egypt: Estimates of past incidence and future morbidity and mortality," *Journal of Viral Hepatitis* 16(9): 650–658.

Levin, N., R. Lugassi, U. Ramon, O. Braun, and E. Ben-Dor. 2007. "Remote sensing as a tool for monitoring plasticulture in agricultural landscapes," *International Journal of Remote Sensing* 28: 183–202.

Lindley, Keith. 1982. *Fenland Riots and the English Revolution*. London: Heinemann Educational Books.

Lorimer, Jamie and Clemens Driessen. 2013. "Bovine biopolitics and the promise of monsters in the rewilding of Heck cattle," *Geoforum* 48: 249–259.

Lybbert, Travis J. and Heather R. Morgan. 2013. "Lessons from the Arab Spring: Food security and stability in the Middle East and North Africa." In *Food Security and Sociopolitical Stability*, edited by Christopher B. Barrett, pp. 357–380. Oxford: Oxford University Press.

Lynton-Evans, John. 1997. "Strategic grain reserves: Guidelines for their establishment, management and operation," Food and Agriculture Organization (FAO) Agricultural Services Bulletin no. 126.

MacFarquhar, Neil, David Rohde, and Aram Roston. 2011. "Mubarak family riches attract new focus," *New York Times*, February 12.

Mahmoud, Rasha. 2022. "Egypt claims wheat self-sufficiency despite Ukraine war," *Al-Monitor*, October 7.

Major, Claire. 2008. "Affect work and infected bodies: Biosecurity in an age of emerging infectious disease," *Environment and Planning A* 40: 1633–1646.

Makki, Fouad. 2015. "Reframing development theory: The significance of the idea of uneven and combined development," *Theory and Society* 44(5): 471–497.

Mansour, Sameeh A. 2008. "Environmental impact of pesticides in Egypt," *Reviews of Environmental Contamination and Toxicology* 196: 1–51.

Manyanga, Taru, Hesham El-Sayed, David Teye Doku, and Jason R. Randall. 2014. "The prevalence of underweight, overweight, obesity and associated risk factors among school-going adolescents in seven African countries," *BMC Public Health* 14 (887).

Margolis, Jonathan. 2012. "Growing food in the desert: Is this the solution to the world's food crisis?," *Guardian*, November 24.

Marsden, Terry K, Josefa S. B. Cavalcanti, and Jose F. Irmão. 1996. "Globalisation, regionalization and quality: the socio-economic reconstitution of food in the San Francisco Valley, Brazil," *International Journal of Sociology of Agriculture and Food* 5: 85–111.

Marx, Karl. 1967. *Capital, Volume 3*. New York: International Publishers.

Marx, Karl. 1979. *Capital, Volume 1*. Middlesex: Penguin Books Ltd.

Mather, Charles and Amy Marshall. 2011. "Living with disease? Biosecurity and avian influenza in ostriches," *Agriculture and Human Values* 28: 153–165.

Maye, Damian, Jacqui Dibden, Vaughan Higgins, and Clive Potter. 2012. "Governing biosecurity in a neoliberal world: Comparative perspectives from Australia and the United Kingdom," *Environment and Planning A* 44: 150–168.

Mayer, Jane. 2016. *Dark Money: The Hidden History of the Billionaires Behind the Rise of the Radical Right*. New York and London: Doubleday.

McGill, Julian, Dmitry Prikhodko, Boris Sterk, and Peter Talks. 2015. "Egypt: Wheat sector review," Country Highlights, FAO Investment Centre. Rome: Food and Agriculture Organization of the United Nations.

McGowan, Bruce. 1981. *Economic Life in Ottoman Europe: Taxation, Trade and the Struggle for Land, 1600–1800*. Cambridge: Cambridge University Press.

McGrath, D. J. 1981. "Controlled environment agriculture: A growing industry," *Agribusiness Worldwide* Oct./Nov.: 46–50.

McMichael, Philip. 2000. "The power of food," *Agriculture and Human Values* 17: 21–33.

McMichael, Philip. 2009. "A food regime genealogy," *Journal of Peasant Studies* 36(1): 139–169.

McMichael, Philip. 2012. *Development and Social Change: A Global Perspective* (5th ed.). London: SAGE.

McMichael, Philip. 2013. *Food Regimes and Agrarian Questions*. Halifax & Winnipeg: Fernwood Publishing.

McMichael, Philip. 2017. *Development and Social Change: A Global Perspective* (6th ed.). London: SAGE.

Meadows, Donella H., Dennis L. Meadows, Jorgen Randers, and William W. Behrens III. 1972. *The Limits to Growth: A Report for the Club of Rome's Project on the Predicament of Mankind*. New York: Universe Books.

Meleigy, May. 2007. "Egypt battles with avian influenza," *Lancet* 370(9587): 553–554.

Mennerat, Adèle, Frank Nilsen, Dieter Ebert, and Arne Skorping. 2010. "Intensive farming: Evolutionary implications for parasites and pathogens," *Evolutionary Biology* 37(2-3): 59–67.

Merchant, Carolyn. 1980. *The Death of Nature: Women, Ecology, and the Scientific Revolution*. San Francisco: Harper & Row, Publishers.

Meyer, Günter. 1998. "Economic changes in the newly reclaimed lands: From state farms to small holdings and private agricultural enterprises." In *Directions of Change in Rural Egypt*, edited by Nicholas S. Hopkins and Kirsten Westergaard, pp. 334–353. Cairo: American University at Cairo Press.

Mielants, Eric H. 2007. *The Origins of Capitalism and the "Rise of the West."* Philadelphia: Temple University Press.

Mikhail, Alan. 2011. *Nature and Empire in Ottoman Egypt: An Environmental History*. Cambridge: Cambridge University Press.

Miller, Brittney J. 2022. "Why unprecedented bird flu outbreaks sweeping the world are concerning scientists," *Nature*, May 26.

Ministry of Finance. 2009. *Egypt Response to the Global Crises*. Macro Fiscal Policy Unit, Cairo, Egypt, June.

Mintz, Sidney. 1996. *Tasting Food, Tasting Freedom*. Boston: Beacon Press.

Mitchell, Timothy. 1991. *Colonising Egypt*. Berkeley: University of California Press.

Mitchell, Timothy. 1998. "The market's place." In *Directions of Change in Rural Egypt*, edited by Nicholas S. Hopkins and Kirsten Westergaard, pp. 19–40. Cairo: American University at Cairo Press.

Mitchell, Timothy. 1999. "Dreamland: The neoliberalism of your desires," *Middle East Report* 210, Spring.

Mitchell, Timothy. 2002. *Rule of Experts: Egypt, Techno-Politics, Modernity*. Berkeley: University of California Press.

Mitchell, Timothy. 2011. *Carbon Democracy: Political Power in the Age of Oil*. London and New York: Verso.

Moneim, Doaa A. 2020. "Egypt's pharmaceutical industry suffering, multinational companies have lion's share: SHUAA Securities report," *Al-Ahram Online*, January 8.

Monteiro, C. A., J-C. Moubarac, G. Cannon, S. W. Ng, and B. Popkin. 2013. "Ultra-processed products are becoming dominant in the global food system," *Obesity Reviews* 14 (Supplement 2): 21–28.

Monteiro, Carlos A., Geoffrey Cannon, Renata Levy, et al. 2016. "NOVA. The star shines bright," *World Nutrition* 7 (January–March): 1–3, 28–38.

Montgomerie, Johnna. 2008. "Bridging the critical divide: Global finance, financialisation and contemporary capitalism," *Contemporary Politics* 14(3): 233–252.

Moore, Jason W. 2010a. "Madeira, sugar, and the conquest of nature in the 'first' sixteenth century, Part II: From regional crisis to commodity frontier, 1506–1530," *Review: A Journal of the Fernand Braudel Center* 33(1): 1–24.

Moore, Jason W. 2010b. "The end of the road ? Agricultural world-ecology, 1450–2010," *Journal of Agrarian Change* 10(3): 389–413.

Moore, Jason W. 2011. "Transcending the metabolic rift: A theory of crises in the capitalist world-ecology," *Journal of Peasant Studies* 38(1): 1–46.

Moore, Jason W. 2015. *Capitalism in the Web of Life: Ecology and the Accumulation of Capital.* London and New York: Verso.

Moore, Simon. 2019. "How the African swine fever crisis could disrupt global food companies," *Forbes*, June 15.

Moss, Michael. 2013. *Salt Sugar Fat: How the Food Giants Hooked Us.* New York: Random House.

Mossallem, Mohammed. 2017. "Egypt's debt trap: The neoliberal roots of the problem," Committee for the Abolition of Illegitimate Debt, June 5.

Moukheiber, Zina. 2011. "Egyptian billionaire family caught in the crosshairs of Egypt's history," *Forbes*, February 1.

Mowafi, Amy. 2009. "The strongest link," *Enigma Magazine.*

Mowafi, Mona, Zeinab Khadr, Ichiro Kawachi, S. V. Subramanian, Allan Hill, and Gary G. Bennett. 2014. "Socioeconomic status and obesity in Cairo, Egypt: A heavy burden for all," *Journal of Epidemiology and Global Health* 4: 13–21.

Müller-Mahn, Detlef. 1998. "Spaces of poverty: The geography of social change in rural Egypt." In *Directions of Change in Rural Egypt*, edited by Nicholas S. Hopkins and Kirsten Westergaard, pp. 245–266. Cairo: American University at Cairo Press.

Multari, Salvatore, Derek Stewart, and Wendy R. Russell. 2015. "Potential of fava bean as future protein supply to partially replace meat intake in the human diet," *Comprehensive Reviews in Food Science and Food Safety* 14: 511–522.

Murdoch, Jonathan. 1998. "The spaces of actor-network theory," *Geoforum* 29(4): 357–374.

Nahmias, Petra. 2010. *The Social Epidemiology of Maternal Obesity in Egypt.* PhD: Princeton University.

Najjar, Dina, Bipasha Baruah, and Aman El Garhi. 2020. "Gender and asset ownership in the old and new lands of Egypt," *Feminist Economics* April: 1–25.

Nash, Linda. 2006. *Inescapable Ecologies: A History of Environment, Disease, and Knowledge.* Berkeley: University of California Press.

Nerlich, Brigitte, Brian Brown, and Nick Wright. 2009. "The ins and outs of biosecurity: Bird flu in East Anglia and the spatial representation of risk," *Sociologia Ruralis* 49(4): 344–359.

NNI. 2000. *Food Consumption Pattern and Nutrients Intake among Different Population Groups. To update Food Consumption Pattern Survey conducted in 1981.* National Nutrition Institute Final Report, Supported by WHO/EMRO.

OECD. n.d. "Crude oil import prices," Organization for Economic Co-operation and Development Data.

OECD. 2015. "Hearing on oligopoly markets—a note by Egypt." Directorate for Financial and Enterprise Affairs, Competition Committee, Organisation for Economic Co-operation and Development, May 29.

Ong, Aihwa. 1999. *Flexible Citizenship: The Cultural Logics of Transnationality.* Durham: Duke University Press.

Osterlund, Paul B. 2022. "MENA faces a crisis at the world's key wheat producers are at war," *Al Jazeera*, March 1.

Otero, Gerardo. 2018. *The Neoliberal Diet: Healthy Profits, Unhealthy People.* Austin: University of Texas Press.

Ouma, Stefan. 2010. "Global standards, local realities: Private agrifood governance and the restructuring of the Kenyan horticulture industry," *Economic Geography* 86: 197–222.

Ouma, Stefan. 2015. *Assembling Export Markets: The Making and Unmaking of Global Food Connections in West Africa*. Walden and Oxford: John Wiley & Sons.

Owen, Roger. 1969. *Cotton and the Egyptian Economy 1820–1914: A Study in Trade and Development*. Oxford: Clarendon Press.

Owen, Roger. 1999. "A long look at nearly two centuries of long staple cotton." In *Agriculture in Egypt: From Pharaonic to Modern Times*, edited by Alan K. Bowman and Eugene Rogan, pp. 347–365. Oxford: Oxford University Press.

Owen, Roger. 2006. "The rapid growth of Egypt's agricultural output, 1890–1914, as an early example of the green revolutions of modern South Asia: Some implications for the writing of global history," *Journal of Global History* 1: 81–99.

Pamuk, Şevket. 2000. *A Monetary History of the Ottoman Empire*. Cambridge: Cambridge University Press.

Patel, Raj. 2022. "Our global food system was already in crisis. Russia's war will make it worse," *Boston Review*, May 4.

Patel, Raj and Philip McMichael. 2009. "A political economy of the food riot," *Review* 32(1): 9–35.

Patel, Raj and Jason W. Moore. 2017. *A History of the World in Seven Cheap Things: A Guide to Capitalism, Nature, and the Future of the Planet*. Oakland: University of California Press.

Payne, Anthony and Nicola Phillips. 2010. *Development*. Cambridge: Polity

Pearce, Fred. 2012. "Saudi Arabia stakes a claim on the Nile," *National Geographic*, December 19.

Phillips, Catherine. 2013. "Living without fruit flies: Biosecuring horticulture and its markets," *Environment and Planning A* 45: 1679–1694.

Philpott, Tom. 2019. "A nasty swine flu in China means big trouble for US farmers," *Mother Jones*, June 15.

Piketty, Thomas. 2014. *Capital in the Twenty-First Century*. Translated by Arthur Goldhammer. Cambridge, MA: The Belknap Press of Harvard University Press.

Pioppi, Daniela. 2004. "From religious charity to the welfare state and back. The case of Islamic endowments (*waqfs*) revival in Egypt," European University Institute, Working Paper RSCAS No. 2004/34.

Pisani, Donald J. 1992. *To Reclaim a Divided West: Water, Law, and Public Policy, 1848–1902*. Albuquerque: University of New Mexico Press.

Pisani, Donald J. 2002. *Water and American Government: The Reclamation Bureau, National Water Policy, and the West, 1902–1935*. Berkeley: University of California Press.

Ponte, Stefano. 2009. "Governing through quality: Conventions and supply relations in the value chain for South African wine," *Sociologia Ruralis* 49(3): 236–257.

Population Council. 2011. "Survey of young people in Egypt: Final report," Population Council, West Asia and North Africa Office, Cairo, January.

Potter, Clive. 2013. "A neoliberal biosecurity? The WTO, free trade and the governance of plant health." In *Biosecurity: The Socio-politics of Invasive Species and Infectious Diseases*, edited by Andrew Dobson, Kezia Barker, and Sarah L. Taylor, pp. 123–135. London and New York: Routledge.

Prashad, Vijay. 2007. *The Darker Nations: A People's History of the Third World*. New York and London: The New Press.

Prebisch, Raúl. 1950. "The economic development of Latin America and its principal problems," Economic Commission for Latin America (ECLA), UN Department of Economic Affairs, New York.

Prentice, Andrew M. 2006. "The emerging epidemic of obesity in developing countries," *International Journal of Epidemiology* 35: 93–99.

Radwan, Samir M. 1977. *Agrarian Reform and Rural Poverty, Egypt, 1952–1975*. Geneva.

Ramadan, Racha. 2015. "Food security and its measurement in Egypt," *CIHEAM Watch Letter* no. 32, April.

Rashad, Ibrahim. 1939. "The co-operative movement in Egypt," *African Affairs* XXXVIII, Issue CLIII (October): 469–476.

Rennison, Joe. 2022. "War, climate change, energy costs: How the wheat market has been upended," *New York Times*, August 1.

Richards, Alan R. 1980. "Egypt's agriculture in trouble," *Middle East Report* 84: 3–13.

Richards, Alan R. 1987. "Primitive accumulation in Egypt, 1798–1882." In *The Ottoman Empire and the World-Economy*, edited by Huri İslamoğlu-İnan, pp. 203–243. Cambridge: Cambridge University Press.

Richards, John F. 2003. *The Unending Frontier: An Environmental History of the Early Modern World*. Berkeley: University of California Press.

Rignall, Karen E. 2021. *An Elusive Common: Land, Politics, and Agrarian Rurality in a Moroccan Oasis*. Ithaca and London: Cornell University Press.

Rivlin, Helen Anne B. 1961. *The Agricultural Policy of Muhammad 'Ali in Egypt*. Cambridge, MA: Harvard University Press.

Rogan, Eugene. 1999. *Frontiers of the State in the Late Ottoman Empire*. Cambridge: Cambridge University Press.

Rohac, Dalibor. 2013. "Solving Egypt's subsidy problem," *CATO Institute Policy Analysis* no. 741.

Roitman, Janet. 2014. *Anti-Crisis*. Durham and London: Duke University Press.

Roll, Stephan. 2010. "'Finance matters!' The influence of financial sector reforms on the development of the entrepreneurial elite in Egypt," *Mediterranean Politics* 15(3): 349–370.

Roos, Jerome. 2019. *Why Not Default? The Political Economy of Sovereign Debt*. Princeton and Oxford: Princeton University Press.

Rosenberg, Justin. 2005. "Globalization theory: A post mortem," *International Politics* 42: 2–74.

Russ, Hilary. 2021. "U.S. fast food chains cash in, seize market share during pandemic," *Reuters*, April 30.

Saad, Reem. 1988. "Social History of an Agrarian Reform Community in Egypt," *Cairo Papers in Social Science* 11(4).

Saad, Reem. 1999. "State, landlord, parliament and peasant: The story of the 1992 tenancy law in Egypt." In *Agriculture in Egypt: From Pharaonic to Modern Times*, edited by A. K. Bowman and E. Rogan, pp. 387–404. Oxford: Oxford University Press.

Saad, Reem. 2004. "Social and political costs of coping with poverty in rural Egypt." Paper presented at the Fifth Mediterranean Social and Political Research Meeting, European University Institute, Florence.

Sadek, Karim. 2012. "Concord doing good for Sudan," *The Star*, March 21.

Sadowski, Yahya M. 1991. *Political Vegetables? Businessman and Bureaucrat in the Development of Egyptian Agriculture*. Washington, D.C.: The Brookings Institution.

Sakr, Bashir. 2010. "On the organizational forms of Egyptian agrarian struggles [An al-Ashkal al-Tanzimiyah Lil-Kifah al-Felahi]," Peasant Solidarity Committee, Egypt.

Salem, Sara. 2020. *Anticolonial Afterlives in Egypt: The Politics of Hegemony*. Cambridge: Cambridge University Press.

Sarant, Louise. 2013. "Biotechnology Report: 1000 hectares of genetically modified maize grows in Egypt," *Egypt Independent*, March 14.

Sarant, Louise. 2020. "In the Land of the Pharaohs, can Faba be king again?," *IFPRI*, March 31.

Sawahel, Wagdy. 2008. "First Egyptian approval of genetically modified corn raises questions," *Intellectual Property Watch*, June 16.

Schechter, Relli. 2019. *The Rise of the Egyptian Middle Class: Socio-Economic Mobility and Public Discontent from Nasser to Sadat*. Cambridge: Cambridge University Press.

Scheper-Hughes, Nancy. 1995. "The primacy of the ethical: Propositions for a militant anthropology," *Current Anthropology* 36(3): 409–440.

Schewe, Eric. 2017. "How war shaped Egypt's national bread loaf," *Comparative Studies of South Asia, Africa and the Middle East* 37(1): 49–63.

Schoenberger, Erica. 2008. "The origins of the market economy: State power, territorial control, and modes of war fighting," *Comparative Studies in Society and History* 50(3): 663–691.

Schrader, Wayne L. 2000. "Plasticulture in California vegetable production," University of California Division of Agriculture and Natural Resources Publication no. 8016.

Schurgott, Andrew. 2008. "Private accord," *Business Today Egypt*, September.

Scott, James C. 2009. *The Art of Not Being Governed: An Anarchist History of Upland Southeast Asia*. New Haven, CT: Yale University Press.

Sekine, Kae and Alessandro Bonanno. 2016. *The Contradictions of Neoliberal Agri-food: Corporations, Resistance, and Disasters in Japan*. Morgantown, WV: West Virginia University Press.

Selwyn, Ben. 2007. "Labour process and workers' bargaining power in export grape production, north east Brazil," *Journal of Agrarian Change* 7: 526–553.

Sfakianakis, John. 2004. "The whales of the Nile: Networks, businessmen, and bureaucrats during the era of privatization in Egypt." In *Networks of Privilege: Rethinking the Politics of Economic Reform in the Middle East*, edited by Steven Heydemann, pp. 77–100. New York: Palgrave Macmillan.

Shaw, Ian G. R., John Paul Jones III, and Melinda K. Butterworth. 2013. "The mosquito's umwelt, or one monster's standpoint ontology." *Geoforum* 48: 260–267.

Shokr, Ahmad. 2016. *Beyond the Fields: Cotton and the End of Empire in Egypt, 1919–1956*. PhD: New York University.

Siegel, Seth M. 2015. *Let There Be Water: Israel's Solution for a Water-Starved World*. New York: St. Martin's Press.

Sims, David. 2018. *Egypt's Desert Dreams: Development or Disaster?* (2nd ed.) New York: American University in Cairo Press.

Sjerven, J. 1986. "Ismailia Misr Poultry sets example for private sector initative in Egypt," *Agribusiness Worldwide*, Nov./Dec.: 6–10.

Slackman, Michael. 2008. "Egypt's problem and its challenge: Bread corrupts," *New York Times*, January 17.

Soliman, Ahmed. 2004. *A Possible Way Out: Formalizing Housing Informality in Egyptian Cities*. Dallas: University Press of America.

Soliman, Samer. 2011. *The Autumn of Dictatorship: Fiscal Crisis and Political Change in Egypt under Mubarak*. Translation by Peter Daniel. Stanford, CA: Stanford University Press.

Soliman, A. S., M. L. Bondy, A. A. Raouf, M. A. Makram, D. A. Johnston, and B. Levin. 1999. "Cancer mortality in Menofeia, Egypt: comparison with US mortality rates," *Cancer Causes Control* 10(5): 349–354.

Soliman, A. S., X. Wang, J-D. Stanley, N. El-Ghawalby, M. L. Bondy, F. Ezzat, A. Soultan, M. Abdel-Wahab, O. Fathy, G. Ebidi, N. Abdel-Karim, K-anh Do, B. Levin, S. R. Hamilton, and J. L. Abbruzzese. 2006. "Geographical clustering of pancreatic cancers in the northeast Nile Delta region of Egypt," *Archives of Environmental Contamination and Toxicology* 51(1): 142–148.

Son, Hugh. 2022. "Morgan Stanley aims to serve the richest of the rich as family offices grow to $5.5 trillion in assets," *CNBC*, April 10.

Sowers, Jeannie. 2011. "Remapping the nation, critiquing the state: Environmental narratives and desert land reclamation in Egypt." In *Environmental Imaginaries of the Middle East and*

North Africa, edited by Diana K. Davis and Edmund Burke III, pp. 158–191. Athens: Ohio University Press.

Springborg, Robert. 1979. "Patrimonialism and policy making in Egypt: Nasser and Sadat and the tenure policy for reclaimed lands." *Middle Eastern Studies* 15(1): 49–69.

Springborg, Robert. 1990. "Agrarian bourgeoisie, semiproletarians, and the Egyptian state: Lessons for liberalization," *International Journal of Middle East Studies* 22(4): 447–472.

Stanley, Daniel J. and Andrew G. Warne. 1998. "Nile Delta in its destruction phase," *Journal of Coastal Research* 14: 794–825.

Stoll, Steven. 1998. *The Fruits of Natural Advantage: Making the Industrial Countryside in California*. Berkeley: University of California Press.

Stoltenberg, Clyde, Barbara C. George, Kathleen A. Lacey, and Michael Cuthbert. 2011. "The past decade of regulatory change in the US and EU capital market regimes: An evolution from national interests toward international harmonization with emerging G-20 leadership," *Berkeley Journal of International Law*, no. 577.

Summers, Lawrence H. and Masood Ahmed. 2022. "IMF-World Bank meetings are the last stop before a coming economic storm," *Washington Post*, October 5.

Swinburn, Boyd A. et al. 2019. "The global syndemic of obesity, undernutrition, and climate change: The Lancet Commission report." *Lancet* 393: 791–846.

Syvitski, James P. M. 2008. "Deltas at risk," *Sustainability Science* 3: 23–32.

Syvitski, James P. M., Albert J. Kettner, Irina Overeem, Eric W. H. Hutton, Mark T. Hannon, G. Robert Brakenridge, John Day, Charles Vörösmarty, Yoshiki Saito, Liviu Giosan, and Robert J. Nicholls. 2009. "Sinking deltas due to human activities," *Nature Geoscience* 2(10): 681–686.

Tanchum, Michael. 2022. "The Russia-Ukraine war has turned Egypt's food crisis into an existential threat to the economy," *Middle East Institute Policy Center*, March.

Thompson, Edward P. 1971. "The moral economy of the English crowd in the eighteenth century," *Past and Present* L: 76–136.

Tooze, Adam. 2018. *Crashed: How a Decade of Financial Crises Changed the World*. New York: Penguin Books.

Tooze, Adam. 2022. "Welcome to the world of the polycrisis," *Financial Times*, October 28, 2022.

Toth, James. 1998. "Beating plowshares into swords." In *Directions of Change in Rural Egypt*, edited by Nicholas S. Hopkins and Kirsten Westergaard, pp. 51–72. Cairo: American University at Cairo Press.

Tseng, W.-C., H.-A. Li, W.-C. Huang, and L-H. Liang. 2010. "Potential number of human cases of H5N1 avian influenza in Egypt," *Public Health* 124(8): 452–459.

Tsing, Anna L. 2005. *Friction: An Ethnography of Global Connection*. Princeton: Princeton University Press.

Turnbull, Chrystal, Morten Lillemo, and Trine A. K. Hvoslef-Eide. 2021. "Global regulation of genetically modified crops amid the gene edited crop boom–a review," *Frontiers of Plant Science* 12: 1–19.

Tvedt, Terje. 2004. *The River Nile in the Age of the British: Political Ecology and the Quest for Economic Power*. London: I.B. Tauris.

Tyrrell, Ian. 1999. *True Gardens of the Gods: Californian-Australian Environmental Reform, 1860-1930*. Berkeley: University of California Press.

Udasin, Sharon. 2012. "Feed the world: The CIPA plasticulture for a green planet conference looks at agricultural practices for farming," *Jerusalem Post*, May 16.

UN. 2022a. "Billions of people face the greatest cost-of-living crisis in a generation." Brief No. 2, UN Global Crisis Response Group on Food, Energy and Finance. United Nations, June 8.

UN. 2022b. "The Black Sea Grain Initiative: What it is, and why it's important for the world," United Nations, September 16.

UNCTAD. 2001/2004/2005. *World Investment Report: FDI Policies for Development: National and International Perspectives*. New York and Geneva: United Nations Conference on Trade and Development.

UNDP. 2011. "Food security challenges in the Arab States/MENA region in the context of climate change: The role of the regional directors team," Regional UNDP, Arab States/Middle East and North Africa Position Paper: Nexus of Climate Change and Food Security, March.

USAID. n.d. "US overseas loans and grants and assistance from international organizations: Obligations and loan authorizations, July 1, 1945–September 30, 2001," Greenbook, U.S. Agency for International Development.

USDA. 2009. "Egypt grain and feed annual 2009," USDA Foreign Agricultural Service *GAIN Report EG9002*, March 10.

USDA. 2010a. "Egypt: Retail foods." USDA Foreign Agricultural Service *GAIN Report*.

USDA. 2010b. "Peru: An emerging exporter of fruits and vegetables," *Economic Research Service USDA FTS-345-01*.

USDA. 2012. "Egypt: Grain and feed annual; Wheat and corn production on the rise," USDA Foreign Agricultural Service *GAIN Report*, April.

USDA. 2015. "Egypt: Food processing ingredients, annual," USDA Foreign Agricultural Service *GAIN Report*, November 9.

USDA. 2021. "Grain and feed annual: Egypt is able to secure a steady supply of grains during the COVID-19 pandemic," USDA Foreign Agricultural Service *GAIN Report*, March 17.

van Cruyningen, Piet. 2014. "From disaster to sustainability: Floods, changing property relations and water management in the South-western Netherlands, c. 1500–1800," *Continuity and Change* 29(2): 241–265.

van Dam, Petra J. E. M. 2001. "Sinking peat bogs: Environmental change, Holland, 1350–1550," *Environmental History* 6(1): 32–45.

van de Ven, Gerard P. 1996. *Man-Made Lowlands: History of Water Management and Land Reclamation in the Netherlands* (3rd ed). Utrecht: Matrijs, International Commission on Irrigation and Drainage.

van der Ploeg, Jan D. 2009. *The New Peasantries: Struggles for Autonomy and Sustainability in an Era of Empire and Globalization*. London and Sterling, VA: Earthscan.

van Kerkhove, Maria D., Elizabeth Mumford, Anthony W. Mounts, Joseph Bresee, Sowath Ly, Carolyn B. Bridges, and Joachim Otte. 2011. "Highly pathogenic avian influenza (H5N1): Pathways of exposure at the animal-human Interface, a systemic review," *PLoS ONE* 5(1): 1–8.

van Tielhof, Milja. 2015. "Forced solidarity: Maintenance of coastal defences along the North Sea coast in the early modern period," *Environment and History* 21(3): 319–350.

van Veen, Johan. 1962. *Drain, Dredge, Reclaim: The Art of a Nation*. The Hague: Martinus Nijhoff.

Veinstein, Gilles. 1991. "On the Çiftlik debate." In *Landholding and Commercial Agriculture in the Middle East*, edited by Caglar Keyder and Faruq Tabak, pp. 35–53. Albany: State University of New York Press.

Vitalis, Robert. 1995. *When Capitalists Collide: Business Conflict and the End of Empire in Egypt*. Berkeley: University of California Press.

Voll, Sarah P. 1980. "Egyptian land reclamation since the revolution," *Middle East Journal* 34(2): 127–148.

Wahid, Walaa. 2012. "Badou yaqtaaoun tariq Al Ismailia-Zagazig (Bedouin block Ismailia-Zagazig road)," *Alwafd.org*, January 18.

Wallace, Robert G. 2009. "Breeding influenza: The political virology of offshore farming," *Antipode* 41(5): 916–951.

Wallerstein, Immanuel. 1979. *The Capitalist World-Economy: Essays by Immanuel Wallerstein.* Cambridge, UK: Cambridge University Press.

Wallerstein, Immanuel. 2011a. *The Modern World-System 1: Capitalist Agriculture and the Origins of the European World-Economy in the Sixteenth Century.* Berkeley: University of California Press.

Wallerstein, Immanuel. 2011b. "The contradictions of the Arab Spring," *Aljazeera,* November 14.

Wallerstein, Immanuel, Hale Decdeli, and Reşat Kasaba. 1987. "The incorporation of the Ottoman Empire into the world-economy." In *The Ottoman Empire and the World-Economy,* edited by Huri İslamoğlu-İnan, pp. 88–97. Cambridge: Cambridge University Press.

Warriner, Doreen. 1957. *Land Reform and Development in the Middle East: A Study of Egypt, Syria, and Iraq.* London and New York: Royal Institute of International Affairs.

Waterbury, John. 1979. *Hydropolitics of the Nile Valley.* Syracuse: Syracuse University Press.

Waterbury, John. 1983. *The Egypt of Nasser and Sadat: The Political Economy of Two Regimes.* Princeton: Princeton University Press.

Waterbury, John. 1989. "The political management of economic adjustment and reform." In *Economic Adjustment in Algeria, Egypt, Jordan, Morocco, Pakistan, Tunisia, and Turkey,* edited by Alan Roe, Jayanta Roy, and Jayshree Sengupta. The World Bank EDI Policy Seminar Report 15.

Watson, Andrew M. 1983. *Agricultural Innovation in the Early Islamic World: The Diffusion of Crops and Farming Techniques, 700–1100.* Cambridge and New York: Cambridge University Press.

Watts, Michael. J. 2009. "The Southern question: Agrarian questions of labour and capital." In *Peasants and Globalization: Political Economy, Rural Transformation and the Agrarian Question,* edited by A. Haroon Akram-Lodhi and Cristóbal Kay, pp. 262–287. London and New York: Routledge.

Watts, Michael J. and David Goodman. 1997. "Agrarian questions: Global appetite, local metabolism: nature, culture and industry in fin-de-siècle agro-food systems." In *Globalising Food: Agrarian Questions and Global Restructuring,* edited by A. Haroon Akram-Lodhi and Cristóbal Kay, pp. 1-23. London and New York: Routledge.

Watts, Susan and Samiha El Katsha. 1995. "Changing environmental conditions in the Nile Delta: Health and policy implications with special reference to schistosomiasis," *Journal of Environmental Health Research* 5(3): 197–212.

Weatherspoon, Dave D. and Thomas Reardon. 2003. "The rise of supermarkets in Africa: Implications for agrifood systems and the rural poor," *Development Policy Review* 21(3): 333–355.

Weis, Tony. 2007. *The Global Food Economy: The Battle for the Future of Farming.* London and New York: Zed Books.

Weis, Tony. 2010. "The accelerating biophysical contradictions of industrial capitalist agriculture," *Journal of Agrarian Change* 10(3): 315–341.

Weis, Tony. 2013. *The Ecological Hoofprint: The Global Burden of Industrial Livestock.* London and New York: Zed Books.

Welton, George. 2011. *The Impact of Russia's 2010 Grain Export Ban.* Oxfam Research Reports, June 28.

Werbner, Prina, Martin Webb, and Kathryn Spellman-Poots, eds. 2014. *The Political Aesthetics of Global Protest: The Arab Spring and Beyond.* Edinburgh: Edinburgh University Press.

Werr, Patrick. 2015. "Making the most of Egypt's subterranean sea," *The National,* December 2.

Westad, Odd A. 2007. *The Global Cold War: Third World Interventions and the Making of Our Times*. Cambridge: Cambridge University Press.

WFP. 2008. "Vulnerability analysis and review of the food subsidy program in Egypt," World Food Programme (WFP), Egypt, October.

WFP. 2022. *War in Ukraine Drives Global Food Crisis*. World Food Programme, June 24.

White, John W. 1979. "Energy efficient growing structures for controlled environment agriculture," *Horticultural Reviews* 1: 141–171.

Whiting, Kate. 2022. "Here's how the food and energy crises are connected," Sustainable Development Impact Meetings. *World Economic Forum*, September 20.

WHO. 2004. "Avian influenza and human health." Report by the Secretariat, World Health Organization. Executive Board 114th Session, Provisional agenda item 4.5, April 8.

WHO. 2005. *Preventing Chronic Diseases: A Vital Investment*. Geneva: World Heatlh Organization.

WHO. 2016. "STEPwise approach to NCD risk factor surveillance (STEPS)," World Health Organization, Geneva.

Winders, Bill. 2009. *The Politics of Food Supply: U.S. Agricultural Policy in the World Economy*. New Haven: Yale University Press.

Winders, Bill. 2011. "The food crisis and the deregulation of agriculture," *The Brown Journal of World Affairs* 18(1): 83–95.

Winders, Bill. 2017. *Grains*. Cambridge and Malden, MA: Polity Press.

Winders, Bill, Alison Heslin, Gloria Ross, Hannah Weksler, and Seanna Berry. 2016. "Life after the regime: Market instability with the fall of the US food regime," *Agriculture and Human Values* 33: 73–88.

Woertz, Eckart. 2013. *Oil for Food: The Global Food Crisis and the Middle East*. Oxford and New York: Oxford University Press.

Woertz, Eckart, Eduard Soler, Oriol Farrés, and Anna Busquets. 2014. "The impact of food price volatility and food inflation on southern and eastern Mediterranean countries," CIDOB Barcelona Centre for International Affairs, Union for the Mediterranean, October.

World Bank. n.d. "GNI per capita, Atlas method (current US$)," World Bank data.

World Bank. 2012. *The Grain Chain: Food Security and Managing Wheat Imports in Arab Countries*. Washington, DC: World Bank.

World Economic Forum. 2008. "The global economic impact of private equity report 2008," *Globalization of Alternative Investments Working Papers* 1.

Wright, Brian and Carlo Cafiero. 2011. "Grain reserves and food security in the Middle East and North Africa," *Food Security* 3 (Suppl 1): S61–S76.

Wynn, L. L. 2007. *Pyramids & Nightclubs: A Travel Ethnography of Arab and Western Imaginations of Egypt, from King Tut and a Colony of Atlantis to Rumors of Sex Orgies, Urban Legends about a Marauding Prince, and Blonde Belly Dancers*. Austin: University of Texas Press, Austin.

Xu, Guanmian and Leonard Blussé. 2019. "Land reclamation in the Rhine and Yangzi deltas: An explorative comparison, 1600–1800," *Fudan Journal of the Humanities and Social Sciences* 12: 423–455.

Yanagisako, Sylvia J. 2002. *Producing Culture and Capital: Family Firms in Italy*. Princeton and Oxford: Princeton University Press.

Yau, Yvonne Y. C. and Marc N. Potenza. 2013. "Stress and eating disorders," *Minerva Endocrinology* 38(3): 255–267.

Youssef, Mohamed H. 2008. *Role of Food Subsidies on Poverty Alleviation in Egypt*. Cairo: American University of Cairo.

Zaalouk, Malak. 1989. *Power, Class, and Foreign Capital in Egypt: The Rise of the New Bourgeoisie*. London: Zed Books.

Zanetti, Cristiano. 2017. *Janello Torriani and the Spanish Empire: A Vitruvian Artisan at the Dawn of the Scientific Revolution.* Leiden, Netherlands: Brill.

Zeitlin, Maurice. 1974. "Corporate ownership and control: The large corporation and the capitalist class," *American Journal of Sociology* 79(5): 1073–1119.

Zeitlin, Maurice and Ratcliff, Richard E. 1988. *Landlords and Capitalists: The Dominant Class of Chile.* Princeton: Princeton University Press.

Index

For the benefit of digital users, indexed terms that span two pages (e.g., 52–53) may, on occasion, appear on only one of those pages.